A PALACE FOR A KING

Diego de Velázquez, *Count–Duke of Olivares on Horseback* (Madrid, Prado)

A PALACE FOR A KING

The Buen Retiro
and the Court of Philip IV

Jonathan Brown and J. H. Elliott

YALE UNIVERSITY PRESS
NEW HAVEN & LONDON
1980

Published with the assistance of the F. B. Adams, Jr., fund.

Designed by Caroline Williamson
and set in Monophoto Bembo.
Printed in Great Britain by
BAS Printers Limited,
Over Wallop, Hampshire.

Published in Great Britain, Europe, Africa, and
Asia (except Japan) by Yale University Press
Ltd., London. Distributed in Australia and
New Zealand by Book & Film Services, Artarmon,
N.S.W., Australia; and in Japan by Harper & Row,
Publishers, Tokyo Office.

Library of Congress Cataloging in Publication Data

Brown, Jonathan.
  A palace for a king.

  Bibliography: p.
  Includes index.
  1. Felipe IV, King of Spain, 1605–1665—Art patronage. 2. Madrid. Buen
Retiro. 3. Olivares, Gaspar de Guzmán, conde-duque de, 1587–1645. I.
Elliott, John Huxtable, joint author. II. Title.
  DP185.B76   946′.052′0924   80-13659
  ISBN 0-300-02507-6

For Sandra, and for Oonah,
whose kinsman General Pakenham
helped destroy the palace
which we here attempt to reconstruct.

PREFACE

Throughout the history of Western civilization, the princely palace has been a potent political and social symbol. In addition to serving as the abode of the ruler and the center of government, the palace was the most impressive manifestation of the wealth and glory derived from the power of dominion over men and land. By its nature, the palace served as a repository of the values of the ruling class. Here ideas were collected, ordered and expressed in visual form. By reconstructing the history of these buildings and analyzing their architecture, decoration and use, the historian can recapture spiritual and cultural attitudes that are important to the understanding of the past.

The great palaces built in Europe during the Renaissance and Baroque periods lend themselves to this kind of study. This was the age of the prince, when enormous human and financial resources were concentrated in the hands of a few men and women. It was also a time of intense political rivalry, which gave new importance to propaganda and display. These conditions favored the rise of palace building and court life on a grand scale. Political theorists promoted the ideal of magnificence as an indispensable attribute of the prince, and magnificence was most effectively displayed in splendid buildings that housed lavish courts. Many of the palaces built or rebuilt in fulfillment of this ideal are famous—Fontainebleau, the Louvre and Versailles; the Vatican, the Pitti and the Barberini; Whitehall and St James's.

Less well-known, but no less impressive, were the palaces built by the kings of Spain, who for nearly one hundred and fifty years dominated European politics. Charles V, Philip II and Philip IV were among the greatest builders and patrons of early modern Europe, but their achievements in these spheres of activity are largely unrecognized. There is little to inform the reader who wishes to know the history and significance of the buildings of Charles V and Philip II—the Escorial, the Alcázares of Madrid, Toledo and Seville, the palace of Charles V in Granada, and the country houses of Aranjuez and the Pardo. Similarly, the building and decorative enterprises of Philip IV have only recently begun to attract attention. By studying one of these projects in detail, we hope to encourage the awakening interest in the subject, and to assign to Spain its due place in the political and cultural history of palace-building.

The Palace of the Buen Retiro was created in the 1630s on the outskirts of Madrid. Beginning as a small addition to the royal apartment attached to the church of San Jerónimo, it quickly became a sizable palace set in an immense garden–park. Seen from the outside, the Retiro was rather an unimpressive structure. But the interior was richly decorated and furnished, and adorned with a large collection of pictures assembled from several European cities. Rubens, Claude and Poussin were well represented on the walls of the Retiro, and the *Surrender of Breda* by Velázquez, that masterpiece of seventeenth-century painting, was specially commissioned to occupy a place in its great central hall, the Hall of Realms.

The Retiro was built for two purposes, the first of which is suggested by its name. It was to be used by the king as a convenient place of retreat and recreation, where he could find relief from the cares of office without the trouble and expense of a journey into the countryside. The suburban palace or villa, as this type of building is called, was a common feature of European capitals which was lacking in Madrid. The second purpose, related to the first, was to create a setting for the king to act as a great patron of the arts. The king would patronize the arts and the arts would glorify the king. As it happened, Philip IV was a knowledgable, avid connoisseur of painting and the theater. To satisfy his taste, the Retiro became the setting for plays and spectacles, the best of which were written by Calderón and brilliantly staged by the Florentine scenographer Cosimo Lotti. These court amusements did much to promote the image of the king in other courts, where liberality, as it was known, was numbered among the princely virtues.

But in Spain it was not a season for liberality. A splendid court and palace were brought into being during a decade when Spain was racked by military reverses and economic crisis. In the midst of poverty and defeat, the Retiro and all it contained became a symbol of bad government and of the wasteful expenditure of financial resources desperately needed to defend the Monarchy. Events had suddenly overtaken traditional ideas of kingly comportment; courtly splendor was tarnished by crisis and decline.

Caught in the eye of the gathering storm was the king's minister, the Count–Duke of Olivares, the protagonist of this book. The complex, contradictory personality of Olivares shaped the Retiro as it did the destiny of Spain in the 1620s and 1630s. He conceived the plan to build the palace, raised the money to carry it out, and oversaw every detail of its planning, construction and administration, until inevitably it became a symbol of the failure of his regime.

It is this period of the Buen Retiro's history on which we have chosen to concentrate, ending in 1643 with the fall of Olivares, because it seems to us to illuminate the complex relationship of art and politics at a critical moment in the history of Western European monarchies. The Retiro has a subsequent history, although of a rather melancholy character. The fabric of the building was so poorly made that it was soon decaying. By the middle of the nineteenth century, after a period of neglect, war, and further neglect, little remained but the park, and even this was hardly more than a pale reminder of past splendors.

Yet even though the palace is gone, it has left its mark on the history of European civilization. Olivares wanted to create a brilliant court around his monarch and planned the Retiro as its setting. The money that he diverted from the needs of state to create this court went into the pockets of painters, sculptors, architects, poets, playwrights, actors and musicians who displayed their arts at the Retiro. The names of Velázquez, Zurbarán, Quevedo, Calderón, Lope de Vega, Francisco de Rioja, Giovanni Battista Crescenzi, Cosimo Lotti and lesser-known artists figure in the history of the Retiro. They also figure in what is known as the Golden Age of Spain. It would be claiming too much to say that the two histories are synonymous. But within the precincts of the Retiro, we can see a sample of the artistic activities that gave luster to this period of Spanish history and come closer to understanding the causes of this remarkable upsurge of cultural vitality in an age of economic decline.

A word about the approach adopted in this book may be of help. It is not "architectural history" or "art history," as these terms are often understood. Nor is it simply a study of the political, social and cultural background to the building of a palace. Instead, we have sought to present as "total" or integrated a history of the circumstances attending the construction and first occupation of a major European palace as the fragmentary character of the surviving evidence allows.

Over the years the Buen Retiro has attracted the attention of a number of scholars, and our first acknowledgements must be to those authors, ranging from architectural to literary historians, whose work has made our own task easier. None of them, however, has tried to bring together all the elements of the story in quite the way attempted here. In almost every instance, we have gone back to the archives for the original documentation, even where it has been previously cited, and we have incorporated fresh documentary material to fill out the story. We owe a deep debt of gratitude to the many archivists, both inside and outside Spain, who have given us unstintingly of their time and attention, and only regret that they are so numerous that it would be invidious to single out names. But we should like to make special mention of the archivists and staff of the Archivo General de Simancas, and of the Archivo Histórico de Protocolos in Madrid, where we spent many rewarding hours.

We are also grateful to David Coffin for sharing with us his unique knowledge of Renaissance villa and garden design, and to René Taylor and Catherine Wilkinson Zerner for information on the architecture of the Spanish Habsburgs. Enriqueta Harris has generously exchanged ideas with us on many points relating to Spanish painting in the reign of Philip IV. Felipe Ruiz Martín and José F. de la Peña provided us with valuable suggestions during numerous conversations on seventeenth-century Spain which took place at the Institute for Advanced Study during the academic year 1978–9. Irving Lavin and Kathleen Weil-Garris gave us information which helped us to formulate some of the ideas in chapter VI. Some of the material in this book was first tried out in two seminars given by Jonathan Brown at the Institute of Fine Arts of New York University, and we are grateful to the members of those seminars, and especially to Barbara von Barghahn, Marcus Burke and Steven Orso, for scholarly contributions which have considerably lightened our task.

Felix Gilbert kindly read an early draft of the book and gave us many excellent ideas for its improvement. Richard Ollard and Rosalie Siegel also read it at this stage and were most helpful with advice and encouragement. Peggy Van Sant typed and retyped our chapters with unfailing patience, accuracy and good humor. We are indebted to Sergio Sanabria for providing the architectural drawings and to Philip Evola for his photographic work.

Jonathan Brown gratefully acknowledges financial support from the National Endowment for the Humanities, the Commission for Educational Exchange between the United States and Spain, and the Institute for Advanced Study. Finally we wish to thank our editor, John Nicoll, for the enthusiasm and care with which he has transformed our manuscript into a book.

Princeton, December 1, 1979.

CONTENTS

LIST OF ILLUSTRATIONS

TABLES

PHOTOGRAPHIC SOURCES

Photographs have been supplied by owners, with the exception of the following:

Prologue

The selection of Madrid as the capital of the Spanish Monarchy represented the triumph of policy over plausibility. When Philip II moved his court there from Toledo in 1561, only he seems to have known that a far-reaching decision had been definitively made. Until that year, it had been customary for the kings of Castile to hold court in the principal cities of the central Castilian plateau. Toledo, Valladolid and Segovia housed the court more often than the other cities of the realm, and it was therefore expected that Philip's move to Madrid would only be temporary. But a perambulating court has its inconveniences, not least when the sovereign possesses a world-wide empire and lives in daily expectation of dispatches from the farthest corners of the earth. This time, as the court settled into Madrid and the months passed into years, it began to look as though the days of wandering were done. Spain, like France and England, would have its capital.

But why Madrid? The question has been asked from that day to this, and has never received an entirely satisfactory answer.[1] Several cities of Castile had stronger claims than this unimpressive little town on the banks of a minor river, the Manzanares, in the middle of the parched Castilian tableland. As the seat of the chancellery, Castile's highest legal tribunal, Valladolid in particular had seemed destined for greatness. The court frequently resided there, and it served more often than any other Castilian town in the fifteenth and early sixteenth centuries as a meeting place for the Cortes, or parliament, of Castile. In 1521–2 the Emperor Charles V, who never stayed long in any one place, spent a whole year in Valladolid. His son Philip was born there in 1527, and lived there from 1536 to 1538, and again, as regent for his father, from 1543 to 1545. Valladolid increasingly assumed the appearance of a political and administrative capital in these middle years of the sixteenth century; and the high nobility, in recognition of this fact, built or rented large town houses to be near the seat of power.[2]

Yet the prize which seemed to be within Valladolid's grasp in the 1550s unexpectedly eluded it. In the eyes of Philip II (1556–98), Valladolid was tainted by the discovery of a clutch of heretics, who were sent to the stake in 1559. That same year he moved his court to Toledo, and never brought it back. Under Philip III (1598–1621) Valladolid made a final bid to reverse the verdict of nearly half a century. In 1601 the Duke of Lerma, the favorite of the new king, had the court moved back for reasons of political and personal convenience. But the move was not a success, and in 1606 the king and government returned to Madrid, which thereafter was the court's definitive residence.

As the site for a capital, Madrid had a few, if modest, assets. The Guadarrama mountains were within easy reach, and the surrounding countryside abounded in game for the royal hunts. Although scorched by the summer sun and swept by icy north winds in winter, Madrid at least had a dry climate, whereas Toledo, which housed the court from 1559 to 1561, was found to be too damp for the queen's health. Unlike mid-sixteenth-century Toledo, Madrid also had ample supplies of wood to keep the charcoal braziers burning. Its water was praised as being unusually pure, and was thought to be available in sufficient quantities to meet the needs of a growing town, although this proved less true of the rising ground to the east—a fact which greatly complicated the work of the building contractors when the palace of the Buen Retiro came to be built and its gardens planted. But these various assets hardly added up to a decisive case in favor of Madrid. Set on a parched plateau which would all too soon be stripped of its trees, the town had only one real advantage over its nearest competitors—its central location within the Iberian peninsula. At the moment when Philip II settled his court there, this advantage may well have tipped the balance.

By the middle of the sixteenth century the economic center of Castile was shifting away from the northern cities to a south that was showing signs of prosperity as a result of trade with the Indies. A courier on horseback needed six days to reach Valladolid from Seville, the emporium of the Spanish Atlantic. Although Madrid was still far enough away, it was at least equidistant from Seville in the south and Laredo in the north.[3] For a man as addicted as Philip II to geometrical principles and rational planning, this centrality represented a powerful attraction. The placing of his seat of government at the very center of the peninsula nicely symbolized his ideal of a Solomon-like equity in the government of his numerous kingdoms. "It was right," wrote his biographer, Cabrera de Córdoba, "that so great a monarchy should have a city fulfilling the function of a heart, located in the middle of the body, to minister equally to all its states in war and peace."[4]

The king's desire for centrality, then, weighed heavily in Madrid's favor. It also was a town with some significant links to the monarchy. There was a royal castle, the Alcázar (fig. 1), which with some modifications could be used to house the court and the government; and on its eastern outskirts it had, in the monastery of San Jerónimo, a ceremonial center and major religious foundation on which the kings of Castile had lavished their patronage. Finally, Madrid was convenient to excellent country houses. The Pardo to the north had superb hunting and Aranjuez to the south, beautiful gardens and forests.

When the court moved to Madrid in 1561, it was a town with only some 2,500 houses,[5] and the arrival of a swarm of royal officials and courtiers naturally placed an acute strain on its limited resources. The unfortunate inhabitants were ordered to reserve the upper stories of their houses for the accommodation of officials, and responded by building houses with only one storey, known as "malice houses" (*casas de malicia*), which would be exempt from this burdensome obligation. Expanding outward rather than upward, Madrid under Philip II assumed the appearance of a boom town, as hastily constructed dwellings went up along the edges of the highways that led toward Segovia, Toledo and Alcalá de Henares. As the town spread, it tended to grow away from the Alcázar, perched on the western edges above the Manzanares, and to press eastward along the principal thoroughfare, the

1. Anthony van der Wyngaerde, *Madrid and the Alcázar*, 1563–70 (Vienna, Nationalbibliothek Cod. Min. 41.)

Calle Mayor, toward the central meeting-point, the Puerta del Sol, and then eastward again until it reached the wooded meadowland known as the Prado (fig. 2).[6]

The removal of the court to Valladolid between 1601 and 1606 slowed down only momentarily the rapid expansion now under way. After 1606, when it became clear that the court was back to stay, people flocked into Madrid from all over Castile, to the growing alarm of the government. The Crown attempted to check the immigration by ordering landowners to return to their estates, hoping that this would clear the court of the hordes of dependents and parasites; but its efforts met with no success. By 1617 Madrid had a population of around 150,000—double its size of twenty years before.[7] Feverish building failed to keep pace with the demand for new houses, most of them mean constructions of brick and mud, reflecting the local shortage of lime and the lack of stone quarries any nearer than the Escorial. The streets were filthy and crowded, and the town spilled out into the countryside, for— as foreign visitors were surprised to discover—Madrid had gates but no town walls. It was not until 1625 that the Crown ordered the construction of a low adobe wall in place of the medieval walls torn down in the rush to build.[8]

The opening decades of the seventeenth century, therefore, were a time of building and urban expansion in Madrid, as they were in London and Paris. But construction in the capital of Spain, unlike the capitals of England and France, began almost from nothing. In theory, this created a great opportunity for rational city planning of the kind that Henry IV and Sully undertook for Paris.[9] In practice, Madrid was allowed to grow with economic forces in control. Only in one instance was a well-ordered urban space created, the Plaza Mayor, which was built between 1617 and 1619 by the court architect, Juan Gómez de Mora.[10] The plaza, a vast open space measuring 434 by 334 feet, was lined with four-storey houses built over granite colonnades and was used occasionally for major public spectacles. Otherwise, Madrid was shaped by circumstance. The nobility, who had flocked to court, built themselves town houses along the Calle Mayor—houses with severe brick facades, embellished only by their granite doorways and their iron balconies, ostentation otherwise being reserved for the interiors, which were hung with tapestries and pictures and adorned with handsome pieces of furniture. Near the town gates, however, and especially on the eastern border of Madrid, it became fashionable to

MANTVA, CARPE

2. Pedro Texeira, Map
of Madrid, 1656
(Madrid, Biblioteca
Nacional)

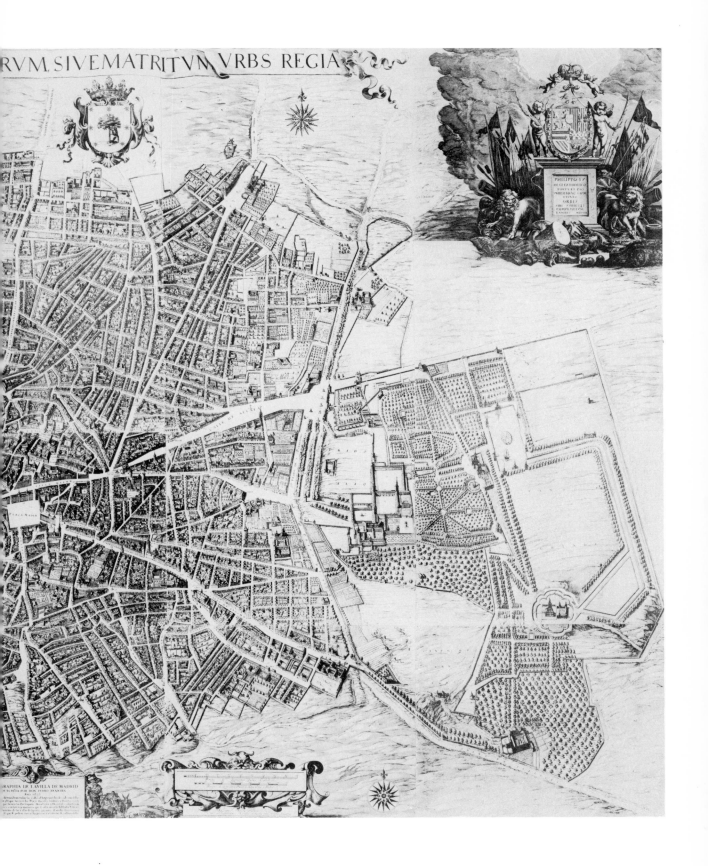

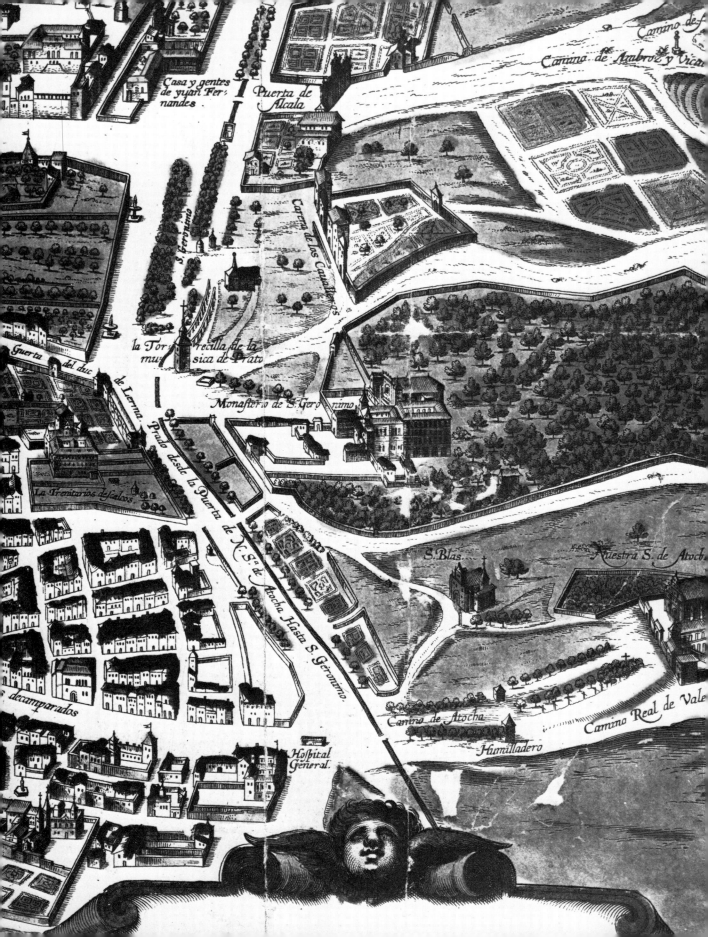

build large private houses or palaces with delectable gardens, well-suited for entertainments.[11]

In the early seventeenth century, the eastern border of Madrid was defined by an avenue called the Prado de San Jerónimo, and its extensions, the Prado de Atocha and the Prado de los Recoletos Agustinos. This was a long thoroughfare lined with trees and fountains that was a favorite site of recreation for the populace. Access to the Prado de San Jerónimo was provided by two major arteries that radiated from the heart of the city, the Calle de Alcalá and the Carrera de San Jerónimo. The amenities of the Prado were essentially suburban. Here the citizens of a crowded, foul-smelling city could enjoy clean air and open spaces without having to travel far from the urban center. Before long, the nobility and court officials had begun to build the houses and gardens which formed a buffer zone between the town and countryside.

Beyond the Prado to the east the ground rose gently and was vacant except for a few structures. A map of the city done around 1630 shows this area in somewhat compressed form (fig. 3). In the northern sector, at the top near the Puerta de Alcalá, are two small enclosed gardens, owned by noblemen. The northernmost belonged to the Marquis of Tavara; the one to the south, to the Marquis of Povar. The principal structure, however, was the monastery of San Jerónimo, which had given its name to the Prado that ran below. As seen on the map, the monastery consisted of a church flanked at the south by two cloisters. Behind this complex was a large enclosed and wooded area called the Huerta de San Jerónimo.

It was here, around the nucleus of the monastery of San Jerónimo, that the Crown built in the 1630s the enormous complex of palace and gardens known as the Buen Retiro. It was a vast, if hasty, undertaking which permanently changed the face of the capital, and greatly enlarged its boundaries. Just as the old royal palace of the Alcázar marked the western limits of Madrid, so the new royal palace of the Retiro came to mark its eastern limits. The Retiro, indeed, may be regarded as the most significant legacy of the seventeenth-century House of Austria to the life of Madrid.

The Retiro of today, however, is not the Retiro created by Philip IV (1621–65) and his principal minister, the Count–Duke of Olivares. They built a royal pleasure-palace, set amidst spacious gardens, for the enjoyment of a great royal court. The palace was largely destroyed in the Peninsular War, and the gardens, utterly transformed, have become a large municipal park.

The story of the Retiro in its great days—the age of Philip IV and the Count–Duke of Olivares—consequently becomes a more than usually delicate exercise in the art of reconstruction. In its time the Buen Retiro was extravagantly eulogized, and as extravagantly condemned; since then its history has been overtaken by neglect. In Calderón's allegorical drama of 1634, *El nuevo palacio del Retiro*, one of the characters asks in bewilderment: "What building is this? For whom? Who has this house been prepared for, this temple, this matchless marvel?" Even now it is not too late to offer him some answers.

3. De Wit, Prado and Monastery of San Jerónimo, from Map of Madrid. *c.* 1630 (Madrid, Biblioteca Nacional)

I

The Great Reformer

A Wasted Inheritance

Hangings of black velvet draped the walls of the monastic church of San Jerónimo el Real. In the chapel, illuminated by the flickering light of some two thousand candles, stood a majestic catafalque. Its twelve Doric columns, three to a side, were surmounted by four pediments supporting sixteen enormous statues which represented the virtues of the deceased: Glory and Fame; Faith and Prudence; Continence and Meekness; Liberality and Religion; Piety and Clemency; Justice and Victory; Peace and Benignity; Truth and Honor. The monument culminated in a superb obelisk and crown. The tomb itself was covered with a rich brocade, and the elegant epitaph to *Philippo III. Hispan. Regi potentissimo* made the most of the rather modest achievements of this 42-year-old man who for twenty-two years, six months and eighteen days had occupied the most exalted throne in the western world.[1]

Philip III had been taken seriously ill on returning to Madrid from a state visit to Portugal in 1619, but later he appeared to have made a reasonable recovery. His premature death on March 31, 1621 after a short illness came as a surprise. In accordance with the procedure followed on the death in 1598 of his father, Philip II, his body was laid to rest in the Escorial, where a royal pantheon was being built. The new king, the sixteen-year-old Philip IV, retired with his brother, the Infante Carlos, for thirty-six days of official mourning to the royal apartments in the monastery of San Jerónimo, which was to be the scene of the royal exequies.

On Sunday May 2 the royal councillors paid a formal visit to San Jerónimo to express their condolences, and on the following day the obsequies were performed with pomp and circumstance. On the 4th the royal standard was raised in various parts of Madrid—the Plaza Mayor, the Plaza de la Villa, the convent of the Descalzas, where the new queen was spending the period of mourning with the king's sister Maria and the younger of his two brothers, the Cardinal Infante Ferdinand[2]—and the new king's style and titles were publicly proclaimed. Two days later Philip IV, clearly in need of some relief after the oppressive weeks of mourning, made a temporary escape to the hunting field before returning to his monastic retreat for the night.[3] From here, on Sunday the 9th, he made his public entry into Madrid, proceeding through richly decorated streets to his palace of the Alcázar.[4]

The king's return to the Alcázar marked the end of the solemn rituals surrounding a royal death and accession, for which San Jerónimo had come to provide the traditional setting. A few weeks later he gave orders for the community to be paid 360 ducats to make good the damage done to the floor of the church by the heavy catafalque.[5] Comparative peace now returned to San Jerónimo—a peace which the prior and brethren would soon wistfully recall. For it was not long before the cloisters again resounded to the sound of hammering, and the rural tranquillity of the monastery gardens was shattered by the noisy construction of a new suburban palace.

Before a new palace was built beside San Jerónimo, however, there was other more urgent work of demolition and construction to occupy the court. Tirso de Molina, one of the most dazzling dramatists of the age, was later to write of those April days of 1621: "The Catholic and most pious Philip died, the third of his name. The structures which, thanks to his favor, were venerated through the Monarchy, were now dismantled. New architects acceded with the new king."[6] For Tirso, thinking nostalgically back to an age that was gone, the new architects were wreckers, wilfully destroying the ancient edifice of the Spanish Monarchy. But, as was only to be expected, they saw their own activities in a very different light. For them, the young king had succeeded to a bankrupt estate. The edifice consigned by the late monarch to the hands of incompetent and corrupt caretakers had fallen into ruin. It was their task to strengthen the foundations and shore up the crumbling walls, to demolish some extravagant new superstructures which threatened to bring the building down, and then by degrees restore the house to its ancient splendor.

This once splendid edifice now fallen on bad times is known to later generations as the Spanish Empire, but to contemporaries as the *monarquía*, the Spanish Monarchy. It was in reality a composite structure, somewhat accidental in design, which had acquired new and disparate additions over the course of the years and consequently lacked the uniformity that appealed to modern tastes. It had its origins in 1469 when Ferdinand, the heir to the crown of Aragon, and Isabella, the heiress to Castile, came together in marriage and agreed to unite their joint inheritances (Table 1). Thereafter new parts were added in rapid succession: Granada, taken from the Moors in 1492; the Indies of America, starting from small beginnings in the same year, and gradually extending to embrace an enormous expanse of land; and in 1515 Navarre, to the indignation of the neighboring French. New and impressive additions came in the following year when the inheritance passed to the young Charles of Ghent, soon to acquire the Imperial title as the Emperor Charles V.

By Charles V's later years the structure had grown cumbersome, and he was unable to fulfil his original intention of transferring it intact to his son, Philip II. Part of it, together with the Imperial title, had to be surrendered to Philip's Austrian cousins who belonged to the younger branch of the Habsburgs, although Philip retained an outlying extension in the Netherlands which was to cause him much trouble. But even after its division the inheritance remained exceptionally impressive, and Philip made further additions, including Portugal and its possessions, to which he succeeded through inheritance in 1580. The Spanish Monarchy was now at its fullest extent, a vast and rather rambling property, but run with an extraordinary eye for detail by an owner who was also the full-time overseer of his own estate.

All this, however, was to change when Philip III inherited from his father in 1598.

Table I. The Spanish Habsburgs (simplified version)

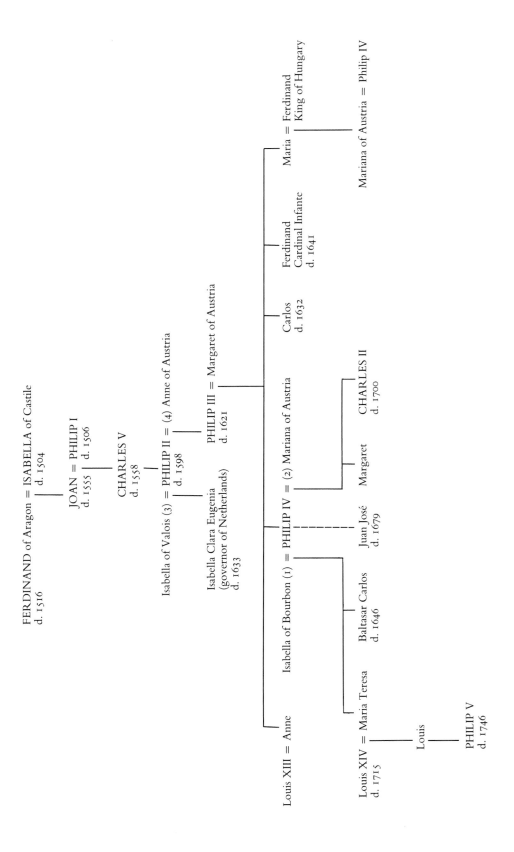

The new king lacked his predecessor's intelligence and his unlimited capacity for work, and promptly transferred his responsibilities to a member of the nobility, don Francisco Gómez de Sandoval y Rojas, soon to be created first Duke of Lerma. In selecting a favorite Philip was acting in what was to prove the pattern of early-seventeenth-century kingship. James I of England had his Duke of Buckingham; the young Louis XIII of France had his Duke of Luynes; and Philip III had his Duke of Lerma.

In the opening decades of the seventeenth century, when a Europe exhausted by the long wars of the later sixteenth century had relapsed into a precarious peace, the dazzling figure of the favorite seemed an appropriate symbol of the new and more relaxed times. Victorious in the backstairs intrigues for the favor of the prince, he had the world at his feet. Part minister, part courtier, part royal confidant, he made the most, like a brilliant butterfly, of the transient days of sunshine before the return of winter. Throughout western Europe these early years of the seventeenth century were years of lavish spending—on buildings and court spectacles, on jewels and rich clothing, on pomp and pageantry—and the favorite, digging deep into the royal coffers, could easily outdistance his rivals in this febrile competition.

The Duke of Lerma conformed perfectly to the pattern, which indeed he helped to set. Shrewd, indolent, rapacious, he lavished patronage on his innumerable Sandoval relatives and on an eager crowd of suppliants, while simultaneously amassing a splendid private fortune. On this he lived in princely magnificence until being reluctantly compelled to retire in 1618, consoled by a cardinal's biretta, to the palace built for him by the court architect, Francisco de Mora, on his ducal estates at Lerma. He suffered the humiliation of being supplanted at court by his own son, the Duke of Uceda, but the son lacked the political skills of the father, and in any event the temper of the times was already beginning to change. In Spain, at least, the age of the easy-going favorite had in reality ended before it was officially interred along with Philip III, and it was entirely fitting that Uceda should promptly follow his royal master into the oblivion which was his natural habitat.

What had happened to bring about this change? Lerma, who, for all his apparent aversion to the business of government, possessed undoubted political abilities, had succeeded in steering his country back to peace after the long wars of Philip II—peace with England in 1604, and peace, in the form of a twelve-years' truce, with the rebellious provinces of the Netherlands in 1609. But the peace once achieved was not put to any good purpose. The Crown's finances, suffering from a staggering burden of accumulated debt, remained in disarray; and during the second decade of the century the annual remittances of silver to Seville from the mines of America, which in the past had done so much to keep the Crown afloat, began to fall alarmingly.

The situation was made worse by the fact that the burden of taxation was distributed so unequally within the Monarchy. The constitutional arrangements by which at different times the various kingdoms and provinces of the Monarchy had transferred their allegiance to the kings of Spain meant that there were sharp disparities in the fiscal burdens they were called upon to bear.[7] The Italian viceroyalties—Naples and Sicily—could be exploited with relative ease, but the bulk of their revenues was liable to be consumed on the spot. The Crown of Aragon—consisting, on mainland Spain, of the kingdoms of Aragon and Valencia and the principality of Catalonia—retained strong parliamentary institutions which sharply limited the Crown's ability to interfere with its forms of government or tax its peoples more heavily. Portugal, too, was well protected by the arrangements under which it gave its allegiance to Philip II in 1580. As a result, the Crown had made a practice of resorting to Castile, the largest and most populous of the peninsular kingdoms, for money to fill its coffers and men to fight its wars.

Although Castile had its Cortes, or parliament, composed of the thirty-six representatives of eighteen major towns, this body had not proved strong enough to resist effectively the Crown's incessant tax demands. By the early seventeenth century the consequences of this were plain for all to see. In a bleak and arid countryside where, as the Count of Gondomar once remarked, one could travel for days on end without finding a bed for the night,[8] an over-taxed peasantry eked out a miserable existence. Alternatively it chose to join the swelling ranks of the under-employed or the unemployed in the overgrown cities of Seville and Madrid. In a society of some five millions, with around 170 titled nobles at its apex,[9] a large and powerful clerical estate and a swollen bureaucracy, the potentially productive elements were savagely penalized by a grossly inequitable fiscal system under which the well-born and the well-placed were absolved from paying taxes.

The corrupt and profligate government of the Duke of Lerma lacked the political will to address itself to problems which were now becoming the subject of widespread and anxious commentary. Indignant voices were raised in the Castilian Cortes about the crippling consequences of taxation and the intolerable burdens placed on the rural laborer. Pamphleteers and projectors peddled their pet nostrums, and propounded ingenious solutions for a multitude of problems. During the final years of the reign of Philip III the demand for reform was becoming irresistible— reform of the Crown's finances, and of the whole system of government by favorite; economic reform, which would bring about the restoration of Castilian agriculture and industry; and the reform of manners and morals, the corruption of which were held responsible for Castile's *declinación*.[10]

Reform appeared all the more urgent because the years of peace were visibly drawing to a close. The *pax hispanica* which had prevailed through western Europe during the reign of Philip III had always been something of a sleight of hand. The assassination of Henry IV of France in 1610 and the pacific policies followed by the regency government of Marie de' Medici during the minority of Louis XIII had temporarily left the Spanish Crown without an effective challenger, and Philip III's diplomats were adept at trading on the Monarchy's legendary reputation for unlimited riches and invincible power. But this sleight of hand could not forever conceal the harsh realities. Sooner or later Spain's capacity for war would again be put to the test, and the more responsible ministers of the Crown knew that the prospects were far from encouraging. The fleet had been neglected; the fortresses and garrisons which sustained the Spanish military presence in northern Italy and Flanders—the Spanish Netherlands—were grossly undermanned. The Crown's expenditure even in times of peace was running at nine million ducats a year, and the shortfall in supplies of silver from America made it hard to raise additional sums from bankers already justifiably sceptical of the Crown's ability to meet its commitments.

By 1618 the alarm bells were ringing even in Madrid. The revolt of the kingdom of Bohemia against the emperor seemed to portend a combined onslaught by the forces of Protestant Europe against the Catholic church and the Habsburg ascendancy. In 1621 the twelve years' truce with the Dutch was due to expire, and Spain's commanders and diplomats were deeply concerned about the safety of the military routes that linked Milan to Brussels. Spanish forces were sent to the emperor's aid; and, as the conflict extended through Germany, so Spain's involvement grew.

In this Europe which now stood on the brink of the Thirty Years' War, victory or defeat would be determined by the relative capacity of states to mobilize men and money for the battle. The Spanish Monarchy, with its widespread dominions, would seem at first sight to enjoy a clear advantage. But the Castilian economy was staggering beneath the weight of fiscal mismanagement; a corrupt administration was gripped by the creeping paralysis of bureaucratic inertia; and the very extent and disparity of the King of Spain's territories greatly complicated the task of mobilizing their resources. Yet sooner or later the effort must be made. As the reign of Philip III drew to its premature close amidst the gathering clouds of war, it was clear that the opulent abandon of those feckless years was increasingly out of tune with the times. Austerity and reform were to be the order of the day. Sterner times were coming, and with them sterner men.

THE CONQUEST OF POWER

"New architects," as Tirso de Molina had written, "acceded with the new king." Philip was only sixteen at the time of his accession, a callow and rather petulant youth with what ambassadors described as a choleric temperament. In the first flush of excitement at finding himself a king, he made it clear that he had no intention of following in the steps of his father, who, he had been told, was weak, if virtuous. His model was to be his grandfather Philip II, the image of rectitude and application to duty. But even if he possessed the character, and this remained to be seen, he certainly lacked the training to assume the heavy cares that were inseparable from this style of kingship. Although "favorite" was no longer an acceptable word at the Spanish court, he still needed one or more counsellors in whom he could repose a special confidence, and on whom he could rely to put his house in order.

The choice of the "new architects" came as no surprise. The first act of the new king was to order the Duke of Uceda to surrender his keys and hand over his state papers to the royal tutor, don Baltasar de Zúñiga. Don Baltasar was a respected and rather austere figure with a long record of foreign service, which had taken him in particular to Brussels and Prague. In the last years of Philip III he returned to Madrid from his post as ambassador at the Imperial court to occupy one of the coveted seats in the council of state, the supreme governing body of the Spanish Monarchy. But it was generally suspected that don Baltasar, for all his long experience of diplomacy and politics, was likely to prove little more than a front man for his nephew, don Gaspar de Guzmán, the Count of Olivares.

Now aged thirty-four, don Gaspar had been born in 1587 in Rome—in Nero's palace, his enemies alleged—where his father was Spanish ambassador to the papal court.[11] His earliest years had been passed outside Spain, first in Rome, and then successively in Palermo and Naples, since his father moved on to become viceroy first of Sicily and then of Naples, one of the best appointments in the gift of the King of Spain. In 1600, at the age of thirteen, he travelled with his father to the native land he had never seen, and for the rest of his life did not set foot outside the Iberian peninsula.

As a second son, don Gaspar was sent to Salamanca University to prepare for an ecclesiastical career. If he had persisted in it his family connections would probably in due course have secured him a cardinal's hat, and the rival of Cardinal Richelieu would have been known to history as Cardinal Guzmán. But the sudden death of his elder brother left him heir to the Andalusian title and estates of the counts of Olivares—a title to which he succeeded, as third count, on his father's death in 1607. The family income was moderate by the standards of the Andalusian nobility, for the counts of Olivares were only a cadet branch of that great Guzmán family whose most distinguished representatives were the dukes of Medina Sidonia. But this did not deter the new count from encumbering his estates with enormous debts as he set about spending on a ducal scale, in a bid to outshine his fellow-aristocrats in his native Seville in lavish hospitality and the patronage of men of letters and learning.

If fortunes were to be spent in Seville, they were best made in Madrid, where the spectacular rise of the house of Sandoval had shown what glittering prospects awaited those lucky enough to secure the royal favor. Don Gaspar from the first had his sharp eyes fixed on the court. On his father's death he set out to make his mark by ostentatiously wooing his cousin doña Inés de Zúñiga, a lady-in-waiting to the queen. The marriage was one of convenience, strengthening the ties between two branches of the family. Doña Inés, a devout and rather forbidding woman, was the daughter of the fifth Count of Monterrey, who had died in the previous year while serving as viceroy of Peru; and her brother, don Manuel de Acevedo y Zúñiga, the new Count of Monterrey, now married Olivares's sister, thus completing a close family alliance. This union of families produced no lasting succession. The marriage of Monterrey was childless, and of the children born to Olivares only one, a daughter, María, survived infancy, and she died in childbirth in 1626 together with her infant. Politically, however, it was to prove a powerful combination, building up a Guzmán–Zúñiga connection which would challenge, and finally overthrow, the dominance of the Sandovals.

Between 1607 and 1615 Olivares moved restlessly between Seville and Madrid, always watching for an entry to the antechambers of power. His ambitions were measureless—ambitions not merely for himself but for his house. His father, in spite of all his services to the Crown, had been consistently denied the supreme prize, the grandeeship which would raise his own branch of the Guzmán family to the highest ranks of the Spanish nobility. Don Gaspar was determined to succeed where his father had failed, but the Duke of Lerma, who was quick to spot potential rivals, was a master of smooth words and empty promises. In 1615, however, in a moment of weakness, Lerma agreed to the appointment of Olivares as one of the gentlemen of the chamber to the ten-year-old Prince Philip, who was now being given his own household on the occasion of his marriage to Isabella of Bourbon, the daughter of Henry IV of France.

4. Diego de Velázquez, *Count–Duke of Olivares* (São Paolo, Museu de Arte)

5. Rodrigo de Villandrando, *Philip IV and the Dwarf Soplillo* (Madrid, Prado)

The appointment gave Olivares what he most needed—regular entry to the palace. The prince had a suite of rooms running off the northern wing of the Alcázar, rooms which were later to be occupied by Olivares himself. As a gentleman of the prince's household, Olivares was now in a position to capture the affections and confidence of the heir to the throne. The process was far from smooth. Don Gaspar, arrogant and overbearing, was not an immediately sympathetic figure (fig. 4); and the prince, although weak-willed, had his moments of petulance (fig. 5). Olivares's rivals could be counted upon to do their best to turn the prince against him, and Philip soon made it clear that he had little liking for his new gentleman of the chamber. A series of snubs and humiliations culminated in a disdainful remark from the prince that the count's presence wearied him. At this moment Olivares happened to be carrying the prince's chamber pot. In a gesture that would long be remembered, he kissed the sacred object and withdrew in silence from the room.

He was refused his request, however, to abandon the prince's service and retire to Seville. By a carefully contrived mixture of firmness and fawning self-abasement he gradually made himself an indispensable figure in the prince's entourage, playing in particular on Philip's passion for riding and his taste for the theater. There were still dark days when he saw no future for himself at court, and would despairingly decide to leave at once, and forever, for Seville. With a king still under forty and in reasonably good health, the favor of his heir could not in any event be regarded as more than a long-term investment. But the king's sudden illness in 1619 changed all this, and a new element of uncertainty was added to the life of a court already thrown into disarray by the fall of the Duke of Lerma. Through the intense intrigues and maneuvering of the two succeeding years, the faction of Zúñiga and Olivares steadily consolidated for itself a base at court from which it could launch its bid for power when the hour struck.

"Now everything is mine," said Olivares to Uceda as the king lay on his deathbed at the end of March 1621. "Everything?" asked Uceda. "Yes, everything, without exception," Olivares replied.[12] The events of the first weeks of the new reign proved that he was right.

Even though Uceda's papers were given to Zúñiga, and Olivares ostentatiously refused any office of state, it was clear from the first where the new king's favor lay. On April 10 he was given the coveted grandeeship for himself and his descendants, and so joined the select rank of those high nobles who were entitled to the supreme privilege of wearing their hats in the presence of the king. A new regulation that no one could in future hold more than one office in the household neatly deprived Uceda of his position as the king's *sumiller de corps*, or groom of the stole. The post went to Olivares. Its duties included the dressing and undressing of the king, and gave its occupant privileged access to the royal person, symbolized by the golden key which he carried at his waist. At the end of 1622, in flagrant contravention of the new regulation, Olivares was also appointed master of the horse. As such it was his duty to accompany the king whenever he moved outside the palace, either by coach or on horseback. These two offices had previously been combined in the person of the Duke of Lerma, who was keenly aware that the right of constant access to the king was an indispensable guarantee for the retention of power.

During those opening months of the reign Olivares and Zúñiga were clearly working in unison to a prearranged plan. The first task was to make sure of the royal household and the important offices of state. This involved the dislodging of the old Sandoval connection, and the appointment to vacant or newly-created offices of men whom they could trust—which meant in practice members and dependents of the three interrelated families of Zúñiga, Haro and Guzmán, all of which had been left to eat the crumbs from the Duke of Lerma's table. Matías de Novoa, a disaffected courtier who kept a secret journal, traces with unconcealed venom the rise of what he called the *parentela*, the clan.[13] Of Olivares's three brothers-in-law, one, the Count of Monterrey, was promptly given a grandeeship, and launched on what was to prove a highly remunerative career, which carried him to the viceroyalty of Naples and a seat on the council of state. Another, the Marquis of Alcañices, who had none of Monterrey's political talents, became the principal huntsman to the king. The third, the Marquis of Carpio, received a household appointment, as did his son, don Luis de Haro; and don García de Haro, the brother of the marquis and a graduate of Salamanca University, was to be rapidly promoted up the ministerial ladder until he became (as Count of Castrillo) a dominant figure in the royal administration.

Another of Olivares's relatives, his cousin don Diego Mexía, who was serving at the time in the Spanish army of Flanders, hurried back from Brussels on the news of the king's death to lay the foundations of a spectacular career. Although probably a year or two older then Olivares, the latter came to treat him as the son he never had. He was given a seat on the council of war, was appointed a gentleman of the chamber in 1624, and became a councillor of state in 1626. In the following year he was created Marquis of Leganés, and made a splendid marriage to doña Policena Spínola, a lady-in-waiting to the queen, and daughter of Ambrosio Spínola, the great Genoese commander of the army of Flanders. Although military service took him away from Madrid repeatedly during the next few years, he remained one of Olivares's closest and most trusted confidants. The owner of a fine Madrid house and of a superb collection of paintings, this amiable, easy-going man, born the fourth son of a relatively minor nobleman, rose effortlessly to become one of the richest and most influential men in the Spain of Philip IV—a living witness to the supreme advantage of enjoying the favors of the favorite.[14]

The more unscrupulous members of the Olivares clan would soon learn, like their predecessors, the judicious use of power and patronage for personal enrichment. But at least during the early years of the new regime they had to move with care. Olivares and Zúñiga had come to power as reformers who saw it as their mission to cleanse the Augean stables. Their own hands remained clean, at least by seventeenth-century standards, and Olivares missed no opportunity to emphasize, perhaps a shade too vehemently, the disinterested character of his service to the Crown. The proclaimed intention of the new rulers was to restore the high standards of equity and justice of the reign of Philip II, when the Crown was respected and its authority obeyed. This restoration was to be achieved both by personal example and public exhortation, suitably reinforced by the rigor of the law.

One of the first actions of the new rulers was to create a special reforming Junta with the avowed purpose of "eradicating vices, abuses and bribes."[15] Judicial inquiries were begun into the activities of Lerma and his colleagues; royal officials throughout the Monarchy were ordered to produce inventories of their possessions; and, to set a public example, one of Lerma's principal henchmen, don Rodrigo Calderón, was executed amidst scenes of extraordinary popular emotion in the Plaza Mayor. The execution proved to be a psychological mistake. Calderón's noble bearing on the scaffold instantaneously expunged from the public mind the record of his crimes, and the villain became the first martyr of the new regime.

Don Baltasar de Zúñiga died in October 1622, but the unrelenting vigor of the campaign for the reform of manners and morals suggests that the moving spirit behind it had from the first been Olivares. He is known to have been heavily occupied from the early months of the reign with attempting to bring some order to the royal finances—a task made all the more necessary by the sharp increase in military and naval expenditure that followed on the resumption of the war with the Dutch. Financial austerity was now the order of the day, and the cornucopia which had flowed so liberally under Lerma suddenly ran dry. Olivares, by imposing strict limitations on the award of those honors and favors which imposed a burden on the treasury, did nothing to endear himself to the old nobility. But he was not the kind of man to be deterred by unpopularity, least of all among the old grandee families of Castile, most of which he despised.

Austerity, discipline, the restoration of the old moral values—these were the watchwords of Olivares's campaign. It culminated in February 1623 in the publication of twenty-three "articles of reformation." These constituted a strange medley of fiscal, institutional and moral reforms, ranging from a prohibition on the import of foreign manufactures to the closing of brothels.[16] But the intention behind them was clear. They were all designed to bring about the restoration of Castile. But was Castile—the old Castile—capable of restoration, and was the new austerity compatible with the image that had to be sustained of the King of Spain as the richest and most powerful monarch in the world? It was a dilemma that was to haunt Olivares for the rest of his career.

THE COUNT–DUKE AND HIS PROGRAM

The death of don Baltasar de Zúñiga in 1622 had left Olivares as the sole architect in charge of the reconstruction of the Monarchy. Tirso's use of the word "architect" was singularly appropriate when applied to Olivares. *Arquitecto* had entered the Spanish language in the sixteenth century, and was defined in Covarrubias's dictionary of 1611 as being the equivalent of *maestro de obras*, or master of the works: "he who provides the designs (*trazas*) of buildings, forming them first in his mind." Olivares was above all a man of grand designs.

On his uncle's death he finally moved out of the shadows and accepted a seat on the council of state. He was now a minister, and in effect the first minister, of the Spanish crown. Like Richelieu, who became first minister of the King of France in 1624, he saw it as his first duty to elevate the authority of his royal master both at home and abroad. He appreciated, as did Richelieu, that the Crown's national and international standing were intimately related, and he was acutely aware that economic prosperity was essential for the exercise of power—a lesson that had been forcefully driven home by the spectacular successes of the Dutch. The decay of Castilian trade and industry could only be reversed, he believed, if the full weight of the Crown's authority was placed behind reform. As a result, there sprang from his powerful if disorderly mind a profusion of measures designed to encourage a revival of economic activity—plans for the founding of trading companies and for radical fiscal reform, for repopulating the countryside and making rivers navigable, and for relaxing the discriminatory laws against those of his countrymen who bore the "taint" of Jewish ancestry.[17]

In order to relieve the fiscal burden on Castile and mobilize more effectively the resources of the Monarchy he also planned a major revision of its constitutional

6. (left) Diego de Velázquez, *Count–Duke of Olivares* (New York City, Hispanic Society of America)

7. (above) Detail from Diego de Velázquez, *Count–Duke of Olivares on Horseback* (Madrid, Prado)

structure. Beginning with the Iberian peninsula itself, he looked forward to the day when it would be possible to demolish the institutional barriers dividing its different kingdoms and peoples; do away with the laws and privileges that impeded the exercise of effective royal government in Portugal and the Crown of Aragon; and establish a new system whereby Spaniards would all be ruled by the same laws (those of Castile) while offices at court and in the Monarchy at large would be awarded on merit irrespective of the kingdom or province of origin. It was, therefore, a more coherent and more integrated Monarchy which he aspired to create—a Monarchy in which the burdens and the profits were more equitably shared.[18]

OLIVARES AND THE KING

Olivares's program was an ambitious one, difficult enough to achieve in time of peace, and still more difficult in time of war. But this was entirely in character. Once he had decided on a course of action he was not a man to let himself be diverted by objections and difficulties. Foreign ambassadors in Madrid, who tended to find him unsympathetic, described him as a man with the ambition to dominate;[19] a man "by nature very inclined to novelties, without taking account of where they may lead him."[20] He was forever scheming and contriving, bullying and cajoling,

19

determined to be the master in everything he did. This made him a harsh task-master, arrogant, overbearing, constantly fussing over details—a man who could never bear to leave anything alone.

The arrogance of a man born to command is well captured in the "official" portraits of him by Velázquez. Already in the first of these, the São Paolo portrait of 1624 depicting Olivares with the golden key of his office of *sumiller de corps*, the massive physical presence is firmly established (fig. 4). But it is the Hispanic Society portrait of 1625, in which he holds in his right hand the riding whip symbolizing his position as master of the horse, that introduces the Olivares best known to posterity (fig. 6). The Olivares of 1625, with his large head, his bulbous nose, his squat but heavy body, already has the traits of the definitive image. Here is the famous thick black moustache, the wide splayed beard (which in later years would be reduced to cover only the center of the chin) and the artificial hairpiece concealing the incipient baldness, mentioned by Matías de Novoa, who describes Olivares addressing the council of state in this same year, 1625, and inserting his cane between the hairpiece and the bald patch as he harangued his fellow-councillors.[21]

Some ten years later, in the great equestrian portrait in the Prado, the gaze has become still more imperious, the assertion of command more complete (fig. 7). This is the portrait of a man who firmly controls the destiny of the Spanish Monarchy, and guides it safely amidst the perils of war. But there was another Olivares whom Velázquez also knew. In the extraordinarily vivid portrait drawing of 1625–6, which appears to be by the hand of Velázquez, the face seems softer and more

8. Attributed to Diego de Velázquez, *Count–Duke of Olivares* (Paris, École des Beaux-Arts)

9. Diego de Velázquez, *Count–Duke of Olivares* (Leningrad, The Hermitage)

vulnerable (fig. 8). This is a more reflective, and perhaps less confident, Olivares, more like the man who wrote in 1625 to the Count of Gondomar: "I am not rigorous by nature, even though my duties compel me to appear so."[22] This Olivares seems more conscious of the burdens than the splendors of office, and also more conscious of his own fallibility. The eyes reveal a melancholy that is still more marked some fifteen years later in the Hermitage portrait of around 1640 (fig. 9). By now the cares of office have taken a heavy toll. The eyes have lost their alertness, the face is puffier, the body more obese. In 1640 Olivares was a man nearly overwhelmed by care and misfortune, a statesman struggling to turn back what looked to be an inexorable tide of disaster.

If the images seem contradictory, so also was the man. Olivares was subject to exceptionally sharp changes of mood. Moments of euphoria would give way to times of deep depression, when he wanted no more than to be allowed to retire to some remote corner where he might die in peace. But while ambassadors would comment on his natural impulsiveness, he was in many ways a deeply cautious statesman, who held his instincts under tight rein. On the surface he appeared impulsive because he was much addicted to the theatrical manner and the grand gesture. He was liable to sudden violent outbursts of temper; he was a compulsive talker; he would threaten and bludgeon and bully. But behind the violent gestures, the sudden strange movements of head and body which perhaps betrayed an epileptic inheritance,[23] there was a mind of unusual astuteness and a sharp, appraising eye. The grand pronouncements often bore little relation to the careful moves of a master player who knew in intricate detail the disposition and potential of every pawn on the board.

Olivares's notorious capriciousness may therefore have been a capriciousness more of style than of substance. Much of what he did was done for effect. There was calculation behind the wild spending and lavish display of the early years in Seville and at court; and once he had made his point and achieved his aims he settled down to an abstemious style of life, in which he allowed himself few distractions from the ceaseless round of work. There came to be an established pattern to his day.[24] The hours before seven in the morning were devoted to his religious exercises, including daily confession. From seven to eleven, with the help of four secretaries, he would go through the *consultas*—the documents recording the discussions and recommendations of the various councils, which would then go up for decision by the king. Next he would hold audiences for those who had already received a royal audience on the preceding day. At lunch he ate little, without ceremony, and by three he would be back at work, reading and dictating state papers and letters, holding juntas or meetings of ministers, and preparing business with his secretaries until eleven at night. If he went out in his coach for a turn in the countryside, he took his secretaries with him, determined to lose no time from affairs of state.

There were few distractions from the austerity of this regime. In his early years he was an outstanding horseman, and riding was one of the great pleasures of his life. But his official duties left him less and less time for exercise, and an increasingly sedentary existence helped to undermine his constitution. By the early 1630s his gout and his growing corpulence made him a martyr to ill-health. "I am so racked by illnesses," he wrote to the Marquis of Aytona in 1633, "that when I tried to mount a

10. Anonymous seventeenth-century artist, *Duke of Medina de las Torres* (Madrid, Prado)

horse the other day I simply could not manage it. This is the worst thing that could happen, because I always used to recover my spirits and vitality once I was on horseback."[25]

Indifferent health was certainly one explanation for his increasingly austere style of life. But another and probably more potent cause was the terrible shock of the death of his daughter, María, in childbirth in 1626. All the hopes for the family succession had been placed on this seventeen-year-old girl. Since coming to power in 1621 Olivares had been assiduously building up his Andalusian estates with the intention of creating a family fief to outmatch that of the Duke of Medina Sidonia. In 1624 he found a husband for his daughter in the young Marquis of Toral, who came from an impoverished branch of the house of Guzmán which could claim greater antiquity than Medina Sidonia's. Then on January 5, 1625 Olivares himself was raised to a dukedom, that of San Lúcar la Mayor. As Count of Olivares and now Duke of San Lúcar as well, he acquired the sobriquet of "count–duke" by which in future he was to be universally known. With the title and the entail established there lacked only an heir; but the happy prospects for succession were dashed forever with María's death on July 30, 1626. His daughter's death left Olivares distraught. His plans for the establishment of a great new house of Guzmán had been irreparably shattered, and one of the great driving forces of his existence was suddenly removed.

He continued to further the career of his son-in-law, who was created Duke of Medina de las Torres (fig. 10); and he sought, and apparently found, consolation in his faith. In the words of his biographer and panegyrist, the Count of La Roca, "he embraced God with frequent recourse to the sacraments, and with spiritual exercises whenever public affairs gave him a respite."[26] His thoughts were much on death and salvation—"*solo salvarse importa*," he wrote in a letter of 1628, "salvation is all that counts."[27] He found his confessors among the Jesuits, especially Hernando de

22

Salazar, who became one of his most intimate advisers and whom he described as "the cleric in Spain to whom I owe most and whom I love most, and a man who, in my fallible judgment, is a person of rare and superior parts both in virtue and letters."[28] Although a devotee of the Jesuits, his first allegiance, as a member of the house of Guzmán, was to the Dominican Order, because, in his own words, "it runs in my blood."[29] He and his wife, who were great patrons of religious foundations, established in 1625 on his Andalusian property of Castilleja de la Cuesta a convent of Dominican Recoleta nuns.[30] The contemplative life obviously exercised a powerful fascination over Olivares, essentially a man of action, and from the late 1620s or early 1630s he made it his practice to spend every Holy Week in retreat in the monastery of San Jerónimo, where he indulged to the full his insatiable appetite for sermons.[31]

He had one other great passion in his life, his books. He was an avid—indeed an obsessive—book collector, whose library became one of the most famous of the age.[32] When catalogued in the mid-1620s it contained some 2,700 printed books and 1,400 manuscripts, and was notably rich in its ancient codices. Although the count–duke was obviously well-informed about painting and architecture, he is not known to have shared the passion of other members of the Spanish nobility, such as his cousin the Marquis of Leganés, for the acquisition of pictures. Books were his great delight, and as soon as they were acquired they were bound in handsome bindings stamped with the Olivares arms. The range of his library was extraordinarily impressive. Subdivided into Latin (including Greek and Hebrew), Spanish, French and "Tuscan," it was particularly strong in religion, in works of history and political treatises, although it also contained an extensive medical collection, and a certain amount on the *ars amatoria*.

An enthusiastic book collector is not invariably an enthusiastic reader, but the impression created by the library is of a man with lively curiosity, wide geographical and historical interests, and a broad and tolerant humanist culture. In his Seville days Olivares was famed as a patron of men of letters, and he carried the habit of patronage with him to Madrid. Even during the years when his time was largely occupied with matters of state, he seems to have maintained his interest in literary and scholarly discussion. Learned questions of classical philology would be debated in his presence,[33] and he would spend long periods closeted with his librarian, Francisco de Rioja, who had come with him from Seville.[34] Rioja was a poet and a classical scholar whose numerous friendships in the world of Spanish scholarship and letters would stand Olivares in good stead. To judge from a letter written by Olivares to Cardinal Barberini in 1623 requesting a benefice for Rioja, the relationship between the two men was close. Olivares described him as "a person of great virtue and excellent parts, to whom I have a special obligation because of the good company he has given me for many years now. . . He is a person of singular learning with a deep knowledge of Greek and Latin authors, and I am extremely obliged to him and want to see him well settled."[35] Apart from acting as the count–duke's librarian, he seems to have served as his amanuensis, helping with the drafting of some of his most important state papers. His intimacy with Olivares and his classical learning made him in effect the scholar-in-residence at the court of Philip IV. Before the end of 1624 he had been appointed to the official post of chronicler of Castile, which made him the equivalent of a historiographer royal, and ten years later he was given custodianship of the royal library in addition to Olivares's own.[36]

If books and the company of learned men provided Olivares with a little respite from the cares of state, the fact remained that his entire life, especially after the death of his daughter, was unremittingly dedicated to his governmental duties. He thought of himself as a "minister"—"the king's faithful minister"[37]—whose task was to serve his royal master to the limits of his ability by formulating policies, mastering all the details of governmental business at home and abroad, and presenting the king with the recommendations on which his decisions would be based. The Spanish Crown, with its far-flung dominions, had pioneered the art of government by paper; and Olivares, in the tradition of Philip II, was never happier than when surrounded by his papers. Indeed he was rarely without them, and it was a common sight to see him bustling along in the palace with documents stuffed into his hatband and dangling from his belt, looking for all the world like a scarecrow.[38]

In the circumstances it is not surprising that he overworked his secretaries, just as he overworked himself. "It seemed impossible," wrote the Count of La Roca, "that the count–duke should be able to survive this punishing daily routine, so contrary to nature, and he visibly killed four secretaries in their attempts to keep up with him."[39] One of these unfortunates, however, survived to the end. This was Antonio Carnero, of mixed Spanish–Flemish parentage, who was brought back from Brussels by Baltasar de Zúñiga, and then inherited by Olivares on Zúñiga's death. Described by the English ambassador as "a very honest man and a very good friend (though he stole my dog),"[40] Carnero rose rapidly to become the count–duke's most confidential secretary. Olivares's major state papers and a large part of his private correspondence were dictated to Carnero, whose rewards for his many services would in due course include the lieutenant–governorship of the Palace of the Buen Retiro.

By taking over the papers on Zúñiga's death and making himself master of the intricacies of government, Olivares was deliberately emphasizing the ministerial nature of his relationship with the king. While the Duke of Lerma had also run the government, although with a certain characteristic indolence very distinct from the bustling activity of Olivares, Lerma was always regarded as the favorite, and this was an image that Olivares hoped to avoid. This was in fact a vain hope. However much he might insist that he was no more than the king's faithful servant in the day-to-day business of government, he was in reality no less the royal favorite than Lerma, since it was his influence with the king that had made him what he was.

The tenure of a favorite rested on royal caprice; that of a minister on the quality of his service. It was as a royal servant that Olivares wished to be judged, and the quality of their service to the king was the criterion by which he judged his fellow-men. But here he consistently met with cruel disappointment. How often he had to complain that the king's will was not done! Obedience was lax and resistance widespread, as he discovered all too soon when he attempted to put his reform program into effect. There were too many vested interests, too much insistence on privilege and status, which to Olivares seemed matters of little consequence where the service of the Crown was involved.

To make matters worse, the existing machinery of government proved a very imperfect instrument for introducing change. The Monarchy was administered by a massive bureaucracy, with twelve royal councils in Madrid at its summit. Some of these councils, like the council of state, embraced the entire Monarchy in their concerns. Others, like the councils of Castile, Aragon, Italy and the Indies, devoted themselves exclusively to the affairs of their respective territories. As a device for providing the king with recommendations for action, this conciliar system, although cumbersome and time-consuming, worked reasonably well. But as a device for securing action it was painfully inadequate.

For all Olivares's efforts, the conciliar system proved impervious to change. By degrees he was able to alter to his own advantage the composition of the council of state, as the older generation of councillors disappeared and his own relatives and dependents were nominated to take their place. But the council of state consisted of nobles, prelates, generals and diplomats, whereas the other councils were staffed by members of a professional bureaucracy who had worked their way slowly through a standard *cursus honorum* until attaining, at a relatively advanced age, their exalted conciliar status. To introduce outsiders into this self-perpetuating caste of royal ministers and officials, drawn from a few privileged colleges in the universities, proved an almost impossible task. Olivares did succeed in securing a seat on the council of Castile in 1629 for his personal lawyer, José González, but in general the system defeated him.[41]

Since the bureaucratic citadel proved impervious to assault, the count–duke's only remaining option was to subvert it from within. Increasingly he resorted to the expedient of taking business away from the councils and placing it in the hands of expert committees or juntas, composed of his own hand-picked men. Some of these men were friends and dependents from his years in Seville; others were members of the professional bureaucracy or of the royal secretariat who for one reason or another had attracted his attention. Typical of these was Jerónimo de Villanueva, a member of a dynasty of Aragonese officials, who held the office of protonotary of the Crown of Aragon. Once the count–duke had spotted his talents his rise was spectacular. In 1626 he was given a secretaryship of state, which made him the intermediary between the king and Olivares. In December 1627 he was entrusted with the management of the king's secret expense account, and soon there was no secret which he did not know. He was appointed to all the more important juntas; increasingly, as protonotary, he appropriated to himself the management of all business relating to the Crown of Aragon; and, as the suave official ever at Olivares's service, he eventually became in all but name the second most important man in the royal administration.[42]

We know a little about Villanueva because he was arrested by the Inquisition after Olivares's fall, and became the subject of an interminable trial.[43] Through its documentation we get occasional glimpses, not of the official but the man: a wealthy bachelor, a dabbler in astrology, and above all the founder and patron of the Madrid convent of San Plácido, which became a source of grave scandal to the faithful in the late 1620s when the nuns took to having mystical revelations and consorting with the devil. Here we catch him making an incautious reference to his Jewish ancestry, or glimpse him—in an unusual juxtaposition of cleanliness and godliness—being deloused by the mother superior while he sat on her lap. But all too quickly, even with Villanueva, the shutters come down, and most of Olivares's hand-picked men remain lost among the shadows.

Yet these men, now forgotten—Villanueva and José González, Francisco de Tejada, Diego Suárez, Antonio de Contreras—were the men who, in the 1620s and 1630s, managed the affairs of the greatest power in Europe. They were the count–duke's men, his "creatures" in the terminology of the day. It was they who staffed the juntas, helped devise and execute the policies, and devoted more and more of their time to inventing new financial expedients to keep the Crown in cash. They formed a close and rather self-conscious little coterie, priding themselves on their loyalty to the count–duke and the king. It was to this coterie that Olivares turned for both business and pleasure. When the Buen Retiro was being built, he relied upon these men to help him raise the money, supervise the construction, and assist with schemes for decorating the empty rooms. It was to become their palace almost as much as his; and when the king took his pleasure at the Retiro he took it amidst the Olivares circle, with its intimacies and its private jokes and its self-satisfied pastimes.

Along with a handful of the count–duke's friends, relatives and dependents among the aristocracy, the little circle of secretaries and officials constituted, in effect, the Olivares regime. As seen by themselves they were struggling against every kind of adversity to bring salvation to the Monarchy. But to others they appeared in a less flattering light. To the representatives of the old houses of Castile, in particular—families like the Pimentels and the Toledos—they were arrogant upstarts whose very claim to speak in the name of the king was an affront to their honor. Above all, they were the instruments of Olivares, a man whom the old families detested.

Enmity between Olivares and the powerful families of the Sandoval connection was inevitable from the circumstances of his rise to power, but he did not take long to antagonize the larger part of the Spanish nobility. Partly this was a result of his own abrasive manner, which may itself have sprung from the inherited resentments of the cadet branch of a great house which believed that it had not received its due. But it also reflected his profound belief that, in the years since the death of Philip II, the balance of social and political power had tilted dangerously against the Crown and in favor of the high nobility. It was an essential part of his program to redress this balance, and if this meant alienating grandees who put their own interests above those of the king, so much the worse for them. Most of them reacted with open, or barely concealed hostility, and during the 1630s they increasingly withdrew from a court where they found themselves held in such low esteem. But Olivares held unflinchingly to his criterion: "I have neither father, child nor friend except for him who serves the king well."[44] For at the center of his program was the greatness of his king.

"PHILIP THE GREAT"

Olivares tended to write and speak of his sovereign with an extravagance of language that bordered on idolatry. He possessed an unbounded reverence for the majesty of kingship, and no king on earth was called to a higher mission than the King of Spain. Philip was the heir to the great tradition of Hispanic kingship which began in the mists of antiquity with Tubal and Hercules, and was transmitted by way of the Visigoths and the Catholic Monarchs to his glorious progenitors of the House of Austria. He was the guardian of the faith, the right arm of the church, and the ruler of the largest empire the world had ever known. If the Spanish Monarchy were to be restored to its former splendor, the centerpiece of its spectacular revival must be the king himself.

Nothing, in Olivares's eyes, was too good for the king, but at the same time he felt a profound sense of responsibility for the precious trust that had been committed to his charge. Philip at the time of his accession was exactly half his age—a still unformed youth who needed careful training if he were to occupy with distinction the high office to which God had called him. Olivares saw the most important of all his tasks, therefore, as that of royal schoolmaster, initiating his young pupil into the craft and mysteries of kingship.

For Olivares, three men above all provided the true model of kingship: Ferdinand the Catholic, whom he called the king of kings; Charles V, the image of the Christian knight, victorious in his wars; and Philip II, who from his narrow study in the Escorial governed the world with his pen. The young Philip must emulate these ancestors and in due course surpass them all; but the only way to achieve this was by unremitting work.

Philip was to begin his royal education by acquiring a first-hand knowledge of his Iberian kingdoms. As a prince he had already visited Portugal, to be sworn in at Lisbon as heir to the throne. Olivares's native province of Andalusia was chosen for Philip's first major excursion from Madrid once he became king. He left Madrid on February 8, 1624, and the high point of the journey was his visit at the beginning of March to Seville. He was lodged in the Alcázar, that splendid Moorish palace set about with gardens, the governorship of which was vested in the counts of Olivares. For eleven days he stayed in Seville, enjoying firework displays and other festivities worthy of that most opulent of cities, still basking in the fading sunset of the riches of the Indies.[45]

The king's tour of Andalusia was to have been followed almost at once by a visit to the eastern provinces of the peninsula, where he had still to take the oath to observe the laws and privileges of his Aragonese, Catalan and Valencian subjects. But royal tours were expensive and there was no money in the treasury. The visit to the Crown of Aragon therefore had to be deferred. There was pressing business, too, to keep the king and Olivares at court, as news arrived of negotiations for an alliance between the French and the Dutch, with the prospect of a great anti-Habsburg coalition in the making.

But how far the king could be persuaded to devote his attention to such matters was very much an open question in those early years of the reign. Philip seems to have grown quickly bored with the more routine duties of kingship in which the count–duke was attempting to train him. In a famous letter of 1626 Olivares made it plain to the king that his own situation, and that of the Monarchy, was being made impossible by his unwillingness to attend to affairs of state. Philip's penitent reply was that of an erring pupil who promises to do better in the future, and he returned the letter to Olivares so that his descendants might see how a faithful vassal should speak to his king.[46] But repentance always came more easily to Philip than reform. His intentions were of the best; he was by no means lacking in intelligence; but while the spirit was willing, the flesh was very weak. He knew that he should spend more time with his papers, but the distractions of the court and the pleasures of the chase (whether of women or of wild beasts) seemed incomparably more alluring.

In the autumn of 1627, however, Philip was struck by a sudden and alarming illness, which for a few days seemed likely to end in death.[47] Religiously very impressionable, he came to see the illness as a solemn warning. His father, after all, had died in a state of terrible remorse over his failures as a king. Once he was recovered, Philip began to take his duties more seriously. He was now seized with the conviction which was to haunt him for the rest of his life that the misfortunes of the Monarchy were directly attributable to his private sins. While the conviction may not have done much to reduce the number of these sins, it certainly increased the contrition that followed in their wake. It also led him to spend longer and longer hours at his desk, poring over the endless succession of documents sent for perusal and decision by his ministers and councils.

Olivares therefore succeeded in creating, if not another Philip II, at least a conscientious royal bureaucrat. This success might have seemed to endanger his own position as the effective master of the Monarchy. But the count–duke knew his prince. There were moments of restlessness in these years, when Philip seemed to chafe at the domination of his overbearing minister. But although more intelligent and capable than his father, he suffered from the same acute lack of self-confidence. At times he could be obstinate, but his obstinacy was the obstinacy of the congenitally weak-willed. He found it difficult to reach decisions, and the very extent of the paperwork increased his dependence on the count–duke, by underlining his own inability to cope single-handed with the multitude of problems that assailed a King of Spain. He was therefore happy to have a minister whose capacity for work appeared to be boundless, and who could sift the material for him and guide his decisions. Olivares was always careful to represent these decisions as his master's, but the occasions on which the king took an independent decision of real importance seem in fact to have been few.

Since the temperaments of the two men complemented each other very nicely, the working relationship which they finally achieved after a few stormy passages proved to be highly satisfactory for both. The king reigned; Olivares ruled. They were constantly consulting each other—the king, walking through the north gallery of the palace, would even visit Olivares in his rooms—and the bonds of mutual dependence in due course created a genuine partnership and even perhaps a certain affection between a grateful king and a profoundly respectful minister.

But the count–duke was not merely concerned with turning Philip into a dedicated bureaucrat. He wanted to make him a king more powerful at home than any of his predecessors, and no less respected than Charles V and Philip II by his foreign enemies. The groundwork for achieving both these ambitions was laid in 1625 and 1626.

Seventeenth-century statesmen intent on exalting the majesty of kingship had little patience with those ancient laws and institutions which prevented the free and unfettered assertion of royal authority. Olivares, like the proponents of more effective kingship in Bourbon France and Stuart England, chafed against the restraints imposed by parliaments and corporate bodies, which seemed more concerned to protect their own privileges than to further the interests of the king. In a now famous secret memorandum on the government of Spain which he presented to Philip at the end of 1624, he told him that, although he might be King of Portugal, Aragon, and Valencia and Count of Barcelona, he was not yet King of Spain. The supreme objective of his reign must be to make himself a real King of Spain, the ruler not of disparate kingdoms but of a unified peninsula.[48]

But this was not an objective that could be achieved by issuing an edict. The Portuguese and the Catalans were extremely jealous of their traditional laws and privileges, and if they were to be persuaded to surrender them for the higher good of the Monarchy as a whole, it was essential that the ground should first be carefully prepared. It was here that the wars and the rumors of war which threatened the very survival of the Monarchy might be turned by skilful statesmanship to good account. For it was obvious—at least to Olivares—that the highest of all laws was the law of self-defence.

The remarkable events of 1625, that *annus mirabilis* of the reign of Philip IV,

PHILIPP·S·IIII·HISPANIAR·REX·

I de Courbes F

IMPERIVM SINE FINE FIDES ASSERTA PARABIT: ASSERO, ET IMPERIVM, NON MIHI, SED FIDEI.

11. Jean de Courbes, *Philip IV on Horseback*

29

enabled Olivares to prepare the appropriate scenario. The year began with the Monarchy beleaguered and embattled. Pernambuco in Brazil had fallen to the Dutch; the war in the Netherlands since Ambrosio Spínola's capture of Jülich in February 1622 seemed once again to be settling into a costly stalemate; the combined armies of France and Savoy were closing in on Spain's ally and client, the republic of Genoa; and the English were preparing a fleet for the invasion of Spain.

In the face of all these dangers Spain had to gird itself for battle under the leadership of its king. Philip put on armor and was portrayed armed and on horseback "like a Caesar." (fig. 11)[49] Olivares also donned his arms and was appointed captain–general of the cavalry in November.[50] By the end of the year the immediate danger was past, and the king and his minister could look back on a string of glorious successes. The Marquis of Santa Cruz had relieved the city of Genoa; a combined Spanish–Portuguese naval expedition under the command of don Fadrique de Toledo forced the surrender of the Dutch garrison at Bahía in Brazil on May 1; the allegedly impregnable fortress of Breda in the Netherlands surrendered to the besieging army of Spínola on June 5; and at Cadiz the English invading force beat a hasty retreat at the beginning of November. These were triumphant days, which would allow Olivares to unveil to the world a victorious monarch, *Felipe el Grande*, Philip the Great. It was an image later to be brilliantly depicted by Maino in his painting for the Hall of Realms.

With all the prestige of victory behind him the king could now set out on his long-deferred visit to the Crown of Aragon. He left Madrid with Olivares on January 7, 1626, travelling first to Zaragoza. His intention was to present to the Cortes of Aragon, Valencia and Catalonia a project of Olivares's devising called the "Union of Arms." Each kingdom of the Monarchy would provide its quota of paid soldiers, who would be sent to the assistance of any of its fellow-kingdoms under attack. This scheme for mutual defense had obvious advantages. It would rationalize the use of manpower in the Monarchy, relieve Castile of part of its burdens, and greatly improve the defense capabilities of the Monarchy as a whole. It also had the further long-term advantage of accustoming kingdoms and provinces which had hitherto lived in relative isolation to the idea of mutual assistance in time of need. In this way it would serve as the first stage toward achieving the Monarchy's closer integration, and toward making Philip IV a true "King of Spain."

But the scheme met with more resistance, especially from the Catalans, than Olivares had anticipated, and when the king returned to his capital on May 14, the visit to the Crown of Aragon had to be regarded as less than a total success.[51] In spite of this, the count–duke could look back on his first five years in command of the fortunes of the Monarchy with a certain satisfaction. Castile had not sunk beneath the accumulated weight of its troubles, and the first modest steps toward recovery had been taken. Ministers were busy with projects for financial reform and economic revival, and in 1625 Spain had emerged victorious from its trial of strength with its enemies. His reputation secured by these glorious victories, it might now be possible for the king to negotiate an honorable settlement with the Dutch. Once this had been achieved, his peoples could look forward to a new golden age— an age in which Philip the Great, victorious in his wars, could hold court amidst all the splendors of a Spain at peace.

II

The King on Stage

THE THEATER OF THE COURT

The court of the King of Spain resembled a magnificent theater in which the principal actor was permanently on stage. The stage instructions were meticulously detailed; the scenery was imposing, if a little antiquated; and the supporting cast was impressively large. All that was needed was a director of genius to orchestrate the action and make the necessary dispositions to secure the most brilliant scenic effects. In the Count–Duke of Olivares, who had learned his craft in Seville, that most theatrical of cities, the perfect director was ready to hand.

The etiquette and protocol of the Spanish court as they had developed under the House of Austria were exceptionally formal, even for an age as obsessed with ceremony as the seventeenth century. The Emperor Charles V had introduced Burgundian ceremonial and organization into the court life of Spain in 1548. Since that time a series of written regulations known as *etiquetas de palacio* had come to prescribe in minute detail the exact ordering of ceremonial functions, and the duties, wages and perquisites of every official in the complex court hierarchy. The purpose of these regulations was to ensure the observance of an order and decorum which would enhance the remote grandeur of the monarch as a semi-divine being who was not as other men.[1]

So exalted was the King of Spain that much of the time he was withdrawn from public view. Once a week he ate ceremonially in public, but otherwise he would take his meals alone, served by a gentleman of the household who brought and removed the dishes. The queen, who had her own separate household, also ate alone; but on special occasions, like the marriage of a lady-in-waiting, the king and queen would eat together in public, waited upon by court functionaries whose every movement was guided by the most exacting ritual.

Among the courts of seventeenth-century Europe the Spanish court was notable for this curious combination of the very public and the very private. On certain fixed occasions the king was presented to the world. The rest of the time he was screened from it by a barrier of protocol vigilantly guarded by a select group of court nobles and officials. The supreme custodian of the protocol was the king himself. No one was more conscious of the requirements of etiquette and ceremonial than Philip IV, who carefully revised and amended the *etiquetas* over the course of his reign, in order to ensure that the highest standards of decorum were observed. These standards could be disregarded only by the court dwarfs and buffoons, licensed jesters who made free with their right to cross the boundaries between the

31

king's public and private worlds. For the rest, Philip, who was endowed with innate dignity and an instinctive sense of what was fitting and proper, trained himself to present to the world that outward appearance of rigid self-control which had come to be expected of a king of Spain. Foreign envoys, after proceeding through a succession of dark but handsomely appointed rooms in the king's suite at the Alcázar, would enter the audience-chamber to find him standing alone beside a console table. He would raise his hand to his hat as the ambassador made his entry, and then stand motionless through the audience, which he would bring to an end with one or two anodyne remarks whose exquisite courtesy never failed to impress.

Behind the public mask was a private man, still very unsure of himself at the beginning of his reign (fig. 12). As a prince he had lived a withdrawn life in the palace, one enlivened nonetheless by the company of brothers and sisters. His mother, Margaret of Austria, had died in childbirth in 1611, when he was six. Four years later, at the age of ten, he was married to Isabella of Bourbon, and in an exchange of brides across the river Bidasoa his elder sister Anne was married to Isabella's brother, Louis XIII of France. It was forty-four years before Philip saw his sister again. Because of the extreme youth of the bridal couple the marriage was not consummated until late in 1619, when Isabella was seventeen and Philip fourteen and a half. In the meantime, Isabella joined a household of children: the Infanta Maria, born in 1606, a year after Philip; the Infante Carlos, two years his junior, and a backward youth who never emerged from beneath the shadow of his older brother; and the Infante Ferdinand, created a cardinal in 1619 at the age of ten—a singularly inappropriate destiny for the liveliest of the three royal brothers, whose demeanor suggested that he would have been better with a baton in his hand than a biretta on his head.

Philip's married life appears to have started well enough. He was captivated by Isabella's beauty and vivacity, and they shared a common enjoyment of plays and pageantry. But the marriage seems quickly to have soured, and the queen's initial inability to provide him with an heir proved an additional source of disappointment. Their first child, a daughter, was born in August 1621, and lived only a few hours; and two other daughters, born in 1623 and 1625, did not survive infancy. Philip soon showed that he had a roving eye, and the queen, who resented the influence of Olivares over her husband, suspected the favorite of encouraging him in his extra-marital affairs. When it was learned in the opening months of the reign that Olivares was accompanying the king on sorties from the palace to savor the night life of Madrid, the obvious conclusions were generally drawn. Olivares himself indignantly denied charges that he was corrupting the king, and protested that nothing improper occurred on these nocturnal excursions, which were simply intended to show Philip how his subjects lived. This may or may not have been true. Kings who roamed the streets by night for reasons both licit and illicit were common enough both in Spanish historical literature and in the contemporary Spanish theater; and court life and drama were never far apart.[2] In any event the king had ample opportunity to gratify his impulses; and a succession of mistresses provided him with fleeting amusement and a number of bastard children, who were carefully placed in private households, their educational progress regularly reported through Olivares to the king.

12. Diego de Velázquez, *Philip IV* (Dallas, Southern Methodist University, Meadows Museum)

The pursuit of women occupied some relief from the tedium of those long hours of emptiness ticking slowly away on the palace clocks. So, too, did the pursuit of animals. Philip was a passionate hunter, an outstanding horseman, and a first-class shot with the arquebus (fig. 13).[3] Accompanied by Olivares as his master of the horse, he would spend long days in the hunting field, in pursuit of deer, wolves and wild boar. Excelling in these open-air sports, and capable of spending long hours in the saddle, he found in the wide expanses of the Castilian countryside and in the parks and gardens of his country houses a welcome release from the gloomy confinement of the Alcázar of Madrid.

For it was in the Alcázar that he was condemned to spend the larger part of his life, and it was the Alcázar that was regarded as the seat of the court. This old Moorish fortress, rising above the banks of the river Manzanares, had been partly reconstructed by Charles V and then remodelled by Philip II as a permanent royal residence after the selection of Madrid as his capital. It was a massive rectangular building constructed around two courtyards, known respectively as the courtyards of the king and of the queen, and separated from each other by the royal chapel. The king's state apartments and private quarters were on the upper floor on the west side, while in the eastern wing were those of the queen, remodelled under the direction of the court architects Francisco de Mora and his nephew and successor Juan Gómez de Mora in the years following the return of the court from Valladolid in 1606 (fig. 14). Further improvements followed during the later years of Philip III and the opening years of the new reign. The principal facade, facing south, was reconstructed to give

33

it a more impressive appearance, and at the same time to provide a new suite of state rooms (fig. 15). Gómez de Mora also made skilful use of the great vaulted spaces beneath the Alcázar to carve out summer quarters for the royal family, where they would be better protected from the oppressive summer heat.[4]

The Alcázar, especially after the completion of these improvements, was not

13. Peter Snayers, *Philip IV Hunting* (Madrid, Prado)

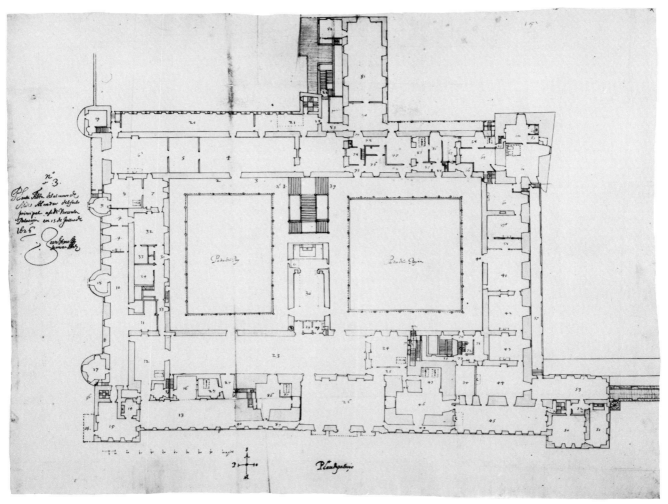

14. Juan Gómez de Mora, Plan of Main Floor, Alcázar of Madrid (Vatican, Biblioteca Apostolica)

entirely devoid of charm. The king's apartments in the southwest corner of the palace looked out over the Garden of the Emperors, named after the two series of statues with which it was graced. The garden itself was a pleasant one, and the garden galleries, adorned with jasper tables, were hung with some of the most precious paintings in the royal collection, the Fables of Titian.[5] But the Alcázar as a whole, with its small, fortress-like windows and its dark rooms, remained obstinately gloomy, and it was no doubt a relief to the king to escape down the tiled passageway that led from the Garden of the Emperors to the Casa del Campo, his rural residence on the other side of the river (fig. 16).

While the Alcázar was the permanent residence of the king, it was also the seat of his government. There was a constant traffic through the king's courtyard, not simply to the booths and shops that were housed beneath its arcades, but also to the secretarial offices and the council chambers of the various royal councils which occupied the ground floor of the northern wing. This constant coming and going served as a vivid reminder of that intermingling of royal household and royal

35

administration which was so characteristic of the courts of early modern Europe.

Indeed, the very word "court" embraced the members both of the royal household and of the central government. In this sense, language and architecture kept company. Ministers and palace officials worked in close proximity, and sometimes, like Olivares himself, combined governmental and ceremonial duties. The exact composition and size of the Spanish court therefore escape easy definition. Too many functions were duplicated, and there were too many blurred edges at the points where specific functions ended but privileged rights of access were nonetheless allowed. "Court" was, by its nature, an imprecise word, expressing at once the place, the pomp and the persons associated with the presence of the king.

The core of the court consisted of those whose duty it was to attend to the needs of the royal family. The Alcázar contained two distinctive households, one for the king and one for the queen, each of them presided over by a principal majordomo (the *mayordomo mayor*). In 1623, palace dignitaries, officials and attendants totalled nearly seventeen hundred, of whom over four hundred looked after the king's sister and his brothers, still considered too young to have households of their own.[6] Of the seventeen hundred, some four hundred—all of them housed on the top floor of the palace—were the ladies-in-waiting and *meninas*, or maids of honor, to the queen and the infanta. These women were in the charge of the mistress of the queen's bed-chamber, the *camarera mayor*, a post held from 1626 by the Countess of Olivares, whose austere presence seems to have cast a blight over the spirits of the queen. The Duke of Infantado, as the king's principal majordomo, supervised the noblemen who served as the king's majordomos on a weekly rota. Olivares, in his capacity as groom of the stole (*sumiller de corps*)—an office which he transferred to his son-in-law, the Duke of Medina de las Torres, in 1626—was in charge of the gentlemen of the chamber, whose duty was to help dress and undress the king, attend upon him, and act as his personal bodyguard.

If the "court" as royal household numbered around seventeen hundred people, the "court" as central government numbered perhaps four hundred, consisting of members and officials of the royal councils, and the king's secretaries.[7] But beyond these two thousand or so people, whose names figured on the books of the *aposentadores*, the officials whose duty it was to ensure that they had accommodation either in the palace or the town, there was a large but indeterminate body of people more loosely associated with the court—high ecclesiastics and court preachers, and members of the titled nobility who had either taken up residence in the capital, or owned or rented town houses to which they paid regular visits. There was also an important foreign community with close links to the court. This consisted of resident or visiting diplomats, ranging from the papal nuncios to the envoys of petty states like Modena and Lucca, and it also included certain members of the foreign financial community associated in one way or other with the Crown's finances. The Fuggers no longer possessed the pre-eminence they had enjoyed under Charles V, and their place had been taken by Genoese bankers, such as Carlos Strata, who had settled in Madrid in the 1590s, married a Spanish wife, and lived the life of a merchant prince in a splendid house in the fashionable district of the Carrera de San Jerónimo, near the palaces of the Duke of Lerma and other members of the high aristocracy.[8] These men enjoyed privileged access to the court, were in constant

But cause thou hearst ye mighty king of Spaine
Hath made his Inigo Marquess, wouldst thou fayne
Our Charles should make thee such? T'will not become
All kings to doe ye self same deeds with some!
Besyds, his man may merit it, and be
A Noble honest Soul! What's this to thee?
He may have skill & judgement to designe
Cittyes & Temples! thou a Caue for Wyne,
Or Ale! He build a pallace! Thou a shopp
With slyding windowes, & false Lights a top.[39]

It appears likely that Jonson's reference to Crescenzi as a palace builder was typological and not intended to evoke a particular building. But just at this time Crescenzi was involved in the remodelling of the Royal Apartment of San Jerónimo, soon to become the Palace of the Buen Retiro.

The elevation of Crescenzi and Maino to power may have been as much the king's doing as the count–duke's. Quite apart from their merits as artists, they commanded attention because they were familiar with recent artistic developments in Italy, the country to which Spain looked for leadership in painting.[40] As the decade wore on, it became apparent that Philip's taste in painting was not confined to the "old masters," and that he had a great interest in collecting works of the leading painters of the day. His knowledge and taste in the paintings of his contemporaries may well have been shaped by Maino and Crescenzi. These two sometime artists also played a decisive role in Velázquez's advancement at court. Without their assistance, the young painter from Seville, who represented the forces of artistic innovation, would have had to struggle more than he did to secure his place in the royal favor.

When Velázquez was appointed painter to the king (*pintor del rey*) in October 1623, court painting was dominated by two senior painters who worked in a conservative, somewhat outdated style. Vicente Carducho and Eugenio Cajés had been painters to the king since the reign of Philip III.[41] By the 1620s, time had caught up with their manner of painting, at least as far as those with advanced taste were concerned. Velázquez's arrival at court must have been unwelcome to them, and even more so the favor bestowed on him by the king and the minister. The rivalry appears to have reached a climax in 1627, when Velázquez, Carducho and Cajés participated in a competition to paint a picture of the *Expulsion of the Moriscos*.[42] The winning composition was to be installed in a new picture gallery being formed in one of the principal staterooms in the south wing of the Alcázar. The judges selected for the competition were Crescenzi and Maino and their choice of winner was Velázquez. This verdict was a personal triumph for Velázquez, who was rewarded with the post of usher to the chamber (*ujier de cámara*), his first appointment in the king's household.[43] And it may also be interpreted as a triumph for the forces of modernism, championed by Crescenzi and Maino. If any doubts remained about the direction of Philip's taste, they were laid to rest in the following year by the arrival in Madrid of Peter Paul Rubens.

The story of Rubens's diplomatic mission to Spain is well-known, but perhaps his impact on Philip and Velázquez is less fully understood.[44] Rubens was in Madrid for nine months, from August 1628 to April of the following year. When he was not involved in discussing the negotiations with England, Rubens painted, working in a room set aside for him in the Alcázar.[45] From different sources, we know that Rubens was often in the company of the king and his painter and came to know them well. He made a profound impression on them both. Here was a man of cultivation and learning who was also a profoundly original, powerful painter; a man who had carefully studied the art of the past, and then distilled what he had learned into a new way of painting that was subtle in its outlook and dazzling in its execution. Philip, who already owned a few paintings by Rubens, now became his most devoted admirer and patron. For Velázquez, Rubens was the model of the artist–courtier and inspired him to renew his own art by studying the great masterpieces of Italy. Three months after Rubens left Madrid for Brussels, Velázquez was on his way to Italy. Thus, Rubens's stay in Madrid marks a turning point in the career of Philip as a patron and Velázquez as a painter. With his example before their eyes, they were inspired to make the Spanish court into a showplace for masterpieces of painting old and new.

Philip's interest in painting was matched by his love of music and the theater. He was taught the theory and practice of music by an official of the royal chamber, Mateo Romero. He conducted his own compositions, and one of the rooms in his suite was reserved exclusively for his musical books and instruments.[46] As for the theater, this entranced him, and it was his passion for painting and the theater that put a special stamp on his court. Sometimes it was amateur theater, especially in the carnival season, with courtiers, ladies-in-waiting and members of the palace entourage. At other times professional troupes were called in to play before the court. There were two public theaters in Madrid, the Corral del Príncipe and the Corral de la Cruz, and Philip—whose interests included the actresses as well as the plays—would occasionally honor them with his presence.[47]

Numerous productions were also staged in the Alcázar itself. The room used for these productions was the large hall near the king's apartments known as the Salón Grande or the Salón de Comedias, which also provided the setting for banquets, *saraos* or court balls, masquerades, ballets, and other court festivities, like those given in honor of the Prince of Wales in 1623. The seating arrangements for these court plays followed those laid down in the official rules of etiquette. In the middle, at one end of the hall, was a carpet on which the king's chair was set. There were seats, too, for the king's brothers, while the queen, the Infanta Maria and the ladies-in-waiting reclined on cushions to the king's left. The ladies of the court sat on cushions reclining against two rows of benches running along either side of the Salón. The gentlemen, grouped by rank—grandees, councillors of state, gentlemen of the household, majordomos, the eldest sons of grandees, other palace officials, and the royal secretaries—stood by the doorway to the left, with the court pages kneeling in front of them, while lesser members of the nobility and household officials were grouped behind the benches against the wall that adjoined the royal chapel.[48]

The curtain went up on the court theater of Philip IV with three spectacular productions staged at Aranjuez in 1622. These plays—one of them by the Count of Villamediana, and the other two by Antonio de Mendoza and Lope de Vega—were better called *invenciones* than *comedias*, since they incorporated many features of the

46

pageant and the masque, and demanded the most elaborate scenic effects. Villamediana's play, setting a pattern which would later be followed at the Buen Retiro, was performed on an island on the Tagus, where a stage with a Doric facade had been especially constructed.[49]

The elaborate theatrical machines required for such productions were known as *tramoyas*. Writing in the middle of the century about the fashion for machine plays (*comedias de tramoyas*), Alonso Núñez de Castro explained that their attraction lay in the *mudanzas totales del teatro*—the spectacular changes of scene—"first a palace, then a garden, then a wood, then a fast-flowing river, and then a stormy sea followed by a calm."[50] Plays which depended on mechanical devices for their effects were already being written in the early years of the century, and came to be particularly associated with the name of Luis Vélez de Guevara, whose connections with Seville, and with Olivares, were close. Vélez de Guevara's fortunes were made with the change of regime in 1621. He was appointed gentleman usher to the Prince of Wales in 1623, and doorkeeper to the king's chamber in 1625; and the machine play which he had done so much to promote came into its own at court.[51]

Much ingenuity was required to transform gardens into palaces, or to make gods and goddesses descend from the clouds in triumphal cars, but in the late 1620s the court found its *tramoyista*. Olivares had sent orders to Spain's ambassador extraordinary to the papal court, the Duke of Pastrana, to bring back from Italy a skilled *fontanero*—an engineer who specialized in constructing fountains and garden water-works—along with a number of gardeners for the gardens of the Alcázar, the Casa del Campo and Aranjuez. Pastrana returned in 1626 with Cosimo Lotti, whom he had acquired with some difficulty from the Grand Duke of Tuscany. While two gardeners who had accompanied him were despatched to Aranjuez, Lotti was retained at court with his assistant, Pietro Francesco Gandolfi. Like most court employees Lotti was soon complaining about the inadequacy of his salary, but did not find an entirely sympathetic hearing in the Committee of Works. One of its members, the Count of Ericeira, considered that the Crown might well dispense with the services of all the Italians and other foreigners employed at "exorbitant salaries" at Aranjuez and the Casa del Campo, and on the building of the Pantheon at the Escorial. Spaniards, in his view, were much more skilled in the arts they professed, and foreign artisans were no longer required. Lotti, however, refused to settle for the paltry wages offered him, and in July 1628 the king granted him an annual salary of five hundred ducats, and Gandolfi two hundred.[52]

The raise in Lotti's salary was a tribute to his services. These were not confined to the royal gardens. The Tuscan *fontanero* had shown himself to be a brilliant designer of stage sets and machinery, and it was he who was to be responsible for the decor of the spectacular machine plays so lavishly staged at the Retiro in the 1630s. In 1629 he displayed his skills in a production of Lope de Vega's *La selva sin amor*, a pastoral eclogue which, with its sung dialogue, came close to opera. The production was notable for its remarkable perspectives, its *trompe l'oeil* devices, and its spectacular shifts of scene. A seascape, for instance, in which the waves rose and fell with alarming realism, was replaced by a scene of a grove on the banks of the Manzanares, with a perspective of Madrid.[53]

Productions like this were extremely expensive, and they raised in a particularly vivid form a problem that was to be central to the whole history of the Olivares regime. Olivares had come to power as the champion of austerity and economy. The articles published in February 1623 by the reform Junta[54] reflected this concern, imposing as they did strict sumptuary legislation in an attempt to reduce personal and national expenditure on superfluous embellishments. But hardly had they been published when the arrival of the Prince of Wales forced a suspension of the pragmatics relating to austerity of dress.[55] Royal example in any event was likely to prove more effective than royal decree, as Philip IV proved when he abandoned the elaborately starched ruff for the simple cardboard *golilla* and changed the fashion overnight.[56] But the fact remained that there existed a fundamental incompatibility between the regime's desire for economy and its equally strong desire to impress the world with the unique splendor and majesty of the King of Spain. It would have taken the ingenuity of a political *tramoyista* of the first order to reconcile the puritanical fiscal program of Olivares with his plans for a brilliant court life revolving around the person of the Planet King. His enemies were not slow to note the discrepancy between the regime's professions of fiscal austerity and its daily practice. As a result, the government was soon faced with a problem of credibility which would become increasingly severe as Spain plunged deeper into war and debt.

But the immediate impression of the court in the early years of Philip IV was of glitter and liveliness under the patronage of an increasingly cultivated monarch. This is the impression conveyed by the diary of Cassiano dal Pozzo who accompanied Cardinal Francesco Barberini on his mission to Madrid in 1626.[57]

19. Peter Paul Rubens, *Philip IV* (Bayonne, Musée Bonnat)

Rubens, who was no mean judge of princes, commented favorably on the king after observing him in Madrid. "He really takes an extreme delight in painting, and in my opinion this prince is endowed with excellent qualities. I know him already by personal contact, for since I have rooms in the palace, he comes to see me almost every day."[58] It is clear that the king profited from Rubens's presence to enlarge his understanding of the arts. A world of aesthetic experience was opening up before him, and it was a world that he was eager to enter. If the duties of his office prevented him, at least for the time being, from undertaking that journey to Italy which was the goal of every cultivated man, he did the next best thing. By sending Velázquez to Italy in 1629 he sought to ensure—like James I in sending Van Dyck to Italy in 1621[59]—that the most recent advances in style and taste were represented at his court.

Philip IV was obviously coming to fill the role for which Olivares had been sedulously grooming him. By the late 1620s the parts of royal bureaucrat and royal aesthete seem to have been satisfactorily combined. But Rubens, watching him at close quarters, was clearly uneasy. "The King alone arouses my sympathy. He is endowed by nature with all the gifts of body and spirit, for in my daily intercourse with him I have learned to know him thoroughly. And he would surely be capable of governing under any conditions, were it not that he mistrusts himself and defers too much to others" (fig. 19).[60] The count–duke had perhaps made of Philip all that could be made of him, but in the process had increased his self-mistrust and his innate indecisiveness. Philip by the late 1620s was restless, moody, prone to melancholy; an uneasy figure overshadowed by a powerful minister whose policies seemed increasingly far from realizing his ambition of restoring the Monarchy to glory.

The Theater of the World

Philip was twenty-four in 1629. The restlessness which he was beginning to display was partly that of a young man who had been kept on leading-strings beyond his time, and was anxious to exercise the authority for which he had been trained. But it also reflected a growing awareness, borne in on him as he perused the state papers that passed across his desk, that all was far from well with his Monarchy.

Both at home and abroad the problems of the regime had been multiplying. The reform program on which Olivares had embarked with such determination in 1621 had very little to show in the form of positive results. At every turn he had come up against resistance and obstructions which had compelled him to retreat, or to postpone some cherished measure until a more propitious time. In 1626 the Crown of Aragon had made clear its deep distrust of his project for a Union of Arms. In Castile the Cortes persistently obstructed his plans for tax reform. The Castilian ruling class, which controlled the city councils, blocked every measure which threatened its monopoly of power; and the bureaucracy resorted to the time-honored bureaucratic device of deferring or sabotaging dangerous innovations. Moreover, both silver and credit were in short supply, and prices rose sharply in the opening years of the reign, in part at least because the Crown minted large quantities of copper coins (vellón) to cover its deficits.[61]

Attempts at tighter censorship could not entirely silence the murmurings against

Olivares and his government, but it took the king's illness in September 1627 to bring home to the count–duke the extent of his unpopularity. When public prayers were ordered for Philip's recovery, foreign envoys in Madrid were astonished to find that the churches remained almost empty.[62] The populace could clearly contemplate with equanimity the death of the king if it brought about the downfall of his favorite. Heavy taxation, high prices, the chaotic state of the copper currency, and the count–duke's harsh and authoritarian style of government all contributed to the detestation in which he was held.

As soon as the king recovered, Olivares took steps to reinforce his position. A pretext was found for removing from court don Manuel de Moura, Marquis of Castel Rodrigo (fig. 20), whose influence with the heir presumptive, the Infante Carlos (fig. 21), made him a potentially dangerous rival. A ringing defense was prepared of the government's record during its first six years of office. The councils were instructed to present specific reform proposals, and Olivares challenged the council of Castile to come up with a prompt remedy for the rise in prices, or else accept his own plans for a drastic deflation.[63]

The sudden exposure of his own vulnerability gave the count–duke an added incentive to ensure that the key posts, both in the palace and the government, were filled by men he could call his own. By placing them in the most critical posts, Olivares hoped to outflank the bureaucrats who stood in the way of his reforms. But, in the nature of things, reform took time, and Olivares was well aware that nothing would restore his domestic fortunes more dramatically than some spectacular success in the field of foreign policy. The triumphs of the *annus mirabilis* of 1625 had disappointingly failed to secure the peace with England and the United Provinces that Spain so badly needed. Although Spínola's capture of Breda had helped edge the Dutch into informal peace discussions, the count–duke was convinced that they would never agree to settle on terms more favorable to Spain than those of 1609 unless he could undercut the commercial prosperity which was the secret of their power. In the enigmatic figure of Wallenstein, the victorious general of the Emperor Ferdinand II, he thought that he had found a providential instrument for his grand design. In 1627 Wallenstein agreed to lay siege to one of the Baltic ports, which would then be converted into a base for a trading company founded to wrest the Baltic trade from the hands of the Dutch.[64]

The count–duke's Baltic design would take time to mature, and he needed a quick success to impress the world with Spain's overwhelming power. The death of the Duke of Mantua at the end of 1627 seemed to provide the perfect opening. Exploiting the uncertainties over the Mantuan succession Olivares allowed don Gonzalo Fernández de Córdoba, the governor of Milan, to move his army into the Mantuan territory of Montferrat and lay siege to the fortified stronghold of Casale on the river Po. The capture of Casale would be a spectacular triumph, giving Spain an almost unchallengeable dominance over northern Italy.[65]

Unhappily for the count–duke, the plan miscarried. Don Gonzalo's army moved too slowly and then stuck fast outside the walls of Casale. The siege dragged on throughout 1628, consuming vast sums of money from the Crown's depleted treasury. The Mantuan war played havoc with the government's plans for financial stabilization based on a halving of the nominal value of the copper currency; and any remaining prospects for financial solvency were shattered in September 1628 when the returning silver fleet was captured by a Dutch squadron under the command of Piet Hein. From week to week Olivares hoped to hear that Casale had surrendered. If it held out much longer there was a real danger that the French would come to its assistance, especially if Louis XIII could free himself of his most pressing domestic preoccupation by reducing the Huguenot stronghold of La Rochelle. At the end of October La Rochelle surrendered, and four months later Louis XIII startled Madrid by leading his army in person across the Alps through deep snows. With the French bearing down upon him don Gonzalo had no choice but to raise the siege of Casale.

Everything, then, seemed to have gone wrong for Olivares. His bluff had been called in Italy; the Dutch, fortified by their haul of Spanish silver, were planning a spring offensive; and Spínola, who had arrived in Madrid from Flanders in February 1628, was orchestrating a campaign for a peace settlement with the United Provinces on terms that promised to be no better than those of 1609. His foreign policy failures encouraged the count–duke's enemies to mount an offensive at court. In June 1629 an anonymous manifesto was placed in the hands of the king. Olivares, it asserted, was destroying Spain with his futile proposals for reform, his ill-timed

20. Anonymous seventeenth-century artist, *Marquis of Castel Rodrigo* (Madrid, Princess Pio of Savoy)

21. Diego de Velázquez, *Infante Don Carlos* (Madrid, Prado)

currency devaluation of August 1628, and his wars in Italy. As for Philip himself, he was no more than a "ceremonial king." The time had come for him to imitate his "most prudent" grandfather, Philip II, and his "invincible great-grandfather," the Emperor Charles V, by dismissing his favorite and taking personal control of affairs of state.[66]

In terms of the king's psychological development, Olivares's enemies had timed their campaign with considerable skill. Almost two years had passed since Philip had begun to devote himself conscientiously to his state papers, and the temptation to exercise a more direct personal authority must have been strong, especially at a moment when his Monarchy seemed threatened with shipwreck. It was, after all, for this that Olivares had trained him. He was at last coming to maturity. The queen was once again pregnant, and there were renewed hopes of an heir. Moreover the military successes of his brother-in-law, Louis XIII, had piqued him, and fired his ambitions to excel where kings were expected to excel—on the battlefield. Why should not he, like his brother-in-law, go to the wars? He was not, it seems, prepared to consider seriously, at least at this moment, the dismissal of a favorite whose value he had come to appreciate and whose energy and dedication he admired, but he did inform a horrified count–duke that he intended to lead his armies personally into Italy. Having learned his part in the theater of the court, the king now wanted to cut a figure in the theater of the world.

A tense struggle ensued between king and minister, as Olivares attempted to restrain the martial enthusiasm of his impetuous monarch and to impress upon him the unpalatable fact that the Crown for the present lacked the resources for so risky, and expensive, a venture (fig. 22).[67] Reluctantly Philip allowed himself to be overruled, although he did not abandon his intention of one day taking personal command of his armies. During the autumn of 1629 the dispatches from Brussels indicated that the military situation was rapidly deteriorating and that the Spanish Netherlands were on the verge of collapse. This time the king startled his ministers by announcing that he intended to go to Flanders in person as soon as an heir to the throne was born. On October 17 the queen gave birth to a son, Baltasar Carlos. The king could be forgiven for thinking that this was a sign from heaven that God looked with favor on his plans.

Olivares was deeply concerned, and wrote a worried letter to Ambrosio Spínola, who had been sent to replace don Gonzalo de Córdoba as commander of the army of Milan.[68] In it he explained that the idea of a trip to Flanders had come to Philip as the result of a proposal that one of his brothers should be sent to Brussels to assist, and eventually succeed, the king's aunt, the Infanta Isabella, in the government of the Netherlands. "The king," he continued,

is as ambitious for fame as Your Excellency knows him to be, and it has proved quite impossible to get him to agree to the prospect of one of his brothers becoming a soldier before him; and I am afraid that nothing in the world will make him abandon his plan. God give us peace this winter and so help calm these unfortunate royal humors. The best thing would be a general peace, and for the king to retire for most of the time to San Lorenzo [del Escorial] or to one or other of the woods round here, and try to save money and reform expenditures and see to the execution of the orders he has already given for the war. And I believe that, if this happens, I shall be in a position to put forward proposals to His Majesty

22. Memorandum of Olivares to Philip IV, June 17, 1629, with king's reply in left-hand margin (Madrid, Archivo Histórico Nacional)

which, when examined by the experts and approved by him, will enable His Majesty, if implemented (as one can presume they will be, with God's help), to find himself the most powerful and glorious king that Spain has ever had, excluding none. . .

The drift of Olivares's thinking in these autumn months of 1629 is clear enough. His vision of the glory of Philip IV remained undimmed. But its realization needed time, and meanwhile Philip himself, by his heroic impetuosity, was endangering the carefully laid plans that would bring it to pass. Somehow, while continuing to work at his papers, he must be distracted, and be persuaded to take life quietly in some rural dwelling. Is there here perhaps the germ of the idea that was soon to grow into that house of rural retreat, the Buen Retiro?

Whatever happened, it was clear that a royal visit to Flanders was out of the question until new treasure fleets arrived from the Indies. In the meantime the king had set his mind on another journey, this time inside Spain. After the failure of the English match, the Infanta Maria had been married by proxy to Ferdinand, King of

Hungary, the son of the emperor. The time had come for her to leave for Vienna where her husband impatiently awaited her arrival. Philip insisted that he must accompany her to the port of embarkation. Again Olivares resisted, on the grounds that a journey to Cartagena could endanger the king's health. It was finally settled that Philip would accompany the Queen of Hungary on the first stage only of her journey, with Olivares remaining in Madrid to look after government business. The queen and her brothers left Madrid on December 28, 1629, with the king expected to return in a matter of days.[69]

It was generally assumed that Philip would take leave of his sister in Guadalajara; but instead of turning around at this point he continued to the Aragonese frontier, and then, to everyone's surprise, gave orders that the whole party should move on to Zaragoza. Matías de Novoa, who lost no opportunity in his secret diary to vent his spleen against Olivares, wrote gloatingly that this was the first occasion on which the king had ever deceived his favorite.[70] The news of the king's decision caused intense excitement, both inside and outside Spain. Was he at last preparing to jettison his minister? By 1630 the hatred of Olivares and his regime was so intense that the least hint of royal displeasure was taken as evidence that the deluded monarch had at last seen the light. But again the count–duke's enemies were to be disappointed. Having reached Zaragoza and entrusted his sister to the temporary care of don Fernando de Borja, the viceroy of Aragon, the king slipped out of the city with his two brothers, and was back in Madrid by January 19.

The three-weeks' drama was over, and the monarch was back in Olivares's control. It seems highly improbable that he had ever had the slightest intention of severing himself from his favorite—the bonds of trust and dependence were now too tightly drawn. A minor demonstration of independence was good enough. But it was a demonstration which Olivares had to take into account as he pondered ways to satisfy Philip's growing ambition to be a king. For the time being at least Philip's energies must be diverted away from the battlefield to the *bureau*. Philip was now becoming accustomed to the heavy routine of paperwork, and the count–duke was impressed by the intelligence that he displayed. But it was clear that he must be given some relief from the exercise of his burdensome duties—duties from which no conscientious king could ever escape.

Philip, as the result of Olivares's efforts, had become the model of a conscientious king. During the later 1620s he had also developed his taste in art and letters to the point where his recreational interests embraced the aesthetic as well as the sensual. This, too, was a development that Olivares could only applaud. Just as he had been eager to see Philip assume the responsibilities of kingship, so also he had cherished the vision of Philip as the resplendent central figure in a glittering court. Naturally, the realization of these aspirations paid the count–duke a dividend, for a king at work at his desk in the Alcázar, or attending a play, was easier to control than a king who left his capital for the provinces or who led his armies into battle in Flanders. The ministrations of a favorite, then, and the education of a prince were converging in such a way as to inaugurate a new age for the arts in the court of Spain. The actor had been successfully groomed for his part. It only remained to provide him with a stage on which he could perform it to the most brilliant effect. This stage was to be provided by the Palace of the Buen Retiro.

III

A Theater for the Arts

The Palace of the Buen Retiro was created by a curious mixture of premeditation and improvisation. The very choice of the site seems almost to have been an accident. At first glance, the king was not in want of a royal house near Madrid which might serve his purposes.[1] Aranjuez, about thirty miles to the south, and the Pardo, only five miles to the north, must have been considered.[2] Set beside the river Tagus on the road to Toledo, the Palace of Aranjuez (fig. 23) had been started by Charles V after a visit to the Duke of Mantua's Palace of Marmirolo. Philip II had further embellished it with fountains, gardens and wide, shaded avenues which made it the most beautiful thing of its kind in Spain "and perhaps in the whole world," according to the papal nuncio Camillo Borghese who visited Spain in the late sixteenth century.[3] The Pardo (fig. 24) was a country house surrounded by excellent hunting country and was much frequented by the kings in the months of November and December, as its woods abounded with deer, wolves, foxes and wild boar.[4] But Aranjuez was too distant from the capital to serve as a showcase for the king, while the Pardo was too valuable for hunting to be compromised by other uses.

Just across the Manzanares River stood the Casa del Campo, which had established gardens, ample water and plenty of room for new construction. Over this royal residence, however, there hovered the shadow of the Duke of Lerma, who had done so much to improve it, and whose family held the governorship in perpetuity.[5] Rather than wrestle once more with this figure from the past, Olivares turned his gaze to the eastern border of Madrid, to the site of the church and monastery of San Jerónimo.

Here an important event was impending—the swearing of the oath of allegiance to Prince Baltasar Carlos. The heir to the throne had been born on October 17, 1629. Following a custom begun in 1528, the ceremony of fealty, in which the nobles and the Cortes of Castile pledged allegiance to the crown prince, was held in the church of San Jerónimo.[6] The act of homage to Baltasar Carlos was an ideal pretext for a great state occasion, and Olivares determined not to squander it. Taking the matter into his own hands, as he always did when matters counted, he secured for himself, on July 10, 1630, the position of governor (*alcaide*) of the Royal Apartment of San Jerónimo.[7]

The Royal Apartment was attached to the eastern and northern side of the church (fig. 26).[8] It had been constructed in 1561–3 by Juan Bautista de Toledo on the orders of Philip II, to provide lodgings for the times when the king retreated to San Jerónimo for Easter services or when he participated in the state occasions which were organized there, like royal exequies and solemn entries into the city.[9] The

Royal Apartment consisted of only a few rooms, one of which had a window overlooking the main altar where the king would sit to hear mass. During the 1620s, the Apartment had been used sparingly by the king, and its governance had been assigned successively to the Counts of Gondomar and Arcos.[10] In persuading Arcos to renounce the appointment in his favor, Olivares took the first step toward the creation of the Retiro.

During the rest of 1630, and all of the next year, a project to enlarge the Apartment was carried out under the supervision of Giovanni Battista Crescenzi, with money supplied from the king's secret expense account, administered by Jerónimo de Villanueva.[11] The date for the swearing of the oath was eventually set for February 22, 1632. In the event, the prince fell ill and the ceremony was postponed until March 7, when it was staged with great pomp and splendor.[12] The oath of allegiance was commemorated in a magnificent portrait by Velázquez of the two-year-old prince dressed in the military uniform he wore for the occasion (fig. 25).[13] In a clever conceit, Velázquez included a dwarf holding a rattle in one hand and an apple in the other. By means of this playful analogy Velázquez evoked the time when the toys of a prince would become scepter and orb, the symbols of a monarch. He also hinted at the choice between duty and pleasure which would eventually confront the youthful heir to the throne.

The work accomplished on the Apartment in 1630–1 was modest in scale. In addition to remodelling the existing rooms (fig. 26), which were used by the king, a second apartment for the queen was created by appropriating ten of the friars' cells in the east wing of the upper cloister (fig. 27).[14] Enough was done, however, to make Olivares realize that an excellent building site had been found. San Jerónimo was already identified with the Crown and considered by one and all as a royal church. Behind the monastery was a spacious grove of olive trees stretching into the countryside, so that no obstacles stood in the way of expansion. And yet the town lay right at the doorstep, thus sparing the king a journey to a place of recreation and ensuring that the glow of his magnificence would still illumine the capital.

23. Anonymous seventeenth-century artist, *Palace of Aranjuez* (only southern portion was completed at the time of this representation) (El Escorial)

24. (facing page) Anonymous seventeenth-century artist, *Palace of El Pardo* (El Escorial)

Following the ancient Roman example, which had been spectacularly revived in the sixteenth century by members of the papal court, Olivares decided to create a suburban villa of the kind described by the great architectural theorist of the Renaissance, Alberti, as a "private house, in which the dignity of the town house, and the delights and pleasures of the country house, are both required. . ."[15]

The date of the decision to build is unknown, but it was confirmed on July 22, 1632, when the governorship of the site was perpetuated in the house of Olivares.[16] In the decree of appointment, one function of the new royal house was made explicit. The count–duke and his successors were to ensure the maintenance of the "house and gardens and other things that might be added to the site for recreational purposes." The use of the words "recreational purposes" suggests that the idea of creating a pleasure palace was now beginning to take form.

These new plans required a reorganization of the administration, and led to the appointment of a master of works to assist Crescenzi, who continued to serve as supervisor of the project. The choice was unexpected. In June, Alonso Carbonel appeared at the Retiro in the capacity of what would now be called site architect.[17] Logically, the appointment should have gone to the master of the royal works, Juan Gómez de Mora, the leading architect of the time. But Gómez de Mora had perhaps been too closely associated with the Duke of Lerma's building projects for Olivares ever to feel entirely at home with him. He had also succeeded in making enemies in high places by his implacable opposition to the growing tendency to entrust Crown building projects to men like Crescenzi, whom he regarded as amateurs.[18] Gómez de Mora chose his opponents unwisely and was made to pay by an inevitable loss of favor. In 1636, he was found guilty, perhaps on trumped-up charges, of stealing a painting by Titian from the royal collection. He was deprived of his office and banished to the remote city of Murcia to oversee the construction of an irrigation system, and there he remained until Olivares's fall.[19]

Carbonel played his hand with greater skill, although for lesser stakes. He was a plodder, who was concerned only with winning perquisites, not professional battles.

25. Diego de Velázquez, *Baltasar Carlos and a Dwarf* (Boston, Museum of Fine Arts)

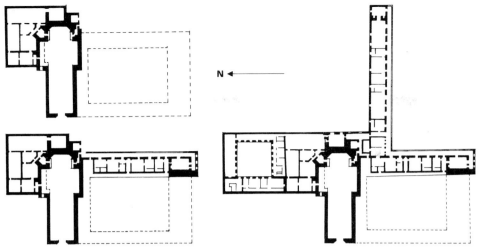

N ←

26. (far left, above) Church of San Jerónimo and Royal Apartment of Philip II, completed 1563 (after Carlier)

27. (far left, below) Additions to Royal Apartment of San Jerónimo for Oath of Allegiance Ceremony, completed March 1632 (after Carlier)

28. Royal Apartment of the Buen Retiro, completed January 1633 (after Carlier)

The son of a carpenter who lived in Albacete, Carbonel was born around 1590.[20] After spending the early part of his career as a sculptor and maker of altarpieces, he became involved in the royal works in 1619 as an *aparejador*, or architectural assistant in charge of making working drawings and supervising their execution. During the 1620s, Carbonel served under Gómez de Mora at the Escorial and the Alcázar. His conscientious service was rewarded first by the appointment as *aparejador* to the royal works in 1627, and then as *aparejador mayor* three years later.[21] When he received the call to come to the Retiro in 1632, Carbonel was well equipped for the office of master of the works, which initially made him Crescenzi's lieutenant, and later, after Crescenzi's death in March 1635, the count–duke's architectural executive.[22] His long association with Gómez de Mora had enabled him to master the court style while his submissive personality qualified him to work with a headstrong master.

The expansion of the Apartment was limited and by early January 1633 had largely been accomplished (fig. 28). On the fifteenth of that month, Bernardo Monanni, the secretary of the embassy of the Grand Duke of Tuscany, and a valuable eyewitness to the construction of the Retiro, sent a dispatch describing what had been done.[23] The first thing to be finished, he wrote, was a chapel in the middle of the garden. With his customary perspicacity, Monanni expressed doubts about the wisdom of building on the sloping terrain behind the monastery. His description of the new construction is brief but still informative. "Two apartments, each of a different plan, have been erected and roofed. All that remains to be done is to finish the inside. It ought to be ready for habitation by spring."

Besides the apartments, there were other features that had been nearly or entirely completed. The first of these was a formal garden with an artificial pool. Then there was a cage for wild animals.[24] And finally there was an iron aviary known as the Gallinero, or chicken coop. Olivares's enemies had already seized on the Gallinero as a derisive nickname for the whole enterprise and satires and broadsheets had been posted almost on the doorstep, comparing the flimsy chicken coop to the great buildings of antiquity.[25] Olivares's reaction to the criticism was immediate if ineffectual; he changed the name of the house from the Royal Apartment of San Jerónimo to the Royal House of the Buen Retiro, a name that preserved the idea of a religious retreat, while also conveying the sense of a place designed for relaxation, away from the cares of office.[26] Although "Buen Retiro" gradually achieved currency, it never succeeded in replacing Gallinero during Olivares's lifetime, except in official documents. In the minds of the populace, the new palace remained a gilded chicken coop.

Monanni's prediction that the building would be ready for spring occupancy proved to be accurate. By May 1633, all seemed ready for the inauguration of the Retiro. But the dispatch of May 14 reported a new and dramatic development.[27] A huge workforce, numbering more than a thousand men, had descended upon the site to begin another phase of construction. The remodelling of the small apartment of Philip II undertaken in 1630–1 had given way in 1632 to a substantial expansion of the Royal Apartment and the construction of gardens and dependencies. Now a third amplification was about to begin, with results that would prove to be startling.

As Monanni observed the new burst of building activity, he was struck by the way in which the palace and gardens were being rapidly and recklessly enlarged: "Every day, as they build, they expand the project, which is not the one they started with. The site has been enlarged and enclosed by a wall, and now covers the ground between . . . the Carrera de San Jerónimo and the Calle de Alcalá. . ."[28] The Crown had in fact acquired earlier in the year additional plots of land to the north of San Jerónimo, which extended the grounds, as Monanni noted, to the Calle de Alcalá. The two most important properties were the garden plots of the Marquises of Tavara and Povar, both of them relatives of the count–duke. A third property, located near Povar's land, belonged to a certain Juan Gaytan de Ayala.[29] These purchases came to constitute the northwest sector of the expanding park and gardens.

In the same dispatch, Monanni reported further important work in the gardens: the removal of a small artificial pond and the construction of a larger one, closer to the buildings; the planting of a new formal garden, to be known as the Queen's Garden, which was to include a maze; and preparations for the transfer of the notorious aviary to the further reaches of the site. But the most important news contained in the dispatch was that the formal garden, built at such vast expense, was being demolished, "because they want to put in its place a *piazza*—a courtyard—for bullfights and jousting, conveniently situated for the king to be able to watch from his room."

Before it had ever come into use, therefore, part of the new Royal Apartment complex was already being demolished, in order to make way for a large courtyard—a *plaza de fiestas*—for bullfights, jousting and other spectacles (fig. 29). A comparable courtyard, but on a smaller scale, had been built at the Alcázar around 1630, and was used both for equestrian exercises and the staging of plays.[30] That a similar purpose was intended for the building now under way at the Retiro is indicated by the wording of a royal decree of November 5, 1633: "I have ordered the construction at this site of a courtyard where fiestas and entertainments can take place."[31]

How are we to explain this further expansion of the building in the spring of 1633? There is one simple and logical explanation, namely that Olivares, along with his royal master, was succumbing to building fever. For a statesman, whose most

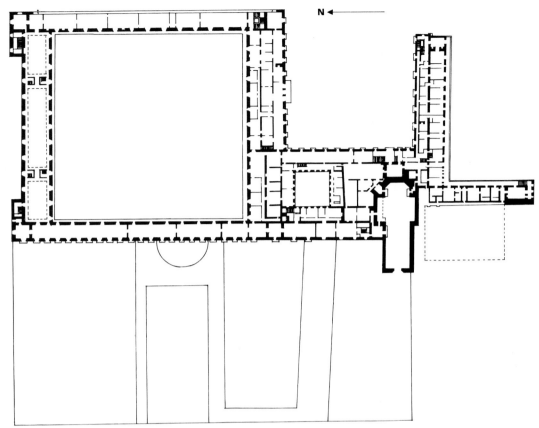

29. Principal Court and Dependencies, Palace of the Buen Retiro, completed December 1633 (after Carlier)

elaborate structures possess an inevitable air of impermanency, there is no doubt a special pleasure to be gained from building something other than castles in the air. It hardly seems a coincidence that, in the spring of 1633, as the new expansion of the Royal Apartment of San Jerónimo began, the count–duke purchased the small town of Loeches some six leagues from Madrid. Soon the masons were at work here too, constructing a convent and a modest house for Olivares under the direction of Alonso Carbonel.[32]

But there are other possible explanations of the great new expansion of 1633, all of which seem to have played a part in the decision to convert a modest suburban apartment into a grandiose palace. The criticism of what had so far been done may well have provided a stimulus to further action. Money had been raised in difficult times for a royal chicken coop, a building unworthy of a king. The insulting name of chicken coop had made it a laughing-stock, and Frenchmen were said to be shouting "chicken" at the sight of passing Spaniards.[33] These criticisms naturally prompted the thought that, if a palace were to be built at all, it should be built on a scale and in a manner befitting a King of Spain. Olivares may well have come to share this view as he saw what had been accomplished by the end of 1632 and compared it to the

61

nearby noblemen's houses along the Prado de San Jerónimo, some of which were indubitably grander than what he had contrived for the monarch.

One house in particular would have been seen as a challenge to his powers as a builder. Right across the road from San Jerónimo was the large estate consisting of house and gardens created by the Duke of Lerma after the return of the court from Valladolid. Lerma had been a builder on the grand scale, but Olivares was determined to outbuild him. The Retiro, once expanded, would cut down Lerma and his palace to size.

Any such psychological motives, however, were no doubt secondary factors in the decision to create a new palace. More important was the fact that, while the program of royal patronage of the arts was beginning to bear fruit, it was in someone else's garden. Already in June 1631, the papal nuncio had observed that court entertainments were on the increase, for reasons that he was unable to fathom.[34] It seemed, he wrote, as if the count–duke was beginning to imitate the Duke of Lerma, who had organized countless diversions for Philip III. On June 23, the eve of St John's day, Olivares invited their majesties to the house of the Count of Monterrey on the Prado de San Jerónimo for a performance of two new plays, one by Lope de Vega, the other by Quevedo. A magnificent fiesta was staged after the conclusion of the plays. Then, a few days later, the Duke of Medina de las Torres followed suit with another fiesta in honor of the king. These two events revealed the possibilities of open-air festivities in a town house setting, for which the king obviously needed a proper house of his own.

As host and patron in his own house the king would not only be fulfilling in a fittingly regal manner the duties expected of him, but might also be able to cast off some of the melancholy which had recently descended upon him. In 1632 he was deprived in quick succession of the company of both his brothers. A few weeks after the ceremony of homage to Baltasar Carlos, Philip left Madrid with his two brothers for Valencia and then Barcelona, where the Catalan Cortes had again been called into session. While the king and the Infante Carlos returned to Madrid in May, the Cardinal Infante Ferdinand was left behind as viceroy of Catalonia, a post in which he was to be groomed for the succession to his aunt in the government of the Netherlands. The farewell was painful, for the brothers must have been well aware that their chances of meeting again were slight. In fact the trio was to be permanently sundered sooner than anyone could have anticipated. The Infante Carlos, who had always been considered robust, suddenly fell ill at the end of July, and died within a few days at the age of twenty-four.

The expansion of the palace with a view to more splendid festivities might help to take the king's mind off these personal sorrows. But a king could not shine without the presence of his nobility, and in June 1632 the Tuscan ambassador, Francesco de' Medici, was reporting that many nobles were failing to put in an appearance at court festivities, while those who came displayed a marked lack of enthusiasm for the proceedings.[35] The old aristocracy had found a means of expressing its disapproval of Olivares, and this obvious disaffection of the nobility may well have played a part in the decision to expand the Retiro and make it the focal point of a court so brilliant as to be irresistible.

At heart, the count–duke despaired of winning the lasting support of the heads of the great noble houses. Instead, his thoughts turned toward the younger generation, which it was not too late for him to mold. In a lengthy memorandum sent to the council of Castile in September 1632 he expressed his concern with the educational deficiencies of these young men, who were expected to provide leadership in the future.[36] In this paper, Olivares lamented the decline of the arts of war and peace among the scions of the aristocracy. Following the example of His Majesty, they should study riding and fencing, learn to play *pelota*—a ballgame which was considered excellent for developing agility and alertness—and practice equestrian exercises which would prepare them for the battlefield. If the court were to become, as Olivares intended, a nursery of chivalry for young aristocrats, it would be necessary in due course to create a "playground" where they could compete before the king in jousting, tilting and other noble pursuits.

The erratic way in which the building operations developed between 1630 and 1633 undoubtedly reflects these changing priorities and preoccupations of Olivares. There was obviously a desire to build afresh on a larger scale. But why specifically at the beginning of 1633 should a decision have been taken to concentrate financial resources on a major new expansion of the work? The Spanish Crown was not noted for its ability to tailor expenditure to income, but certainly nothing had happened since the building began to give the count–duke more latitude for financial maneuver. The relatively modest construction of 1630–2 had forced a resort to financial expedients which flew in the face of all that the count–duke had said in 1629 about the need for economy. Nor had the Crown's financial position shown any marked improvement since the difficult days of the Mantuan War. It was true that the count–duke's inner circle of ministers had launched a massive fiscal drive, and that the combination of new grants from the Castilian Cortes of 1632 with some clever financial devices had done something to increase the depleted royal revenues.[37] But commitments rose faster than income, and in the spring of 1633 a junta was discussing yet again how to free the king from debt.[38]

On the other hand there were some grounds for revived optimism at the end of 1632 about the Monarchy's long-term prospects. Gustavus Adolphus of Sweden had thrown Europe into turmoil in 1630 by landing his army in Germany, and marching inland on a campaign that swept everything before him. The Austrian Habsburgs, and the cause of Catholicism itself, seemed on the brink of catastrophe when, as if by a miracle, Gustavus was killed on the battlefield of Lützen in November 1632. The news of his death reached Madrid on Christmas day and was celebrated by bonfires, firework displays, and a Te Deum in the royal chapel.[39] On January 26, 1633 the king and the count–duke went to the theater incognito to see a play on the defeat and death of the King of Sweden, especially written by Lope de Vega. The production had to be immediately withdrawn because it contained indecorous material, but the popular demand for it was so great that Antonio de Mendoza produced a hastily revised version which was performed before enthusiastic audiences.[40]

It was therefore in a jubilant atmosphere that the count–duke contemplated the advent of the new year. In a session of the council of state on January 9, 1633, he gave his colleagues a *tour d'horizon*, outlining the opportunities and requirements of the situation. It was, he told them, "the moment to finish off everything—to settle matters in the Empire, secure the election of (the emperor's son as) the King of the

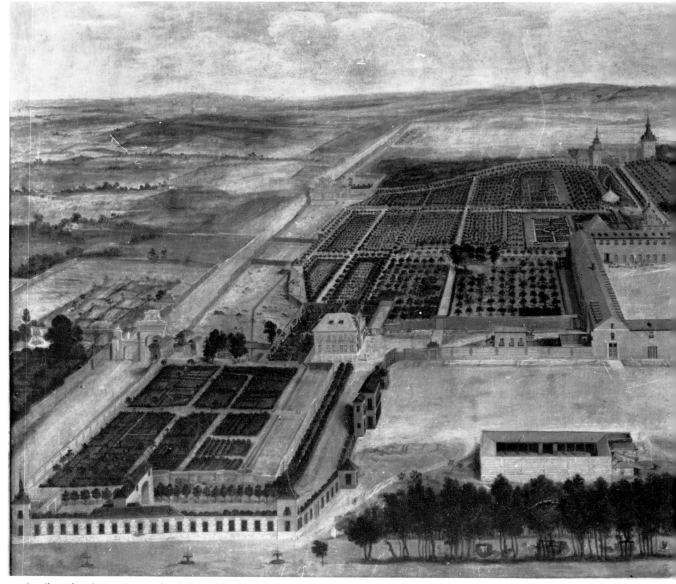

30. Attributed to Jusepe Leonardo, *Palace of the Buen Retiro in 1636–7* (Madrid, Museo Municipal)

Romans, secure an honorable peace with the Dutch, reach a settlement in Italy, restore the Duke of Lorraine, and sow in France the discord that it so handsomely deserves."[41] Even if the euphoria lasted no more than a few weeks, and the growing prospects of war with France were already making him talk again in March of the dangers of "final ruin,"[42] the sudden upsurge of confidence in that triumphant winter may well have provided the stimulus to think more expansively of the possibilities of the Royal Apartment of San Jerónimo as a site for celebrating in a truly regal style the glories of a victorious dynasty. Olivares's idea for a grandiose theater of the arts of war and peace could now become a reality.

This purpose determined the plan of the new structure, which can be seen in

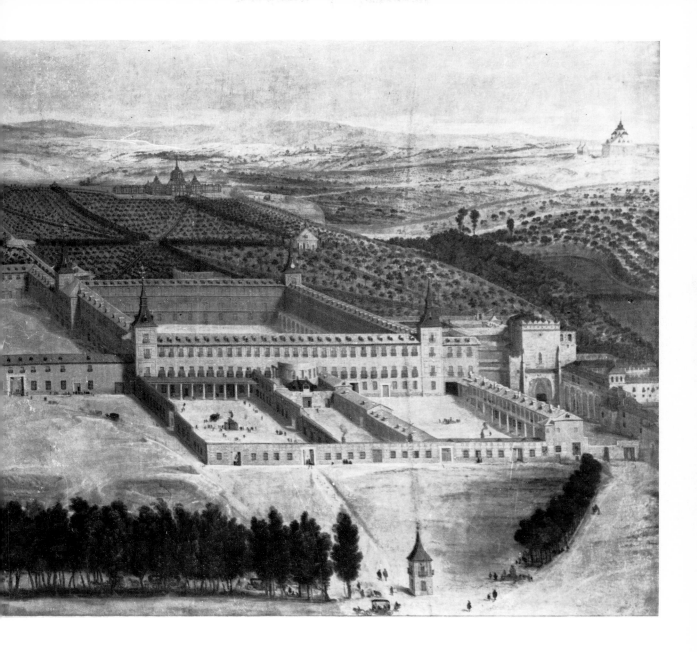

contemporary views of the Retiro (figs. 30 and 31). To the north of the Royal Apartment of San Jerónimo there is a large square building with slate-roofed towers at the corners, and a spacious inner court. This was the new Principal Court, or *plaza de fiestas*. It had three stories (except in the southeast section of the south wing, where there were only two) and an attic, and was built of brick and timber with granite moldings around the doors and windows, rather humble materials whose choice was later to be regretted. The principal facade, which looked to the west in the direction of Madrid, was the most imposing and had thirty-two windows. The other three exterior facades had fewer windows, the number varying from wing to wing. The interior court facades, however, were identical, each one having thirteen

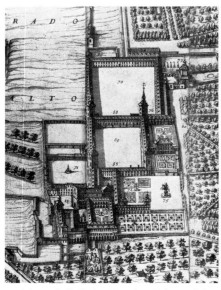

31. (above left) Pedro Texeira, Palace of the Buen Retiro, from Map of Madrid, 1656

32. (above right) Orazio Scarabelli, *Naval Battle in the Pitti Palace*, 1589 (London, British Museum)

33. (below) René Carlier, Cross-section of Principal Court (detail) (Paris, Bibliothèque Nationale)

34. (bottom) René Carlier, Cross-section of Terrain and Palace of the Buen Retiro (Paris, Bibliothèque Nationale)

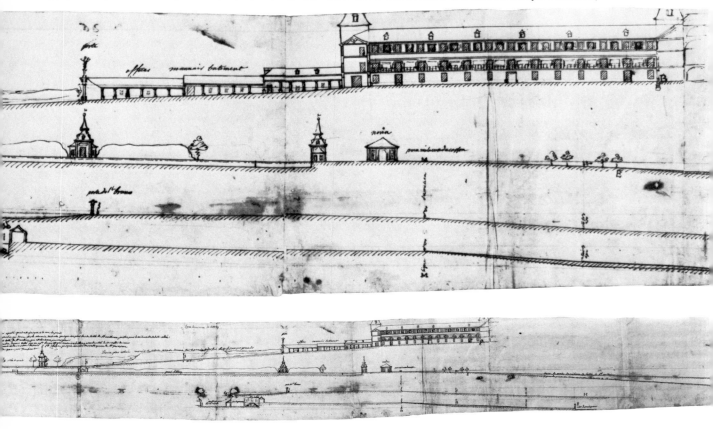

66

windows on the main floor. Around the entire perimeter of this floor ran a continuous iron balcony.

The three sides of this complex consisted of spacious rooms to accommodate the members of the royal councils and guests who attended the spectacles. In the center of the north wing was the royal box, the Salón Grande, later to be known as the Hall of Realms. When a spectacle was planned, spectators would assemble in the state rooms and then go out to the balcony once the show had started.

Although this type of building was new in Spain, it belonged to a well-established type of Italian suburban villa with theater, which had begun with the construction of the Belvedere Court in the Vatican in 1505 and was best exemplified by the Pitti Palace.[43] An engraving of the famous mock naval battle staged at the Pitti in 1589 shows the courtyard being used exactly as the courtyard of the Retiro was designed to be used (fig. 32). On the two flanking wings of the palace, spectators stand on a narrow balcony to observe the event. The court of the Retiro was fitted with just such a balcony and used in just this way (fig. 33).[44]

If the concept of the palace was not especially remarkable, the speed of its realization was generally considered to be extraordinary. Work began on the courtyard and its surrounding rooms in mid-May 1633. In June the two main building contractors, Juan de Aguilar and Cristóbal de Aguilera, and the excavating contractor, Juan Ramesdique, received their first payments.[45] Ramesdique had a huge undertaking on his hands because the new structure was to be built on a hillside which had to be levelled before the building could begin (fig. 34). But this was a time to move mountains and to make miracles happen. Ramesdique began to excavate the ground for the eastern wing, called the Gallery of the Prado, around the end of May. By early July, it was being covered with a slate roof.[46] The astonishing rate of construction is confirmed in a letter from the papal nuncio, Monsignor Monti, to Cardinal Francesco Barberini which says that on June 23, the eve of St John, following dinner in the Royal Apartment of San Jerónimo, the king and queen went to the "*nuova galleria*" overlooking the Prado to listen to music.[47] Between mid-May and late June, then, sufficient work was done on the extensive Gallery of the Prado to make it ready for at least partial use. And by July 30, the exterior of the complex had been completed.[48] The first fiesta was held there in August, despite the fact that construction was still going on inside.[49] Other work was also in progress. A payment of August 23 records that the walls of the Servants' Quarters (*Patio de los Oficios*) were being erected.[50] On September 17, according to Monanni, an octagonal pool was completed and filled with water.[51] At the same time, a new hermitage (*ermita*) was being constructed in the northwest corner of the gardens, the hermitage of San Juan.[52]

Arthur Hopton, the British envoy (fig. 35), was also observing the building with interest. His letter of October 26 reports that the frantic pace of construction had not slackened. "The business seems to be a matter of the king's or Conde's affection or both, for to have it ready against the time there are about 1,000 men at work, without sparing the nights or Sundays or holy days."[53] Monanni confirmed the huge size of the workforce in early December, estimating that there were now almost 1,500 men at the site.[54] Hopton, like every contemporary observer, also remarked on the widespread hostility toward the project. "It is the speech of the whole court, every man speaking according to his affection, some well but most to the contrary, the charge thereof being taken out of the belly of the people by an imposition laid upon flesh and wine. They suffer worse because it is attributed to a fancy of the Conde's, whose judgment they approve not in this as in many things."[55]

By late November 1633, the new building had progressed to the point where the decoration of some rooms was now well-advanced, although it would take years for the interior to be completely finished.[56] On December 1, Olivares was observed at the site "much occupied with putting the final touches upon the work, trotting around on a pony giving orders everywhere he went."[57] Later that day, the king and queen paid a visit and were greeted by the count–duke, who presented them with the keys to the building on a silver plate. The king graciously returned the keys to his governor, and led the court off to a sumptuous meal.[58] In a lengthy dispatch written two days later, Monanni described the newly-finished courtyard complex in detail.[59] He was not impressed with the quality of the design, but he and everyone could not but marvel at the speed of construction. Lope de Vega found the right words to express the general amazement in his dedicatory sonnet: "The building was no sooner mentioned than it was built."[60]

The inaugural fiestas, which took place on Monday and Tuesday, December 5 and 6, were marked by equal measures of splendor and precipitation.[61] Sunday the 4th was a day of continual rain that threatened to cancel the jousting and bullfighting scheduled for the next day. But Olivares was determined that the show should go on, and at six in the morning was on the scene overseeing the arrangements. The king's balcony was fitted with glass panels to protect him from the downpour and adorned with red velvet and gold damask hangings. To one observer, the seated king looked like a holy relic in a reliquary.

The first event was bullfighting, with bulls for eight noblemen, led by Olivares. This was followed by jousting in which the king himself took part. The choice of games of physical skill led by the king himself may have been a way of emphasizing one of the programmatic functions of the new structure. But the arts of peace were not forgotten either. After the jousting, a play was staged by two companies of actors, and was followed by a banquet. Presents were given to the king and queen and ladies of the court. On the following day, the rain had turned to snow, but still the festivities went on. In the morning, the king went to see a magnificently ornate cabinet offered by a consortium of noblemen and was also presented by Jerónimo de Villanueva with three large purses of red velvet, each containing 2,000 ducats.[62] In the afternoon, the king again took to the jousting field and won two prizes, which he gave to the queen and the prince. Then the court went to the menagerie to watch a fight between a bull and a lion (won by the lion). With these festivities, the golden age of the Retiro was inaugurated.

One other event worthy of note had occurred on December 1; the name of the building was changed once more. On this date, a royal proclamation announced that

---

35. Attributed to Fray Juan Rizzi, *Sir Arthur Hopton and Attendant* (Dallas, Southern Methodist University, Meadows Museum)

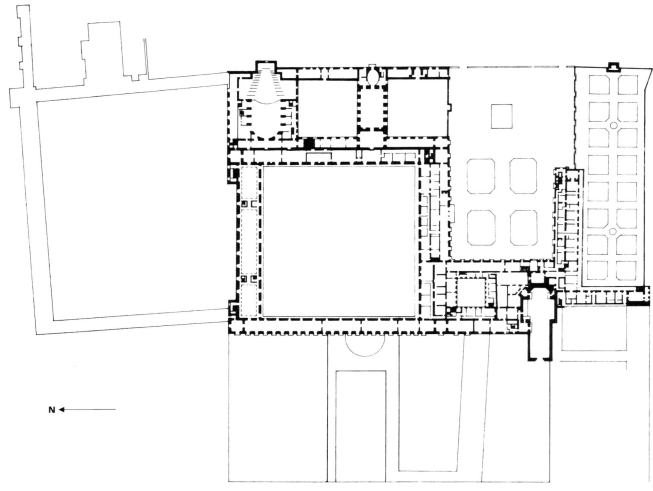

36. Palace of the Buen Retiro, with additions of 1634–40 (after Carlier)
37. Domingo de Aguirre, *Palace of the Buen Retiro from the Queen's Garden* (Madrid, Biblioteca Nacional)
38. (facing page) Robert de Cotte, Cross-section of the Casón (detail) (Paris, Bibliothèque Nationale)

henceforth it was to be known as the Palace of the Buen Retiro.[63] In the minds of the king and the minister, it must have seemed that the new court had become an imposing edifice in its own right and, thanks to the surrounding rooms, could even be used like a palace for indoor activities. The change of function implied by the new name was reflected in the reallocation of the rooms. The Royal Apartment of San Jerónimo became the private apartments of the king and was henceforth called the King's Quarters. The south wing of the court was designated for the use of the queen and her ladies and became known as the Queen's Quarters. The Prince's Quarters were established in the Gallery of Toledo that jutted out into the garden behind the cloister of the monastery. And the apartments of the councils, while still continuing to serve this purpose as the occasion arose, became the public rooms of the palace. Below, on the ground floor, were rooms for members of the court and the household staff.

Not everyone was convinced that the new structure deserved the exalted name of "palace." Novoa wrote scathingly in his journal of this building adjoining the royal monastery of San Jerónimo as "ridiculous, unprofitable and absolutely useless, with thin walls and weak foundations, unfavored by nature and the heavens, built on sterile, sandy soil. . ."[64] Monanni was more restrained and pithily formulated his Italianate opinion: "It looks more like a monastery than a royal dwelling."[65] Hopton agreed about the lack of external magnificence. In addition, he thought that the rapid construction had been achieved at the expense of solidity. "Only I wish it had been built with less haste, both for the security thereof as also that it might have had therein a little more of the prince."[66] It was not long before Philip and Olivares came to see that it would take more than a stroke of the royal pen to transform their courtyard into a palace.

On May 13, 1634, Monanni wrote to Florence that the two men had just been meeting at the Retiro to discuss ideas for improving the appearance of the main facade.[67] Philip and his minister were talking about increasing its size so that the building would have greater majesty and scale. If nothing was done on this occasion, the idea was by no means dead. In May 1637, almost exactly three years later, Olivares was proposing to remake the facade in Italian marble and had had a design

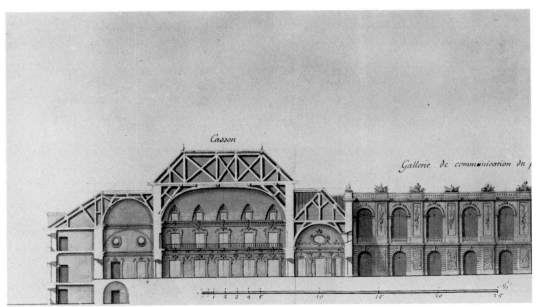

drawn by a Venetian architect which would have cost the huge sum of 400,000 ducats to build.[68] Once again, the plans were shelved, probably because Olivares sensed that a magnificent marble construction would have been more than the king's impoverished subjects could bear.

The opportunity for grandeur that was lost on the outside, however, was recouped within. As the palace was nearing completion, Olivares's agents began to assemble the extraordinary collection of paintings, furniture and tapestries that would be the glory of the Retiro.[69] The effect of the splendid interiors was reported by Hopton in a letter of July 17, 1634: "The Conde of Olivares took great pains, all things being ordered by himself and so well it savored of his excellent judgment in all things, especially in the furniture of the house which was such as it was not thought there had been so many curiosities in the whole kingdom."[70] By a fortunate coincidence, the plan of the main floor was ideally suited for the display of artistic treasures. The long, narrow rooms for the councils, once decorated, were almost like museum galleries.

The miscalculation about the external appearance of the building was equalled, if not surpassed, by the failure to make the Principal Courtyard large enough for some of the events that it was intended to accommodate. Monanni saw the problem immediately and noted it in his dispatch of December 3, 1633.[71] The remedy led to a number of additions to the palace complex during the succeeding seven years (fig. 36). The first of these was a new Large Courtyard, a simple structure that incorporated the northern wing of the palace as one of its sides.[72] Monanni reports that construction was under way in August 1634 and was completed by March 1635, except for the pavement, which was not laid until the middle of 1636.[73] Henceforth, the Principal Courtyard would be used for smaller private fiestas, and the Large Courtyard for great public entertainments. In 1637, stables were added to the north of the Large Courtyard in the form of a small square attached to its northwest corner.

39. Pedro Texeira, Palace and Park of the Buen Retiro, from Map of Madrid, 1656

PALACE
1. Church and Monastery of San Jerónimo
2. *Plaza Principal* (Principal Court)
3. *Plaza Grande* (Large Court)
4. *Patio del Emperador* (Emperor's Court)
5. *Patio de la Leonera* (Menagerie Court)
6. *Patio de los Oficios* (Servants' Court)
7. *Casón* (Ballroom)
8. *Coliseo* (Theater)
9. *Caballeriza* (Stables)

GARDENS
10. King's Garden
11. Queens' Garden
12. Prince's Garden
13. Octagonal Garden
14. Aviary
15. *Estanque Ochavado* (Octagonal Lake)

16. *Estanque Grande* (Large Lake)
17. *Islilla* (Island)
18. *Pescaderos* (Fishing Pavilions)
19. Watermills
20. *Río Grande* (Grand Canal)
21. *Río Chico* (Little Canal)
22. *Juego de la Pelota* (Ballcourt)

HERMITAGE CHAPELS
23. San Antonio de los Portugueses
24. San Pablo
25. San Jerónimo
26. San Bruno
27. San Isidro
28. San Juan
29. Santa María Magdalena

30. Nuestra Señora de Atocha

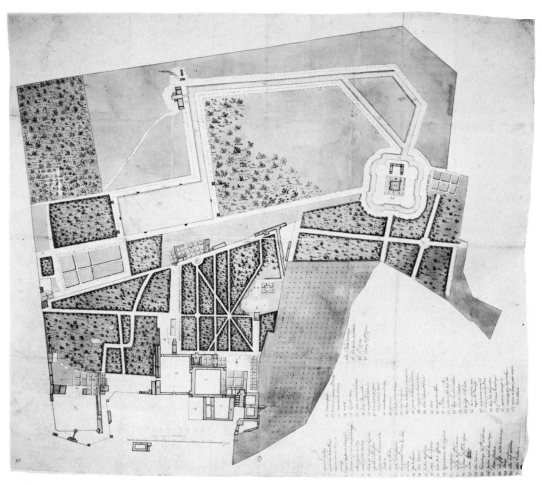

40. René Carlier, Palace and Park of the Buen Retiro (Paris, Bibliothèque Nationale)

The attractions of the palace were also augmented by the addition of a ballroom and a formal theater. The Casón, or ballroom, designed by Carbonel, was constructed in 1637.[74] It still stands, although the exterior was entirely remodelled in the nineteenth century, and is used as the Museum of Nineteenth-Century Art. The original exterior was an elegant design, consisting of two stories of pedimented windows resting on a granite arcade (fig. 37). The plan was rectangular, with two smaller rooms flanking a central hall covered by a high vaulted ceiling, beneath which ran an iron balcony for spectators (fig. 38). The theater, called the Coliseo, was built between 1638 and 1640, and had all the equipment and machinery needed to stage the spectacles designed by Cosimo Lotti.[75]

The architectural charms of the Retiro by no means exhausted its amenities. Indeed, once the main building had been completed, attention was directed to the gardens and park which underwent continual expansion and refinement from 1634 to the end of the decade (figs. 39 and 40). Nearest the palace were the enclosed formal gardens or *parterres*, and beyond them lay the park, which was crisscrossed by wooded alleys and dotted with various small structures. This was separated from the third zone by a long diagonal promenade that ran in a north–south direction from the hermitage of San Antonio to the Calle de Alcalá. This further part of the grounds, the water-gardens, was dominated by the Large Lake (*Estanque Grande*) and its tributary, the Grand Canal (*Río Grande*), which merged with the moat surrounding San Antonio.

In its general concept, the Retiro followed the latest ideas of Italian villa planning in which the garden and park predominated over the house. Indeed, up to a point, the layout of the grounds was strongly determined by Central Italian ideas. Crescenzi, of course, must have been responsible for some of the Italianate features.[76] The Octagonal Garden, for example, partly resembles the octagonal garden of the Villa Mattei, on Monte Celio, which he would have known. Another agent of transmission was Cosimo Lotti, who, during his early years, had worked as an assistant to Bernardo Buontalenti at the Boboli Gardens of the Pitti Palace.[77] His intervention in the design of the Retiro gardens has long been supposed and there is some evidence to confirm his participation.

On March 14, 1634, Francesco de' Medici reported that Lotti had told him of a commission to design a beautiful grotto for the Retiro gardens.[78] A week later, however, he told Monanni that the grotto project had been abandoned as too costly.[79] Undaunted, Lotti was proposing to design a *ragnaia*, an evergreen wood for trapping garden warblers with nets, which would be less expensive to create. It is not certain that the *ragnaia* ever came into being, but grottoes were constructed in some of the hermitage gardens. Again in 1636, a grotto was planned and partially built in the formal gardens behind the palace, only to be dismantled in February 1637 to make way for the Casón.[80]

Yet, for all these foreign accents, the Retiro park was informally composed and organized in comparison with Italian models.[81] The lack of unity and coherence resulted from the haphazard way in which the site had been expanded, for new land was continually being acquired on which new attractions were built. Between 1637

41. Louis Meunier, *Octagonal Pond* (London, British Library)

Le petit estang du Retir   el pequino estanque del Retiro

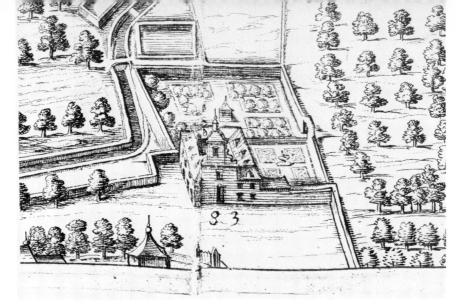

42. Pedro Texeira, Hermitage of
San Juan, from Map of Madrid,
1656

43. Pedro Texeira, Hermitages of
San Bruno and San Jerónimo,
from Map of Madrid, 1656

44. Pedro Texeira, Hermitage of
Santa María Magdalena, from
Map of Madrid, 1656

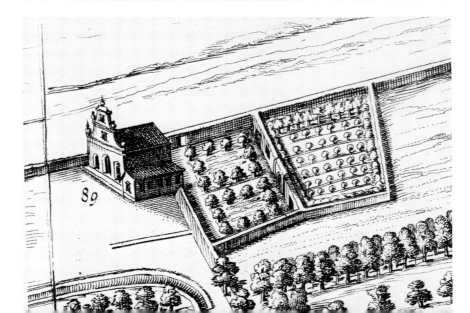

45. Anonymous seventeenth-century artist, *Enclosed Garden* (Madrid, Biblioteca Nacional)

and 1641, over twenty-five small tracts were purchased along the borders of the site.[82] There was also a sizable area to the south that was annexed to the park. This comprised the church and precinct of Nuestra Señora de Atocha, a Dominican foundation for which the king had a special affection. In 1636, an alley was laid out that linked the garden of the monastery to the grounds of the Retiro, considerably enlarging them at little cost to the Crown.[83]

As in the construction of the palace, there appears to have been no overall advance plan for the design of the park that could be implemented as land and money became available. Nevertheless, the grounds were impressive, and delightful for recreation, and their very size contributed greatly to the effect. By 1640, the Retiro had taken on kingly proportions and covered an area almost half as large as the entire town of Madrid. Within the walls, there were lakes, canals, ponds and fountains (fig. 41), groves of fruit trees, flower and vegetable gardens, covered walkways and long, shady alleys. There was also a ball court, a riding school, a menagerie, an enormous aviary, boat-houses and a series of six hermitages.

The hermitages were the most distinctive feature of the park and appear to have been purely Spanish in origin.[84] Hermitages had been incorporated into the park of the estate at Lerma, built by the Duke of Lerma in the 1610s.[85] But the immediate inspiration may have been provided by the little oratories at the Catalan monastery of Montserrat, which the king visited on his return journey from Barcelona in 1626. Later that year he ordered the construction of thirteen hermitages on the model of Montserrat in the gardens of Aranjuez.[86] The creation of the Retiro gave him a new opportunity to establish the kind of rural devotion which was obviously very much to his taste. But while the hermitages of the Retiro had a religious function, secular activities were by no means excluded from their precincts. The hermitage of San Juan (fig. 42), which was finished in 1634, was the official residence of the governor and contained a small apartment with a library.[87] It was frequently used by Olivares as a retreat within the Retiro. The hermitage of San Isidro, just behind the palace, had a small pool for boating and fishing.[88] Other hermitages, such as San Bruno (finished in 1635, fig. 43)[89] and Santa María Magdalena (built in 1634–5, fig. 44),[90] had gardens and grottoes and were used as picnic sites or occasionally as outdoor theaters. An anonymous architectural drawing of the mid-seventeenth century

77

VEVE DE L'HERMITAGE DE SAINCT PAVL DANS LE RETIR DE MADRID   Vista de la Hermita de San Pablo que esta en el buen retiro de Madrid

VEVE DE L'HERMITAGE DE St ANTOINE DANS LE RETIR ... MAIS BATI PAR LES   Hermita de San Antonio que esta en el buen retiro de Madrid
DORTVGAIS ...

ueue du grand es tang du Retir

VEVE DV GRAND ESTANG DV RETIR OV LES ROIS DESPAGNE   Vista del Estanque grande del buen retiro de Madrid.
SE DIVERTISENT DANS DES GALEERS ET NAVIRS

46. (facing page, above) Louis Meunier, *Hermitage of San Pablo* (London, British Library)
47. (facing page, center) Louis Meunier, *Hermitage of San Antonio* (London, British Library)
48. (facing page, below) Louis Meunier, *Large Lake* (London, British Library)
49. Attributed to Juan del Mazo, *Large Lake* (Madrid, Prado)

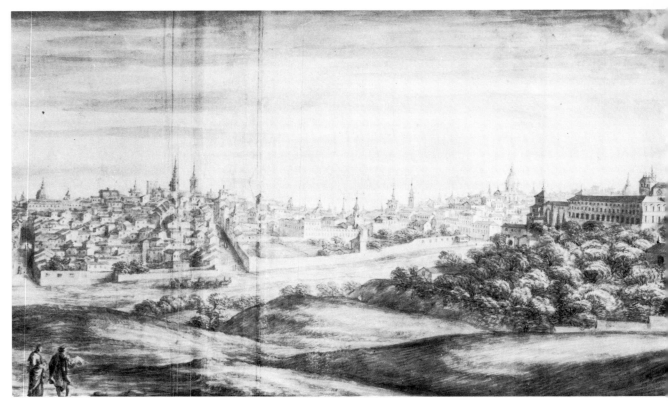

50. Pier Maria Baldi, *Palace and Park of the Buen Retiro* (Florence, Biblioteca Laurenzana)

(fig. 45) furnishes a general idea of how the enclosed hermitage gardens may have appeared, although none of them can specifically be related to the sketch.[91]

The exterior designs of the hermitages used the same basic elements of design and construction as were used in the palace. They were built of brick, with stone moldings around the doors and windows. The roofs were made of slate and terminated in the characteristic high, pointed towers common to Spanish royal buildings. The only exception to the rule was the hermitage of San Pablo, the first of the hermitages to be built (fig. 46).[92] Its highly ornate facade, with elaborate decorative motifs and sculptures in niches, was reminiscent of Roman villas such as the Casino of Pius IV in the Vatican or the garden facade of the Villa Medici. The Italianate design may well be attributable to the hand of Crescenzi, who was working alone as the architect of the site when San Pablo was built.

On the interior, each hermitage had at least one chapel decorated with paintings and sculpture. The altar of the chapel of San Pablo, for instance, was probably the original location of Velázquez's painting *Landscape with St Anthony Abbot and St Paul the Hermit* (fig. 86).[93] The rooms devoted to secular purposes were naturally decorated with secular themes. This fact explains the otherwise bizarre commission of the sculptor Antonio de Herrera, who was asked in 1635 to make two figure groups for the hermitage of San Jerónimo. The first was to represent the three Magi, the second, Venus and Adonis.[94]

80

The most vivid idea of the appearance of the hermitages is conveyed by the contract for the largest of them, San Antonio de Padua or "de los Portugueses" (fig. 47). The contract was signed on July 25, 1635 by Carbonel, who promised completion of the building by June 16 of the next year.[95] According to the terms, the hermitage was to be built, as usual, of red brick. The main portal was to be made of four white marble columns with black marble bases and capitals, and to be crowned by the statue of the patron in white marble. Inside, three altars were planned for a chapel constructed of brick and tile, the main altar dedicated to St Anthony, the two side altars to Sts Isabella and Gonzalo. The altar of St Anthony was designed to have a jaspar altar frontal similar to the one already in place at San Bruno. The other rooms on the first floor, which were arranged in a circle around the chapel, were to be made of Toledo brick, faced with decorated tiles to the height of eight tiles. The rooms on the second and third floor were to be treated in the same way.[96]

San Antonio had another distinctive feature, its lobular surrounding moat which formed part of the ambitious network of artificial lakes, ponds and canals that were used for irrigation, as well as for boating and fishing.[97] The centerpiece of the system was a huge body of water called the Large Lake, which was completed in 1637 and survives in much modified form in the Retiro Park today.[98] The Large Lake was frequently used for royal boating parties, which navigated its waters in ornate gilded gondolas sent from Naples (fig. 48). Along its banks were six fishing pavilions, from which the courtiers could fish in the abundantly stocked waters (fig. 49).[99] The Large Lake fed two rivers, the Little Canal (*Río Chico*), which wound a crooked course through the northwestern sector of the park, watering plants and trees as it went, and the Grand Canal, a sizable waterway that flowed through the eastern perimeter and terminated at the hermitage of San Antonio.[100]

The elaborate waterways kept the king amused and the plants and trees alive, for the soil of the Retiro was notoriously difficult to cultivate. Yet, while the Modenese poet Fulvio Testi in apostrophizing Olivares somewhat overstated the case when he wrote, "at your command the plants grow,"[101] they did somehow succeed in growing, thanks to the labors of an army of gardeners brought from Aranjuez and even from as far away as Italy. In June 1638, a Genoese gardener named Benedetto Babestreli arrived as the escort of forty-four boxes of plants and trees.[102] He decided to stay on, and three years later was supervising the transplanting of trees in the long alleys near the Large Lake.[103] Shipments of plants and trees were forever arriving at the Retiro—orange and lemon trees from Valencia, poplars from the forest of the Pardo, almond trees from Andalusia. In the end, the triumph of man over nature was complete. A drawing of 1668, made by an Italian artist, shows the park grown to maturity (fig. 50).[104] In the midst of the dry, dusty tableland of central Castile, an oasis of lush greenery had managed to survive the baking sun of summer and the freezing winds of winter.

This conquest of nature did not, unfortunately, meet with universal applause. From Olivares's political critics the worst could be expected, and they did not disappoint. But there was also a group of "art critics," who disapproved of the Retiro as a work of architecture. The position of this group is best represented by Bernardo Monanni, in a critique of the palace written in December 1633.

The building is suitably large for the site, but the architecture, in general, is not pleasing because they have not followed the advice of the architects, although they were Italian and eminent. They have only paid attention to comfort and to finishing quickly, not to the majesty and durability of the work, qualities that should be observed in royal buildings. Thus, the building is too low; the windows, too small, simple, and ordinary; the rooms, too long and narrow. In comparison with a well-made house, this one looks more like a monastery than a royal dwelling. And because they had laid foundations only for what has been built, they will find it difficult to enlarge in the future, although they are now changing the plan and making it larger every day.[105]

Monanni's objections are hard to refute, especially if one accepts his Italianate viewpoint. However, what cannot be refuted can sometimes be explained. The Retiro was created by circumstances, traditions and personalities that were never fully reconciled, which explains why it became such an eloquent symbol of its times.

Monanni's first criticism related to the lack of majesty and splendor of the exterior. Visitors from abroad never failed to express disappointment at the appearance of the palace, and it is easy to see why they reacted as they did. The main facade of the palace was drastically flat, simple and unadorned, and was built of modest materials (fig. 51). Amazingly, too, it was devoid of references to classical architecture at a time when architects throughout the rest of Western Europe were adapting recent Italianate models to local traditions and customs. The architectural

51. North Wing, Palace of the Buen Retiro in the nineteenth century

vocabulary of the Retiro excluded columns, pilasters, friezes and sculptural relief. To eyes that had seen the magnificent princely palaces of Italy and France, the Retiro was austere to a fault.

This outward austerity, however, was deliberate and consistent with the tradition of Spanish Habsburg architecture. It was even a trait affected by the kings themselves. Philip IV, who was rhetorically likened to the sun, habitually wore a black costume and an icy expression. In this he was following the tradition of his grandfather Philip II, who set the austere style of comportment and architecture that became obligatory for Spanish Habsburg kings. Philip II's architectural style was confected of two disparate elements that were first successfully synthesized in the Escorial (1561–83, fig. 52).[106] One part was a chaste Italian classicism that was further purified by Philip's cerebral architect, Juan de Herrera.[107] The second component somewhat incongruously came from Flanders, which Philip had twice visited. It was from this source that the king appropriated the hallmark of his architecture, the pointed, slate-roofed tower. This element, combined with the astringent Italian classicism, produced what is now called the *estilo austriaco* (the style of the Spanish branch of the House of Austria), which was also marked by the predominant use of granite and brick as building materials. The Escorial set the style for future Crown construction and it is no wonder that the Retiro looked to Monanni like a religious establishment. The slate-roofed towers at the corners of the main courtyard emulated the Escorial and functioned like signposts. This building, they proclaimed, was the abode of His Catholic Majesty.

The plan of the palace was equally traditional. It was arranged as a series of courtyards, following the scheme of the Escorial, the Alcázar and many private palaces.[108] The only novelty was the arrangement of the large halls on three sides of the courtyard. They were disposed *enfilade*, with center doors that linked them into a long axial view. The enfilade arrangement was typical of sixteenth-century Italian palaces, including the Palazzo Crescenzi, but was unprecedented in Spanish royal palaces.[109] Obviously, the design of these rooms was the idea of Crescenzi, who seems to have tried in vain to escape the burden of the Escorial.

Yet it was a far cry from the stern magnificence of the Escorial to the careless informality of the Retiro. The construction materials had something to do with it. Once Olivares had decided to go ahead with the project, there could be no delay, and rapid construction was best accomplished by using simple, inexpensive materials. Also, the count–duke may have sensed initially that the creation of a dazzling new palace was not appropriate and decided on a compromise that was entirely characteristic of the times: to build a palace with a modest exterior, but to spare no cost in adorning it. This was a formula that was also used in two important counterparts of the Retiro—the Luxembourg Palace and the Pitti Palace, behind whose sedate facades were exuberant decorations by Peter Paul Rubens and Pietro da Cortona respectively.[110]

The validity of these explanations of the deficiencies of the Retiro is partly contradicted, unfortunately, by the notorious demand for speed, which swept all before it. Planning is a thoughtful, time-consuming business, and haste is its mortal enemy. While the Escorial followed a meticulous plan, the Retiro lurched forward from whim to whim. The lack of planning shows up best in the early stages of the

52. Anonymous seventeenth-century artist, *The Escorial* (El Escorial)

project, when every new phase of construction was preceded by demolishing something that had only recently been finished. It also led at times to serious lapses and omissions. The Retiro, for instance, had no grand principal entrance. The central forecourt, its logical location, was incongruously occupied by the menagerie. It appears that the king used the northern court, the Emperor's Courtyard, when he visited the Retiro. Thus he entered his palace in the northwest corner through a portal that was really a side door, and then ascended to the main floor by a simple staircase, rather than a monumental one of the kind that would have been built in an Italian palace of this category. This is but one example of how improvisation could lead to confusion. Throughout the entire building history, Philip and Olivares seemed to draw fresh inspiration as each new addition to the site neared completion. There was a general guiding idea, namely to build a suburban palace suitable for lavish entertainment and luxurious recreation. But the process of thought and design, as the pell-mell evolution of the Retiro shows, was realized in an additive, not a premeditated way.

This manner of execution meant that the patron had extraordinary power to shape the design of the palace and gardens. At its best, the architect–patron relationship is an organic one. The patron establishes the program, the architect gives it form, and in so doing inspires the client to try new ideas and expand his conception of the project. At its worst, the relationship can collapse into tyranny on the part of either architect or client. Unfortunately, the construction of the Retiro seems to have conformed to the second model. Olivares, as tyrannical a patron as ever lived, put speed before all other considerations. And with speed came impetuosity. Crescenzi and then his successor Carbonel worked under the dual swords of whim and impatience, which must have made their lives a misery. Monanni went so far as to suggest that Crescenzi was cut down by these weapons. In his report of March 15, 1635, he noted the death of his compatriot. "The Marquis of la Torre, who served as His Majesty's principal architect, has died. And the troubles that he suffered in building the Pantheon of the Escorial, but especially in building the new Retiro, in which he often had to deal with Olivares and suffer indignities, may have abbreviated his life."[111] Carbonel, who had learned to succeed at court by following orders, was better able to withstand his patron's capriciousness. But his suggestions, too, went largely unheeded. In the autumn of 1637, an indictment of Olivares circulated in the court accusing him, among other things, of disregarding the advice of his architects and insisting on doing things his own way.[112] These charges are believable and are confirmed by the way that the project progressed by fits and starts. And they lead inevitably to the conclusion that the Retiro was fundamentally the inspiration of an enthusiastic, impetuous and headstrong amateur.

The Retiro, therefore, became a projection in three dimensions of the personality and policies of the count–duke. In his eagerness to revive the image of the Monarchy, he dictated adherence to an architectural model created by Philip II in the hope of identifying his monarch with a great ancestor. But the times had changed, and Philip II's lofty disdain for outward show, based on the limitless confidence of his power and the steely conviction of his righteousness, would not serve the needs of the moment. Now doubt and dissension were abroad in the land and were undermining faith in the Monarchy's capacity to fulfill its historic mission. The Retiro was therefore designed as a monumental diversion. It might serve to divert attention from political reality to political imagery. It was certainly meant to divert the attention of a royal aesthete from a tendency to melancholy that deepened with the years. But it also proved to be a diversion of another sort, for large sums of money, painfully extracted from an impoverished populace, were diverted from the pressing needs of state to create an oasis of splendor in the midst of misery.

IV

Behind the Scenes

BUILDING THE PALACE

"Who is the architect of this affair, of this marvelous prodigy?" asked the student in Carducho's *Dialogue on Painting*. "I regard it as certain," replied his master, "that it reveals the illustrious mind of the most excellent count–duke, his discrimination, his wisdom and understanding, and his success in disposing everything that relates to the service, comfort and taste of His Majesty—the purpose being that he should have a seemly place of retreat for such occasions as may present themselves, and where perhaps he may be able to get away from business, without having to suffer the usual discomforts and costs of travel."[1]

While it was obligatory upon those who moved in court circles to glorify the count–duke as the inspiring genius of the marvelous complex of palace and gardens now miraculously arising on the unpromising terrain round the monastery of San Jerónimo, all the available evidence suggests that they were right. But this does not imply that the king himself, with his discriminating eye and his aesthetic sensibility, followed with anything less than the closest interest the progress of the building works and the decoration of his palace. He also followed it with considerable impatience. Monanni reported at the end of July 1633 that Philip had ordered Olivares to have the work finished as soon as possible, doubling the work force so that building operations planned to last a year would be completed in six months. The reason for this royal impatience, he said, was that the king and queen had taken such a liking to the site that they no longer wanted to be entertained in any gardens but their own.[2] Matías de Novoa overheard Philip asking the foremen: "When is all this going to be finished? When shall we be free of all this dust and earth, and have the workmen out?" Characteristically, Novoa saw this sign of exasperation—normal enough when clients follow with dismay the slow progress of their builders—as evidence that the king had been dragged into an undertaking for which he felt no inclination. "*Basta lo hecho*"—"enough is enough"—he said on another occasion when the count–duke came to him with further suggestions.[3]

The king, not unreasonably, was anxious to take up residence in his new palace. On November 8, 1633 he gave instructions that, so far as considerations of health and cleanliness allowed, the royal quarters might now be occupied, except for the bedrooms and the rooms immediately adjoining them.[4] After recovering from a brief indisposition he was expected to take up residence himself on November 19, but this proved impossible because the mortar was still damp.[5] Frantic last-minute preparations were needed to have the royal apartments ready for the king and queen to move into the palace at the beginning of December. They only stayed a few days, but from that moment the new royal residence, so impatiently awaited, was an established fact.

During those last hectic days before the inauguration, the count–duke was constantly at the site, barking out orders and fussing over details. Often the Countess of Olivares accompanied him, and everyone in the count–duke's circle was pressed into service. In addition to those professionally concerned with the site in one capacity or another, some of the count–duke's closest colleagues and dependents, like the Count of Castrillo, the Marquis of Leganés, and the indispensable protonotary Jerónimo de Villanueva, were all kept busy making ready the rooms and galleries.[6] "The house," reported Hopton shortly after the opening, "is very richly furnished and almost all by presents, for the Conde hath made the work his own, by which means it hath not wanted friends."[7]

This deep personal commitment of the count–duke to the Buen Retiro naturally reflected his obligation as governor to see that everything was properly ordered. But it also reflected the fact, recognized by friends and enemies alike, that from the moment of its inception it was peculiarly his own enterprise, and one which he was determined to push through to a triumphant conclusion. The very way in which the palace had grown, starting from a modest extension of the Royal Apartment of San Jerónimo, and ending as a vast complex designed for a whole variety of purposes, bore the hallmark of the count–duke's personality, which contemporaries often described as "capricious." But not all the capriciousness was necessarily on the count–duke's side. If, as seems probable, the king became increasingly enthusiastic about the possibilities of his new palace, Olivares, as a loyal servant, was keen to do whatever gave his master pleasure.

In recognition of Olivares's achievement and of his accustomed "zeal" in his service, the king issued a decree on January 23, 1634 conferring full powers upon him to dispose and order whatever he considered necessary for further work on the Retiro.[8] It was a clear sign both of his confidence and his satisfaction, but Olivares was much too skilled a courtier not to keep his master fully informed about each new phase of the work. Early in May 1634, for instance, when Philip was just back from Aranjuez, the count–duke went to the Retiro gardens to meet him and report on the latest developments.[9] But there is more than mere formality in Olivares's constant and continuing preoccupation with the Retiro. Having launched the king on such a large and expensive enterprise, he was naturally committed to making it a success, and all the more so when it was becoming the object of criticism by his enemies. He was also immensely proud of what he had achieved. On what was formerly arid and desolate terrain he had wrought a modern miracle, a handsome, superbly appointed palace, set about with gardens, lakes and shady walks. The desert had literally been made to blossom as the rose, and the count–duke was not the man to let people overlook this remarkable accomplishment.

The Italian poet and diplomat Fulvio Testi, who was sent to Madrid in 1635 as the envoy of the Duke of Modena, vividly describes in one of his letters a conversation with Olivares, who had given him a personal and exclusive invitation to attend a play to be performed before the king at the Retiro in May 1636.[10] After Olivares had stepped in to reduce confusion to order in the seating arrangements for the play, he invited Testi to take a seat beside him and then proceeded to talk to him without interruption throughout the entire performance. "He described to me the structure of the Retiro, not without some personal satisfaction; and certainly the building is extremely sumptuous, although more so within than without, and makes a greater impression than its external appearance would suggest. Then he spoke of the buildings and gardens of Rome, and talked of perspectives and painting, of theaters, fiestas and tournaments, and finally of poetry. . ." This unquenchable flow of conversation, which prevented Testi from ever discovering what was happening on the stage, suggests something of Olivares's enthusiasm for a project that he had nurtured and cherished. Testi took the hint. "Knowing how fond he is of the Retiro building and of the delights he has made there," he composed some verses on the Retiro and presented them to the count–duke, who was duly gratified.[11]

Olivares's close identification with the site was strengthened by the fact that it also offered him a secluded residence of his own. In the palace itself he had a set of apartments in which the Duke of Modena was lodged when he came to Madrid in 1638. They are described as double apartments, with one suite of rooms being furnished for winter and the other for summer. The winter quarters were hung with crimson velvet and gold brocade hangings. As for the summer quarters, decorated in white and gold, it was enough simply to look at them to feel refreshed.[12] How far Olivares actually used these apartments is not clear. Probably he found it more peaceful to retire to the hermitage of San Juan, which was designated as the governor's residence. Here he could retreat for Lenten meditations, or work quietly among his books. But even when he was not able to stay overnight at the Retiro, it was near enough to the Alcázar for an afternoon outing by coach; and when important work was under way, as it was in the gardens in the spring of 1635, he would pay almost daily visits.[13]

It may seem strange that a man who was so constantly complaining about his intolerable burden of work should devote so much precious time to worrying about building or decorative schemes, to busying himself with the planting of the Retiro gardens or to wondering whether the fountains were in working order. This kind of activity, however, seems to have provided a welcome relief from the cares of office. For the count–duke the beautification of the Retiro seems to have meant not so much another duty as a pleasant, and therapeutic, distraction. Antonio Carnero suggests as much in a letter he wrote to a colleague on December 4, 1638: "The new method of planting grown trees has been approved here and put into practice, and a large number of them have already been planted in the Retiro. We hope that all this trouble will be justified by the results. In the midst of all my master's cares, this pastime is his only solace and relief."[14] Giving orders to gardeners probably came as a welcome change to giving orders to generals; and, even in the heat of a Madrid summer, trees were sometimes easier to handle than men.

The distracting care of the Buen Retiro undoubtedly consumed a significant amount of the count–duke's time and energies in the 1630s, but he was vigorously supported by his lieutenants, who knew that they stood to gain in his favor if they displayed zeal and dedication in helping with this, his favorite enterprise. It would have been easy enough to hand over the details of planning and furnishing to the Committee of Works and Woods. But this would have been quite uncharacteristic of Olivares. His life consisted of a running battle with the bureaucracy, and he did not want cautious and routine-bound officials blocking his architectural projects any more than his other projects for the restoration of Castile and the Monarchy.

As governor of the Buen Retiro, and one who was vested with absolute powers, he was in a position to organize the construction and administration as he saw fit. The Committee of Works did not like this, and as late as June 9, 1640 the king had to intervene to prevent it from trying to inspect the site.[15] The count–duke was well aware that the massive deployment of men and money required for the building of the palace could only be achieved if the arrangements rested in his own hands and those of trusted subordinates.

The chain of command for building operations is best shown in the form of a diagram[16] (Table II). It will be seen from this diagram that, while Crescenzi supervised the design and construction and reported directly to Olivares, Carbonel had direct control of the large army of contractors, subcontractors and laborers working on the site. Although Carbonel was known as the master of the works, he was in fact an architect, but the word *arquitecto* was not usually applied to him because it implied a higher social status than the Crown was willing to grant to practitioners of the art. His duties tended to reinforce the prejudice; for although he had design responsibilities, he was as much a construction supervisor as he was an artist.

Under Carbonel's supervision there were three primary construction contractors,[17] although in 1635 Juan de Aguilar left the Retiro to begin work on the cardinal infante's palace of the Zarzuela. Thereafter Cristóbal de Aguilera took charge of many of the important undertakings, especially in the gardens. Other building contractors were brought in for the occasional additions to the palace, notably the Casón and the Coliseo. These contractors appear to have operated much as they do today. They agreed to undertake a project for a set amount of money, hoping to make a profit by completing the work within the contract price. The agreements were signed by the contracting parties before a notary, and many of them are preserved in the notarial archives of Madrid. The contractor agreed to finish a certain piece of work by a specified date in strict accordance with the plans he had been given, and frequently a detailed description of the work was included. For his part, the official who represented the Crown guaranteed specific payments on specific dates. The contract also contained a clause arranging for arbitration in case of dispute.

The building materials required by the contractors were obtained by special procurement officers, who scoured the surrounding countryside and badgered local officials into arranging for their transportation to Madrid. Terracotta roof tiles were made in Añover del Tajo, a hillside town between Toledo and Aranjuez which still has an important brick factory. Wood, which was used for the framework of the buildings, came from the forests in the foothills of the Guadarrama mountains. From quarries in the same region came the enormous quantities of stone required to pave the courtyards of the palace. Stonecutters were pressed into service from towns and villages in the neighborhood of Madrid like Barajas, Arganda and Getafe,[18] while other local villages had to provide the necessary transport. In 1634, for instance, twelve villages were ordered to produce a total of 276 carts to carry the paving-stones needed for the Retiro's principal courtyard.[19]

90

Table II. The Construction of the Buen Retiro.

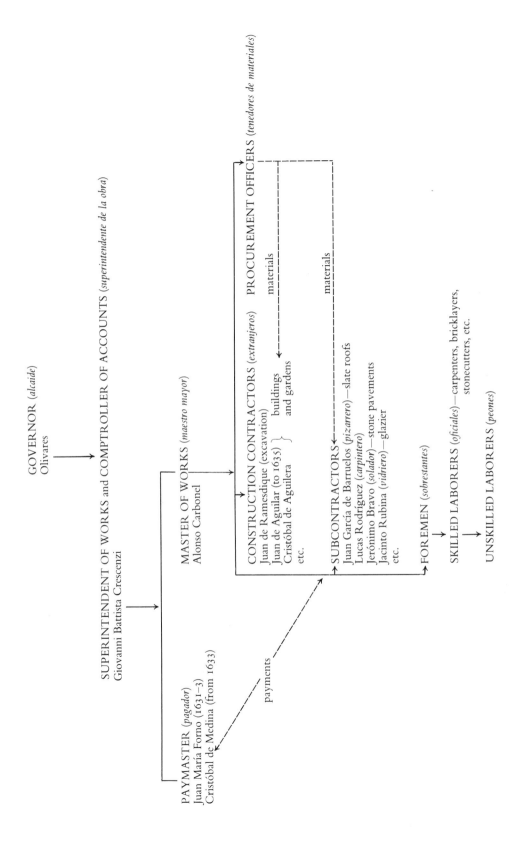

GOVERNOR (*alcaide*)
Olivares

SUPERINTENDENT OF WORKS and COMPTROLLER OF ACCOUNTS (*superintendente de la obra*)
Giovanni Battista Crescenzi

MASTER OF WORKS (*maestro mayor*)
Alonso Carbonel

PAYMASTER (*pagador*)
Juan María Forno (1631–3)
Cristóbal de Medina (from 1633)

CONSTRUCTION CONTRACTORS (*extranjeros*)
Juan de Ramesdique (excavation)
Juan de Aguilar (to 1635) ⎱ buildings
Cristóbal de Aguilera   ⎰ and gardens
etc.

PROCUREMENT OFFICERS (*tenedores de materiales*)

materials

materials

SUBCONTRACTORS
Juan García de Barruelos (*pizarrero*)—slate roofs
Lucas Rodríguez (*carpintero*)
Jerónimo Bravo (*solador*)—stone pavements
Jacinto Rubina (*vidriero*)—glazier
etc.

FOREMEN (*sobrestantes*)

SKILLED LABORERS (*oficiales*)—carpenters, bricklayers, stonecutters, etc.

UNSKILLED LABORERS (*peones*)

payments

It seems that the contractors were not responsible for the finishing work, which was let out to independent subcontractors, including sculptors and painters. During the course of 1633, a substantial amount of architectural and ornamental sculpture was executed by a group of Italian sculptors. These men had worked at the royal Pantheon of the Escorial with Crescenzi, who must have brought them to the Retiro. In the group were Bartolommeo Zumbigo, Giacomo Semeria, Giovanni Antonio Ceroni, Pietro Gatti and Diego de Viana, who despite his name was said to be Italian.[20] Zumbigo, Gatti and Semeria received several payments for stone chimney-pieces, usually totaling no more than thirty or forty ducats an installment, which indicates a modest price for each unit.[21] Ceroni executed a statue of *St Paul the Hermit* for the hermitage chapel of that name, for which he was paid around 100 ducats.[22] In the next year, Zumbigo was working in the gardens, and was given fifty-three ducats for a fountain to be placed in the garden of San Juan, and later 181 ducats for another fountain in the formal garden behind the palace (fig. 53).[23] Several years later, the sculptor Pedro de Tapia was paid 170 ducats for a small fountain for San Bruno.[24] These wages were generally in line with those given to other skilled craftsmen. For instance, the woodworker Juan Garrido was given forty-three ducats to mount a portable stage in the masking room, while the carpenter Francisco Limón received 173 ducats for two sets of doors for the main staircase and six windows for the chapel in San Juan.[25]

The artisan painters fared about as well. Most of the painters who appear on the payrolls did decorative work such as painting balconies and ironwork with gold or green paint. An Italian named Giulio Cesare Semini, who had been employed by the Crown since the reign of Philip III, made a speciality of this work. In 1633, he was paid ninety ducats on three or four occasions for this monotonous chore.[26] The few payments for easel paintings, admittedly by second-rate artists, were also modest. On July 30, 1633, Pedro Núñez, a painter of modest reputation, was given twenty-seven ducats for some paintings he had done for the hermitage chapel of San Juan.[27] That this rate of pay was not exceptionally low for an artist of his caliber is seen in a payment to Juan de Solís, who in 1637 received ninety-four ducats for four landscapes and a painting of Bacchus, and some decorative work in the hermitage of La Magdalena.[28] Clearly the distinction between art and craft did not mean very much either to this class of artist or their employers. To all intents and purposes, they belonged to the group of master craftsmen, along with carpenters, metal workers, and glaziers. Obviously, painters such as Velázquez, Maino and Carducho, artists of reputation and achievement, were much better paid, although their social status, while perhaps more elevated than that of their humble colleagues, was not as lofty as they would have wished it to be.

At the bottom of the ladder were the workmen—the *oficiales*, or skilled laborers, and the *peones*, the unskilled. The skilled labor force consisted primarily of carpenters, bricklayers and stone-cutters. At the Retiro, most of these men were employed by the contractors and sub-contractors, and not directly by the Crown. Beneath them were the unskilled laborers, who did the numerous jobs that required only a strong back. For these men the pay scale was low, and the working day long. The normal practice in the royal works was for the workmen to arrive on the site at 6 a.m. and work until 11 a.m. At 11 a.m. they had a two-hour lunch break and *siesta*

53. Diego de Viana, *Project for Fountain*, whereabouts unknown (from Caturla, *Pinturas*)

away from the heat of the midday sun. Work resumed at 1 p.m. and continued to 4 p.m., when an hour's break was taken. The men returned at 5 p.m. and worked until sunset. In the winter months the working day lasted from 7 a.m. to sunset, with only an hour's break at noon.[29]

The pay scale also followed the path of the sun; and, for the unskilled at least, wages were no more than a pittance. The usual standard of pay at the royal sites in the opening decades of the seventeenth century was eight or nine *reales* a day for the skilled, and five *reales* for the unskilled in summer, and four in winter. (There were eleven *reales* to the ducat.) In his *Restauración de la abundancia de España* of 1631, Miguel Caxa de Leruela writes that the rise in prices had made it impossible for a day-laborer in Madrid to live on the standard wage of eight *reales* a day.[30] But Monanni reports that some of the unskilled men working at the Retiro in 1633 were being paid only four a day in summer and three in winter. These, however, seem to have been an unfortunate minority, presumably doing the most menial work. Most of the workmen at the site were apparently earning eight, ten or twelve *reales* a day, and some as many as sixteen or twenty.[31]

Foremen supervised the work of the laborers, and were required to be on the site before dawn and keep records of the hours worked, for the benefit of the comptroller of accounts. The disappearance of all such records for the Retiro makes it impossible to trace the fluctuations in the size and composition of the workforce at the site. In December 1633, according to Monanni, over 1,500 men were continuously engaged on work for the Retiro, but these included not only the men actually working on the palace and gardens but also those who fetched and carried, and the artisans at work in their houses and shops. At this moment, he wrote, the costs of wages and materials were running at over 2,000 ducats a day—enough to maintain an army of respectable size.

In reporting on the early stages of the construction, Monanni was struck by the fact that most of the work was being done by human hands, although horses, dogs and even camels were also being used at the site.[32] His comment suggests that by Italian standards not much use was being made of mechanical devices in the construction work. But the fact that the Retiro was being built of wood and brick rather than stone makes less surprising the absence of the kind of machines used, for example, in the building of the Escorial. This overwhelming reliance on manpower meant that each decision to add to the palace or extend the gardens led to a drastic expansion of the labor force, especially as the king and Olivares were always in a hurry for the work to be done. In the winter of 1639, for instance, when extensive work was being done on the gardens, it was reported that more than 1,600 men were at work on the site.[33] With some justification Olivares would later defend the building of the Retiro by saying that it gave work to the unemployed.[34] But this convenient argument leaves on one side the delicate question of the social value of the project in relation to other public work enterprises that might have been undertaken with human and financial resources of this magnitude. How, for instance, is the construction of the Retiro to be compared in terms of social and economic benefits with the projects which Olivares planned but never realized for the improvement of river navigation in Castile?

The count–duke's real concern, however, was to give not work to the poor but pleasure to the king. Philip wanted his palace, and he wanted it fast. The decision to by-pass the Committee of Works and set up a structure of command which Olivares could galvanize with his own driving energy made it possible for the royal requirements to be met. This structure of command, however, applied only to the initial building operations. A new and more permanent organization was required for the management of the palace once it was ready for occupation.

On November 5, 1633, the ordinances for the administration of the Royal Apartment of San Jerónimo were superseded by a new set of ordinances for the Buen Retiro.[35] These followed the pattern used in other royal houses, and were intended to govern only the maintenance of the palace and grounds. No special regulations were needed for household staff because the king and queen brought with them from the Alcázar their ladies- and gentlemen-in-waiting, their pages and cooks and kitchen staff whenever they crossed Madrid to stay at the Retiro.

The ordinances gave Olivares, as governor, broad discretionary powers to do whatever was necessary to maintain and improve the physical amenities of the site. He interpreted this charge literally, and never stopped improving and extending the attractions of palace and garden. From February 1634 all payments for new construction were authorized in his name, as they had been authorized in Crescenzi's name since 1631.[36] This arrangement in effect regularized the power which he had wielded from the start of the project.

The count–duke's determination to keep everything firmly in his own hands is further indicated by his choice of a second-in-command. No man was closer to him, or saw more of him, than his faithful secretary Antonio Carnero, and on November 29, 1633, Carnero was appointed deputy governor with an annual salary of three hundred ducats.[37] Among his duties Carnero was expected to have a meeting every Saturday to plan the coming week's work with the comptroller of accounts and the treasurer, who had an annual allocation of 6,500 ducats for salaries and maintenance costs. This allocation, which soon proved inadequate, was established in 1633, and

Table III. The Administration of the Buen Retiro.

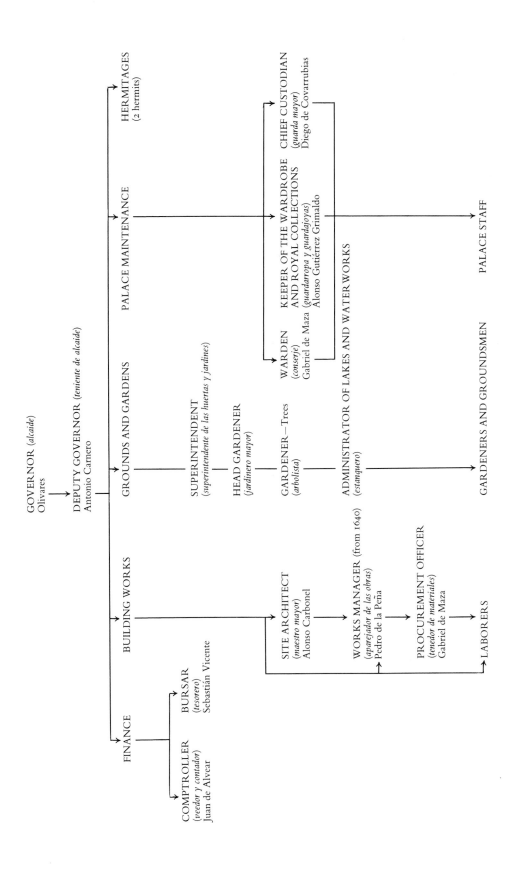

consisted of 5,000 ducats drawn from ecclesiastical dues in Castile and Aragon and 1,500 diverted to the Retiro from the revenues normally applied to the upkeep of the Alcázar of Seville.[38]

Carnero exercised control over an organization divided into different departments[39] (Table III). This organization seems to have worked well; and as new amenities were added new appointments were made. The groundsmen, too, proved inadequate as the gardens were expanded, and in April 1636 a contingent of gardeners was ordered to move from Aranjuez to the Retiro to help with the upkeep.[40] But in one important, if unusual, department, special provision was made from the outset. Two men, one of them in clerical orders, were designated to serve as hermits—perhaps the first official appointments ever made to that demanding calling. The hermitage chapels were placed in their care; and on Sundays and feast days, in one of the chapels designated by the governor, the professionally qualified hermit was expected to hold mass for the Retiro staff.[41] The joys of the spirit were not forgotten in this garden of earthly delights.

PAYING FOR THE PALACE

A pleasure palace suggests the delights of peace, but the Retiro was built in time of war. This unhappy paradox beset the building from the start. It determined its unusual character because Olivares, more and more a full-time war minister, was unable to plan it systematically, as he might have done in time of peace. It determined the public's perception of the Retiro, for should not the king have forgone its pleasures in order to lead his armies in battle? It also determined the methods of funding, since wartime conditions imposed their own special demands.

While it might be argued that no time is ever the right time to spend public money on private pleasures, the 1630s were particularly unpropitious years for the King of Spain to embark on such a costly venture. For this was the decade in which Spain was plunged into the seventeenth-century equivalent of total war. Following the death of Gustavus Adolphus in 1632, the count–duke planned a major offensive in collaboration with the emperor to defeat the Protestant forces in Germany and compel the Dutch to agree to peace. A specially created army of Alsace under the command of the Duke of Feria cleared the military route along the Rhine between Constance and Breisach in the autumn of 1633—a victorious campaign that was to be duly celebrated by no less than three battle paintings for the Hall of Realms.[42]

The way was now open for the cardinal infante to travel overland from Milan to Brussels, where the death of the Infanta Isabella in December 1633 had left the Spanish Netherlands without a governor. On his northward march, after joining forces with the Imperial army, he inflicted a crushing defeat on the Swedes at Nördlingen on September 6, 1634. But the very extent of his victory made it impossible for Richelieu to continue his policy of avoiding direct French intervention in the conflict, and in May 1635 France at last declared war on Spain. It was a war that would last for twenty-four years, bringing untold misery to the peoples of both countries before the island meeting on the river Bidasoa between an ageing Philip IV and his vigorous young nephew Louis XIV brought it to a ceremonious end in November 1659.

To sustain the intense military effort that was now required, new taxes were levied, and offices and privileges created and sold, while Olivares haggled and bartered with the royal bankers to secure loans at manageable rates of interest. "The poor man," wrote Arthur Hopton in May of 1634, "is spent with the burthen of business that lies on him and deserves to be pitied if he would pity himself."[43] Yet the count–duke never spared himself, any more than he spared his compatriots. Satires and broadsheets were circulating in Madrid that summer which portrayed Spain as a mule which Olivares held by the ears, or as a patient being told by his doctor that the knife was the only remedy left. By now it was more than probable that the patient would bleed to death as soon as the knife was applied.[44]

It is hardly surprising in these somber circumstances that the critics of the regime should have singled out the Retiro for special attack. At a time when his peoples were being subjected to incessant demands for money and his armies were going hungry in the field, Philip was spending enormous sums—twenty million ducats, the Portuguese author of the *Arte de Furtar* later alleged—on "the monstrous building of the chicken coop in Madrid."[45] On his side, Olivares, very much on the defensive, would claim that the project had not cost the king even five hundred ducats.[46] Which party to the argument was telling the truth?

Estimates of the sums devoted to the Retiro are inextricably bound up with the mechanisms used to raise and disburse the money. Philip repeatedly insisted that the ordinary revenues of the Crown were not to be used for the palace and gardens— they were to be financed entirely from extraordinary sources of income.[47] This compelled his ministers to resort to a patchwork of fiscal expedients which was as complex as it was untidy, although in this respect it hardly differed from the patterns of financing used for other major enterprises of the Spanish Crown.

It was no accident that the ministers most active in raising money for the war were also the ones most heavily engaged in looking for ways to finance the Retiro. For both purposes Olivares naturally turned to his own small circle of trusted lieutenants, who seem to have been expected to serve simultaneously as fund raisers, art collectors, and overseers of building works. Some of them were no doubt well equipped for all these roles, like don Francisco de Tejada, of the council of Castile, who served as superintendent of the works for the main courtyard of the Retiro, which was independently financed by conciliar contributions. Always at the center of action where questions of money were concerned, he was himself a wealthy collector, whose picture gallery included an *Adoration of the Kings* attributed to Titian. He died in September 1634, and was buried in the church of the Colegio Imperial, in a family chapel being completed to a design by Crescenzi.[48]

The two members of the inner circle most actively engaged in every aspect of financing and adorning the Retiro were probably the Count of Castrillo, and the ubiquitous protonotary of Aragon, Jerónimo de Villanueva. Castrillo was later described by the Earl of Clarendon, who met him on his visit to Madrid in 1649, as "a man of great parts, and a very wise man, grave and eloquent in his discourses. . . He lived within himself, as if he had a mind to be rich"[49]—a not uncommon characteristic among the count–duke's relatives. Promoted by rapid stages to the presidency of the council of the Indies, he was entrusted by Olivares with the responsibility for providing a substantial portion of the furnishings between 1633 and 1636. He had at his disposal the income from the sale of various effects in the Indies—effects which were turned into Indian and Turkish carpets, ornate writing cabinets, tables and clocks, paintings and tapestries. His accounts, which cover the period from November 11, 1634 to the end of 1638, show a total expenditure on the Retiro of approximately 226,000 ducats.[50]

Villanueva was, if anything, even more zealous in his services to the Retiro, which extended far beyond the call of duty. On the inauguration of the palace he is reported as having shown himself "very conscious of his obligations on this occasion, presenting an extremely rich Flemish tapestry and other objects..." These included mirrors, Barcelona glassware, and presents for the queen and the ladies-in-waiting. Their total value was placed at over 10,000 ducats, but Villanueva could afford the money.[51] In September 1634 we find him supervising, at the king's request, the production at the Retiro theater of a play specially commissioned from Quevedo to celebrate the birthday of Baltasar Carlos.[52] But above all he took responsibility for the adornment of the centerpiece of the Retiro, the Hall of Realms. A Portuguese poet, Manuel de Gallegos, who in 1637 published a book of verses in honor of the Retiro, attributes the Hall to the protonotary's "care, determination, prudence and intense activity," and relates how he was to be found wandering around the building at dead of night or in the early hours of the morning, tirelessly inspecting the progress of the work.[53]

Like Castrillo, Villanueva kept a set of accounts. These consisted of the monies disbursed from the king's secret expense account, which had been placed in his charge, and were spent at the sole discretion of the king.[54] The funds for the account were produced by a variety of financial expedients, like the appropriation of the revenues of vacant ecclesiastical benefices,[55] and the sale of offices—something which Villanueva apparently managed with consummate skill, "selling freely and openly all the offices in the realm, not excluding Sardinia and the Balearics."[56] From October 1630 small sums from the secret expense account were being handed over to the paymasters at the Royal Apartment of San Jerónimo.[57] By the middle of 1633 the disbursements had become impressive. Most of them went initially to building contractors, and notably to Cristóbal de Aguilera, who was under contract to do most of the construction work on the main courtyard; but by the end of 1633 Villanueva was also providing funds for decorative work (fig. 54).[58] His accounts (unfortunately incomplete) record the expenditure of some 270,000 ducats on building and decoration at the Retiro.

There was certainly no lack of inventiveness in devising schemes to finance the building work, and Villanueva and his colleagues could have squeezed money from a stone. One of their more ingenious devices was to secure funds for the construction of the principal courtyard in 1633 by selling space on a corporate basis. The Cortes of Castile, the municipality of Madrid, and the various royal councils were all offered a permanent grandstand view of the festivities to be held in the courtyard on the understanding that each of them took responsibility for constructing and decorating one of the great rooms that overlooked it.[59] The municipality of Madrid, for instance, was given a copy of the master plan, on which it was assigned seventy feet of space, at the standard cost of 200 ducats a foot.[60]

This device had the additional advantage of stimulating the endemic rivalry

54. Folio from Secret Expense Account, 1634 (Madrid, Biblioteca Nacional)

among these various corporate bodies, so that each council strove to outshine its fellows in the luxurious splendor of its apartment.[61] But in the end it was the public that paid. The councils could only reimburse the costs of their participation in this and other Retiro projects by finding fresh sources of revenue. This meant selling offices, privileges and Crown effects in the territories under their jurisdiction, generally to the detriment of the local population. Indeed, offices were created and sold faster than the market could absorb them. In 1635 the post of revenue officer at Almendralejo went for 1,000 ducats, and that of Almadén for slightly less. The proceeds of these particular sales helped to pay for "the lakes and canal being constructed at the Buen Retiro."[62] Royal authority was being diluted in the water-gardens of the pleasure palace.

It is not surprising that in the process hostility was aroused to the Retiro as far away as Naples and Sicily. But it was in Madrid itself that the hostility was most sharply felt. As the home of the court, Madrid was expected to make a major contribution to the costs of the Retiro. A precedent had been set in 1606 when the town council, in order to lure the court back from Valladolid, had offered the king

250,000 ducats payable over ten years to construct new apartments for the queen in the Alcázar. The money was raised by the sale of municipal lands and by the imposition of excise duties, notably on sales of meat and fish, which were still being collected in the 1620s.[63]

The count–duke's financial advisers were quick to see the possibilities in this convenient source of income. The excise money, coming in on a regular basis, could be used as security for one or more loans offering interest at eight per cent. No difficulty was expected in finding subscribers, and the loans would make it possible to pay for work at the Retiro while the Crown was awaiting the proceeds from the sale of offices which it would put on the market at not too frequent intervals. A special committee to handle the arrangements was set up in December 1632, and continued to function through the decade.[64] To the great indignation of the citizens of Madrid two new excises were imposed in the spring of 1633—one on meat consumed in the carnival season, and another (expected to yield 40,000 ducats a year) on all the wine sold in the town.[65] In spite of the king's insistence that the excise dues were not to be tapped for the Retiro, but were to serve simply as a guarantee for loans, it proved impossible to hold to this requirement. The sale of offices and other expedients failed to bring in the expected profits, and it was not long before the municipality had run up substantial debts on the whole transaction. Madrid's total contribution to the Retiro was later estimated at 250,000 ducats;[66] and while some of this represented "voluntary" gifts for special purposes, it seems likely that a good part of it came from the failure of the Crown to repay the money which it had borrowed from the excise dues.[67]

Every time, then, that a citizen of Madrid drank a glass of wine, he had cause to remember and curse the Retiro. But for one group of citizens at least, the king's necessities could be turned to account. Portuguese financiers or businessmen, many of them suspected of being *conversos*, or crypto-Jews, had flocked to Madrid in the later 1620s when Olivares had called them in as a counterweight to the Crown's Genoese bankers.[68] These wealthy Portuguese, thirsty for royal favor and social acceptance, lived precarious lives in Madrid, in constant terror that some informer would denounce them to the Inquisition. Already there had been one great *auto de fe*, watched by the king and queen and an enormous crowd of onlookers in the Plaza Mayor on June 20, 1632.[69]

In his extraordinary allegorical drama, *El nuevo palacio del Retiro*, written for performance at the Retiro for Corpus day of 1634, Calderón depicted the new palace as a symbol of the heavenly kingdom, with the wandering Jew (a not entirely unsympathetic figure) being turned away from its gates.[70] Diego Suárez, the adroit secretary of the council of Portugal, could easily insinuate to the Portuguese community that the best way to avoid such a humiliating exclusion was to establish a permanent symbol of its fidelity to church and king inside the grounds of the Retiro itself. Under his aegis large funds were mobilized for the construction in 1635 of the ornate hermitage chapel dedicated to the patron saint of Portugal, Saint Anthony of Padua, and popularly called "of the Portuguese."

The most prominent member of the Portuguese community in Madrid at this time was Manuel Cortizos de Villasante, who had built up a fortune through dealing in wool and spices, and was one of the participants in a consortium of Portuguese businessmen which bought the rights to administer some of the more lucrative royal revenues. During the 1630s the merchant turned courtier. Cortizos was always ready to lend a hand when the crown ran into financial difficulties, correctly calculating that his investments would yield him a rich return.[71] Naturally he found it expedient to make his own contributions to the Retiro, and like every enterprise with which he was associated, they were on a lavish scale. He not only produced substantial sums toward the construction of the lake and its fishing pavilions, but he also assumed responsibility for decorating the hermitage of San Bruno. Here on February 16, 1637, he organized a splendid reception for the king and queen. In spite of the season, the royal visitors were amazed to see the garden in bloom and the trees laden with fruits. After watching a play which Cortizos had arranged for them they sat down to a sumptuous repast in this terrestrial paradise.[72]

Two years later, however, Cortizos suffered a temporary fall from grace. Having laid out in the Retiro a small private garden for the king and queen, he offered the queen a bouquet while she was strolling in it one day. This was a grave social solecism, for only rustics were allowed to present bouquets to royalty. The queen turned her back on Cortizos, and Olivares, when he heard what had happened, forbade him to set foot in the Retiro again.[73] But it is doubtful whether he found himself permanently excluded from paradise. His services, after all, were in great demand. In 1642 he was raising large sums for infantry companies, and in 1644, when the military situation was critical, he saved the queen the embarrassment of having to pawn her jewels. He died in 1650, honored by the court but hated by the country, and escaped through his death the disgrace that overtook his family when the Inquisition produced a formidable dossier on their Judaizing activities during the very years when they stood highest in the royal favor.

By cajoling rich men like Cortizos, and by bullying and bludgeoning and resorting to downright extortion, Olivares succeeded in getting his palace finished, in spite of all the pressures of war. Its last major building, the theater of the Coliseo, opened its doors for the first time on February 4, 1640.[74] After eight years of frenetic activity and enormous expense, the contractors could at last be dismissed and the work force disbanded. Or so at least it seemed. But at 7.45 on the morning of February 20, fire broke out in the southwestern quarter of the palace. The count–duke was promptly on the spot directing the fire-fighting operations, and after three hours the blaze was brought under control. Fortunately there was no wind to fan the flames. The ladies of the court had time to escape from the burning building in a state of *déshabille*, which gave rise to much ribald merriment; and most of the furniture could be saved, although some of it was damaged by being thrown from the windows. The area affected by the fire was around the southwest tower, and included the king's quarters near the church, and part of the queen's quarters in the south wing.[75]

Once again it was necessary to look for money and once again the municipality was asked to help. On March 5, dozens of contracts were issued for the work of reconstruction, which was carried out in Olivares's usual style—without pause and regardless of cost.[76] The rebuilding and repairs cost nearly 100,000 ducats, and the count–duke himself, with the Monarchy on the verge of collapsing about him, was at the site every day to oversee the work. But within six weeks, and in time for

Easter, the Retiro was ready again for royal occupancy. The war might be going badly but the palace was saved.

The multiplicity of sources from which the Retiro was funded explains the extreme difficulty in assessing its total cost. Different officials kept different sets of accounts, and even if all of them had come to light, the jigsaw puzzle would probably still defy solution. But enough figures do survive to allow a rough and ready estimate. If Madrid contributed 250,000 ducats, and the surviving accounts are totalled, with due allowance for overlaps, the documented expenditures on the Retiro during the 1630s come to approximately 2,000,000 ducats.[77] Of this, some 1,750,000 ducats went in construction costs, and the remaining 250,000 in furnishing and decorating. The nature of the records suggests that the surviving figures for the construction costs may be reasonably complete, but this does not hold true for the sums spent on embellishing the palace. Both the Spanish Netherlands and the Italian viceroyalties of Naples and Sicily contributed handsomely in the form of paintings, furnishings and ornaments, which would again have been bought from the sale of offices and other fiscal expedients of the kind used in the Iberian peninsula and the Indies. No accounts have yet appeared for these parts of the Monarchy, and their absence suggests that furnishing and decorative costs in particular are badly under-represented.

In the autumn of 1637 it was being said in the court that over 2,000,000 ducats had been spent on the Retiro over the past six years.[78] This figure is consistent with those that emerge from the surviving records, and suggests that a grand total of 2,500,000 to 3,000,000 ducats may have been spent from official funds on building and decorating the Retiro in the 1630s. This takes no account of expenditures on festivities, which again are extremely difficult to determine with any precision, since they are broken up among the various accounts or else do not appear at all. Villanueva and Castrillo, for instance, shared the costs of a masque performed in May 1636, paying around 1,000 ducats apiece.[79] It also excludes the salaries of Retiro officials, and the ordinary maintenance costs of the palace.

How is this estimated expenditure on the Retiro to be evaluated? The building of the Escorial is said to have cost Philip II 5,260,560 ducats, which would work out at an annual average of 142,000 ducats between 1562 and his death in 1598.[80] If the building and furnishing of the Retiro cost 2,500,000 ducats, the annual average of expenditure on it in the decade 1630–40 was 250,000 ducats. But neither the global figures nor the average annual expenses are really comparable, in view of the monetary depreciation between the reigns of Philip II and Philip IV.

The costs of the Retiro acquire significance only when related to other contemporary expenditures. During the years in question, 1631–40, the average annual expenses of the Crown were of the order of ten to twelve million ducats. About a million ducats—some ten per cent—were assigned to cover the expenses of the court.[81] Even with an additional 250,000 ducats a year for the Retiro, court expenses still remained a relatively insignificant fraction, in relation to the enormous military and naval costs, and the servicing of debts. About the same amount went each year to the Retiro as went to the upkeep of the Spanish galley squadron of twelve galleys, at a rate of about 20,000 ducats a galley.[82] The army of Flanders alone was costing over three million ducats a year, which seems rather more than was spent on the Retiro over a ten-year period. Indeed, between the beginning of 1632 and the end of 1638 the Crown claimed to have sent a total of 21,500,000 ducats to Flanders.[83]

The most expensive building project in the Retiro was the Principal Court, built in 1633 at a probable expense of 400,000 ducats.[84] Other building costs on the site were much lower, as was only to be expected. The contract price for the hermitage of San Antonio was 23,000 ducats, for the Casón 26,000, and for the Coliseo 23,500.[85] Yet Villanueva and his friends presented the king with a writing cabinet worth over 30,000 ducats, and for a rich hanging, don Fadrique de Toledo was offered some 25,000 ducats.[86] It is clear that this was a society in which unskilled labor and building costs were low, at least when the building materials were of the kind used in the Retiro, and in which objects of ornate workmanship, especially when containing gold, silver and precious stones, were very highly prized.

Tapestries and hangings seem to have fetched very large sums, especially in relation to paintings. Villanueva spent 4,403 ducats in 1633 on an eight-panel tapestry of the fables of Diana,[87] and Castrillo bought a tapestry representing a scene from the life of Alexander the Great for 2,121 ducats.[88] Against these figures should be set the cost of eight landscape paintings acquired for the Retiro in 1634 for 840 ducats.[89] In general, landscapes, flower paintings and still lifes were valued more cheaply in seventeenth-century Spain than portraits, and might be acquired for ten or twenty ducats or less, although it clearly made a considerable difference to the price if they were specially commissioned. But even portraits and figure paintings were unlikely to be valued much above 100 ducats.[90] There were, however, important exceptions. A *Satyr* by Ribera cost the secret expense account 472 ducats in 1634,[91] and Maino's painting for the Hall of Realms, the *Recapture of Bahía*, earned him 500 ducats.[92]

The value of these figures acquires significance only when compared with contemporary incomes. The *Recapture of Bahía* cost more than an unskilled worker at the Retiro could earn in almost four years. But even when set against the incomes of the middling ranks of the nobility, some of the individual items that adorned the Retiro seem almost unbelievably expensive. While a handful of dukes like Infantado or Sessa had nominal incomes of well over 100,000 ducats a year (although their heavy indebtedness made their real annual incomes considerably less), many counts, who constituted the lowest rank of the titled aristocracy, had nominal annual incomes of 15,000 ducats or less—some of them, indeed, no more than 7,000 or 8,000, or not much more than the cost of a good set of tapestries. The entailed estate of a gentleman without a title of nobility might yield him one or two thousand ducats a year.[93]

In relation to the Crown's total expenditure over the period 1631–40, which may be crudely estimated as being of the order of a hundred million ducats, a possible three to four million spent on the Retiro and its various festivities was still a figure of some significance. Not unnaturally these additional court and architectural expenses provoked great and growing resentment. In April 1637 a Capuchin, Father Ocaña, was banished from court for preaching a sermon in which he denounced the multiplicity of taxes, and argued that, while they might be acceptable if they were used for the defense of the realm, it was intolerable that they should be spent on "irrelevancies (*impertinencias*) and useless buildings."[94]

But how far was Father Ocaña correct in assuming that the Retiro was paid for from taxation? The citizens of Madrid certainly paid taxes for the privilege of having the new palace within the confines of their town. The perpetuation of the old excise dues, originally levied for the Alcázar, and the imposition of the new excise on wine—an imposition described by Hopton as being "to the eighth part of the value of all the wine that shall be spent in this town without exception of any"[95]—were direct consequences of the need to subsidize the building of the Retiro. Understandably, this provoked bitter resentment in the capital. Contributions, too, from the Cortes of Castile—a modest participation in the building of the Plaza in 1633, and an offer of 90,000 or 100,000 ducats in 1639 for "improvements"[96]—were also drawn from the taxes of the people.

The Crown does, however, seem to have kept its promise to finance the Retiro only out of extraordinary sources of revenue, in the sense that, so far as can be ascertained, it did not draw on ordinary tax income for the purpose. Where possible it had recourse to gifts, in the form either of money, or of objects for the adornment of the interior. Beyond this it resorted, both in Castile and in the other parts of the Monarchy, to fiscal expedients like the sale of offices and privileges. Expedients of this kind represented a form of hidden taxation on those who were for the most part likely to be tax-exempt. Anyone of the rank of noble or gentleman enjoyed exemption from direct taxation in Castile. This category included the courtiers, councillors and high financiers who had to contribute so heavily to the costs of the Retiro, and members of the urban patriciate who saw in the purchase of office and privilege a valuable form of social investment. In addition, those who did not yet possess tax exemption were happy to acquire it by devoting some of their resources to the acquisition of offices which had been put up for public auction. By capitalizing on these social aspirations, Olivares was able to mobilize sources of wealth which would otherwise have remained largely inaccessible to the Crown. Ultimately the poor paid, in the sense that the privileged found innumerable ways of recouping their expenses from the community at large; but the king's requirement that the Retiro should be financed without resorting to the taxes of the poor was—with one exception—nominally observed.

The exception was Madrid, whose inhabitants found themselves subjected to new excise dues. But it could be argued that they obtained at least some return on their money, in terms of the new amenities they involuntarily acquired. Contemporaries had criticized Philip II for building the Escorial far from a principal city, "where all could enjoy it, where small and great alike could enter, and where it could serve as a spectacle and recreation for the people."[97] By building the Retiro on the edge of Madrid, and then opening its gardens to the public, at least for special occasions, Olivares avoided a repetition of Philip II's offense. But at the same time he offered a formidable hostage to fortune. The citizens of Madrid, well known for their mordant wit, could not be expected to spare the gigantic new edifice that had so spectacularly arisen on their very doorstep. Nor would they refrain from endless speculation about the riches and the mysteries that lay concealed behind that plain facade.

V

"Affectioned unto the Art of Painting"

Almost as soon as the Retiro had been inaugurated, the disparity between the interior and exterior of the palace began to be noticed. In December 1633, Monanni, who was not impressed with the architecture, wrote that he thought that the furnishings and decoration were finer than those of the Alcázar.[1] Two years later, the Modenese ambassador, Fulvio Testi, formed the same impression after his visit to the site. "Certainly the building is extremely sumptuous, although more so within than without, and makes a greater impression than its external appearance would suggest."[2] In 1668, another Italian visitor, Lorenzo Magalotti, who was travelling in the retinue of Cosimo III de Medici, echoed the opinion of his countrymen.[3] The entrance of the Buen Retiro, he wrote, had nothing grand or magnificent about it. The facade was lacking in adornment; the construction was of brick and crudely made. But the rooms were entirely satisfactory. Some had beautifully woven rush mats covering the floors; others had carved ceilings and cupolas with foliate designs. The walls, he noted, were encrusted with tiles to the height of a few feet. And the furnishings were rich and well-made.

The marked contrast between the magnificent interior and the plain exterior grew out of circumstances relating to the construction. The desire for extraordinary speed ruled out complicated, ornate architecture and the original intention to build a *plaza de fiestas* invited the use of simple, rustic materials. Later the Plaza, or courtyard complex, was decreed a palace, but it required more than a royal proclamation to make the existing building reflect the elevated aspirations for the site. The interior was another matter. The king and Olivares resolved to make the decoration a paragon of regal magnificence. Once more, the count–duke sent the members of his inner circle to the hunt, this time for furniture and decorations instead of money. They scoured the length and breadth of Europe in one of the best organized, most successful efforts of large-scale collecting of the seventeenth century. Between the years 1633 and 1640, tapestries, paintings, sculptures and elaborate furnishings were purchased, commissioned and appropriated on an enormous scale.

The acquisition of tapestries would have been an important priority. In seventeenth-century Spain, rich tapestries and hangings were an unmistakeable sign of luxury and splendor. The best examples were always considerably more costly than even the greatest masterpieces of painting. Paradoxically, tapestries also played a humbler role in palace decoration since they were used for insulation during the winter. Numerous references both to the Alcázar and the Retiro make it clear that tapestries took the place of paintings once the weather had started to turn cold. At the Retiro, the substitution may have been made only in the northern and western wings, the areas most directly exposed to the chilling winds. Vast sums of money were spent on tapestries, most of which because of their fragility have not survived. But there was hardly a room without a tapestry or decorative hanging of silk or taffeta.

The lead in the acquisition of tapestries seems to have been taken by the Count of Castrillo, although others, whose records have been lost, probably participated in the effort. Among Castrillo's purchases of 1634 were a Florentine tapestry of the *Fall of Phaeton*, purchased from Olivares's cousin, the Count of Ricla, for 4,900 ducats; a Flemish tapestry with a garden scene, purchased from the Marquis of Villena for 6,174 ducats; and a tapestry with the "story of a gentleman in his village," from the Count of Pere, for 2,177 ducats.[4] Two series of nine panels apiece, one depicting the story of Theseus, the other the "story of man" (possibly the Creation), were bought from the royal tapestry-maker, Pedro Biquemans.[5] Monanni mentions additional purchases of tapestries and hangings, including one from the Duke of Alburquerque, which was said to have cost 25,000 ducats.[6] Many of these sales were made by applying pressure to the nobility, who were often decidedly reluctant to part with their treasures. One day, according to Monanni, the agents paid a visit to the house of the Marquis of Leganés with the intention of carrying off his best pieces of furniture for the Retiro.[7] When they began to make an inventory, the marchioness protested violently, claiming that they were part of her dowry, and forced them to desist. As compensation for leaving the furniture, Leganés agreed to give a tapestry valued at 40,000 ducats. The relatives of the king, no less than those of Olivares, became a source of tapestries. On December 1, 1633, the Infanta Isabella died in Brussels. Nine months later, Philip sent an order to choose her best tapestries for the Retiro and to ship them to Madrid as quickly as possible.[8]

Opulent, ornate furniture was collected at the same time and by the same means. Castrillo opened his purse wide, converting the treasure of the Indies into a museum of exquisite furnishings. Undoubtedly the most spectacular, if not the most expensive, of his purchases was the king's bed, executed by the silversmith Jorge de Quevedo at a cost of about 2,500 ducats.[9] It was made of silver with four large columns at the corners and twenty small columns along the sides. At the head was an eagle holding the royal arms. Castrillo's agents also purchased a large quantity of a staple item of furniture—*bufetes de jaspe*, console tables with jasper tops and gilded wooden legs, which were placed against the walls. Another popular type of furniture was the *escritorio*, a writing cabinet with elaborate carving. The most costly of these cabinets was one presented by members of the Committee of Works in concert with Villanueva, José González and other "creatures" of Olivares.[10] This piece, made of ebony and ivory with crystal colonettes and gold and silver figurines, was meant for the king's chambers, and its value was calculated at 30,000 ducats.

Castrillo was also responsible for commissioning the royal table-service of white and gilded silver used at the Retiro. In 1635, he paid the silversmith Juan de Huete about 10,000 ducats for a large service comprising almost two hundred pieces, all bearing the royal coat of arms. Everything was included from a toothpick holder to gilded centerpieces in the shape of fountains through which water could circulate.[11] Small-scale objects of art were bought in great numbers. In 1634, Castrillo paid the Duke of Alburquerque, one of his principal suppliers, the sum of 10,970 ducats for a lot containing two ebony writing desks with silver inlay, a sculpture in silver of a coach and horses, fourteen silver vases with silver flowers, four small boxes of ebony and silver and other assorted pieces.[12] Alburquerque also sold a small bronze sculpture of a galleon and two silver dogs for 2,000 ducats. In addition, Castrillo purchased clocks, mirrors, candelabra and dozens of braziers.[13] No list can adequately convey the opulence of the objects or the magnificent impression they must have created when placed in rooms hung with tapestries and paintings and crowned by carved and gilded ceilings. In the winter of 1654–5 an English merchant, Robert Bargrave, was allowed to visit the palace. After his tour, he wrote a description in his diary of the sights he had seen. His is the best existing eyewitness account of the palace during the reign of Philip IV and brings its magnificence vividly before our eyes.[14] Bargrave's route can be followed in Carlier's plan (fig. 55) although the identification of several rooms, especially in the living quarters, is difficult because the description is sometimes insufficiently precise.

55. Plan, Main Floor, Palace of the
Buen Retiro (after Carlier)

1. Church of San Jerónimo	4. Hall of Realms	7. *Casón* (Ballroom)
2. King's Quarters	5. Masking Room	8. Queen's Quarters
3. Landscape Gallery	6. *Coliseo* (Theater)	9. Prince's Quarters

N ◄—————

Bargrave entered the palace by a staircase in the southwest corner of the patio of the king's quarters and proceeded to the main floor. As he walked along the galleries of the western wing, he saw "four rooms; viz. an audience room, a dining room, a bedchamber of honour [probably for guests] and a retiring room, which four with two long galleries, make one side of the chief quadrangle." Looking back along the path he had just taken, Bargrave remarked on one of the most arresting features of the palace architecture. "The doors of all six [rooms] are made so exactly in the middle, that we see the whole length in perspective, from one end to the other; all of them being adorned with tapestry hangings, of silk, silver, or gold, or with embossed work." The absence of any mention of pictures is at first puzzling, for it is known that they covered the walls. Undoubtedly the paintings had been removed for the winter season and replaced with tapestries.

"Hence we turned into a fair square room, having a stately balcony round within it, and being richly hung." Bargrave's party now entered the north wing of the palace, which contained the Hall of Realms, whose threshold they crossed. "Yet this was but the passage into the council seat, which is a much more spacious room, having likewise a noble balcony round about it, ten rich marble tables at the sides, and a throne of Majesty for the king at the end of it; most gallant hangings round the walls, the roof painted and richly gilded with the several arms of the 24 kingdoms of Spain." Unless Bargrave's memory was confused, it appears that the famous series of paintings had been temporarily removed. The last room in this wing of the palace was "the masking room with a fair balcony also about it, roofed and hanged very richly as befits the place."

Having toured half the palace, Bargrave and his companions began to walk through the eastern or garden wing, beginning in another large room hung with pictures. "Hence I entered a long gallery, hung with fair pictures; and this looks into a large quadrangle, where the king and queen use to engross their pleasure in greater privacy, to see the combating with bulls or other wild beasts." The next stop was the Coliseo. "Then I saw the playhouse gallantly contrived for its purpose; furnished with diverse machines, scenes and handsome representments."

The party continued its walk along the garden wing and entered the first rooms of the private quarters. In this section of the palace, the furnishings became more numerous and luxurious, in contrast to the public rooms which tended to be sparsely furnished in Spanish royal palaces.

Hence we passed into another long gallery, furnished with abundance of pictures in rich uniform frames, and this enters into the queen's billiard room. Next I saw the king's scrittorio (or private counting house) hung with embossed work of gold upon velvet, the richest I have ever seen; furnished with a marble mosaic work-table, four very rich cabinets, two of pure gold and two of gold and ebony. To the scrittorio joins another walking gallery, beside which is likewise another fair gallery, hung with silk and gold tapestry, and a Retiring Room belonging to it.

The rest of Bargrave's description seems to correspond with the south wing where the queen and her household resided when the court was at the Retiro. This consisted of numerous small rooms, of which Bargrave mentions only the most important.

Near this is the red gallery, out of which goes the king and queen's dormitories; in the king's is a single bed; but in the queen's, two beds joining together, made of ebony and gold, with a table suitable. Out of the queen's chamber goes her tiring-room, furnished with rich hangings and pictures. To the queen's stansions [apartments] belongs another stately private gallery, hung with noble tapestry and pictures; a chamber of state, in which is a glorious throne for herself; and this is also hung with very stately hangings; through which she passes into her dining room, hung likewise very richly, having a fair throne wherein her majesty sits at meat.

Bargrave's description, if lacking in detail about paintings and tapestries, makes the richness and opulence of the interior come alive. The walls, hung with countless tapestries, hangings and pictures; the private rooms, full of ornate, colorful furniture made of fine wood and precious metals—all these details help us to imagine the splendor and magnificence that lay behind the plain, unpretentious facade of the palace.

A large collection of sculpture was also assembled that was placed both in the palace rooms and in the gardens. Much of this collection was brought from other royal houses, in accordance with a long-standing practice of transferring works of art from houses and palaces that were seldom used by the king to his favorite residence of the moment. Most of the pieces were taken from Aranjuez, which was made largely redundant as a country house by the Retiro. On May 5, 1634, an order went out to the governor of Aranjuez to deliver thirty-nine pieces of sculpture large and small to the Retiro.[15] The major work was Leone Leoni's *Charles V Conquering Heresy* (fig. 56), which was installed in the Emperor's Courtyard of the palace. A bronze statue of *Philip II*, perhaps the one by Leoni, was also included, in keeping with the motif of dynastic commemoration that would be developed so grandly in the Hall of Realms. Most of the pieces, however, were small in scale and apparently were meant to be installed in the palace. The list mentions ten antique medals of emperors, a Bacchus, a marble relief roundel bust of Charles V, a small Apollo and thirteen unidentified statuettes in marble. A second lot of sculpture, consisting of thirty-seven pieces, was ordered to be sent from Aranjuez by a royal decree of April 29, 1635.[16] More royal portraits were in this group, including a life-size statue of the Empress Isabella, and two portrait busts of Charles V and Philip II. There were also a few replicas of antique sculpture, such as the one in alabaster of the *Spinario* and a bronze *Laocoon and His Sons*. An additional but smaller consignment of sculpture was sent from the Alcázar, under the supervision of Juan Gómez de Mora.[17]

In 1637, an important sculptural group arrived from Flanders, sent by the cardinal infante who was busily acquiring works for the Retiro in the territory under his jurisdiction. By March 20, he must have sent word from Brussels that an extraordinary group of statues had been found and was being shipped to Madrid. In a letter to the cardinal infante on that date, Olivares wrote that they were being anxiously awaited because they had been so lavishly described.[18] With a typical burst of hyperbole he promised, as governor of the Buen Retiro, that the cardinal infante's memory would always be honored in that site for his magnificent gift. The statues arrived on June 22, a group of seven large-scale bronzes representing the seven planets, a subject especially appropriate as a gift to the "Planet King." (fig. 57)[19] Their arrival caught the eye of Monanni, who described them as excellently made.[20] The statues had belonged to the Duke of Aumale, who had installed them in his country house, and then sold them to an Antwerp merchant. This man may have been Jacques van Ophem, the Receiver General of Brabant. In 1647, in the course of a petition to the council of Flanders, he said that he had sold the Planets to the cardinal infante at cost price, forgoing a profit of 48,000 florins, which he now wished to be regarded as a favor to the Crown.[21]

From the existing records, it appears that very little independent figural sculpture was expressly commissioned to be made for the Retiro. Sculptors were employed, but they were only given ornamental work to do—fountains for the gardens and jasper fireplaces for the palace were made in great numbers. But, with the exception of a few reliefs for the altars of the hermitage chapels, the sculptors were not encouraged by patronage to produce ambitious works of art. Only two important sculptural commissions were undertaken, one of which falls halfway between sculpture and the decorative arts. On November 20, 1634, Villanueva commissioned the silversmith Juan Calvo to make twelve large silver lions to adorn the Hall of Realms.[22] In September, Monanni had already heard of the project and was sending back a description to Florence. The lions, he said, were to be rampant, holding a torch in the right paw and, in the left, a shield with the arms of Villanueva's native Aragon.[23] The cost was 2,000 ducats apiece, or 24,000 in all. The

56. Leone Leoni, *Charles V Conquering Heresy* (Madrid, Prado)

57. Anonymous, *Planet Saturn* (Madrid, Palacio de Oriente)

lions remained in the Hall only until 1643 when, in a grandiloquent gesture to raise money for the war, the king ordered all the silver in the palace to be melted and minted into silver *reales*.[24]

The second sculptural commission was of greater consequence and more enduring. On May 2, 1634, Monanni sent with his dispatch a copy of a letter from Olivares to the ambassador, requesting that the grand duke present to the king a bronze statue of Philip on horseback.[25] The statue was to follow the model of some unspecified portraits by Rubens and was intended to be installed in a courtyard of the new palace. In due course, the commission was accepted by Pietro Tacca, then fifty-seven years old and nearing the end of his career. Tacca was already known to the Spanish court for his *Equestrian Statue of Philip III*, which had arrived in Madrid in 1616 and been erected in the Casa del Campo in the following year (see fig. 16). By autumn 1636, Tacca had completed a full-scale model of the king astride a walking horse, only to be told that Olivares insisted on having a rearing horse.

The order was by no means simple to execute; up to that time, no one had ever succeeded in casting a large-scale equestrian statue with a rearing horse because of the difficulty of balancing and stabilizing the weight of the bronze on the narrow base of the two hind legs. Nevertheless, Tacca was willing to attempt the feat and by September 1637 had completed a new model with the horse's front legs raised in the air. The horse had been cast by March 1639. Tacca had managed to solve the technical problems—with the assistance of Galileo, according to one account—and had created the first monumental rearing horse ever to be realized in bronze (fig. 58).[26]

Now Tacca was ready to begin work on the figure. In addition to the portraits by Rubens, Tacca had been furnished with a bust of the king by the most renowned sculptor of the day, Juan Martínez Montañés. Martínez Montañés had been called to court from Seville in 1635, probably at the instigation of his compatriot, Velázquez, who two years before had been instrumental in bringing another important Sevillian artist, Zurbarán, to work at the Retiro.[27] Apparently the Sevillian connection, established when Olivares had come to power, was still operating. Velázquez commemorated the occasion of Montañés's visit by painting a portrait of the sculptor at work on the very bust that would be sent to Florence (fig. 59). But as Tacca started to model the portrait of the king, he obviously felt the need for yet another representation of Philip. This was obtained by the ambassador in Madrid in late January 1640, and is likely to have been furnished by Velázquez or a member of his atelier.[28] The finishing touches were applied and on September 26, 1640, the statue was shipped from Florence to Livorno en route for Madrid.

It took almost as long to transport the piece as it did to make it. The crated sculpture arrived in Cartagena in March 1641, accompanied by Tacca's son, Ferdinando (the father had died on October 26 of the preceding year). As a result of endless delays, caused by the Crown's shortage of ready cash, the statue did not arrive in Madrid until June 10, 1642, twenty-one months after it had left Florence. Even then, there was not enough money to erect it. As a last desperate measure, the fruit and vegetables in the Retiro gardens were put up for sale and the proceeds used to install the statue.[29]

Another problem arose because the image of the king did not quite correspond to

58. (facing page) Pietro Tacca, *Equestrian Statue of Philip IV* (Madrid, Plaza de Oriente)

59. (left) Diego de Velázquez, *Juan Martínez Montañés* (Madrid, Prado)

60. (below) Louis Meunier, *Queen's Garden with Equestrian Statue of Philip IV* (London, British Library)

entre du Retiro de madrid   La Entrada del buen Retiro en Madrid

reality, and Ferdinando Tacca was ordered to remodel the face, a task successfully carried out under the eyes of Prince Baltasar Carlos who came to watch the sculptor at work and declared that the results were indeed lifelike.[30] At long last, on October 29, 1642, the statue was put into place in the Queen's Garden (fig. 60). In 1844, it was moved to its present location in front of the Royal Palace.

The apparent indifference to the art of sculpture at the Retiro was in fact real. It was consistently relegated to a minor role in the decoration of the palace. Painting, by contrast, held the spotlight. Pictures abounded everywhere. The astonished reaction of a French cleric, Jean Muret, who came to Madrid in 1667 in the retinue of the Archbishop of Embrun, eloquently describes the abundance of paintings.

In the palace we were surprised by the quantity of pictures. I do not know how it is adorned in other seasons, but when we were there we saw more pictures than walls. The galleries and staircases were full of them, as well as the bedrooms and salons. I can assure you, Sir, that there were more than in all of Paris. I was not at all surprised when they told me that the principal quality of the deceased king was his love of painting and that no one in the world understood more about it than he.[31]

Muret's guides were not exaggerating when they spoke of their former king, Philip IV, and about his influence on shaping the extraordinary and vast collection at the Retiro. In the seventeenth century, Philip was unsurpassed as a connoisseur and collector of painting.[32] His discernment and taste are nowadays underestimated; they were certainly crucial to the decision to make the Retiro a museum of painting.

The impact of Philip's multifaceted activities as collector and patron is revealed by the impressive growth of the royal collection during his reign. If the precise number of his acquisitions is impossible to calculate, there are ways to estimate the spectacular increase in the holdings. From time to time, and for a variety of reasons, inventories were made of the paintings in several royal seats.[33] In the course of the seventeenth century, the collection in the Alcázar, which with the Escorial had the largest number of works, was inventoried four times. The first inventory, made under Philip III, was completed in 1607 and listed 385 pictures. In 1636, fifteen years after Philip had come to the throne, the number had risen to 885. Most of these five hundred paintings must have been acquired by Philip IV; his father was not known as a collector. Twenty years after Philip's death, in 1686, a third inventory was made, revealing that the collection had grown in size to 1,547 paintings.[34] Almost all of the 662 paintings added since 1636 must also be attributed to Philip's efforts because his son, Charles II, was unfit for art collecting or much else. When he died in 1700, the Alcázar had only twenty-eight pictures more than in 1686.[35]

Between 1621 and 1664, then, the number of paintings in the Alcázar rose from about 400 to over 1500. Even allowing for the fact that some of the paintings were brought to the Alcázar from other palaces, the increase in size of the collection is extraordinary. And to this number must be added the works acquired for the Retiro (about 800), the Torre de la Parada (171) and the Zarzuela (96), all of which were constructed and decorated during Philip's reign.[36] It would not be an exaggeration to say that Philip added at least 2,000 pictures to the Spanish royal collection during the forty-three years of his reign. This is approximately the number of paintings now in the collection of the Museo del Prado. Few collectors of the seventeenth century were able to come close to this record.

Philip's love of pictures inspired a new enthusiasm for collecting among the nobility, especially those aristocrats who were dependent upon Olivares. In a time of economic depression, his friends and relatives, in imitation of the king, amassed formidable collections. By 1638, the phenomenon had become so conspicuous that Hopton thought it worth mentioning to Lord Cottington, himself an avid collector.

They are now become more judicious in and more affectioned unto the Art of Painting, than they have been, or than the world imagines. And the king within this 12 month, had gotten an incredible number of ancient and of the best modern hands, and over with the Conde de Monte Rey came the best of Italy, particularly the Baccanalian of Titian and in this town is not a piece worth any thing but the king takes and pays very well for them, and in his imitation the Admirante [the Duke of Medina de Rioseco, Admiral of Castile], don Lewis de Haro and many others are making collections.[37]

Most of the great aristocratic collections were made by noblemen who enjoyed two important advantages—kinship with the count–duke and a foreign service assignment. The first provided the means to collect, for Olivares took pains to secure

61. Peter Paul Rubens, *Marquis of Leganés* (Vienna, Graphische Sammlung Albertina)

the financial well-being of his relatives; the second, the opportunity, because one had to go to Flanders or Italy to secure masterpieces produced by artists of those countries. One of the greatest among the noblemen–collectors was the Marquis of Leganés, Olivares's cousin (fig. 61). The great strength of Leganés's collection, which had come to include 1,333 works by his death in 1655, lay in Flemish pictures.[38] As a youth, he had spent time at the court in Brussels, to which he returned on a number of occasions in the 1620s and 1630s. There he became acquainted with several artists and commissioned works from Rubens, van Dyck and Jordaens, as well as secondary figures such as Snyders, Paul de Vos and Gaspar de Crayer. He also collected Flemish primitives avidly, and owned works attributed to Jan van Eyck, Roger van der Weyden, Bosch, Patinir and Metsys. The Italian collection was less comprehensive, but included several paintings ascribed to Raphael, Titian and Veronese among the sixteenth-century artists. Seventeenth-century Italian painters seem to have interested him very little and, with the exception of Ribera, that Italianized Spaniard, are not very well represented. There was also a large complement of family portraits, coats of arms and anonymous landscapes.

Leganés had the misfortune to be in Madrid during those hectic months of 1633 before the inauguration of the new palace. He was called upon to furnish three or four rooms and a gallery from his own collection, and was reduced to tears when Olivares, reminding him how much he owed to the king, harshly rebuked him for repaying the royal favor with the gift of mediocre paintings.[39] Olivares's brother-in-law, the Count of Monterrey, may have escaped a similar fate by being abroad at the time. An enlightened patron and a discriminating collector, he used his decade of foreign service in Italy, first as ambassador to the Holy See (1628–31) and then as viceroy of Naples (1631–7) to assemble a small but choice collection. During his stay in Naples, Monterrey played an important part in stimulating the revival of high-level artistic activity in the 1630s and 1640s.[40] The best monument to his taste is the funerary monument that he commissioned from Neapolitan artists and brought back to Spain in 1638. This is the decoration of the church of the Agustinas Descalzas, Salamanca, the family seat.[41] There were tomb sculptures of the count (fig. 62) and his wife, Olivares's sister, executed by Giuliano Finelli and a number of altarpieces by Cosimo Fanzago, which were adorned with paintings by Ribera (one of his favorite artists), Lanfranco, Guido Reni and Domenichino. The works are still together in the church and form the best preserved example of an Italian Baroque decorative ensemble in Spain.[42]

After his return to Madrid, Monterrey took up residence in a palace on the Prado de San Jerónimo, to which he added a small picture gallery in the garden, where he displayed the masterpieces of his collection. Although not large by the standards of the day—it numbered just over 265 pictures when the count died in 1653—the collection contained many important works, most of them Italian.[43] Paintings by Ribera headed the list; there were thirteen by his hand. Then there were the inevitable works by Titian, the mark of distinction for Spanish collectors, of which the count had seven. Monterrey also made more adventurous acquisitions of works by less famous painters. There were three ascribed to Borgianni, five to Luca Cambiaso and one apiece to Pordenone and Francesco Salviati.

62. Giuliano Finelli, *Count of Monterrey*, Salamanca, Agustinas Descalzas

Another keen collector was that discreet courtier don Luis de Haro, Olivares's nephew and his future successor in the government both of Spain and of the Retiro. There is no evidence of any contribution by Haro to the decoration of the palace, although it is not unreasonable to assume that he played at least a modest part. One of the king's closest companions, he shared his aesthetic interests, and the collection which he started became in the hands of his son Gaspar, Marquis of Carpio, the closest rival to the royal collection. But it is not clear how much of the collection was the result of his own efforts, and how much came through his wife and through the activities of his son.[44]

The Duke of Medina de las Torres, Olivares's son-in-law, also appears to have acquired paintings and made splendid gifts to the king as well. Outside the Olivares family circle were the works assembled by the Admiral of Castile, Juan Alfonso Enríquez de Cabrera, who was Neapolitan viceroy from 1644–6, and the Duke of Infantado, ambassador in Rome in the early 1650s, who supplemented an already impressive family collection with pictures acquired in Italy.[45] There were also ambitious commoners like Pedro de Arce, who collected on a large scale.[46] By the middle of the seventeenth century, Flemish and Italian paintings in Madrid were numbered in the thousands.[47]

117

The pictorial decoration of the Retiro took place in the midst of this veritable epidemic of collecting.[48] As Hopton observed in his letter to Cottington, the king, through his own impressive efforts as a collector, had made the pursuit of pictures fashionable. It was inevitable, then, that the decoration of the Retiro would be predominantly pictorial. Olivares himself seems to have had but little interest in paintings; he was a book collector and, as often happens with bibliophiles, may have been more interested in words than images. But the king's interest in paintings was too great to be ignored. Taking a cue from his royal master, as so many of his kinsmen had done, Olivares ordered his men to begin an organized search for paintings. This enterprise, however, was guided by the king's taste. Philip had not only shown what he liked through his own acquisitions; he had also by example educated the tastes of an entire generation of Spanish noblemen, many of whom, as viceroys and ambassadors, were about to become the principal agents in the purchase of paintings for the Retiro.

The task of decorating the palace was by any measure enormous. It must have been decided at the start not to remove paintings from any of the palaces used by the king. This decision effectively proscribed the easy solution of borrowing works from the Alcázar, one of the largest storehouses of paintings. Olivares did attempt to appropriate paintings from the Escorial, the other major repository, but was rebuffed by the friars.[49] As a consequence he had to resort to a program of "new acquisitions" of formidable dimensions, because the number of rooms to be decorated—and it was taken for granted that every wall of every room had to be covered with pictures—was large. There were fourteen galleries in the public part of the palace and numerous suites of smaller rooms in the living quarters. The task was made even more difficult by the inevitable demand for speed. Undaunted by this challenge, Olivares dispatched his agents, who in the course of eight years managed to fill the empty shell with over eight hundred pictures gathered from Spain, Italy and Flanders.

The first line of attack was to appropriate paintings from the one or two palaces which the king seldom if ever visited. The prime candidate was the palace at Valladolid, which had been decorated between 1601 and 1606, when the court was resident there, and had since fallen out of use. Early in 1635, a list of paintings in the palace was dispatched to the king, from which he chose the ones to be brought to the Retiro.[50] On May 12, he sent the list back to the governor of the palace, ordering him to ship the designated pictures and any others that he thought worthwhile. The choice was to be made in consultation with "someone versed in the profession," presumably a local artist. The paintings, sixty-three in number, arrived on July 6, accompanied by the architect Francisco de Praves. In September, Praves delivered another consignment of four paintings from Valladolid. As might be expected, it was a mixed bag consisting mostly of mediocre late-sixteenth-century works. Among them was a series of the seven planets by Pietro Facchetti, which had been brought to Valladolid by Rubens in 1603 as a present to Philip III from the Duke of Mantua.[51] There were also paintings in series—seven battles in the Low Countries by Rodrigo de Holanda, six of the months of the year, the four elements—introducing a format that was much used in the decoration of the Retiro.

There were a few additional acquisitions of paintings in large lots from other

63. Diego de Velázquez, *Joseph's Bloody Coat Brought to Jacob* (El Escorial)

royal palaces. Apparently some pictures were obtained from Aranjuez in 1635, but the king otherwise remained firm in his refusal to lend pictures from the royal collection for the decoration.[52] So the agents were compelled to enter the marketplace both in Spain and abroad, to buy existing works and also to commission new ones.

The Spanish campaign was directed by Villanueva and Castrillo. Armed with the rents of Aragon, Villanueva bought pictures from local collections by the hundreds. In the Madrid Palace Archive is a fragment of a document entitled "Paintings delivered [to the Retiro] by don Jerónimo de Villanueva."[53] Only two of at least thirty folios, those numbered "12" and "13," have survived, but they alone contain ninety-nine pictures, together with marginal notations of their location in the palace added at a later date. Obviously there must originally have been listed hundreds of paintings, some of which are documented in other sources. For instance, in 1634 Villanueva bought eighteen paintings from Velázquez, including the *Forge of Vulcan* and *Joseph's Bloody Coat Brought to Jacob* (fig. 63), a version of *Susannah and the Elders* by Cambiaso, a version, or possibly a copy, of Titian's *Danäe*, an unidentified painting by one of the Bassano family, unidentified portraits of Prince Baltasar

64. Jusepe de Ribera, *Ixion*
(Madrid, Prado)

Carlos and the queen, five flower paintings, two still lifes and four small landscapes.[54] On the list in the Palace Archive, the two paintings by Velázquez are described as hanging in the *guardarropa* (a storage room) along with Cambiaso's *Susannah*. This sale by Velázquez had been preceded by an earlier one. On November 28, 1633, the painter received about 250 ducats for three pictures: *St John the Baptist* by Tintoretto and a pair of anonymous pictures showing processions of a pope and the Grand Turk.[55]

Villanueva's secret expense account contains several other records of purchase. In 1634, prior to the fiestas of San Juan (June 24) and San Pablo (June 29), he bought two paintings by Ribera, a *Satyr* and a *Venus and Adonis*, from a well-known collector, Rodrigo de Tapia.[56] The Marchioness of Charela, the grandmother of one of the king's bastard children sold four paintings, two of which, *Tityus* and *Ixion* (fig. 64), were also by Ribera.[57] Crescenzi, who was also selling paintings to the King of England, parted with a group of forty-two works.[58] They included a painting of *Moses*, two large landscapes, *Noah's Ark* by one of the Bassanos, a dozen still lifes with fruit and another twelve Italian landscapes. Castrillo was also active in the picture market at this time. He bought eight large landscapes from the estate of Cardinal Trejo, a former president of the council of Castile who had once lived in

120

65. Giovanni Lanfranco, *An Emperor Sacrificing* (Madrid, Prado)

66. Giovanni Lanfranco, *Banquet with Gladiators* (Madrid, Prado)

121

67. Domenichino, *An Emperor's Exequies* (Madrid, Prado)

68. Massimo Stanzione, *Beheading of St John* (Madrid, Prado)

Italy; a series of fourteen paintings of the *Plagues of Egypt*, possibly by Pedro de Orrente, from the Marquis of Villanueva del Fresno; twelve more landscapes from García de Pareja; and eight *bodegones* (still lifes) and marine paintings from a collector famous for attributing minor works to great masters, Suero de Quiñones, which were to be placed in the small antechamber, the *saleta del cuarto de Su Majestad*.[59]

At the same time, the king's representatives abroad were also busily acquiring pictures. The lack of detailed information makes it impossible to know the extent to which they bought them from collectors and dealers and how far they commissioned paintings from the artists directly. The main collecting points were Naples and Rome, with Flanders a somewhat distant second.

By a stroke of good fortune, the viceroy of Naples during the critical period of collecting was that discerning connoisseur and collector, the Count of Monterrey. Monterrey organized at least two deliveries of paintings. The first was noted by Monanni who, in a dispatch of November 26, 1633, mentioned the arrival of twelve cartloads of pictures from Monterrey.[60] The second consignment was brought by the count himself when he returned from Naples to Madrid in August 1638.[61] This lot contained not only pictures for the Retiro, but also Monterrey's personal collection and gifts for the king and Olivares. With certain exceptions, it is difficult to know which pictures arrived in 1633 and which arrived in 1638. But there is no doubt that the two shipments included a sizable anthology of painting in Naples between 1633 and 1637.

Monterrey's tenure as viceroy coincided with a particularly fruitful moment in the history of Neapolitan painting, which owed much to his generous patronage.[62] In the year of his arrival, the senior generation of artists was headed by Ribera, Massimo Stanzione and Paolo Finoglio. Behind them was a group of younger men, born in the first decade of the seventeenth century, who included Aniello Falcone, Andrea de Leone and Micco Spadaro. Their number was augmented by the arrival of two major Roman artists, who were invited to Naples by Monterrey. In 1631, Domenichino came to work in the cathedral and resided intermittently in the city until his death in 1641. Three years later, Giovanni Lanfranco accepted Monterrey's invitation to come to Naples, where he was to remain almost to the end of his life. Monterrey, and to a lesser extent his successor, Medina de las Torres, collected works by all these artists for shipment to the Retiro.

The orders that were sent him from Madrid must have laid primary emphasis on quantity,[63] but there is reason to believe that they also specified the commission of at least two thematically coherent series of scenes from ancient Roman life. The first group comprised four splendid, large narrative paintings of the life of a Roman emperor by Lanfranco (figs. 65 and 66) which appear to have been done between 1635 and 1637.[64] Other parts of this series were the elaborate *Emperor's Exequies* painted by Domenichino (fig. 67) and a *Lupercalian Scene* by Andrea Camassei.[65] The second group of works illustrated scenes of a Roman circus, some of which were done by Roman artists.[66] The Neapolitan share was executed by Lanfranco, Falcone, Finoglio, Cesare Fracanzano and Andrea de Leone. The works by Roman artists, which may have been commissioned by Monterrey as well, included a painting apiece from G. F. Romanelli and François Perrier, a former assistant of

69. Claude Lorrain, *Landscape with St Mary Magdalene* (Madrid, Prado)

70. Claude Lorrain, *Landscape with St Anthony Abbot* (Madrid, Prado)

71. Nicolas Poussin, *Landscape with an Anchorite* (Madrid, Prado)

Lanfranco.[67] The significance of this impressive series is uncertain, although it may have been intended to provide antique precedents for a program of royal entertainment. Monterrey also commissioned at least one outstanding group of religious works. This was a cycle of the life of St John the Baptist, four of which were painted by Massimo Stanzione (fig. 68) and one by Artemisia Gentileschi.[68]

There has long been speculation about the identity of the person who assembled the extraordinary group of Roman pictures for the palace. The answer to the mystery is provided in the record of a payment of September 23, 1641, to a certain Enrique de la Fluete, who was given 560 ducats for having transported seventeen crates of paintings sent from Rome by the Marquis of Castel Rodrigo,[69] the ambassador to the Holy See, who was doing an even more spectacular job of collecting pictures for the Retiro. Castel Rodrigo had been launched on a career of foreign service in 1627 in order to reduce his influence with the king's brother Carlos. After a tour of duty in Portugal, he took up the post of ambassador to the Holy See in 1632, which he held until 1641. By 1637, if not before, he had become an important patron of Claude Lorrain, from whom he ordered a series of thirteen etchings depicting the celebrations held in honor of the election of Ferdinand of Hungary as King of the Romans.[70] At about the same time, or perhaps a year or two earlier, Castel Rodrigo also commissioned from Claude and other Northern artists working in Rome one of the most spectacular and beautiful decorative ensembles of the seventeenth century—two series of landscapes, one of pastoral scenes, the other

125

of anchorites in panoramic natural settings. Together the two groups numbered over fifty paintings, about half of which were installed in the long gallery in the northern end of the west wing.[71]

In the inventory of 1701, twenty-three landscapes with anchorites, each measuring about 1.60 meters high by 2.40 meters wide, were listed in the Landscape Gallery. This choice of subject was directly related to one of the architectural features of the site, the hermitages. In effect, the pictures brought indoors the idea of pastoral Christianity embodied in the small garden chapels. The solemn, majestic tone of these works must have been established by Claude, who painted at least three paintings in the series. The *Landscape with St Mary Magdalene* (fig. 69) and the *Landscape with an Anchorite* display the common format of the series.[72] An expansive landscape, bathed in muted light, serves as a backdrop for the small figures of the anchorites. The *Landscape with St Anthony Abbot* (fig. 70), although more dramatic in the light effects, still adheres to the formula.[73]

Claude's countryman Nicolas Poussin was also the beneficiary of Castel Rodrigo's patronage and executed two paintings for the cycle. His *Landscape with an Anchorite* (fig. 71) and *Landscape with St Mary of Egypt and the Abbot Socimas*, known now only in the preparatory drawing, are among his important works of the 1630s.[74] Claude and Poussin invited the collaboration of their younger disciples. Jan Both executed at least six pictures for the Landscape Gallery, in a style that owes as much to the tradition of Flemish landscape painting as it does to Claude (fig. 72).[75] Poussin's followers, Gaspard Dughet, Jean Lemaire and Jacques d'Arthois, also participated in the program.[76] Lemaire's *Landscape with an Anchorite and Classical*

72. Jan Both, *Landscape with Baptism of Eunuch* (Madrid, Prado)

73. (facing page) Jean Lemaire, *Landscape with an Anchorite and Classical Ruins* (Madrid, Prado)

Ruins (fig. 73) departs from the set formula by employing an improbable backdrop of assorted antique architectural forms.

Claude also headed the list of painters who executed the group of twenty-two pastoral landscapes. Although uniform in subject, showing cowherds, shepherds and goatherds in rustic settings, they varied in size and seem in some cases to have been done as pairs. Two of Claude's pastoral landscapes have almost identical dimensions and, from a compositional point of view, complement each other well.[77] Other works in this series, of which only about a dozen have survived, were done by Both, Herman Swanevelt and Jean Lemaire.[78]

Castel Rodrigo's penchant for Claude's landscapes led to a final commission of four landscapes in a vertical format that are considered to be the first works in the grand style of the artist's maturity. The paintings were conceived as two pairs, one with scenes from the Old Testament, the other with scenes from the lives of saints (figs. 74 and 75).[79] Two more paintings were also obtained from Poussin, the *Hunt of Meleager* (fig. 76) and the *Feast of Priapus*.[80] As final testimony to Castel Rodrigo's knowledge of painting in Rome, there is a pair of pictures commissioned from Andrea Sacchi, whose version of *St Paul the Hermit and St Anthony Abbot* (fig. 77) fails to challenge Velázquez's treatment of the theme (fig. 86).[81] The numerous works sent by Castel Rodrigo from Rome, combined with those acquired by Monterrey in Naples, meant that by 1641 the Retiro contained nine or ten large landscapes by Claude, four major works by Poussin, six by Lanfranco, together with paintings by Sacchi, Domenichino and a host of lesser lights. For a brief moment, Central Italian Baroque painting was represented more fully in Spain than anywhere

74. (above left) Claude Lorrain, *Landscape with Burial of St Serapia* (Madrid, Prado)

75. (above right) Claude Lorrain, *Landscape with Embarkation of St Paula* (Madrid, Prado)

76. (below) Nicolas Poussin, *The Hunt of Meleager* (Madrid, Prado)

77. (above left) Andrea Sacchi, *St Paul the Hermit and St Anthony Abbot* (Madrid, Prado)

78. (above right) Anthony Van Dyck, *Cardinal Infante Ferdinand* (Madrid, Prado)

79. (below) Peter Paul Rubens, *Judgment of Paris* (Madrid, Prado)

outside Italy itself. And there was still more to come from Flanders.

The harvest of Flemish pictures was somewhat less rich, at least to judge from the identifiable works. The start of the Northern collection may have been delayed by the death of the governor, the Infanta Isabella, in December 1633. Her successor, the Cardinal Infante Ferdinand, entered Brussels in triumph on November 4, 1634 (fig. 78), but meanwhile a good eighteen months may have been lost while Flanders was without a permanent ruler. And once the cardinal infante was in a position to carry out the charge of picture collecting, his efforts were partly diverted from the Retiro to the Torre de la Parada, a hunting lodge in the grounds of the Pardo. From November 1636 to March 10, 1638, when the paintings for the hunting lodge were dispatched, Ferdinand seems to have been primarily concerned with shepherding this commission of over one hundred paintings through the workshop of Rubens.[82] Nevertheless, it is conceivable that some works for the Retiro were being obtained at the same time. On May 1, when the shipment of March 10 arrived in Madrid, Monanni reported that it contained 112 landscape paintings—"*paesi e pitture boscheresce*"—for the Retiro and the Torre.[83] Without more detailed information, it cannot be known how many works for the Retiro were in the cargo.

In June 1638, the cardinal infante placed another order with Rubens for an unspecified number of pictures.[84] Among them was at least one work destined for the Retiro, raising the possibility that the entire lot was meant for the palace. The identifiable work was Rubens's *Judgment of Paris* (fig. 79), which the cardinal infante thought to be excellent, though he was concerned about the nudity of the

80. Frans Snyders, *Fable of the Tortoise and the Hare* (Madrid, Prado)

81. (facing page) Andries van Eertvelt, *Marine Scene* (Madrid, Prado)

goddesses.[85] This group of works was dispatched to Madrid on February 27, 1639.[86]

By whatever means, a large number of Flemish paintings found their way to the Retiro. Not surprisingly, many of them were done by members of the Rubens workshop, which was kept working at full speed in these years with orders from the King of Spain. A substantial percentage of the paintings must have been landscapes and gamepieces, of which the Retiro had an extraordinary number; in the inventory of 1701, there are listed over 270 landscapes of all schools. Some were hung together in groups to decorate an entire room, while others were interspersed with pictures of other subjects. Frans Snyders, as prolific a painter as ever lived, contributed a series of illustrations of Aesop's *Fables* (fig. 80) as well as a number of pictures of animals in combat.[87] Paul de Vos, another "animal specialist," painted some of the *Fables* and also a version of the *Earthly Paradise*.[88] The Retiro had a great number of hunting pictures whose authors are not identified in the inventory, some of which may have been done by de Vos. Jan Wildens, who painted landscape backgrounds for the Rubens shop, did at least four or five identifiable large-scale landscapes and perhaps more.[89] A large number of unattributed Flemish landscapes are listed in the inventory and may be assumed to have come from Antwerp, where the cardinal infante went once a year to commission new pictures and to hasten the execution of those in progress. Like his brother the king, Ferdinand placed a great premium on speed and had little patience for the delays caused in part by Rubens's ill-health.

Another genre of landscape, the marine scene, was supplied by Andries van Eertvelt (fig. 81).[90] The Rubens shop also produced twelve pictures representing

82. Diego de Velázquez, *"Don Juan de Austria"* (Madrid, Prado)

83. Diego de Velázquez, *Cristóbal de Castañeda, called Barbarroja* (Madrid, Prado)

the months of the year, a theme that was the subject of two or three additional pictorial cycles. Although these pictures were distributed throughout the palace on a sometimes random basis, their presence evoked themes that were appropriate to the amenities and recreations of the site. If lacking the distinction of the paintings produced in Italy, they still achieved a high level of quality and helped to enrich the impression of opulence and splendor of the interior decoration.

The third and final source of pictures by contemporary artists was of course Madrid. The decoration of the Retiro provided an opportunity for Spanish court painters unequalled in the seventeenth century. To some extent, the opportunity outran the ability of the available talent. There was, however, one painter of genius on hand: Velázquez, whose work for the Retiro comprises his largest single commission. Most important were the six paintings for the Hall of Realms, painted in 1634–5, to be discussed in the next chapter. Also in 1634, he executed the

84. Diego de Velázquez, *Pablo de Valladolid* (Madrid, Prado)   85. Diego de Velázquez, *Calabazas* (Cleveland, Museum of Art)

magnificent group of six court jesters, for which he was paid on December 11.[91] They were installed as a group in a room in the queen's quarters known as the court jesters' room, the Pieza de los Bufones. Two of the jesters, *"Don Juan de Austria"* (fig. 82) and *Cristóbal de Castañeda, called Barbarroja* (fig. 83) were conceived as a pair of antagonists. "Don Juan de Austria," with his ill-fitting clothes and meek, tentative expression, hardly looks the match for the exaggerated ferocity of Barbarroja. Also in the room were *Pablo de Valladolid* (fig. 84) and *Calabazas* (fig. 85), the one dramatically posed against a flat, plain background, the other, with vacant smile, holding a portrait miniature and a pinwheel, symbol of a fool. The other two jester portraits, *Francisco de Ochoa* and *Cárdenas*, the *"bufón toreador,"* are lost. Velázquez also painted an important picture for one of the hermitage chapels, the luminous *Landscape with St Anthony Abbot and St Paul the Hermit* (fig. 86).[92] By 1701, the painting was installed illogically in the hermitage dedicated to St Anthony

86. Diego de Velázquez, *Landscape with St Anthony Abbot and St Paul the Hermit* (Madrid, Prado)

87. Diego de Velázquez, *Waterseller of Seville* (London, Wellington Museum)

of Padua, which has led to the suggestion that it had been moved from a more appropriate location in the hermitage of San Pablo, where it could have been in place by the spring of 1633.

In addition to commissioned works, there were paintings done by Velázquez earlier in his career. Besides the two important pictures painted in Italy in 1630, the *Forge of Vulcan* and *Joseph's Bloody Coat Brought to Jacob*, there was also his most famous early work, the *Waterseller of Seville* (fig. 87), which was probably a gift of the cardinal infante, its third documented owner.[93] Two of Velázquez's royal portraits were in the Retiro, too; *Philip IV*, executed just after Velázquez's arrival at court in 1623, and its pendant, *Queen Isabella*, painted some years later.[94] The last painting, now lost, had an enigmatic subject, *Pelican with a Bucket and Donkeys*.[95] In all, the Retiro contained eighteen pictures by Velázquez, at least thirteen of which were painted in 1634–5. If not the leader in quantity among the Spanish masters, he took the medal for quality, for the contribution of his contemporaries is uneven.

In the history of painting in Madrid, the decade of the 1630s is one of contradictory developments. By the time the decoration of the Retiro had begun, Velázquez, just back from Italy, had formed his mature style. His technical virtuosity, his profound understanding of the art of the past and his uncanny capacity for seeing and rendering the effects of light and color put him in a class by himself. He was also a thoroughly modern painter who had made the acquaintance of the most advanced artists of his time and had assimilated their techniques and outlook. At the court, Velázquez worked in isolation from his senior colleagues, the now old-fashioned Vicente Carducho and Eugenio Cajés, who were still practising an Italianate style they had learned forty years earlier.[96] But these artists through their long years of royal service had earned the right to participate in the decoration of the Retiro, and particularly of the Hall of Realms. As it happened, Cajés died in December 1634 and was able to complete only one of the two pictures assigned to him. But Carducho executed not only three pictures for the Hall of Realms, but six more of various subjects.

The presence of the older generation of Spanish painters at the Retiro was even more emphatically asserted by Pedro de Orrente, a painter born in Murcia in 1580, who had probably worked in the Bassano family atelier in Venice.[97] On his return to Spain, Orrente specialized in Bassanesque paintings of rustic Old and New Testament scenes set in extensive landscapes long after the tradition had died out in Italy. From 1617 to 1631, he worked in Toledo, and was then not documented again until 1638, when he appeared in Murcia. The inventory of the Retiro strongly suggests that he spent at least some of the intervening time in Madrid, for it lists thirty-two works attributed to him. In keeping with the taste for pictures in series, Orrente painted cycles from the life of Moses, of Jacob (fig. 88) and of the Passion of Christ. Orrente was an inconsistent painter and his works for the Retiro unmistakably demonstrate this.

The one older painter of great distinction unfortunately did not have to paint for a living and therefore painted very little. This was Philip's former drawing teacher, the Dominican friar Juan Bautista Maino.[98] Maino painted only one picture for the Retiro, the memorable *Recapture of Bahía* in the Hall of Realms (fig. 131). But having done this one great work, he chose to do no more.

88. Pedro de Orrente, *Laban Overtaking Jacob* (Madrid, Prado)

89. Francisco Collantes, *Landscape* (Madrid, Prado)

The younger generation of painters in Madrid included several fine artists, but none of them could approach the originality or modernity of Velázquez. Félix Castelo and Jusepe Leonardo were both content to follow the example of their masters Carducho and Cajés.[99] A more adventurous painter was Francisco Collantes, one of the rare Spanish landscape specialists of the seventeenth century.[100] Collantes, born in 1599, the same year as Velázquez, is given as the author of twenty-two paintings in the 1701 inventory, almost all of which are landscapes. Working in the vein of late-sixteenth-century Flemish landscape specialists, Collantes produced tranquil, limpid scenes of imaginary nature, populated by small foreground figures (fig. 89). All his identifiable works were installed in the private quarters.

The youngest painter to participate in the decoration of the Retiro was Antonio de Pereda, who had been born in Valladolid in 1611.[101] His appearance on the scene was the result of the patronage of Crescenzi, thanks to whom he was assigned one of the battle scenes in the Hall of Realms. Also in 1634, the Count of Castrillo paid him for two small landscapes.[102] Pereda's moment in the limelight was brief, ending with the death of his patron in 1635. The failure to secure his position was unfortunate, for his considerable talent seldom found a suitable outlet thereafter.

Only one painter from outside the capital made an important contribution to the decoration. In 1634, Francisco de Zurbarán, then at the height of his career, was called from Seville to execute a substantial number of works for the Hall of Realms.[103] Zurbarán was in Madrid for less than a year, but his contribution to the decoration of this room was sizable; he painted one of the twelve large battle scenes and also ten episodes from the life of Hercules. Having completed the assignment, Zurbarán returned home with the title of "painter to the king" but without further royal commissions. It is not clear whether his decision to leave the court was the result of his desire to resume a successful career as a religious painter in Seville or of his failure to win the king's approval for what he had done at the Retiro.

Late in the year of 1641, as the last of the Roman landscapes were being hung on the walls of the palace, the king and the count–duke must have looked with satisfaction on the extraordinary collection of pictures that they had gathered over the preceding eight years. The sheer number of paintings, about eight hundred, was impressive. By turning the machinery of a powerful state from politics and war to art, they were able to build a collection of princely proportions in a very short space of time. The achievement was all the more remarkable because so many of the pictures were specifically commissioned for the project.

The desire for haste was certainly an important determinant in shaping the collection, but other forces came into play as well. The Retiro was customarily inhabited by the court for only six to eight weeks a year. As an occasional residence, the palace was not a suitable place to install the treasures of the royal collection. The great paintings by past masters stayed on the walls of the Alcázar, where the king spent most of his time and where the solemn ceremonies of state took place. In addition, the purpose of the Retiro as a suburban pleasure garden suggested the use of themes such as landscape and still life. All these circumstances contrived to put a special stamp on the collection.

It was first of all a collection of "modern" paintings, consisting in large measure of works by living artists. The expedient solution of wholesale acquisition of existing works was employed to some extent. But a large number of paintings were made for the palace. Painters in Naples, Rome, Antwerp and Madrid were put to work for *il Re di Spagna*, to quote the words proudly used by Claude Lorrain in referring to the patron of his landscapes for the Retiro. As a result, the walls of the Retiro became an unusual, and possibly unique, anthology of painting in Italy, Flanders and Spain in the 1630s. Within the confines of the palace could be seen important works by Velázquez, Zurbarán and Ribera; by Poussin, Claude, Cortona, Lanfranco and Sacchi; and by Rubens, Snyders and de Vos.

There were of course valleys as well as peaks of artistic achievement. The desire to complete the decoration in the shortest amount of time meant that standards sometimes had to be lowered. Speed of execution and artistic quality are by no means incompatible; many excellent painters have worked at a breathtaking pace. But it does require a special talent to keep the two in balance. Unfortunately, the scale of the project compelled Olivares's agents to employ several artists who could work quickly but not well. The hackwork produced by Juan de la Corte, for example, did little but fill spaces on the walls.[104] A number of rooms were covered with paintings by Scipione Compagno, an obscure Neapolitan painter. Large series of portraits of the kings of Aragon and the dukes of Milan by anonymous artists are dull and unattractive. The lack of consistency, an important feature of the collection, seems rather alarming today. But the differences in quality were partially reduced by the way in which the pictures were displayed.

Attempts to reconstruct the original hanging of the pictures are frustrated by the lack of contemporary views and detailed descriptions of the interior. The difficulties are compounded by the fact that the earliest inventory was not made until 1701, following the death of Charles II. Yet this inventory has been shown to reflect with considerable fidelity the arrangement of the pictures during the lifetime of Philip IV.[105] Two simple but somewhat contradictory ideas governed the disposition of the collection. The first was to hang the pictures when possible in unified thematic groups. The Landscape Gallery is one application of this idea, as is the court jesters' room. There was also a room with imaginary portraits of the kings of Aragon, whose purpose was to emphasize the dynastic ancestry and legitimacy of the monarch. But consistency often had to give way to the other guiding principle.

In the seventeenth century, quantity ran a close second to quality in establishing the magnificence of an art collection. The walls of the house of a great prince had to be covered from floor to ceiling with paintings in order to create the desired effect of wealth, magnificence and splendor. The sheer number of paintings displayed in a large gallery defeated close scrutiny of individual works and could be counted on to minimize differences in quality. While it would have been possible to achieve quantity, quality and thematic consistency in a few rooms at a time, it was virtually impossible to do so for an entire, large-scale palace, especially when the pictures were being gathered in four collecting points as scattered as Madrid, Rome, Naples and Brussels. So the decorators of the palace were often compelled to make rather strange assortments of pictures, which they harmonized as best they could by using uniform frames. For instance, one of the long galleries in the west wing had mythological scenes, biblical scenes and landscapes. Another had landscapes intermingled with elaborate imaginary views of classical architecture. This practice was by no means unique to the Retiro. The Alcázar and the Pardo both employed comparable schemes, which were inevitable when huge collections formed in different times and places were brought together in a single location.[106]

The lack of tightly-woven programs of ideas expressed in paintings seems not to have disturbed the king and the court. As a profound admirer of art, Philip preferred to sacrifice ideas to beauty when the choice had to be made. Yet neither Philip nor his predecessors were indifferent to the function of art as political propaganda. There was an established repertory of ideas and images that occurred time and again in palace decorations; but often they were employed allusively and unified not by strict relationships to other parts of the decorative ensemble, but by reference to the monarch and his recognized virtues. The Habsburg kings of Spain did not have to advertise their power and majesty in quite the same way as did lesser potentates—as heads of a world-wide empire, they were universally recognized as the most powerful monarchs on earth. The name of the King of Spain was synonymous with political might and grandeur. This may explain why Velázquez, for example, almost always dispensed with symbolic attributes when painting the king. The person of Philip himself was a completely satisfactory symbol of all that was regal. This exalted status, as long as it lasted, permitted the king to make his points by inference and helps to explain the apparently casual approach taken to the use of artistic propaganda in palace decoration.

Still, there were times when it was thought desirable to catalogue explicitly and in detail the virtues of the ruler of Spain. Occasional decorations, especially the ones mounted for solemn entries, royal exequies and public spectacles, could be meticulously conceived and executed in a traditional language of emblems and devices. But once inside the palace, the other mode of expression prevailed. Decorative projects of political intent were carried out mostly with paintings already at hand and perhaps supplemented by a few works ordered for the purpose of completing the adornment. This is why one room in the Retiro stands out as exceptional. In the Hall of Realms, a magnificent cycle of pictures was conceived that proclaimed with unity and clarity the power and glory of Philip IV as manifested in the military triumphs achieved by the head of his government, the Count–Duke of Olivares. The reason for the creation of this decorative program is found at the crossroads of long-standing tradition and the circumstances of the moment.

VI

King and Favorite in the Hall of Realms

THE PAINTINGS AND THEIR SETTING

Al Salón del Buen Retiro

Esta al valor, este al poder sagrado
Palestra imperial, orbe ceñido,
De victorias que el arte ha conseguido,
De reynos que el pincel ha fabricado:
　　Al mayor capitán, le ha destinado,
Al monarcha mayor le ha prevenido,
La atención de un Guzmán esclarecido,
Valiente senador, cuerdo soldado;
　　A este, pues, de el León de dos Españas
Ya festivo teatro a sus victorias;
Infamando su sangre las campañas
　　Vendrá el revelde a tributar dos glorias,
Una a la espada, para las hazañas,
Al pincel otra, para las memorias.[1]

This opaque but ringing sonnet appeared in a collection of verses praising the Palace of the Buen Retiro, which was published in 1635 by the chief custodian of the palace, Diego de Covarrubias y Leyva. As the title of the poem states, the writer, an obscure versifier named Pedro Rosete Niño, was eulogizing the *salón del Buen Retiro*. His encomium was by no means unique; twenty-one of the thirty-three poets represented in the anthology had composed verses in honor of this room. The Salón, "this imperial arena of valor, this sphere of holy might," was clearly an exceptional place. Its walls were "encircled with victories won by art," with "realms devised by the paintbrush." These works of art spoke a message. Through the attention of an illustrious member of the Guzmán family, a tribute had been arranged in honor of the greatest monarch and general in the world. To this theater of the king's victories the rebellious Dutchman would come, there to pay homage to the might of the Spanish sword and to the skill of the painters who, with their brushes, had immortalized its triumphs. Behind this curtain of Baroque hyperbole lies the Hall of Realms.

　　The Hall of Realms was the most significant room in the Retiro. Originally it had been intended for use as the royal box in the days when the palace was used as a theater for fiestas. Once the Retiro had been coverted into a proper palace, the Hall

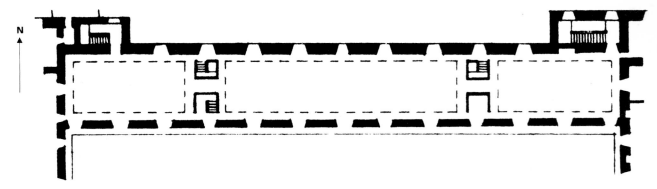

90. Hall of Realms (after Carlier)

91. (facing page) Hall of Realms, *c.* 1900 (from Tormo, *Pintura*)

of Realms became a throne room, in which the king presided over court ceremonies and entertainments. This exalted purpose called for an exalting decoration, which became an epitome of the power and glory of the King of Spain.

No expense was spared to make the room a paragon of regal splendor. The Hall was a long rectangular space in the center of the north wing of the palace, measuring three times as long as wide (34.6 by 10 meters), with a high ceiling (8 meters) (figs. 90 and 91).[2] An iron balcony encircled the room, providing space for courtiers to view the spectacles that took place below.[3] Light flooded into the Hall through twenty windows, illuminating its opulent furnishings and decor. The floor was covered with oriental carpets. Between each of the ten large lower windows and on either side of the two doors stood a jasper console table.[4] Near each of the twelve lateral tables was placed a rampant silver lion holding the shield of Aragon, given by the protonotary Villanueva.[5] Above was a ceiling fresco with ornate gilt grotesques, and, in the vaults above the windows, the escutcheons of the twenty-four kingdoms of the Spanish Monarchy, which ultimately gave their name to the Hall. The most important features of the decoration were the paintings on the lateral and end walls.[6] Between the windows at the side were twelve large battle paintings, specially commissioned from court artists,[7] depicting the great victories won by the armies of Philip IV in every quarter of his worldwide empire (fig. 92). They were complemented by ten scenes of the life of Hercules painted by Zurbarán.[8] Five royal equestrian portraits by Velázquez (fig. 93), which flanked the doors, completed a decoration of almost oriental richness.[9]

During 1634 artists and decorators were hard at work, and by the early part of 1635 the room was nearly finished. In March the queen, who had recently given birth to the short-lived Princess María Antonia, visited the Hall to see what had been accomplished during her confinement.[10] All was in readiness for the inauguration, scheduled to take place after Easter, except for the paintings. Velázquez and Maino were still at work on their canvases at the end of March,[11] but in his dispatch of April 28 Monanni was able to report that the Hall had been completed and the paintings installed.[12]

In the years following its completion, this splendid Hall was used for many purposes, some of them serious, most of them frivolous. When Monanni saw the still uncompleted Hall in March, he noted the preparations for the installation of stage

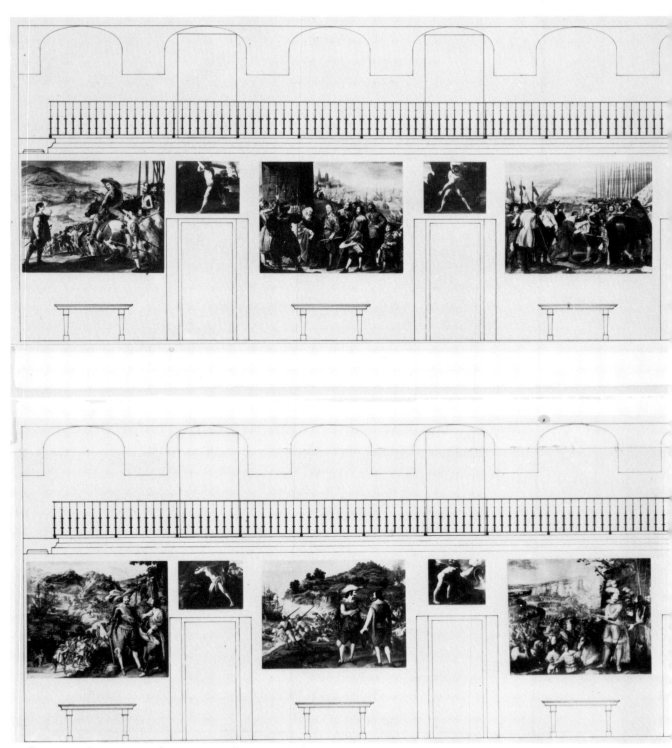

92. Reconstruction, seventeenth–century installation, Hall of Realms. Upper figure depicts north wall; lower figure represents south wall. Pictures are arranged in west to east sequence, reading from left to right.

93. Reconstruction, seventeenth-century installation, Hall of Realms. Upper figure represents west wall; lower is east wall.

machinery, and called the Hall the "*salone principale per le commedie.*"[13] Plays and other entertainments were in fact to be staged there more frequently than ceremonial events, but the discrepancy which we perceive between the function and the decoration of the room was clearly not troubling to the king and the court. For them the Hall was the ceremonial center of the palace, and its decoration showed that it belonged to a tradition almost as old as kingship itself, the Hall of Princely Virtue.

THE HALL OF PRINCELY VIRTUE

Halls of Princely Virtue had long been used to glorify the superior moral and physical qualities of the ruler.[14] They also served to emphasize the antiquity of the dynasty, thus confirming its right to rule, and provided examples of princely conduct for successors to the title. During the sixteenth century, as the prince was elevated to new heights of majesty, the Hall of Princely Virtue attained new heights of splendor. In the courts of Francis I, Henry VIII and especially Charles V, a distinctive language of glory was fashioned[15]—a language that was also spoken by the papacy. The great cycles of glorification created by Raphael in the papal apartments of the Vatican gave a monumental form to age-old ideas.[16] Under the influence of these illustrious examples, the Hall of Princely Virtue became an

94. Sala di Fasti Farnese, Caprarola, Villa Farnese

indispensable component of palace decoration. The Farnese family, for example, commissioned comparable decorative schemes for their palaces in Rome and Caprarola (fig. 94), as did the Grand Duke Cosimo de' Medici in the Palazzo Vecchio at Florence.[17]

The decoration of these rooms used three different modes of expression—allegory, analogy and narration. Great events of family history—military victories, triumphal entries, dynastic marriages, diplomatic coups—tended to be shown in narrative form, while superior moral attributes—for instance Justice, Prudence, Wisdom, Magnanimity—were represented either by symbols or by reference to classical or Biblical heroes who had come to be understood as incarnations of princely virtues. But toward the end of the century, allegory and analogy began to displace narration, perhaps under the influence of another vehicle for princely glorification, the ceremonial or occasional decoration for events like royal marriages. Whatever the reason for the change, the great seventeenth-century works exalting the prince—the decoration of the Banqueting House, Whitehall, and the Medici cycle by Rubens, or the Salone of the Barberini Palace and the apartments of the Pitti Palace by Pietro da Cortona—were either conceived as pure allegory or as allegorized history.[18] This development can be observed in the evolution of the Hall of Princely Virtue at the court of the Spanish Habsburgs, but with significant differences.

If the example of Charles V was important for the kings and princes of sixteenth-century Europe, it was overwhelming for the rulers of Spain. As a consequence of his peripatetic style of rule, Charles never established a permanent ceremonial headquarters. The problem of creating a splendid Hall of Princely Virtue for a wandering ruler was solved by an ingenious expedient. A portable decoration was created in the form of tapestries which could be easily rolled up and packed to accompany Charles on his travels. Two great sets of tapestries depicting the emperor's triumphs were made in Flanders. The first was a series of eight tapestries showing the Battle of Pavia (fig. 95), won in 1525, which was designed by Bernard van Orley and made in 1531.[19] The second and more important was the set of Tunis tapestries (fig. 96).[20] In 1535, when he led his armies on the Tunis campaign, the emperor engaged the services of a Flemish painter, Jan Vermeyen, to make a visual record of events. Almost ten years later, Vermeyen was commissioned to prepare cartoons for a series of twelve tapestries of the *Conquest of Tunis and La Goletta*, which were executed at the factory of Willem Pannemaker and completed in April 1554. The enormous tapestry panels represent a *Map of the Campaign* and eleven scenes which show in episodic fashion the highlights of the expedition. The battle scenes are composed in the panoramic format customarily used for this subject and set within decorative borders that contain Latin and Spanish inscriptions. These monumental tapestries became a part of the imperial baggage and were unfolded for display whenever needed. The tapestries were so heavily used by Charles, and later by Philip II, that a copy had to be made to save the original. Both the old and new sets, as they are called in the inventories, found their way to Spain where they acquired an almost iconic status and continued to be used on all manner of state occasions. Beginning in 1639, one set was permanently installed in the Salón Dorado of the Alcázar.[21]

148

95. *Battle of Pavia* (Naples, Museo di Capodimonte)

96. *Conquest of Tunis and La Goletta* (Seville, Alcázar)

149

1546.

PRINCIPIS ACCESSV BVRANI, TERRITVS HESSVS,
SAXO'QVE, CÆSAREIS SVBITO DANT TERGA MANIPLIS.

The strong emphasis on the emperor's military enterprises established the importance of the battle scene in the repertory of motifs used to glorify the King of Spain. There was of course an equally potent allegorical system devised to exalt the power and achievements of Charles V, but it appears to have led a separate existence from the battle paintings, manifesting itself especially in temporary decorations for the emperor's many triumphal entries and processions. But there was an obvious predilection for narrative depiction, and this was confirmed by an extraordinary series of engravings designed by Martin van Heemskerck, which reviewed in vivid graphic form the major victories of the emperor's career (fig. 97).[22] The series comprised twelve prints, the same number as there were battle paintings in the Hall of Realms, and may well have served as a thematic and compositional source of inspiration for the planners of the decoration.

Philip II kept alive the custom of using battle pieces for palace decoration. In 1584, he commissioned the Italian painters Niccolò Granello, Lazzaro Tavarone and Fabrizio Castello to decorate a long gallery in the king's quarters of the Escorial with battle scenes.[23] On one long wall, there was a copy of a medieval painting in the Alcázar, Segovia, which showed the Battle of la Higueruela. Opposite, in the wall pierced by windows, there were scenes, commissioned in 1590, of the battle of St

97. (facing page) After
Martin van Heemskerck,
*Emperor Charles V's Camp at
Ingolstadt* (New York,
Metropolitan Museum of
Art)

98. Detail, *Battle of St Quentin*,
El Escorial, Hall of Battles

Quentin, a victory pledged to St Lawrence and redeemed by the construction of the
Escorial (fig. 98). The example of the Tunis tapestries must have been etched on
Philip's mind because he had the artists frame the scenes with illusionistic decorative
borders that imitate tapestries, and so made them appear as if they were hung on the
wall with nails.[24]

Philip also adopted the Italian custom of mixing narrative and allegory in the
decoration of the Hall of Princely Virtue, as seen in the state rooms of the Pardo
palace. In the eastern wing of this palace was a suite of three rooms—the *salón donde se
descubre por el rey* (the room where visitors removed their hats before seeing the
king), the antechamber and the audience room. By 1590, the Salón, which was the
largest of the chambers, had an impressive pictorial decoration based on three
themes.[25] First there were the battle pieces showing famous victories of Philip and
his father—the *Conquest of Tunis* and the *Battle of Pavia*, won by Charles, and the
Siege of Antwerp and the *Capture of Sluis*, successes of Philip's army of Flanders in
1584–5 and 1587 respectively. To the battle pieces Philip added another element
which had a long tradition of its own. This was the gallery of family portraits which
expressed the theme of dynastic continuity.[26] The centerpieces of this series were
two famous allegorized portraits by Titian—*Charles V at Mühlberg* and the *Allegory*

151

of Philip's Victory at Lepanto.[27] In the second painting, the dynastic note resounded as Philip, standing before a sketchy view of the battle of Lepanto, raised his infant son Ferdinand toward an angel who carries a banner inscribed *Majora tibi*, or "Greater triumphs await you." These portraits were supplemented by sixteen half-length representations of members of the Habsburg family hung in a frieze just below the cornice. The last group of pictures consisted of four allegorical subjects that unified and extended the meaning of the decoration. Three were personifications of *Faith*, *Hope* and *Charity*, the Christian ideals in defense of which Charles and Philip had fought. And last came *Fame*, trumpet in hand, who spread to the corners of the globe the battle triumphs of the Habsburgs in the defense of the Catholic faith.

By comparison with Italian Halls of Princely Virtue, the program in the Salón at the Pardo is marked by simplicity and explicitness and also by the narrow range of ideas. Military might in defense of the faith and a glorious dynastic succession are the only components of Philip's fame. Philip may have wanted to be known for his *audacia*, *animosità*, *sagacità* and *fortezza*, and for his *prudenzia*, *diligenza* and *honore*, but he, and his successors, must have assumed that the defender of the faith possessed all these virtues in consummate form.

Nevertheless, there were occasions when princely virtues were specifically catalogued in Spanish court decorations, one of the most important of them being the royal exequies. In 1558, an elaborate funeral service for Charles V was staged in the cathedral of Brussels.[28] In front of the church was erected an enormous "ship of state," which was an encyclopedia in emblematic form of Charles's deeds and virtues. From the mainmast hung a gigantic banner which showed Christ on the Cross above, and below, the columnar device of Charles V, the defender of the faith. Personifications of Faith, Hope and Charity rode the decks, separated by a series of flags with the arms of the realms of Charles's empire. The sides of the ship were adorned by representations of twelve of his great battles. Behind the vessel were two hippocamps, pulling the Pillars of Hercules, which identified the deceased ruler with the ancient hero and proclaimed that Charles–Hercules had dominated "monsters, time and himself."[29]

Many of these ideas were recast in Seville, forty years later, when the city erected in the cathedral a gigantic symbolic tomb to commemorate the death of Philip II.[30] The program of this famous monument was devised by a learned canon of the cathedral, Francisco Pacheco, the uncle of the painter of the same name. The funerary structure, which spanned the nave of the church, had eight statues personifying the Church, Faith, Hope, Prudence, Justice, Moderation, Strength and Charity. There were also representations of sixteen famous triumphs, military and diplomatic, of Philip's reign, including Lepanto, St Quentin, Portugal and Granada. Eight altars were adorned with allegories of the kingdoms of the Monarchy. And there was also an arch of Hercules, with the hero holding the globe and a motto *Sufficio Solus*, meaning that Philip had been sufficient unto himself to support this terrible burden.

During the reign of Philip III, a time of peace but also of political stagnation, no new Halls of Princely Virtue were created. But under Philip IV, as Olivares sought to revitalize the power of Spain, this mode of decoration came back into favor. In 1625, plans were laid to decorate the so-called Pieza Nueva in the Alcázar.[31] The

99. Diego de Velázquez, *Baltasar Carlos on Horseback* (Madrid, Prado)

100. Diego de Velázquez, *Philip III on Horseback* (Madrid, Prado)

101. Diego de Velázquez, *Philip IV on Horseback* (Madrid, Prado)

102. Diego de Velázquez, *Margaret of Austria on Horseback* (Madrid, Prado)

103. Diego de Velázquez, *Isabella of Bourbon on Horseback* (Madrid, Prado)

initial suite of pictures, perhaps inspired by the example of occasional monuments, gave increased importance to allegory and analogy to express the traditional ideals and virtues of the King of Spain. The themes of dynastic succession and military power in defense of Catholicism still predominated and were expressed in a series of royal portraits. Two of the portraits were brought from the Salón of the Pardo—Titian's *Charles V at Mühlberg* and the *Allegory of Philip's Victory at Lepanto*—commemorating the triumphs over Protestantism and Islam. A third work by Titian, *Spain Coming to the Aid of Religion*, ensured that the holy mission of the Monarchy was fully understood. Most of the other pictures, including works by Rubens done during his visit to Madrid, and by Ribera, Carducho, Cajés and others, were mythological and religious scenes which used analogy to portray the virtues of the Christian prince.

Thus, in 1633, when the planners of the Hall of Realms started to conceive the decoration, there was a well-established, specifically Hispanic repository of ideas and images on which to draw. The battle piece, which showed the armies of Spain victorious over the heretic, was at the heart of the repertory. No less important was the notion of dynastic succession and its implication of the right to rule. Both of these ideas could best be cast in a narrative or literal form, which meant that the Hall of Realms as a Hall of Princely Virtue would be based on a superannuated format. But as a concession to the now-fashionable use of allegory there were the Hercules scenes, which brought into play the most famous and complex embodiment of princely virtue. Finally, there were the escutcheons of the realms and provinces of the Monarchy which proclaimed in simple emblematic form the vast extension of the power of the King of Spain. The Hall of Realms may have been somewhat old-fashioned in the context of its times, but no more effective declaration of the power, glory and virtue of the Spanish Habsburgs was ever devised.

Seen from the perspective of tradition, the various parts of the Hall of Realms become understandable. Easiest to interpret are the five equestrian portraits by Velázquez, which represented *Philip III* and *Philip IV* and their queens, *Margaret of Austria* and *Isabella of Bourbon*, and the Crown Prince *Baltasar Carlos* (figs. 99–103).[32] By showing the two monarchs and their consorts, together with the heir to the throne, they represent the immediate past, present and future of the Habsburgs and assert the legitimate rights and continuity of the dynasty. The kingship inherited by Philip IV from his father, Philip III, would in turn pass to his son, Baltasar Carlos. The male equestrian portraits are also military portraits and accord with the martial theme that dominates the decoration. In each picture, the king or prince is shown wearing the red sash of the captain–general and holding the baton of command. (The two Philips also wear breastplates.) The themes of dynastic succession and military might are continued and amplified in the Hercules scenes, painted by Francisco de Zurbarán.

HERCULES HISPANICUS

In June 1634, when Zurbarán's commission was first documented, it was to consist of twelve pictures representing the Labors of Hercules. It is clear from the document of final payment and the inventory of 1701 that the number was ultimately reduced to ten.[33] The reduction of the commission must have been related in principle to the decision to place the pictures over the ten windows. At that point, it was presumably decided to change the nature and purpose of this allegorical element in the series. As it now stands, the Hercules cycle seems somewhat disorganized. It contains seven major labors, two minor labors and an unusual representation of Hercules's death. But the apparent untidiness disappears as soon as the customary title, the Labors of Hercules, is discarded and its real meaning is discovered.

To the seventeenth-century mind, Hercules was a polyvalent symbol, a fact that the planners of the scenes for the Hall of Realms exploited to the hilt. First and foremost, Hercules was a popular symbol of Virtue and Strength, meanings which he had represented since antiquity.[34] In the course of the sixteenth century, the virtuous and heroic Hercules was appropriated as a symbol of the prince following the antique example of the Emperor Augustus.[35] Once again, the role of Charles V, the prince of princes, appears to have been important. The invention of the emperor's emblematic device, which was designed around the mythical Columns of Hercules, fixed the association of the ancient hero with the modern ruler firmly in the minds of sixteenth-century princes.[36] In due course, representations of Hercules became a standard part of the repertory of the princely palace decoration.[37]

The connection between Hercules and the prince was strengthened by the numerous claims to Hercules as an ancestor. In the course of his travels in the western Mediterranean, Hercules appears to have stopped in every kingdom, dukedom and

104. Peter Paul Rubens, *Hercules Triumphant over Discord* (London, Whitehall, Banqueting House)

105. (above left) Francisco de Zurbarán, *Hercules Separating the Mountains of Caspe and Abylla* (Madrid, Prado)

106. (above right) Francisco de Zurbarán, *Hercules Slaying King Geryon* (Madrid, Prado)

107. (left) Francisco de Zurbarán, *Death of Hercules* (Madrid, Prado)

108. (below left) Francisco de Zurbarán, *Hercules and Antaeus* (Madrid, Prado)

109. (below right) Francisco de Zurbarán, *Hercules and the Cretan Bull* (Madrid, Prado)

110. (above left) Francisco de Zurbarán, *Hercules and the Erymanthian Boar* (Madrid, Prado)

111. (above right) Francisco de Zurbarán, *Hercules and the Nemean Lion* (Madrid, Prado)

112. (right) Francisco de Zurbarán, *Hercules and the Lernean Hydra* (Madrid, Prado)

113. (below left) Francisco de Zurbarán, *Hercules and Cerberus* (Madrid, Prado)

114. (below right) Francisco de Zurbarán, *Hercules Diverting the River Alpheus* (Madrid, Prado)

principality in western Europe, staying at least long enough to father the ruling line. The Kings of Spain, as it happened, had a better claim than most to Herculean ancestry because one of the major labors, the capture of King Geryon's herd of cattle, was thought to have taken place on or near the coast of southern Spain. The events of ancient and modern history conspired to make Hercules a logical symbol of the Habsburg kings of Spain.[38] Philip IV, following the path blazed by his great-grandfather the emperor, naturally identified himself with Hercules Hispanicus.[39] In Philip's case, the association was exceptionally appropriate because Hercules, like the king, was also identified with the sun, itself another symbol of *Virtù*.[40] The twelve labors were sometimes linked with the twelve signs of the zodiac, through which Hercules moved like the sun. For all of these reasons, the allegorical use of Hercules in the Hall of Realms was singularly appropriate.[41]

The princely connotations of Hercules were by no means exhausted by these interpretations. Hercules was also considered to be a symbol of apotheosis.[42] Having donned the poisoned robe of Nessus, given him by his wife, Hercules sought to end his mortal agony by immolation on a funeral pyre. As the flames consumed his body, he ascended to Parnassus, there to take his place among the gods. The connection of the funeral pyre with immortality had been explicitly evoked by Philip II in the exequies held for his father in Brussels in 1558. There, an enormous *capella ardente* was erected in the cathedral as a symbol of the emperor's immortality. The funeral pyre was also understood to have another meaning, which likewise descended from imperial Rome. When the pyre was ignited, the deceased emperor not only became a god but his son became his successor. In other words, the funeral pyre, real or symbolic, confirmed the rights of imperial succession.[43]

A final idea was applied to the figure of Hercules by sixteenth-century rulers: Hercules as the conqueror of discord.[44] The religious and political struggles of this period, and the divided loyalty of a sovereign's subjects, made the threat of discord loom large over the times. The extension of the Herculean metaphor to include the power to stifle rebellion was almost inevitable, and by the mid-sixteenth century the usual form for the symbol showed Hercules vanquishing a monster.[45] By the time that Cesare Ripa published his influential encyclopedia of emblems, *Iconologia* (1603), the identification between monster and Discordia was universally understood. Discord, he writes, is a woman in the form of an infernal demon (*furia infernale*), dressed in multicolored clothes, with snakes in her hair.[46] The image of Discord was the one used by Rubens in his version of *Hercules Triumphant Over Discord* for the ceiling of the Banqueting House some years later (fig. 104).[47]

All these varied but related meanings were infused into the ten Hercules scenes commissioned by Zurbarán, making them an allegorical index to the ideas expressed in the Hall of Realms. The identification of Hercules with the King of Spain, as we have seen, was widely understood, and had additional significance for Philip IV because he, like Hercules, was likened to the sun. Two of Zurbarán's paintings explicitly evoked the association of the hero with the kingdoms of Spain. In *Hercules Separating the Mountains of Caspe and Abylla* (fig. 105), Zurbarán, by showing the creation of the Straits of Gibraltar, also invokes the Pillars of Hercules, that potent Habsburg imperial symbol. *Hercules Slaying King Geryon* (fig. 106) takes the hero onto Spanish shores, for Geryon was considered to have been the ruler of Iberian lands.[48] These two pictures in consequence also acquire a dynastic meaning because they reinforce the claim of descent from the ancient demigod.

The dynastic motif is reemphasized in the *Death of Hercules* (fig. 107). Zurbarán's rendering of this episode is unusual because it combines two moments of Hercules's death agony into one. In most of the early accounts, Hercules put on the poisoned robe of Nessus, which caused unbearable pain when it came into contact with his skin, but did not break into flames. The robe caught fire only after Hercules had mounted the funeral pyre to end his mortal life and start his ascent to heaven and immortality.[49] In his treatment of the final episode of Hercules's life, Zurbarán sacrifices textual fidelity to concentrate attention on the motif of the flames. By this device, Zurbarán evoked the ancient ritual of apotheosis in which Hercules, and therefore the king, becomes immortal. And he also evoked the theme of dynastic legitimacy which was inherent in the immolation of Hercules. Thus the meaning of the equestrian portraits was reinterpreted in allegorical terms.

The remaining scenes depicted Hercules as a conqueror, and especially as a conqueror of discord. In successive pictures, Hercules dispatches Antaeus, the Cretan Bull, the Erymanthian Boar, the Nemean Lion, the Lernean Hydra and Cerberus (figs. 108–13)—feats which were understood to symbolize the triumph of the just sovereign over his domestic and foreign enemies. The final picture, *Hercules Diverting the River Alpheus* (fig. 114), may be intended to suggest the act of purifying the world of discord.

The symbolic significance of the Hercules scenes is crucial for understanding an artistic question that has long been puzzling. The choice of a specialist in religious art, who commanded an imposing but rigid style of painting, has always seemed somewhat illogical for these pagan subjects that were filled with action. But once the symbolic function of the Hercules pictures is grasped, the commission of Zurbarán makes sense. The Hercules scenes were *emblemas* and therefore invited a schematic treatment. The organizer of the decoration must have seen that Zurbarán's style was well suited to the task. The lack of finesse was offset by an almost blatant legibility of the kind commonly used in emblem books. In addition, the pictures had to be placed ten feet above the floor, which put a premium on clarity. The rough-hewn, unidealized Hercules type invented by Zurbarán captures in an original way the brute force and inexhaustible power of the ancient hero. His ability to triumph over discord is never in doubt.

THE BATTLE PAINTINGS AND THE DEFENSE OF THE REGIME

In Spanish eyes, the sources of discord in the Monarchy and in the world at large were heresy and rebellion, which were everywhere rampant in those dark days of the seventeenth century. They were covertly abetted by the French, and most of all by the Dutch, those disloyal vassals of the Crown, who were to be found across the globe fomenting discord and bringing aid and comfort to Spain's enemies. Between them, heresy and rebellion threatened to sweep away the established order, the House of Austria, and the church universal itself.

Spain's mission, as seen by Olivares, was to stem and turn back the flood. Addressing the council of state in May 1631 on the desperate situation in Germany he said: "Today we see all the power of the heretics united against us," and went on to speak of "religion and its temporal pillar, the House of Austria."[50] Later that same year he urged that even the chalices should be sold, if necessary, to "rescue religion from its present dire straits, and to ensure that this Crown remains firmly established on the principle which it has always professed and ought to profess: to take as the first priority, above the defense of our own states and above every reason of state itself, the defense, preservation and increase of the Catholic religion."[51] The labor was Herculean, making demands on Spain, and most of all on Castile, which might prove its undoing. But if the count–duke's enemies pointed to the terrible costs, he in turn could point to the victories won in the course of Philip's reign under his own wise direction. The Hercules cycle was therefore accompanied in the Hall of Realms by the pictorial representation of twelve victories, a number which itself echoed the theme of the labors of Hercules. The King of Spain was glorified in these battle paintings in terms that also served to vindicate the regime of his minister.

The count–duke was always much preoccupied with the verdict of history. "There are many things which we neglect, not the least of which is the writing of history," he told the council of state in 1634.[52] But the history must be accurate, or in other words officially acceptable. Royal chroniclers existed to write just this kind of history, like Tomás Tamayo de Vargas, who had to produce an account of the recapture of Bahía in 1625 "beneath the eyes of our sovereign the king who ordered the expedition, the count–duke who organized it, and the soldiers who took part in it."[53] It was not easy to write impartial history with so many interested parties looking on.

To satisfy Olivares was the hardest task of all. Very conscious of the power of public opinion, and extremely sensitive to any aspersions against his own reputation, he lost no opportunity to enlist writers—and now painters—to defend his record against his detractors. Faced by what he regarded as a systematic campaign of vilification, he had no hesitations about mounting a counter-offensive which would set the record straight for contemporaries and posterity alike. By the late 1620s he had gathered around him a team of apologists, the three most important of whom were the Count of La Roca, the author of some unpublished "Fragments" on the count–duke's life, which he hesitated to "expose to the battery" of public criticism;[54] Francisco de Quevedo, who wielded the most vitriolic pen in Spain; and the court poet and playwright, Antonio de Mendoza.

The attacks on Olivares reached their first climax during the fiasco of the intervention in Mantua in 1629 with the anonymous manifesto of that summer which ascribed all Spain's misfortunes to his "mistaken policies."[55] It was impossible to ignore this attack any more than the clandestinely published discourses of the organizer of the opposition in the Cortes of Castile, the deputy for Granada, Mateo de Lisón y Biedma.[56] Under heavy fire from his enemies, the count–duke now turned to Quevedo and Mendoza for help. Although Quevedo's excoriating piece of polemic, *El Chitón de las Tarabillas*, entirely eclipses Mendoza's now forgotten essay in apologia, the similarity of their arguments suggests that they were under instructions to answer the same set of charges and that they may have been furnished with ideas from a common source. There is some evidence, at least for the *Chitón*, that this source was the count–duke's confessor, Hernando de Salazar.[57]

115. Antonio de Pereda, *Relief of Genoa* (Madrid, Prado)

116. Francisco de Zurbarán, *Defense of Cadiz* (Madrid, Prado)

Surveying the government's record during the course of the reign, both Quevedo and Mendoza made a point of emphasizing the inevitable fluctuations in the fortunes of war. If Charles V and Philip II had both suffered major defeats, how could Philip IV be expected to obtain an unbroken line of victories? Quevedo was quite prepared to admit the reverses—the loss of Brazil to the Dutch, the attack of the English fleet on Cadiz, the Dutch capture of Bois-le-Duc and Wesel. But it was necessary to set against these reverses the counter-balancing triumphs—the recapture of Bahía, the rout of the English invasion force, the Dutch surrender of Breda.[58] Mendoza argued on similar lines. The Monarchy, which was in desperate straits at the beginning of 1625, suddenly experienced a miraculous recovery: "at one and the same time Breda was captured in the Netherlands, Bahía was recovered in Brazil, the English fleet was reduced to impotence at Cadiz, Genoa was defended and its coastal region recovered, Savoy and the French put to shame, and the glorious banners of Spain and the king raised resplendent and victorious."[59]

Having won their place in the official mythology of the regime, these triumphs of 1625 could be usefully refurbished as arguments in its justification when the count–duke and his policies came under attack. Two of them provided themes for court plays written and performed within a few weeks of the arrival of the news in Madrid: Lope de Vega's *El Brasil restituido* and Calderón's *El sitio de Bredá*.[60] It was therefore natural that the victories of that *annus mirabilis* should figure prominently in any attempt to transfer the apologia of the regime from the printed page to the walls of the Hall of Realms. History-painting as much as history-writing was to be a device for projecting the triumphs of king and minister.

Five of the twelve victories commemorated in the Hall belonged to 1625: the surrender of Breda to Spínola (fig. 125); the expulsion of the Dutch from Brazil by an expeditionary force led by don Fadrique de Toledo (fig. 131); the salvation by the Marquis of Santa Cruz and his fleet of Spain's ally, the city of Genoa, when it was under siege by the Savoyards and the French (fig. 115); the rout of Lord Wimbledon's attack on Cadiz by don Fernando Girón (fig. 116); and a more distant success which neither Quevedo nor Mendoza mentioned—the expulsion of the Dutch from the island of Puerto Rico by its governor, don Juan de Haro (fig. 117).[61] Of the remaining seven paintings, two portrayed victories won before 1625: the capture by Ambrosio Spínola of Jülich (fig. 118) in the Lower Rhineland on February 4, 1622, after a six months' siege, and the victory of don Gonzalo de Córdoba at Fleurus (fig. 119) on August 29, 1622, over the German Protestant forces commanded by Christian of Brunswick and Ernst von Mansfeld—a victory which provided the theme for another of Lope de Vega's plays, *La nueva victoria de don Gonzalo de Córdoba*.[62]

The series also included one further success of the 1620s. On his way out to the Indies in 1629 to escort the returning silver fleet, don Fadrique de Toledo, the savior of Brazil, was under orders to call at the island of St Christopher (St Kitts), one of a number of smaller Caribbean islands where English and French adventurers had recently started to settle. He duly put the intruders to flight and destroyed their tobacco plantations; but since he left no garrison on the island the settlers were back long before Félix Castelo put brush to canvas to celebrate an all too ephemeral success (fig. 120).[63] But the permanency of victory hardly seems to have been a

117. Eugenio Cajés, *Recapture of Puerto Rico* (Madrid, Prado)

118. Jusepe Leonardo, *Surrender of Jülich* (Madrid, Prado)

criterion for inclusion in the series. The Dutch had re-established themselves in Brazil in 1630, five years before the paintings were unveiled.

The remaining triumphs all belonged to 1633, the year in which the decorative scheme of the Hall of Realms was devised. This suggests that Olivares was hoping to represent 1633 as a second *annus mirabilis*, perhaps to score an immediate political point. It may not be entirely fortuitous that the commissioning of the battle paintings appears to date from about the same moment as the circulation at court of a new opposition pamphlet which alleged that the count–duke's disastrous policies were to blame for the decline of Spain's military prestige.[64] Presumably on Olivares's instructions a six-page refutation was produced, answering the original thirteen charges point by point.[65] What better way to drive home the refutation than to depict in the Hall of Realms not only the great victories of the early years of the reign, but those being won at this very time?

The first news of a victory to reach the court during that autumn of 1633 was of a further success in the Caribbean, for which Olivares himself could take some of the credit. In January 1633 the war junta of the council of the Indies had drafted plans for recapturing and fortifying the Antillean island of St Martin, where a party of thirty Dutch were reported to have taken possession, with the intention of exploiting the island's salt flats. In March the count–duke himself drafted a memorandum on the subject, proposing that ten extra galleons with a complement of sixteen hundred infantrymen should be added to the Indies fleet under the command of the Marquis of Cadereita, with instructions to "throw any pirates they find into the sea."[66] The operation worked according to plan. Cadereita's fleet arrived off St Martin on June 24, 1633, and forced the surrender of the settlers after an eight-day siege. It left behind on the waterless island a small garrison which was to remain there for a miserable fourteen years. The letter dispatched from Puerto Rico by Cadereita on July 15 reporting his success was received in Madrid on September 9. No doubt it gave Olivares considerable satisfaction, not least because don Fadrique de Toledo had cast serious doubts at the meeting of the junta on the feasibility of capturing the fort constructed by the Dutch.

The count–duke, then, could legitimately look upon the capture of St Martin, commemorated in the painting (now lost) by Cajés, as very much his own success. He could claim, too, to be behind the other victories of 1633, which were won in Germany by the Duke of Feria (figs. 121–3). For years he had urged upon his colleagues a master plan to clear the Swedes and their allies from the banks of the Upper Rhine. This would relieve the pressure on Breisach, a vital Rhine bridgehead linking the corridors by which Spanish troops and supplies were moved between Italy, Germany and the Netherlands. It was Olivares's persistence which led to the creation of the army of Alsace, just as it was his haggling with the bankers which made it possible to send it on campaign.[67]

One of the disadvantages of contemporary history is that nearness of vision makes it almost impossible to assess the long-term significance even of great events. One or two of the triumphs represented in the Hall of Realms—notably the successes on the islands of St Christopher and St Martin—probably seemed minor affairs to most contemporaries. The Duke of Feria's victories, on the other hand, were widely celebrated, but their importance was ephemeral, and Breisach was lost a mere five

119. Vicente Carducho, *Battle of Fleurus* (Madrid, Prado)

120. Félix Castelo, *Recapture of St Christopher* (Madrid, Prado)

years later, on December 17, 1638. The Dutch had been back in Brazil from the beginning of 1630, and even Spínola's great victory proved to be a triumph without a future. The Spaniards were unable to capitalize on the surrender of Breda; a new and more honorable settlement in the Netherlands slipped through the count–duke's fingers, and the town itself was recaptured by the Dutch on October 10, 1637, little more than two years after the completion of the Hall of Realms.

The purpose of the battle paintings, however, was to magnify the power and glory of Philip IV, ably assisted by his loyal minister; and if some of the victories were not all that they were made to appear, the combined impact of the twelve can only have been to create the impression of a triumphant reign. But behind the obvious intention to defend and vindicate the record of the Olivares government to date, the paintings may also have been intended to convey a program of action and a message for the future. To achieve this they depended on their relation to the overall decorative scheme of which they formed a part.

Although Olivares's great design for the Union of Arms had run into difficulties when he presented it to the Cortes of the Crown of Aragon in 1626, it remained a project very close to his heart.[68] The theme that dominated his state paper of 1625 on the Union of Arms was the inability of the many scattered realms of a world-wide Monarchy to survive in isolation, and the absolute necessity for them to form a close association against the threat of enemy attack.

The day that Castile is a feudatory of Aragon and Aragon of Castile, Portugal of both and both of Portugal—and the same as regards the realms of Spain and those of Italy and

121. Vicente Carducho, *Relief of Constance* (Madrid, Prado)

122. Jusepe Leonardo, *Relief of Breisach* (Madrid, Prado)

123. Vicente Carducho, *Siege of Rheinfelden* (Madrid, Prado)

Flanders, with reciprocal correspondence—it is inevitable that the sterile separation of hearts that has hitherto divided them, should be dissolved in a close natural union by means of an association of arms. Then, when the Portuguese look at the Castilians, and the Castilians at the Portuguese, each will be looking at a friend and a feudatory, ready to shed its blood on the other's behalf.[69]

Olivares was nothing if not tenacious where his own projects were concerned. Once an idea was lodged in his mind it was almost impossible to dislodge it, and it would have been surprising if he had let slip the opportunity offered him by the Hall of Realms to preach the doctrine that was at the heart of his plans for the future of the Monarchy. Everyone by the early 1630s was conversant with his scheme for the Union of Arms, and those who entered the Hall of Realms are likely to have seen it expounded again, this time in visual terms. To look up at the ceiling with its twenty-four escutcheons was to become immediately aware both of the multiplicity of realms owing allegiance to the king, and of the way in which their destinies were inexorably intertwined. Placed at one end of the Hall, above the royal throne, were the kingdoms of Castile–León and Aragon, and facing them at the opposite end the kingdoms of Portugal and Navarre—the four major kingdoms of which Spain was composed. Flanking Castile and Aragon, in the first four ceiling vaults on either side, were eight other peninsular realms forming part of the Castilian crown. Then came a block of four representing the Aragonese inheritance, two on either side— Catalonia and Naples, Valencia and Sicily. There followed another block of four titles added to the Spanish crown by the Emperor Charles V—those of Milan and Austria, Flanders and Burgundy. Two territories were missing from each of these two blocks, Brabant and Sardinia, which were placed one on either side of Portugal and Navarre. Before them came the conquests of Castile in the Indies, the viceroyalties of Peru and Mexico, one on either side.

An effort—not entirely successful because of problems of balance—had clearly been made to group the realms in a logical ordering, but the cumulative effect was also to emphasize that "reciprocal correspondence" between them of which Olivares had written. If the spectator then lowered his eyes to the Hercules cycle, he became conscious of the unremitting labor involved in defending this multiplicity of realms from heresy, subversion and attack. Finally, in the battle scenes, which spanned the oceans from Flanders and Italy to Puerto Rico and Brazil, the king's commitment to the defense of his world-wide Monarchy was vividly apparent. Implicit in this commitment was Olivares's project for the Union of Arms. The king could not continue to defend all his territories, unless they willingly pooled their resources to meet the common peril.

One painting in particular served to make the point—the *Recapture of Bahía*. In making his proposal for the Union of Arms, Olivares had picked on the example of Bahía, whose inhabitants had mistakenly believed that their isolation would save them from enemy attack.[70] This unpreparedness had proved their undoing. Glossing this passage in his *Historical Fragments of the Life of Don Gaspar de Guzmán*, the Count of La Roca wrote that the citizens of Bahía despaired of salvation once they had been driven from their homes by the Dutch. But "to confound their despair, God gave them the mighty arm of Philip IV and the ardent solicitude of the Count of Olivares." Bahía showed that "such dangers can only be guarded against by means of union, with arms at the ready."[71] Fittingly, Bahía was finally saved by just such a union, in the form of a joint Castilian–Portuguese naval expedition. It was a spectacular symbol of the Union of Arms in action—of the willingness of one part of the Monarchy, in this instance Castile, to come to the assistance of another, the Brazilian dependency of the Crown of Portugal. In view of the identification of Olivares with the project for Union it was particularly appropriate that Maino's painting should be the only one in the series to include the figures of the king and his minister. The power of one and the "solicitude" of the other were jointly responsible for this glorious victory.

The presence of these two figures in Maino's *Recapture of Bahía* explains why this was always the painting among the battle scenes that contemporaries singled out for individual praise. But the king's presence was implicit in all the pictures, for it was his generals who were depicted in the moment of victory, and it was the glory of his majesty which filled the Hall of Realms. When he was in the Hall in person, he dominated it from the throne. In his absence he dominated it in the image of Velázquez, who represented him as the supreme commander on horseback, baton in hand. It was a baton handed to him by Philip III, and he in turn would one day pass it to Prince Baltasar Carlos, the scion of a victorious dynasty.

Batons, too, were held by his generals; and in all the paintings, with the partial exception of that by Maino, the emphasis falls on the generals, who figure prominently in the foreground, either alone or in the company of one or two colleagues and subordinate commanders, most of them now impossible to identify with any certainty. The focus on the generals is a departure from the traditional formula for depicting military victories, in which the ruler was always cast in the hero's role. This innovation may have been the result of the decision to concentrate attention on the events of two specific years, 1625 and 1633. Not even the King of Spain could be in two places at once. But more important, Philip was incorporated into the decor as commander-in-chief by means of his equestrian portrait. In context, the generals, for all their prominence, were clearly acting as the king's lieutenants—and also, it might be inferred, acting on the count–duke's instructions.

Although twelve victories are commemorated, only eight commanding generals appear, since Spínola is portrayed twice (at Jülich and Breda), don Fadrique de Toledo twice (Bahía and St Christopher), and the Duke of Feria three times (Constance, Rheinfelden and Breisach). For several of them it proved to be a posthumous portrayal. Don Fernando Girón, a veteran of the Flanders wars, was already old and gout-ridden when he volunteered to take charge of the defenses of Cadiz.[72] Zurbarán's painting appears to depict a scene from the contemporary account of the victory published by Luis de Gamboa y Eraso: "In spite of his poor health and advanced age, don Fernando Girón's stout heart made him go out each day on campaign. Seated on his chair he ran great risks, giving orders which were courageously carried out by that brave and experienced soldier Diego Ruiz, the deputy commander [*teniente de maestre de campo*]."[73] Is it Diego Ruiz who stands before him here?

The great Spínola was also dead. Sent to Italy in 1629 to relieve don Gonzalo Fernández de Córdoba, who had failed so miserably to capture Casale, he died on September 25, 1630, during the course of the siege. Don Gonzalo himself appears in

Carducho's painting as the victor of Fleurus, but his reputation was destroyed by the Mantuan débâcle. In spite of this he was offered, but declined, the command of the army of Alsace after the unexpected death in January 1633 of the Duke of Feria, the principal in Carducho's paintings of Rheinfelden and Constance, and in Leonardo's of Breisach.[74] He died on his estates in Aragon in January 1635, just around the time that the painting of his famous victory was being hung in the Hall of Realms.[75]

Not one of these generals ended his life on good terms with Olivares, but this is hardly surprising. At the best of times in the seventeenth century there was little chance of a harmonious relationship between a supreme minister who expected absolute compliance with his orders, and military commanders who expected the minister to keep them supplied with men, munitions and money. When the minister was Olivares, and the generals drawn for the most part from the ranks of the higher nobility, the prospects for a harmonious partnership were remote. Of all the supreme commanders here depicted, only the Marquis of Santa Cruz can be considered as personally close to Olivares, although the Marquis of Cadereita, who presumably figured as the principal in Cajés's *Recapture of St Martin*, was well enough regarded to be given the lucrative office of viceroy of Mexico in 1635.

Santa Cruz, the son of Philip II's famous admiral, had already seen many years of active service before he brought his galleys to the relief of Genoa in 1625. High in the count–duke's favor he was made a member of the council of state in 1629, succeeded Spínola as governor of Milan in 1630, and then, after a brief spell in Flanders, returned to Madrid in November 1632 to serve as chief majordomo of the queen. Pereda could therefore have painted him from life for his picture of the relief of Genoa—a painting for which the artist received his final payment on June 15, 1635—although he left Madrid again on May 13, 1634 to assume the command of the Mediterranean fleet.[76] After conducting some important naval operations against the French in the opening stages of the war, he was retired from active service in 1636, in his sixty-fifth year, and brought back to Madrid to serve as one of the count–duke's closest confidants in the council of state. He did not die until 1646.

While the supreme commanders at these victories had clearly earned their place in this hall of fame, there must have been some awkward problems of selection when it came to choosing the figures of secondary rank to be included in the paintings. Given the hostile relationship between Olivares and so many prominent figures in the court and the nobility, the depiction—and the exclusion—of so many of the living or recently dead can only have opened new wounds or reopened old ones. Presumably the honor of inclusion in the Hall outweighed the disadvantages of being included on the count–duke's terms. Yet the Duke of Sessa, whose name has been associated with the anonymous manifesto against Olivares in 1629,[77] may well have had divided feelings on seeing his late brother don Gonzalo de Córdoba, the victor of Fleurus, enshrined in Olivares's hall of fame. Olivares, for his part, can hardly have wished to give undue prominence to his rivals or enemies, but at the same time could not so brazenly falsify the record as to omit them from the victories which they had won for the king.

This problem posed itself in an acute form with the figure of don Fadrique de Toledo. The Toledo family, headed by the Duke of Alba, had always looked on Olivares as an arrogant upstart. Don Fadrique de Toledo and his elder brother, the

Marquis of Villafranca, both of them celebrated naval commanders, were proud members of a proud clan, who were inclined at the best of times to disregard orders of which they did not approve. Appointed captain–general of the Atlantic Ocean in 1618, don Fadrique had certainly earned his place in the national pantheon with his famous victories, including the recapture of Bahía in 1625 and the expulsion of the English and French from St Christopher in 1629. But successful commanders had reputations to preserve, and no one was more conscious of his reputation than Fadrique de Toledo. In October 1633, at about the time when the decoration of the Hall of Realms was being planned, he crossed swords with Olivares who wanted him to lead a return expedition to Brazil. Suspecting that he would be given insufficient ships and men, he made it clear that he was unwilling to accept the command, except on terms which Olivares could not possibly approve.[78] The dispute between the two men came to a head in a stormy interview in July 1634 when they bandied insults loud enough to be heard through closed doors. "Look, sir," said Olivares as don Fadrique pressed for further favors, "your entire fortune has been built on posts that His Majesty has given you." To which don Fadrique replied: "Sir, I beg to differ. And even if it were true, I did it by risking life and limb, unlike Your Excellency who by sitting in a chair makes more in a day than I do in a lifetime."[79] Not surprisingly, don Fadrique soon found himself in prison for disobeying royal orders. At once the entire house of Toledo rallied to the cause of their kinsman and made a collective protest by boycotting the fiestas at the Buen Retiro.[80] On November 12 the council of Castile found against don Fadrique, whose health was rapidly deteriorating in his castle prison; and in a savage sentence he was permanently banished from Castile, stripped of his offices and the income of his estates, and fined 10,000 ducats.[81] Olivares, who was endlessly plagued with the problem of aristocratic disobedience, had clearly decided to teach the grandees a lesson.

Don Fadrique died on December 10 in merciful unawareness of his disgrace, but the count–duke's rancor pursued him even beyond the grave. No funerary honors were allowed him, nor even a solemn requiem in the church of the Colegio Imperial; and it was only six months later, on the petition of his widow and his brother, that his sentence was annulled and his honors posthumously restored. The contrast between the splendor of his life and the squalor of his death was brilliantly captured by Quevedo, who was no longer quite the partisan of Olivares that he had been in earlier years. He began his sonnet to the *túmulo*, or catafalque, of don Fadrique de Toledo—that catafalque which was dismantled on royal orders as soon as it was built[82]—with a reference to "the baton that you used to see in his hand": a baton which commanded obedience from the trident of Neptune. "His orders, his arms, his men, brought ignominy to the Dutch and the Lutheran; and with his counsel and his right arm, the Hispanic monarch vanquished Fate." Struggling to find an appropriate epitaph to conclude his sonnet, Quevedo wrote and rewrote the last lines, until at last he hit on a version which contained an ambiguous but bitter reference to the circumstances of his death: "This was don Fadrique de Toledo, and today, undone in the cold shadows, he brings tears to our eyes, and fear to our lips."[83]

It was dangerous, as Quevedo knew all too well, to sing the praises of those who had incurred the anger of the favorite. But Olivares himself must have been in something of a dilemma. Presumably don Fadrique's death helped him to resolve it, although it was unfortunate that it had been arranged for the general to appear not once but twice in the battle paintings. There was an obvious irony in the fact that he was being posthumously honored in the Hall of Realms at the very moment when he was still clouded by the shadow of disgrace. But the count–duke may well have enjoyed a moment of exquisite triumph over the house of Toledo when Maino's *Recapture of Bahía* was finally exposed to the public view. For it would be hard to devise a neater way of indicating don Fadrique's exact status in the hall of fame than to show him at the moment of victory displaying to the vanquished Dutch a tapestry in which it is his enemy, the count–duke, who crowns the king with laurels.

Those who defied the favorite must be kept in their place. But the most intimate of his friends had also to be found a niche of his own. No one stood closer to the count–duke than his cousin the Marquis of Leganés, and yet he had not so far won any famous victory. There was, however, a possible way of introducing him. One of the architects of the victories in the Netherlands was Count Henry de Bergh, the Walloon noble and army commander who played a leading role at the sieges both of Jülich and Breda. But in the summer of 1632 de Bergh turned against Spain and fled to Liège, where he tried to rally his compatriots in revolt.[84] As a traitor who—as Olivares said—deserved to be torn to pieces,[85] de Bergh could not possibly be included in the paintings of Leonardo and Velázquez. Leganés had participated in the Jülich campaign, although his contribution had not been as important as that of de Bergh. But his presence was enough to justify inclusion, and Leonardo shows him splendidly on horseback at Spínola's right hand.

Leganés was at court in late 1633 and early 1634, when Leonardo was probably working on his painting, but he left Madrid on April 2, 1634 to succeed the Duke of Feria as commander of the army of Alsace and escort the cardinal infante on his journey to Flanders. It was in the course of this journey, on September 6, 1634, that the cardinal infante won his great victory at Nördlingen, and Leganés made a triumphal entry into Madrid as the homecoming hero on January 29, 1635.[86]

Nördlingen was such a famous victory that it would have seemed to deserve an immediate place in the Hall of Realms, and all the more so since it was won by the king's own brother. The fact that it was not included suggests that, by the time the news of the victory reached Madrid on September 30, 1634, the paintings and the general decorative scheme were so far advanced that it was inconvenient to make major last-minute changes. Moreover, unlike the other victories displayed in the Hall, Nördlingen was not a purely Spanish victory, and therefore did not fit exactly into a program designed to illustrate the massive power of a well-led and united Spanish Monarchy. Monanni makes these points in his letter describing the Hall of Realms: "When the commission was given, the victory of Nördlingen had not yet occurred, and it was won not by Spanish arms alone, but in collaboration with those of the emperor. All the same, it will be depicted in another large room, in honor of the cardinal infante."[87] This painting, a copy of Rubens's portrait of the *Cardinal Infante at Nördlingen* (fig. 124), was in fact placed in the anteroom of the Hall of Realms.[88] The representation of one further victory, the *Relief of Valenza del Po*, painted by Juan de la Corte, was installed in the masking room, and commemorated

124. Peter Paul Rubens,
Cardinal Infante at Nördlingen
(Madrid, Prado)

the triumph won in the autumn of 1635 by that veteran commander and
soldier–scholar don Carlos Coloma. The portrait of Coloma was said to have been
painted into the picture by Velázquez himself.[89]

The battle paintings had obviously been carefully planned. The choice of battles,
the depiction of the commanders and their subordinates, the relation of the paintings
to the overall decorative scheme—all bore witness to a general design. The same
careful planning was carried over into the internal organization of the paintings,
with only Maino's picture departing from a standard format, in which the generals
appeared in the foreground either conducting operations or at the moment of
victory, while the battles or sieges were shown in the middle ground, with distant
views to the horizon. This type of composition followed the time-honored method
of depicting clashes of arms, evolved during the fifteenth and sixteenth centuries.
Examples of this format abounded in paintings and prints, and the planners of the
decoration would only have to refer, for instance, to one of Heemskerck's
inventions for the Victories of Charles V (fig. 97), or to Giovanni Stradano's
comparable series of engravings of the Victories of the Medici, published in 1583.[90]
Looking closer to home, there would have been the multitude of battle scenes in the
royal collections.

125. Diego de Velázquez, *Surrender of Breda* (Madrid, Prado)

126. Peter Snayers, *Siege of Breda* (Madrid, Prado)

127. Jacques Callot, *Siege of Breda*, detail (Princeton, The Art Museum of Princeton University)

The use of this standardized format for the battle scenes in the Hall of Realms solved the problem of unifying the work of eight artists with disparate styles. But uniformity unavoidably fettered the imagination. As a result, most of the pictures can be described as competent rather than inspired. There were only two exceptions to the rule of conformity—Velázquez's *Surrender of Breda* and Maino's *Recapture of Bahía*, the first of which transcended the constraints of the format, the second of which brilliantly transformed it. These pictures, each in a different way, succeeded in capturing the spirit rather than the mere letter of the commission, and in so doing raised to a different plane the artistic significance of the Hall of Realms.

THE SURRENDER OF BREDA

In order to understand Velázquez's representation of the *Surrender of Breda* (fig. 125), it is necessary to look at the event as it transpired. The siege of Breda had been decided upon by Ambrosio Spínola, in the face of considerable scepticism among his own captains and in the court at Madrid.[91] The war in the Netherlands, resumed in 1621 after the twelve years' truce, had begun well with Spínola's capture of Jülich in 1622, but then, as so often happened in the past, threatened to bog down in the waterlogged fields of Flanders outside the walls of cities impregnable to assault. Spínola was well aware of the need for a new and spectacular success to restore the morale of his army, and selected Breda in Brabant as the objective of his 1624 campaign, in spite of the fact that it was famous for the strength of its fortifications.

The decision looked a foolhardy one, but there were good reasons, both strategic and psychological, for selecting Breda for attack. Situated in low-lying terrain at the junction of the rivers Mark and Aa, it was the gateway to Holland. Its capture would enable the Spaniards to interfere with Dutch river navigation along the borders of Holland and Zealand, and would deprive the Dutch of the base from which they made their incursions into Brabant. Breda also had a special symbolic significance as a patrimonial possession of the Dutch ruling family of Nassau. Its governor since 1601 had been Justin of Nassau, the illegitimate son of William the Silent and older half-brother of the Stadholders Maurice and Frederick Henry.[92]

The infanta wrote to Philip IV on September 12, 1624 to report that the siege had begun and that the perimeter being occupied by Spínola's besieging army was three and a half hours' travelling time in length.[93] Distinguished visitors came from all over Europe to watch the progress of the operations, which were conducted with great skill and technical ingenuity by both Spaniards and Dutch. Trenches were dug, complicated engineering schemes undertaken, and both sides attempted to turn the rivers to their own account. The Dutch, in the hope of relieving the city by water, set out to dam the river Mark and flood the countryside. Spínola responded with clever channelling operations by which he diverted the water back upon the city, and so frustrated the Dutch relief scheme. The results of these various diking and damming operations can be clearly seen in a later painting of the siege by Peter Snayers (fig. 126), and less clearly in Velázquez's picture, although the famous Black Dike across the artificially flooded Vucht polder is easily visible in the line across the waters above the head of Justin's horse.[94]

The siege continued through a cold winter, Spínola braving the elements with his men, and never relaxing his attention to details. The Dutch failed to relieve their weakened garrison, and by the end of May 1625 both sides, equally exhausted, were ready to negotiate a surrender on honorable terms. The articles of surrender were formally agreed on June 2. According to article 1, Justin of Nassau would be allowed to leave the city with his officers and the survivors of the garrison, "after the accustomed manner of war with their colors displayed, the drums beating, after the accustomed sound. . ." The surrendered city, too, was to be treated with remarkable clemency. Indeed some contemporaries thought Spínola too lenient, but, in the words of Gerrat Barry's English rendering of the account of the siege published by Hermannus Hugo in Latin in 1626:

Spínola, holding them to be more wise who are more gentle in cruelty, and that the fame of clemency, was to be preferred before the name of severity . . . made more account of the gaining of a little time, than of the no great spoils of all Breda . . . And truly he judged it more expedient to prefer the majesty and clemency of his king (whose person he bore in this place) than either his own glory, or desire of revenge.[95]

The defeated garrison, reduced to 3,500 men, marched out with colors flying on June 5, 1626. Don Carlos Coloma, one of the Spanish army commanders, noted the contrast between the vanquished, still well-turned out in spite of the rigors of the long siege, and the "misery and nakedness" of the victorious Spanish soldiers.[96] The scene of Justin's departure from the city is vividly described by Barry:

Spinola, attended upon with a notable troupe of nobilities, betwixt the inward circle of the city, and the trench, the conqueror himself beheld the beautiful pomp of his glorious triumph. He courteously saluted all the captains at their going forth, and first Nassauius the governor, venerable for his gray hairs, his wife and children, the son of Emanuel of

Portugal, and two bastards of Prince Maurice's and they again with constant composed countenances and voices, and with a modest inclining of the banners, saluted him. No ignominious voice of provoking one another was once heard, but smiled with favorable countenances.[97]

Velázquez's depiction of the surrender takes considerable liberties with the details but not with the spirit of the event, which it greatly magnifies.[98] The topography of the scene is the only undistorted part, the result of its having been depicted in numerous paintings and prints of the epoch.[99] The appearance of the Spanish troops has been significantly improved. Not only are they well-clothed and content, but their might is emphasized by the famous motif of the lances, more accurately called pikes, which has given the picture its popular name of *Las Lanzas*. But the representation of the ceremony of surrender is the biggest of all changes. A more or less faithful version of it appears in one of the most famous views of the siege of Breda, Jacques Callot's six-sheet engraving made for the Infanta Isabella after he had personally surveyed the terrain in July 1627. In the print (fig. 127), Spínola sits on horseback (just to the left of number 98), impassively watching the well-ordered withdrawal of the Dutch toward the north. Justin of Nassau and his family lead the procession in a coach. In his painting, Velázquez no more than hints at the marching files of Dutch troops, who are seen in the middle ground behind the orange, white and blue tricolor to the left of Justin's head. Instead he concentrates attention on the curiously benevolent and imaginary scene of surrender.

Justin, at the head of the Dutch column, has just come up the hill and dismounted his horse, which is held by a groom. He is accompanied by an armed escort of his soldiers, who are identified by the orange pennons on their pikes. On the right is a detachment of Spanish–Burgundian troops, their checkered banner, with its red St Andrew's cross, a graceful tribute to the memory of the infanta, who had used it as her standard. Nassau advances in Spínola's direction, inclining toward him as if about to bow or kneel, and starts to hand over the keys to the city. At that moment, Spínola places an arm on the Dutchman's shoulder.[100] These two understated actions—the aborted genuflection and the restraining countermovement—reveal the heart of Velázquez's conception. By drawing on a tradition of representations of surrender, and then turning it inside out, Velázquez manifested the underlying meaning of the event and thereby added new glory to the might of the King of Spain.

The ceremony of surrender could take many forms. But in art it was almost always represented as a pageant of triumph and humiliation, in which the victor was shown as standing or seated on a throne or horseback and accepting tribute from the kneeling and submissive vanquished general. One of the prints in Heemskerck's *Victories of Charles V* shows a typical surrender scene (fig. 128). Or, to take an example from France, the painting of the *Submission of Milan to Francis I* (fig. 129), attributed to Antoine Caron, repeats the formula in a particularly lucid way.[101] But in order to make the point unmistakably clear, there was a version of the traditional composition furnished right alongside the *Surrender of Breda*. In Jusepe Leonardo's *Surrender of Jülich* (fig. 118) the same commander, Ambrosio Spínola, leans down from his horse to accept the keys offered by the defeated general who, unaccompanied, kneels on the ground, his hat and baton placed at his side as further

128. After Martin van Heemskerck, *Surrender of John Frederick of Saxony to Charles V* (New York, Metropolitan Museum of Art)

129. Attributed to Antoine Caron, *Submission of Milan to Francis I in 1515* (Ottawa, National Gallery of Canada)

signs of submission. The comparison of this picture to the *Surrender of Breda* reveals the telling clues that Velázquez used to show the extraordinary nature of his conception.

First is the armed escort of Dutch troops. A defeated commander customarily would have met his conqueror unescorted.[102] The presence of the Dutch troops is a sign that the surrender of Breda is an exceptional event. More important, Spínola has dismounted and meets Nassau on equal footing, not as the triumphant victor (fig. 130). The significance of this gesture is underscored by one of the most unusual features of the picture, the prominence of the horse in the right foreground which is always noted but never explained. The horse in this setting is a sign of an extraordinary act of military courtesy precisely because Spínola is not mounted on its back. And so, too, are Nassau's standing position and the hat he holds in his hand. Justin has come forward to perform the customary act of submission. He starts to kneel; hence the slanting posture of his body. But Spínola dismounts and restrains his former adversary, treating him as an equal. In a flash, the surrender has been changed from an act of submission to an act of clemency and magnanimity.[103]

Velázquez's version of the surrender of Breda is grounded in interpretations of Spínola's generous terms that were circulated just after the news had been received in Madrid. As Barry mentions, Spínola was criticized in some quarters for his kind treatment of the Dutch. But in terms of the prevailing conduct of war, his attitude was not exceptional. Courtesy and magnanimity toward the defeated were expected of seventeenth-century generals, although the expectation all too often went unfulfilled. Three years after the *Surrender of Breda* was painted, the Portuguese Francisco Manuel de Melo published in Madrid his *Política Militar*, with a dedication to Olivares. After discussing the importance of preserving the life and honor of the vanquished, he writes that to treat the enemy with "urbanity" in victory is no less brave than to treat them with disdain in the course of the battle. The captain–general should therefore look carefully over the prisoners, and make sure that all persons of quality among them should receive the honors which were their due, in accordance with their degree of nobility and rank.

For there is no doubt that such men would feel more deeply their decline in fortune as the result of receiving insufficient esteem, than they feel the loss of their possessions. Therefore it is just that the man who has been instrumental in depriving them of the latter should preserve them in the former. This is to enhance valor and to magnify the happy circumstance of victory. Consequently any noble and brave actions attempted by the vanquished should be referred to the prince, and this will provide him with the occasion to display kindness rather than wrath, if this is what princes and monarchs ought truly to possess. And also because in this way the glory of the victory is increased.[104]

Spínola's action, therefore, conforms closely to the conceptual context of warfare in a seventeenth-century Europe from which medieval and Renaissance ideals of chivalry had not yet been expelled. These ideals were especially cherished in Spain and had been displayed in the most famous surrender in the history of Spain—the surrender of Granada to Ferdinand and Isabella in 1492. On that occasion the Moorish king Boabdil, in the words of a contemporary, "came out on horseback accompanied by many *caballeros*, with the keys in his hands; and he wanted to dismount to kiss the king's hand, and the king would not let him get off his horse, nor would he allow his hand to be kissed. And the Moorish king kissed his arm and gave him the keys, and said: 'Take, sir, the keys of your city. I, and all of us within it, are yours.'"[105] It is no wonder that the chivalrous aspects of the surrender of Breda were selected for special emphasis at court.

Within five months of the arrival of the news from Flanders, which happened on June 15, 1625, a play by Calderón entitled *El sitio de Bredá* was performed at court under the count–duke's auspices. The surrender scene as represented by Calderón shows the Dutch soldiers and a few women leaving the city while the Spanish soldiers enter by the same gate; and, as they enter, Justin of Nassau comes out with a salver containing keys, protesting that it is not through fear that he has surrendered the fortress, but only as a consequence of the fortunes of war. Spínola, taking the keys, replies: "Justin, I receive them in full awareness of your valor; for the valor of the defeated confers fame upon the victor."[106] In building the scene around the delivery of the keys, Calderón was merely following a well-established formula for picturing a surrender scene. If he had not read an account of the surrender of Granada, then he would have seen a representation of one that resembled those illustrated here. More important are the words spoken by Spínola, which capitalize on the chivalrous implications of the surrender. These same sentiments were taken by Velázquez as the focal point of his conception of the momentous occasion.[107]

The core of the picture is of course the encounter between Spínola and Nassau. The Dutchman offers the key to his conqueror who, rather than accepting it, lays a conciliatory hand on his enemy's shoulder. Spínola's face fairly radiates the benevolence of clemency. Like Calderón, Velázquez interpreted the surrender as a triumph of the spirit as well as a triumph of arms. At the same time, he imparted an uncanny sense of verisimilitude to the picture that stands out all the more when compared to the ritualized compositions of the other battle scenes. Velázquez saw the scene as a drama, but as a drama shorn of theatricality, which he then arrested at a

---

130. Detail, Diego de Velázquez, *Surrender of Breda* (Madrid, Prado)

182

random moment before the participants could freeze in histrionic poses. For the onlookers, the ceremony seems to be one of those important but fleeting moments of history that come and go before they can take it in. A few of the soldiers turn toward the two main figures, but most of them seem to be caught by inner or outer distractions. Three or four faces look toward us while others look away completely from the surrender. A few men appear as if lost in thought. To emphasize the flow of life that eddies around Justin and Spínola, Velázquez, with a remarkable stroke of daring, gave great prominence to the hindquarters of Spínola's horse, a device so much in keeping with the apparently casual nature of the composition that its symbolic significance has gone unnoticed. The sum of these small but telling observations is to transform not only the military ritual, but also the whole dreary history of surrender scenes in art. In this way, Velázquez brought the scene to life and made it unforgettable. And by injecting convincing humanity and feeling into Spínola's *beau geste*, he ensured that the message of the picture would not be missed. Victories of arms made a king powerful; clemency and magnanimity made him great. This same idea pervades the other great battle picture in the Hall of Realms, Maino's *Recapture of Bahía*.

THE RECAPTURE OF BAHÍA

The *Recapture of Bahía* (fig. 131) is a picture of stunning originality.[108] Alone among the battle pieces in the Hall of Realms, it gives the victorious generals and the glories of war second place. The foreground is occupied by a touching scene of mercy, as a woman cleans the wounds of a fallen combatant. Maino's concern for the horrors of war is exceptional in battle pictures of the epoch, where death and suffering were subsumed under power and glory. No less unusual is the episode depicted in the near distance. Standing on a platform, don Fadrique de Toledo points to a tapestry with images of the king and the count–duke surrounded by several allegorical figures. At don Fadrique's feet kneels a group of Dutchmen, who raise their hands as if to implore mercy or offer thanksgiving. This unconventional composition, like that of Velázquez's *Surrender of Breda*, seems to have more to say than the other ten battle pictures, although it speaks in a recondite language of emblem and allegory that needs to be decoded.

Accounts of the event itself were abundant, for Bahía was a famous victory.[109] There were visual representations, too, like the engraving done by Alardo de Popma, to illustrate a broadsheet description of the engagement that was on sale in Madrid in 1625; and there was at least one large-scale canvas (fig. 132), which presents a panoramic view of the Bay of All Saints, and shows in careful detail the major points of military reference.[110]

Maino, however, was apparently not interested in this kind of exact topographical and military detail. Nor, at first sight, did the actual events of the loss and subsequent recovery of Bahía offer much help to Maino for the distinctive work he obviously had in mind. In the early 1620s the newly-founded Dutch West India Company prepared a grand design for occupying Bahía and Pernambuco in Portuguese Brazil, while also dispatching subsidiary expeditions to capture the principal Portuguese slave markets in West Africa. The slaves would work the sugar

131. Juan Bautista Maino, *Recapture of Bahía* (Madrid, Prado)

plantations which the Dutch hoped to seize in Brazil.[111] The opening stages of the
design worked according to plan. The arrival of the West India Company's invasion
force in the Bay of All Saints in May 1624 took the Portuguese inhabitants of the city
of Salvador de Bahía by surprise. Panic-stricken they fled into the surrounding
countryside.

The news of the Dutch occupation reached Madrid in July, and the count–duke's
concern at the loss of this lucrative possession of the Portuguese Crown was reflected
in the urgent orders given for the preparation of two fleets, one in Cadiz and the
other in Lisbon. The combined Spanish and Portuguese fleets, consisting of fifty-
two ships and carrying some twelve thousand men, set sail from the Cape Verde
islands under the command of don Fadrique de Toledo on February 11, 1625. They
reached the Bay of All Saints in Brazil on March 29, and began to disembark on
April 1. For the next four weeks the expeditionary force besieged the Dutch-held
city of Salvador, without provoking much reaction from the garrison, apart from

one major sortie in which the Spaniards and Portuguese suffered some notable casualties. The garrison finally surrendered at the end of the month, on terms which one of the participants, Juan de Valencia y Guzmán, describes as the best achieved by a Spanish besieging force in many years.[112] The Spaniards and Portuguese entered the city on May 1, the day of St Philip and St James; and, in spite of the harshness of the terms, don Fadrique treated the defeated garrison with a courtesy and moderation which made them sing his praises when they finally arrived in their native Holland.

Don Fadrique set sail for home on August 1 leaving a garrison in Bahía, but the first news of the victory reached Madrid early in July. Although the returning fleet, buffeted by storms, was not able to cast anchor in the bay of Málaga until October 24, Lope de Vega's play *El Brasil restituido* is dated the 23rd, and was clearly written on the basis of the reports that had arrived ahead of the main body of the fleet. Approved for presentation six days later and especially recommended for the exemplary lessons that it could teach to the youth of Madrid, it was performed at court on November 6.[113] It is this play which gave Maino the inspiration for the treatment of his theme.

The climax of the play comes when the garrison presents its initial terms for surrender, which don Fadrique tears up with contempt. He had, he said, been sent to punish them for their insolence and not to extend to them a mercy which they did not deserve.[114] "But," he continued, in Lope de Vega's words, "because I know the true character of that divine monarch, who, while a severe judge, also knows how to be a pious father conscious of his power, I wish to speak to him from here, for I have his portrait in my tent. On your knees while I talk to him." Don Fadrique then unveils the portrait of the king and addresses him as follows: "Great Philip, these people ask pardon for their sins. Does Your Majesty wish that on this occasion we

132. Anonymous seventeenth-century artist, *Recapture of Bahía* (Seville, private collection)

186

133. Detail, Juan Bautista Maino, *Recapture of Bahía* (Madrid, Prado)

should pardon them?" The portrait obligingly appears to signify its assent, and don Fadrique is able to tell the garrison that they will be given the necessary ships to return home to Europe.

If this long-distance communication between don Fadrique and the king represents an ingenious flight of the poetic imagination, the inspiration of having the Dutch kneel before the portrait may in fact derive from an actual episode. Valencia y Guzmán reports that on June 5 a procession through the streets of Bahía was organized in honor of the Holy Sacrament. As it passed, they "got down on their knees like us, although we do not know whether this was an act of devotion, or because they were afraid we would treat them badly if they did not offer due reverence to Our Lord."[115] Whatever the source of Lope's inspiration, the image of the Dutch kneeling before a portrait of the king provided Maino with the drama that he had forfeited in eschewing a conventional battle scene.

Maino's debt to Lope, however, does not end here; two other elements in the picture may be traced to *El Brasil restituido*. In the foreground lies the wounded soldier (fig. 133), presumably one of a number of nobles in the expeditionary force

187

who were killed or wounded when the garrison made its sortie. Lope names some of them in the course of the play: don Diego de Guzmán, wounded in the right thigh, and—"oh muses, be sorrowful!"—don Diego Ramírez, struck by a bullet in the chest.[116] The woman who tends his wounds is one of a group which may well represent the Portuguese inhabitants of Bahía, driven out by the Dutch in 1624, and returning to the city as it is recovered for the king. In Lope's play an escaped soldier says how he saw in "these deserted fields old men, children and women, a pitiful sight."[117] It would have been logical for Maino to include these returning refugees as a counterpoint to the defeated and departing Dutch who had deprived them of their homes. It would also have been appropriate to show a Portuguese woman tending a Castilian who had shed his blood on her behalf, as a further symbol of that union of hearts which Olivares was striving to encourage through his Union of Arms. But the Dominican Maino has transformed the scene by subtly casting it in Christianized terms. The group with the wounded soldier resembles standard representations in seventeenth-century paintings of St Irene tending the wounds of the martyred St Sebastian. The woman with three children at the left evokes the traditional representation of Charity.[118] And the woman carrying a bundle of clothes brings to mind one of the seven acts of mercy, clothing the naked.

Also in the course of the play Apollo appears on stage, wearing a laurel crown, and at the very end don Fadrique himself is crowned with laurels by the figure of Brazil. Given the recent disobedience and disgrace of don Fadrique there was no question of showing him as depicted by Lope, with a wreath of laurels on his brows. But Apollo was frequently equated with Philip in court festivities, and it was perfectly natural to portray the glory of the king in this setting, rather than that of don Fadrique. In the painting, however, he receives the honor not—as does don Fadrique in the play—from an allegorical figure of Brazil, but from the count–duke, who makes his one and only appearance in the Hall of Realms at this critical moment. Olivares timed his entrance perfectly, for the scene on the tapestry is like a tableau pointing to the significance of the decorative scheme (fig. 134).

The major theme is naturally the king as conqueror, and especially as conqueror of discord, repeating an idea contained in Zurbarán's *Hercules* pictures. Philip is shown as a soldier, dressed in armor, wearing the sash of command and holding a stick. At his right, Minerva, goddess of war, hands Philip the palm of victory and helps to place the crown of laurels on his brow.[119] The crown of laurels was a commonly used symbol of virtue, the quality also denoted by Hercules, which above all others characterized the prince.[120] At the king's feet lie in defeat the personifications of his enemies—Heresy, holding a broken cross in its hands and mouth; Discord, the *"furia infernale"* with snakes in its hair; and Treachery, or Fraud, a two-faced creature, with left and right hands reversed, who offers peace and then stabs in the back.[121]

Philip's triumph over Heresy, Discord and Treachery, better known in those days as the Dutch, the English and the French, was made possible through divine assistance—*sed dextera tua*, as the quotation from Psalm 43 (Vulgate) says on the

<hr>

134. Detail, Juan Bautista Maino, *Recapture of Bahía* (Madrid, Prado)

panel held by two putti.[122] If God was on Philip's side, so too was the count–duke. In a motif of considerable audacity, Olivares had himself depicted with Minerva as the joint author of Philip's victories. With one hand he lays the laurel wreath on the king's brow, and with the other he holds a sword and the olive branch, a symbol both of the olive groves of his title and of reconciliation.[123] Olivares offered victory to his sovereign and clemency to his defeated enemies. The scene thus becomes an emblematic synopsis of a leading idea of the Hall of Realms. A powerful and virtuous king defeats his enemies; a merciful king offers them peace and reconciliation. And behind it all, in this perfect representation of the concept of rule by favorite, or *valimiento*, is the figure of the minister.

The sword and the olive branch, victory and clemency—these are the themes that unite the plays by Calderón and Lope and the paintings by Velázquez and Maino, and link them to Olivares. In all four works, the victorious generals offer their enemies the forgiveness of a wise, just king. The concept of magnanimity in victory represented in the plays and battle pieces may be traced back to Olivares, who explicitly interpreted the two victories in this light. In July 1625, he wrote two letters to the Count of Gondomar which include observations on Bahía and Breda. On July 3, when the euphoria about the capitulation of Breda was still in the air, he reported to Gondomar that Fadrique de Toledo's forces had landed at Bahía, and wrote as a postscript in his own hand: "Courage, *señor mío*, God is Spanish and fights for our nation these days."[124] Five days later, when the news of don Fadrique's capture of Bahía had arrived, he wrote again of the rejoicings caused by the news of the recent victories.

The victory in Brazil is not less good than that of Breda. It was recaptured on the day of St Philip and St James, and although at the beginning much blood was shed and we had some distinguished casualties, the enemy finally yielded to the clemency of the general, and so saved their lives and enhanced our reputation; for to pardon those who surrender confers glory on His Majesty's arms, and—God willing—clemency will work more to our advantage than the sword. These are events in which God is visibly helping His cause, and as His Majesty's aims are directed solely to its defense, with no other human pretension, and as we his ministers strive to imitate him in everything that concerns us, we can expect that everywhere He will favor this Monarchy and cause its fortunes to prosper. . .[125]

By 1633, it was clear to many that God had not favored the Monarchy nor caused its fortunes to prosper, and Olivares, as he planned the decoration of the Hall of Realms, was as much concerned with the defense of his regime as he was with the defense of religion. Opposition to his policies from within the court was becoming increasingly evident, and the count–duke wanted to trample it under his feet, as with Discord in the *Recapture of Bahía*. The paintings in the room were conceived in part to help accomplish this purpose. In framing his defense of the regime in pictorial form, Olivares turned for assistance to two members of his circle. Francisco de Rioja and Diego de Velázquez were to play roles in the pictorial defense of the count–duke comparable to those of Quevedo and Mendoza in the written defense of 1629.

The intervention of Rioja and Velázquez can only be supposed, but the grounds for supposition are firm. Rioja was one of Olivares's closest friends and had the learning, intellect and experience required to formulate the sort of program of ideas expressed in the Hall of Realms. He even knew one of its prototypes at first hand. In

1598, when he was fifteen, Rioja saw the funeral monument for Philip II in his native Seville and had made the acquaintance of the author of the program, the Canon Pacheco, whom he greatly admired.[126] The influence of the canon on Rioja is suggested by the fact that the poet became an iconographical advisor in his own right while still living in Seville, often helping the painter Pacheco to plan his religious compositions.[127] On top of this circumstantial evidence is one concrete fact. Rioja is documented as having devised the program of a decorative project at the Retiro. On April 18, 1635, the painter Jusepe Leonardo signed a contract to execute a series of pictures for a ground floor room of the hermitage of San Jerónimo, agreeing to paint them in accordance with the instructions and to the satisfaction of Rioja.[128] From this document it may be inferred that Rioja was active at the site as an overseer of artistic programs. The weight of these circumstances makes it plausible to suppose that Rioja was responsible for turning Olivares's ideas into instructions for the painters of the Hall of Realms to follow.

Velázquez's participation in a supervisory capacity also seems likely. Someone was needed to plan the installation, to determine the picture sizes and to co-ordinate the work of the other artists. Velázquez would have been the obvious candidate because of his position at court and his long association with Olivares and Rioja. That he had a penchant for this kind of work was demonstrated later in his career by his participation as overseer in the redecoration of certain state rooms in the Alcázar.[129] With the poet and painter at his side, and no doubt in close consultation with the king, Olivares conceived this remarkable monument of political propaganda. By skilfully blending elements of tradition with the needs and deeds of the moment, Olivares and his team found a way to broadcast the achievements of ten years of rule in pictorial form. But was anyone listening to the message and, if so, what did they hear?

The effect of political propaganda depends to a large extent on the established positions of the audience. Supporters of a government applaud its self-proclaimed successes even as its opponents reject them. The opinion of the largest group of people, the uncommitted and the indifferent, waxes and wanes as events unfold. While it is to be assumed that the populace was excluded from the Hall of Realms, it seems likely that those who saw it represented a cross-section of what passed for public opinion, for anyone of sufficient standing could presumably gain entry if he wished. But, more than anything else, the Hall was one of the great centers of reunion for the court. Although it was used on occasions for state functions, it seems to have been primarily reserved for festivities and entertainments to which members of the court came both to see and to be seen.

In the Olivares years, a major element in the "court" was constituted by those nobles, government officials and literary and artistic personalities who were closely identified with the favorite and depended on his patronage. Their reaction to the decoration was predictable and is recorded in the laudatory poems published by Diego de Covarrubias. But the court also included many figures, ranging from grandees to palace functionaries like Matías de Novoa, who actively disliked Olivares and constituted a covert opposition. If the first group hardly required the message conveyed by the paintings, the second group was likely to reject it out of hand.

191

Yet there must also have been a considerable body of people, either in the court or on its fringes, who were hostile to the government or at best lukewarm, but who still believed—or wanted to believe—in the high destiny of Spain. For such people the Hall, with its reminder not only of recent but of continuing glories, could offer reassurance that God was still on the side of the king, and His promise would not fail. Between the enemies and supporters of the regime, then, should be set an intermediate body of public opinion, still amenable to persuasion by court propaganda if it was skilfully deployed. If the count–duke's propaganda exercises were primarily directed at this influential sector, which extended beyond the court to the provincial capitals, then the high patriotic note struck by the Hall of Realms was well calculated to fall on receptive ears. And the impending war with France, which would become a reality within months of the inauguration of the Hall, would make these ears all the more receptive.

In addition to the public, there was an audience of one person for whom the Hall of Realms was especially significant: the prince and heir Baltasar Carlos, whose image as future king was present in the room. Inherent in the Hall of Princely Virtue were the concepts of commemoration and instruction. The historical events and moral qualities that had made the ruling line great also added up to a lesson in kingship for future generations. The royal chronicler José Pellicer poetically made the point in his sonnet dedicated to the Hall: an "eloquent lesson that is taught without words has been built for you, Baltasar, born to the purple."[130]

Finally, there were the king and the count–duke, because no one pays closer attention to political propaganda than its perpetrators, especially when the propaganda is cast into monumental form by worthy artists. For, in the end, the Hall of Princely Virtue is an exercise in self-congratulation. Engravings, woodcuts and broadsides, which were cheap to produce and reproduce, carried the message of power and glory to the great public. Tapestries, frescoes and large paintings, objects of great intrinsic and extrinsic value, were put on the palace walls, speaking their reassuring message in grandiloquent terms for the enjoyment of those in power. As an essay in political egotism, the Hall of Realms was thoroughly satisfying. In an age when war was the most effective instrument of foreign policy, twelve victories of arms were portrayed, each carefully chosen to advance the claims of the Habsburg kings of Spain as universal defenders of the faith and promoters of peace with justice. The paintings had also been chosen to show friends and enemies of the regime alike that the affairs of the Monarchy were in capable hands. The king had at his side a minister to assist him with the Herculean tasks of government, a minister in whom he had every confidence and whom he was determined to retain.

The reality was rather different: the King of Spain ruled his realms and Olivares ruled the king. The Hall of Realms beautifully reflected a central paradox of these years of European history—that, while the power of kings was being exalted as never before by all the rhetorical devices of literature and art, it was simultaneously being consigned to the hands of other men. The age of the prince had given way to the age of the favorite; and it was entirely appropriate that this splendid room, designed to enhance the glory of the monarch, should so triumphantly express the glory of the minister.

VII

The King Takes his Pleasure

RESIDENCE AND SHOWPIECE

For all the solemnity of the Hall of Realms when solemnity was required, it belonged to a complex of palace and gardens primarily designed to delight the senses. With its superb picture collection, its magnificent furnishings, its lakes and gardens, the Retiro formed an ideal setting for the festivities and recreations of a royal aesthete who found in the patronage of the arts a royal duty that was greatly to his taste. Although it has been said that another royal aesthete, Charles I of England, reigned over "the most brilliant and civilized court in Europe" during the 1630s,[1] it is difficult to judge this claim when the rival court of Philip IV is, by comparison, so poorly documented. Few foreign visitors to Madrid during this decade recorded their impressions of court pageantry; contemporary Spanish descriptions are sparse and undistinguished; there was no school of engravers at court to preserve the sights for posterity; and it is almost impossible to recapture the magic of masques once the stage is darkened and the last notes of the music have faded away. Something of the character of the masques staged by Inigo Jones at the court of Charles I can still be gleaned from his drawings; but no sketches survive from the hand of Cosimo Lotti, no less a master of mechanical marvels than Jones, and only the happy discovery of eleven drawings (see below figs. 138–47) by Lotti's successor, Baccio del Bianco, allows us to catch a fleeting glimpse of the lost world of Spanish court spectacle.

The Retiro was at once a part-time royal residence, a monument to royal taste, and an arena for the encouragement and display of those arts of peace which would give new glory to the name of *Felipe el Grande*. It differed from the king's other part-time residences in that it was kept fully furnished—a point noted by Robert Bargrave when he described that other pleasure palace, Aranjuez, in 1655: "It is altogether unfurnished, as indeed are most of the king's palaces, except that in Madrid and the Retiro; his custom being to send his harbingers before him to the other palaces, with only such necessaries as will barely suffice his short stay."[2] While there may have been a desire to surround the king with familiar objects when he was away from the Alcázar, there were also good economic reasons for furnishing the country residences with necessary items only in the event of a royal visit. Paintings and furniture were unlikely to fare well in deserted palaces, and the costs of upkeep were high.

The Retiro, however, was in a category of its own among the royal residences. It would have been absurd to go to the trouble and expense of moving the contents of the Alcázar from one side of Madrid to the other every time the king wanted a change of air. Admittedly the initial cost of furnishing the Retiro was heavy, even taking into account the large number of gifts. But it was possible to think of this outlay as a good long-term investment. The Retiro gave the king all the convenience of a country retreat without the inconvenience of having to move from Madrid, and this represented a substantial saving both in travelling costs and wages. It was customary for servants of the royal household to draw double rations when the court moved to one of the country houses, but this practice did not apply to the Retiro, which was regarded as being within the municipal boundaries of Madrid. In the 1650s, however, the palace staff claimed that the Retiro was in fact situated outside the town walls, and that they were therefore entitled to receive the higher rates of remuneration paid in the country houses. A possible response would have been to bring the Retiro technically within the town boundaries by closing its outer gates and opening a gate into the town wall of Madrid at the point where it did double duty by serving also as the wall of the palace complex. But Philip regarded this as a deceit beneath his dignity, and his servants were awarded their double rations.[3]

The figures given by Núñez de Castro in *Sólo Madrid es corte* (1675) suggest that it was still considerably cheaper, even with double rations, for the court to take up residence in the Retiro than to move further afield. By that date a month at the Retiro, covering living expenses and servants' portions, cost 80,000 ducats. The comparative figures for transport costs and living expenses at the authentic country residences were as follows:

Escorial (20 days)	120,000 ducats
Pardo (26 days)	150,000 ducats
Aranjuez (1 month)	170,000 ducats

Moving the animate and inanimate contents of the court around the Castilian countryside was clearly an expensive undertaking.[4]

There were other arguments, too, for maintaining a fully furnished pleasure palace in Madrid. It could be used to entertain and impress foreign visitors, and also, if necessary, to house them. "Is it right," asked Manuel de Gallegos in one of his Retiro poems, "that the King of Spain should have no home to offer a foreign prince?"[5] When the Prince of Wales came to Madrid in 1623, apartments had to be found for him in the Alcázar. It would obviously be an advantage to have a well-appointed second palace in the capital to provide lodging and hospitality for such a distinguished guest, and this certainly seems to have been an important consideration in the early stages of the building of the Retiro. When the king insisted in December 1632 on the urgent need to complete the rooms being built at San Jerónimo for the accommodation of important visitors,[6] he may well have had a specific visitor in mind—perhaps his cousin, Princess Margaret of Savoy, Dowager Duchess of Mantua, whose position at the Mantuan court became impossible once the French-supported Duke of Nevers had succeeded to the dukedom.[7]

Yet when Princess Margaret finally arrived in Madrid on November 4, 1634, on her way to take up the viceroyalty of Portugal, she was not housed in the Retiro but in the Casa del Tesoro, adjoining the Alcázar. The Retiro was used only for the initial reception, with the king and the count–duke waiting for her at the hermitage of San Juan, from where they accompanied her to the Alcázar to be received by the

135. Diego de Velázquez, *Francesco d'Este, Duke of Modena* (Modena, Galleria Estense)

queen.[8] Similarly the Casa del Tesoro was used to accommodate the Princess of Carignano, the wife of Prince Thomas of Savoy, who arrived in Madrid with her children in November 1636. Again the formal entry was made from the Retiro, with the king awaiting the princess at the hermitage of the Magdalena.[9] Another distinguished lady, the Duchess of Chevreuse, who had made a spectacular flight from France, made her entry into Madrid on December 5, 1637, watched by the king and queen from the Retiro, but she too was housed elsewhere in the capital.[10]

Although all three visitors were taken to see the sights of the Retiro, there seems to have been no question of using it for anything more than occasional entertainments. Indeed, only once in the 1630s did the Retiro house an important foreign guest; and even then, far from the palace being ready to receive him, much last-minute improvisation was needed. The occasion was the visit of Francesco d'Este, Duke of Modena, from September 23 to October 30, 1638 (fig. 135). For all the talk about the importance of being able to accommodate visitors in style, no visitor's suite had been built. Plans to house the duke in the king's apartments were abandoned when it was realized that the king might want to spend time at the Retiro while his guest was in residence, and finally the count–duke's apartments were taken over and redecorated for the occasion.[11] To house the duke's entourage, Villanueva, Carbonel, Antonio de Mendoza and Antonio Carnero all had to give up their rooms.

Don Carlos Baudoquín, comptroller of the household for the duke's visit, seems to have had a busy time importing furniture and hangings. Among other items, he had to hire twenty-two beds, at a total cost of some 200 ducats, sixteen chairs, six console tables, and a number of pictures—ten, for instance, from Cristóbal de Herrera, at ten *reales* (nearly a ducat) a picture for a month's hire, to be hung over the doors and windows in the rooms assigned to the duke's gentlemen.[12] To hire paintings for the decoration of a palace which already contained hundreds of pictures may seem a little excessive; but appearances counted for everything, especially when it came to entertaining a foreign prince. Blank spaces on the walls would be both a dishonor to the host and a discourtesy to the guest. The lavish attentions, at least on this occasion, had the desired effect. The duke and his entourage were overwhelmed by the Retiro—"this most marvellous palace, the most beautiful in Europe for its buildings and its pictures . . . Of immense size, as is to be imagined of so great a king and queen . . . So many rooms that one gets lost . . . A most beautiful garden, and the site itself larger than a big city."[13]

Had these been times of peace, there might have been more distinguished foreign visitors in Madrid, and the Retiro have been put to greater use. As it was, it served almost exclusively as a residence for the king and the court, but a residence of a very temporary character. It was, after all, a second palace, complementing but not replacing the Alcázar, and it was as a second palace that it had to be justified. Was it not essential, inquired the loyal Manuel de Gallegos in his limping verses, that Philip should have in Madrid "this noble edifice, this jewel, this sphere, where he can forget Aranjuez, and avoid going to the Pardo? . . . And if—which God forbid—the palace should catch fire, or if violent sickness should sweep down on contagious wings, is it not right that the first king in the world should have a second palace?"[14] The infant heir to the throne, Baltasar Carlos, obviously had to be carefully shielded in the event of the outbreak of infectious disease. Yet ironically, when sickness and fire struck, they struck in the Retiro. In July 1637 the king was forced to return prematurely to the Alcázar after contracting a fever at the Retiro, which was attributed to the excessive heat in that part of Madrid.[15] The great fire of February 20, 1640, which damaged his apartments at the Retiro, also drove him back to the palace.

While there is no exact record of the total amount of time that the king and the court spent in residence at the Retiro between its inauguration in December 1633 and the fall of Olivares in January 1643, the surviving records of visits suggest that it was strictly limited. The king and queen went into residence for the first time early in December 1633 when the new palace was formally inaugurated. It was apparently intended that the festivities should extend into the Christmas season, but the news of the death in Brussels of the Infanta Isabella, which reached Madrid on December 18, brought them to an abrupt halt, and the members of the royal family remained in the Alcázar for the period of mourning.[16] In 1634 they celebrated the fiestas of St John's day (June 24) at the Retiro, and remained in residence for two weeks.[17] The following year, which saw the outbreak of war with France, they went there on Ascension day, May 17, and stayed for a month—their longest stay to date.[18] It was not the ideal moment for the king to be seen enjoying himself, and a satirical piece making the rounds early in June spoke mordantly of the King of France being on campaign, and the King of Spain in retreat (*en el Retiro*).[19] In response to the public mood the usual St John's day festivities were suspended, but Calderón's new play for the occasion, *El mayor encanto amor*, was put on a few weeks later, at the end of July.[20]

196

On May 5, 1636 the court returned to the Retiro for a period of two weeks, followed by another four days in June for the fiestas of St John.[21] In 1637, however, the routine was altered to allow for a special round of festivities. Lord Aston, the British ambassador, reported on February 25 that on the 7th "the king returned from the Pardo to this court, and hath ever since remained in the Buen Retiro, where there hath been some time in hand great preparations for fiestas of joy upon the election of the King of the Romans. On the 15th of this present, the entertainments begun, which the king honored with his own person in a large place levelled for that purpose before the Buen Retiro [the Prado Alto], and built about with uniform scaffolds of two stories high, the posts and divisions all beautified with paintings and gildings."[22] The king was back again on June 17 for the fiestas of St John.[23]

Philip's delight in his new palace was apparently not shared by his queen, partly perhaps because of its association with Olivares, whom she did not like. A Retiro season was planned for January 1638, but to humor the queen the court went to the Pardo instead.[24] It spent a month at the Retiro in the spring, however, returning to the Alcázar on May 19.[25] On June 12 it was back again—it was thought for a shorter season than usual because the queen was pregnant, but in fact the royal family was still there on July 5.[26] The Infanta Maria Teresa, whose marriage in 1659 to Louis XIV was to symbolize the reconciliation of France and Spain, was born on September 20.

Monanni wrote in a letter of February 12, 1639 that the king's favorite recreation was to get away to the country. That week he visited the count–duke's village of Loeches, which he had already honored with his presence in the preceding November during two days of hunting in the Guadalajara woods.[27] If the Retiro was not exactly the country, it was the nearest available substitute, and Philip's affection for it appears to have been growing. In 1638 he seems to have spent over fifty days there, and in 1639 rather more, moving in on February 15, and staying for Carnival and Lent, and then coming back again into residence from May 8 to around June 25.[28] In 1640 he moved to the Retiro on February 3, following his customary visit earlier that day to the hermitage of San Blas, just outside the Retiro precincts. But his plans to stay there through Lent were ruined by the great fire of February 20. While the repairs were under way, the royal family spent two weeks at Aranjuez. This was the first time that Baltasar Carlos had been there, and it must have been deeply mortifying for the count–duke when the twelve-year-old prince asked him why Aranjuez had been kept from him, and pronounced its most insignificant garden to be worth more than the entire Retiro. It was perhaps in a special effort to disprove him that the royal family was persuaded to spend an entire month at the Retiro from May 2. This year, too, the usual summer visit for the fiestas of St John was prolonged through most of July because of the exceptionally cool weather. The court, therefore, must have been in residence at the Retiro for around seventy days in the course of 1640.[29]

Yet 1640 was also apparently the last year of royal occupation of the Retiro during the Olivares period. By June 1640 Catalonia was in open revolt, and Portugal seized its independence in December, proclaiming the Duke of Braganza as king. The political and military situation of the Monarchy was by now so desperate that further court entertainments on any but the most modest scale were out of the question. There is no indication that the court moved to the Retiro in 1641 for the usual festivities of Carnival and St John, which anyhow would have been muted. But even now, as Olivares looked down into the abyss, he was in no mind to abandon the palace on which so much money and labor had been spent. In August 1641, in spite of all his other pressing occupations, he was still going there once or twice a day to oversee the construction of four new hermitages.[30] Scarce funds were no doubt more appropriately spent on hermitages at a time of national crisis than on plays and bullfights. But there was one final moment of splendor in January 1642 when the entire court went to the Retiro to congratulate the count–duke's recently legitimized bastard son on the occasion of his marriage.[31] It was a suitably bizarre swan song for the Retiro of Olivares. In April the king left for the Aragonese front to join his armies on campaign, realizing at last—although in pathetic circumstances—his thwarted ambition to be a soldier. The count–duke went with him, and Monanni noted that the Retiro would suffer greatly from his absence, "because those buildings and gardens require continuous attention."[32] Within the year Olivares had fallen, and orders had been given to melt down all the Retiro silver.[33] It was the end of the first, and greatest, age of that remarkable palace.

Over a period of nine years, then, the royal family seems to have resided in the Retiro for some forty days a year on average, although tending to spend more time there in the final years of the decade. During that period a pattern was apparently established, the court's visits coinciding with Carnival, the feast of the Ascension, and the festive season that began on June 23, the eve of St John. It looks as though the royal family never returned in the autumn, when the king preferred to go hunting in the woods outside Madrid. The climate, too, helped to dictate the Retiro seasons. Monanni reported that the queen had no great liking for the palace, which was too hot in summer and too cold in winter, leaving it suitable for residence only in the intermediate seasons, which could just as well be enjoyed elsewhere.[34]

But it was precisely to prevent their being enjoyed elsewhere that the Retiro had been built. The need was for a retreat close enough to the Alcázar to enable the king and the count–duke to keep in touch with affairs of state. During periods of residence at the Retiro the king would continue to hold his public audiences,[35] and meetings of the council of state would, if necessary, be held there, as on December 8, 1633, when the councillors were called into session to discuss the latest dispatches from Flanders.[36] Once at least the Retiro was also used for a major state occasion. Normally, when a new session of the Cortes of Castile was convened, the king opened it in the Alcázar. But in June 1638 he was at the Retiro; and, not wanting to delay the start of the Cortes, he presided over the opening ceremony on June 28 in the Hall of Realms. It must have been an impressive scene, with the battle paintings to remind the deputies of the high—if expensive—destiny of the Monarchy. But all the subsequent meetings of this Cortes were held, as usual, in the room in the Alcázar traditionally reserved for its sessions.[37]

While the Retiro was probably too close to the Alcázar to serve as the ideal pleasure resort for an extended season, its proximity did make it a suitable place for the occasional day's escape from the routine of business. For Olivares the Retiro was a perfect retreat, and sometimes he would go there simply for dinner, returning to the Alcázar in the evening to work.[38] A royal visit was inevitably much more elaborate, and amusements had to be provided. But one of the great virtues of the Retiro was that it lent itself to a whole variety of diversions with a different setting for each—and if, for any reason, the facilities appeared inadequate for some new form of entertainment, it was always possible to add to them.

FIESTAS AND SPECTACLES

The Retiro came into its own most of all during the great seasons of fiestas. These provided an excuse for a medley of entertainments, which displayed both the versatility of spectacle which the Retiro could provide, and the capacity of the Spanish Crown for apparently unlimited expenditure. The first great fiestas held there were those of December 1633, which celebrated both the inauguration of the palace and the birth during the summer of a son and heir to the king's sister, the Queen of Hungary.[39] The count–duke seems to have been eager to hold fiestas at the Retiro in the autumn of 1634 to celebrate the cardinal infante's victory at Nördlingen, but on this occasion he appears to have been overruled at the request of the queen, and they were held instead at the Alcázar.[40] But thereafter the Retiro became the accepted setting for major celebrations. The most spectacular of these were undoubtedly those held between February 15 and 24 of 1637, which were described in several contemporary accounts, both in prose and verse.[41]

There were various pretexts for these 1637 festivities. The summer of 1636 had been a triumphant season for Spanish arms, with the cardinal infante's forces advancing into France along the road to Paris and the armies of the Marquis of Leganés victorious in northern Italy. Originally it was intended to celebrate these victories simultaneously with the seventh birthday of Prince Baltasar Carlos on October 17 (fig. 136). The Madrid town council was asked to organize the celebrations, but it was impossible to have everything ready on time, and they had to be postponed. Olivares seems to have been using the festivities as an opportunity to induce the municipality to bear the cost of the extensive work involved in levelling the Prado Alto of San Jerónimo. This would give the Retiro an enormous new arena for staging tournaments and pageants—larger than the existing Large Court, and larger even than the Plaza Mayor of Madrid. Members of the Madrid town council understandably took exception to the idea; and then, when their resistance was overcome, Juan de Ramesdique, the engineer in charge, ran into trouble with the ground-levelling, which proved to be a long and laborious process. It was not until February 1637 that the new arena, 600 Castilian feet long, and 530 wide, was completed.[42]

But the delay had its compensations. The celebrations could now be treated in part as a tribute to the Princess of Carignano, who had arrived in Madrid in November. Better still, they could be used to commemorate a major event in the annals of the house of Habsburg—the election at Ratisbon on December 22, 1636 of Philip's brother-in-law, the King of Hungary, as King of the Romans, which virtually assured him the succession to the Imperial title. Olivares now brought to bear all his formidable powers of persuasion and command in order to have everything ready for a major round of festivities during the carnival season, from

February 15 to 24. Speculating later on the reasons for the unusual number of celebrations this season, Monanni thought that they reflected Olivares's anxiety to banish the king's congenital melancholy, and also to prove that he was just as capable of organizing recreations, tournaments and burlesques as he was of handling affairs of state. He also believed that they were intended to sustain morale, and to show the Princess of Carignano, who was French by birth, that Spain still had money to spare for other things than war.[43] Others seem to have shared this view, agreeing that one of the objects of the festivities was to impress international opinion: "so that our friend Cardinal Richelieu should know that there is still money to spend, and money to punish his king."[44]

This explanation is not implausible. Olivares had always shown himself alive to the importance of managing public opinion, and the Retiro festivities of 1637 take their place as another move in the propaganda campaign that he was waging against the French.[45] On this occasion at least he certainly managed things in style, and the facilities of the Retiro were never displayed to better advantage. Each day saw one or more different kinds of entertainments in different parts of the great Retiro complex, although, rather unexpectedly, they began outside the Retiro itself. The king chose to open the festivities on Sunday February 15 in an unprecedented manner by going to attire himself in a private house in the Carrera de San Jerónimo—that of the Genoese banker Carlos Strata, who had come to his financial rescue on so many occasions, and for whom he seems to have had a special liking.[46] Strata gave him a grand tour of his splendidly appointed mansion, and then entertained him to a lavish banquet. Anything which he admired—a bed, a glass cross, the tapestry hung in his rooms—was at once given him and duly dispatched to the Retiro. The king could well afford his gracious words on leaving: "Carlos, you have entertained and treated me royally. God preserve you."[47]

From Strata's house the king and the count–duke made their way to the Retiro by torchlight, accompanied by two hundred members of the nobility. A masquerade was to be held in the new arena of the Prado Alto at eight o'clock at night, to celebrate the election of the King of the Romans. The arena, illuminated by over six thousand torches and glazed lanterns, was surrounded by a two-tiered wooden structure divided into 488 loggias.[48] The woodwork was painted to make it look like silver, bronze, jasper and marble, and the arena was decorated with emblematic devices. Monanni picked out the king's device of the sun, with its inscription "I warm and shine" (*foveo, lustro*), and the count–duke's of the sunflower, inclining toward the sun.[49] Fifteen bands of horsemen, dressed in black and silver, then rode into the arena to the sound of music. The king made his grand entry, also in black and silver, and the horsemen divided into two groups, one headed by the king and the other by Olivares. At this point two triumphal cars were drawn into the arena by oxen disguised as rhinoceroses and came to a halt on either side of the queen's balcony. They were designed by Cosimo Lotti, who walked in front of his own magnificent creations, one of which represented the triumph of peace, the other the triumph of war. Once the cars had come to a stop, the tournament began. This was

136. Diego de Velázquez, *Riding Lesson of Baltasar Carlos* (Duke of Westminster)

followed by a dramatic colloquy between war and peace, written by Calderón, which explained the allegory of the two cars to the assembled company. There were songs and music, and the festivities ended at midnight with the king and some of his gentlemen tilting at the quintain. The evening was adjudged a spectacular success, although not all the seats, many of them for sale, were taken.[50] "Those that have curiously looked into the entertainments of former times," reported the English ambassador, "say that among the Romans they have not read of any greater ostentation. The charge hath certainly been very great, but hath cost the king nothing, who hath long used this town to defray all extraordinaries that are either for his honor or pleasure."[51] Monanni gives the total cost of the three hours entertainment as 70,000 ducats.[52]

On the following day, Monday February 16, the king, queen and prince were entertained in the hermitage of San Bruno, at the expense of the ever-obliging Manuel Cortizos. The festivities included dances, a Galician peasant wedding, a play, and a *merienda* or collation of fifty dishes. On Tuesday the count–duke entertained the royal party with a masque and plays in the hermitage of the Magdalena. On Wednesday it was the turn of the Countess of Olivares, and of the hermitage of San Isidro, which the king and queen reached by boat, boarded at the landing stage of the Large Lake. On Thursday the royal family watched a bullfight with eighteen bulls from the windows overlooking the Principal Court of the Retiro. The count–duke was probably not with them—Monanni says that he did not go to bullfights.[53] That evening there was an entertainment in the Hall of Realms, described by Monanni as a "poetical competition, which was a very curious dispute between poetry and astrology."

On the Friday night another literary contest was held in the Hall of Realms. This was an *academia burlesca*, presided over by one of Olivares's favorite playwrights, Luis Vélez de Guevara, with Alfonso de Batres acting as secretary and Francisco de Rojas as *fiscal*, or attorney for the prosecution. The records of this burlesque academy convey a vivid, if rather painful, impression of the court's taste in literary wit.[54] In a splendid setting designed by Cosimo Lotti representing Mount Parnassus, Apollo sang verses to his lyre, and listened to the assembled poets reciting their compositions. These were improvised for the occasion on specially selected themes in accordance with the academy's rules. The competitors were asked, for instance, to produce four octaves on the beauty and elegance of Alonso Carbonel, a notoriously ugly man who resembled a hairy bear. Or they had to come up with seven six-line verses on whether the chief custodian of the Retiro, Diego de Covarrubias, could protect the main entrance better with vigilance or with his paunch. A jury awarded prizes, and the proceedings concluded with a *vejamen* or burlesque critique of the compositions, delivered by Batres and Rojas. This provided the opportunity for further witticisms: "Cosmelot (Cosimo Lotti) has made a little *plaza* of bits and pieces."—"Another *plaza*?"—"Yes, at the Retiro there has to be one for everybody."[55]

On Carnival Saturday, the 21st, there were the usual carnival festivities, including the traditional battles in which the ladies-in-waiting threw perfumed eggs at each other. The Retiro accounts for March include an entry for 81,800 *maravedises* (218 ducats) for 2,000 gilded and painted eggs and perfumed water, at 16 *maravedises* an egg, and for 4,000 silver-plated eggs at 12 *maravedises* each.[56] The combatants defended themselves with gold- or silver-plated cork shields.[57] The Sunday entertainments were provided by Jerónimo de Villanueva, who organized a *mojiganga* (a masquerade) in the style of his native Aragon. It consisted of four floats, two of them carrying musicians, the third depicting the fable of Venus and Vulcan, and the fourth an American Indian chief and his entourage. There was clowning and dancing, and all the spectators had to wear masks, a novelty at the court.[58] In the evening the king and queen watched a play. On the following day there was jousting with *cañas* (reed-spears), the horsemen in pursuit throwing eggs at their opponents. Olivares, watching from a balcony, saw soldiers clearing the courtyard while there were still places to let on the stands, and ordered that they should be occupied free of charge—a gesture that earned him cries of *Viva el Conde!*—cries unusual enough to be music in his ears.[59] In the evening there was a performance of *El robo de las Sabinas* by Rojas Zorrilla and Juan and Antonio Coello.[60] The festivities ended on Tuesday February 24 with another masquerade, this time organized by the municipality, watched by the king and queen "with attention and pleasure" as the usual carnival liberties were taken. One figure clothed in sheepskins carried a banner saying that the excise dues, the sales tax and stamped paper had flayed him (*Sisas alcabalas y papel sellado/Me tienen desollado*); another carried habits and crosses of the military orders with a "For sale" notice.[61] The climax of the ten days of entertainments came that evening in a performance in the Hall of Realms of a play by Calderón, now lost, on the adventures of Don Quijote.[62]

The lavish spectacles of the Carnival season of 1637 give a good idea of the kind of uses to which the Retiro could be put. Masques, plays, pageants, dances, bullfights, tournaments, literary soirées, banquets, all succeeded each other in no doubt exhausting profusion during that festive season. But these various activities were by no means limited to the traditional seasons of fiestas. The court would often go to the Retiro for an evening's entertainment, and there were numerous ways in which the king, briefly escaping from the Alcázar, could take his pleasure there.

Over the course of the years the Retiro offered ample opportunities for Philip to indulge his passion for the theater. If his reign saw a gradual shift from the amateur plays performed by courtiers in the Salón of the Alcázar to the professionally performed machine-plays (*comedias de tramoyas*), combining ballet, masque, costume, and spectacular mechanical metamorphoses, the building of the Retiro did much to assist this process.[63] The arrival of Cosimo Lotti in Madrid in 1626 gave the court a professional stage-designer capable of mounting the most spectacular and up-to-date effects. But it was the construction of the Retiro which allowed him to deploy in all their variety his extraordinary theatrical arts.

At the Retiro Cosimo Lotti had at hand not one, but several, locations where he could mount his plays. As early as 1633 he constructed a portable stage, which was used for plays presented in the *patinejo*, probably the small courtyard of the King's Quarters.[64] The accounts of 1636 include a payment in April for the portable stage to be erected in the "little room where the *comedias* are presented."[65] This seems to have been the room leading out of the Salón Grande, the Hall of Realms, and called by Bargrave the "masking-room."[66] The Hall of Realms, too, was used for theatrical productions;[67] and when bad weather drove the entertainments indoors, as it did in March 1635, the Hall was used for puppet shows and for acrobatic displays.[68]

It was either in the patio or in one or other of these rooms that a machine-play by Calderón, *La fábula de Dafne*, was performed on June 1, 1635. According to Monanni all the gods appeared on their machines, "and there were the usual three scenes, one of a cave and the sea, one of a cave and a wood, and the third of palaces and the temple of Pallas."[69] This device of three separate scenes, or stages, each with a different company of actors, was designed to save the spectators from having to change places between acts. It was also used by Lotti for Calderón's play on the theme of Hercules, *Los tres mayores prodigios*, performed in one of the courts of the Retiro on St John's night, 1636.[70] Extremely elaborate changes of scene were technically possible for these dramas, although the construction of the machinery took time and money. In one of the attractions planned for the June festivities of 1637, for instance, there were to be thirteen scene-changes during a one-and-a-half-hour performance. It is not surprising that the performance had to be postponed because the large machines needed for it were not yet ready; nor that two of these machines alone cost 6,000 ducats.[71]

Extensive use of artificial lighting made it possible to perform these plays at night. When the Modenese envoy Fulvio Testi was invited by the count–duke to watch a *comedia* at the Retiro in May 1636, and never discovered what it was about because Olivares was talking so hard, he described the room where the play was performed as being "brilliantly lit with silver lamps and torches, and with other illuminations all of wax."[72] Again it is not clear from his description whether the performance took place in the masking-room or in the Hall of Realms, since the one feature which he mentions—a balcony—was common to both rooms. He does, however, compensate for his neglect of the play by providing a lively description of the setting. He was met by the count–duke's famous doorkeeper, Simón Rodríguez, and taken to a balcony in the room where the play was to be given. Shortly after his arrival the king and queen entered, accompanied by the ladies-in-waiting. When their majesties had taken their seats under the canopy, the twenty-four or twenty-six ladies grouped themselves on the floor on either side of them, "forming a most beautiful theater." "The stage," Testi continued, "was low but most beautiful, constructed with the most exquisite care, and according to all the best rules of perspective, by a Florentine painter who is working here at an enormous salary in His Majesty's service." Cosimo Lotti would have found it difficult, on the strength of those concluding words, to recognize himself.

The king was seated on the right, the queen on the left, and the young Baltasar Carlos wandered to and fro. Four male and four female dwarfs and buffoons, dressed in the style once worn by the kings and queens of Castile, sat on the ground at the feet of the royal thrones. On the queen's side, beyond the canopy and screened by a gilded screen from the Indies, the Countess of Olivares sat on cushions of crimson velvet, while the count–duke, reclining against the wall near the door, was seated on a velvet stool of the same color, behind a latticed screen of gold. There were no men on the floor of the room—irrespective of rank they all stood bareheaded on the balconies. Just as Testi had settled himself on his own balcony, which had wooden benches, and was separated from the others by a wooden partition, the rest of the court ladies—"an infinite multitude"—flocked in to take their places and found that they could not possibly squeeze into the space assigned them. Characteristically, Olivares attempted to reduce chaos to order, and solved the problem by getting the men to give up their places. Once the confusion was over he took Testi by the hand and led him down from the balcony by way of one of the four staircases located in spaces behind the corners of the room. He then gallantly surrendered his own seat to his guest, and ordered a low stool to be brought so that he could sit beside him during the performance.

Although we are as ignorant as Testi of the events on stage, it is probable that, but for the distraction of Olivares's discourse, he would have seen not one but several different entertainments. It was normal for theatrical performances to start with a tune sung by the musicians. This was followed by a *loa* or prologue, to introduce the actors. Then came the *comedia* itself, but between each of the three acts there was a separate entertainment—an *entremés* or interlude between Acts I and II, and perhaps a short ballet between Acts II and III.[73] The finale might consist of singing and dancing. The performance of Calderón's *Fable of Daphne* on June 1, 1635, for instance, was followed by a ballet arranged by Jerónimo de Villanueva at a cost of over 2,000 ducats.[74] During the seventeenth century the *entremés*, as a playlet between acts, became an extremely popular entertainment in its own right; and just as the development of court theater created new opportunities for the writers of *comedias* like Lope de Vega and Calderón, so also it gave new standing to the *entremesista*.

The prince of *entremesistas* in the Madrid of Philip IV was Luis Quiñones de Benavente, who devoted himself entirely to writing short pieces, which owed their success not only to his wit and poetical gifts, but also his musical talent. Many of them indeed were sung to music of his own composition, and he was also a choreographer.[75] Benavente was unique in the faction-ridden world of Spanish letters in being universally popular, and his talents were in great demand for performances at the Retiro. *El mago*, for example, which was an *entremés* with singing, was written for St John's night of 1637,[76] and tells of a magician who brings to the Retiro all the most notable sights in Spain. In a graceful compliment to Villanueva, the question "Which are the most beautiful wild beasts in the Retiro," was answered by, "the lions of the Salón."[77] Another *entremés*, *Las dueñas*, seems to have been written to accompany Calderón's story of Ulysses and Circe, *El mayor encanto amor*, which was eventually performed at the Retiro on Sunday, July 29, 1635, after being postponed because of the outbreak of war with France.[78]

"To the lake! To the lake!" sing the chorus, and then stand spellbound before the sight that meets their eyes.[79] "What a splendid theater! What wonderful *tramoyas*!" "Who made them?" "Cosmelot, famous for all such works." In his newsletter to Florence, Monanni concurs. The performance, he reported, lasted four hours (another correspondent says six), "and it is a long time since anything better was done in Spain. Cosimo Lotti, inventor and director of the machines and the conceits, has given every satisfaction."[80] The enchantment of Lotti's stage effects on this occasion owed a great deal to their setting, for the story of Ulysses and Circe had been staged on the island of the Large Lake, enabling water and artificial lighting to create a magical combination of illusions. "This, young ladies of Vallecas," sang

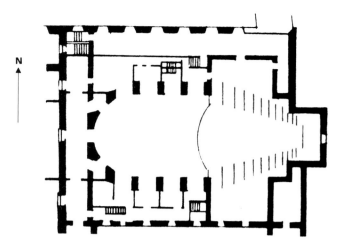

137. Coliseo of the Buen Retiro, from
plan of 1712 (after Carlier)

Benavente's chorus, "is the Lake of the Retiro, where fire and water have made friends."

The use of the island on the Lake for outdoor performances by night obviously created new possibilities for the designers of machine-plays. The public was permitted to attend some of the performances, either free or on payment of an admission charge, and the resulting spectacles became extremely popular. Monanni reported on June 25, 1639 that it was the count–duke's practice to allow only restricted admission for the first performance, so that he might appear more liberal by throwing open later performances to the public. This gesture was clearly a great success. All Madrid turned up during those June days of 1639, and was able to watch either from the lakeside or from boats, although some were too far away to catch the words.[81] But a performance staged on the queen's name-day, July 2, 1640, of another machine-play, *La fingida Arcadia*, presumably Tirso de Molina's comedy of this name, proved less satisfactory. Presented on the island at night, it was seen only by the royal family and by those fortunate enough to be seated on the benches within viewing distance of the stage.[82] '

These out-of-door spectacles of the later 1630s still had about them much of the tradition of pageant from which they originally derived. But by the end of the decade the development of the machine-play, with its professional actors and its Italianate perspective scenery, was relegating the elements of pageantry to a subsidiary role.[83] This shift away from pageantry to theatricals was accelerated by the construction, begun in 1638, of the Coliseo, a properly equipped theater just beyond the masking-room.[84] The doors of the Coliseo were opened on February 4, 1640, with a performance of *Los bandos de Verona*, a version of the Romeo and Juliet story, especially written for the occasion by Rojas Zorilla.[85]

Even though Rojas Zorilla's play required no special stage machinery, the Coliseo was carefully planned to accommodate the machine-play (fig. 137). This meant that, following the Italian model, the stage was designed to take painted backcloths and side wings which slotted into the floor and were operated by hand winches beneath it. There was also special machinery for aerial effects.[86] The general layout of the theater, however, resembled that of the *corrales*, the two public theaters of Madrid. Like the *corrales*, too, it was open to the public on payment, and in the

206

opening season great efforts were made to simulate for the amusement of the king and queen the kind of atmosphere to be found in the public theaters. There were catcalls, whistles and fighting, and—to add a little excitement to the scene—at one of the inaugural performances in February 1640 live mice were released among the women seated in the *cazuela* (the stewpan) on the floor of the theater—"a spectacle more pleasing than decent," as a contemporary newsletter observed.[87]

Although the Coliseo went out of use shortly after its inauguration, first because of the war and then because of the ban on stage plays following the queen's death in 1644, it came to life again after the arrival in Spain in 1649 of Philip's second wife, Mariana of Austria. The fabric, which had fallen into disrepair, was restored in 1650, although it is not known how many modifications were introduced during the process of restoration. A groundplan of 1655, after the restoration was completed, shows that it contained three tiers of boxes on either side, with four boxes to a tier. These were reserved for members of the nobility, ministers and court officials.[88] A royal balcony faced the stage, and beneath it was the *cazuela* for women spectators. Male spectators stood in front of the *cazuela*, facing what seems to have been a proscenium arch. The stage, with its arrangements for perspective scenery, gradually receded towards a rear window which at appropriate moments allowed a final distant perspective, not of artificial trees and shrubs, but of the real Retiro gardens beyond.

Cosimo Lotti died at the end of 1643,[89] but a worthy successor was found in a fellow-Florentine, Baccio del Bianco, who was sent over by the Grand Duke of Tuscany in 1651 at Philip's request. Under Bianco the machine-play reached new heights of ingenuity. In 1653, he designed a brilliant staging of Calderón's *Andromeda y Perseo*, which was presented in the Coliseo in May or June. Following the performance, he was ordered to make a series of eleven drawings, which were proudly sent to the court in Vienna as a record of the event. Through these beautiful drawings, the machine-plays that were so novel and important a feature of life at the Retiro come alive again.[90]

In keeping with the techniques developed at the Medici court, Baccio's machines, like those of Lotti before him, made the most of rapid and dazzling transformations of setting and ingenious aerial effects. As the audience entered the Coliseo, they saw a half-raised curtain before which sat personifications of Painting, Music and Poetry, suspended in the air (fig. 138). Behind was a partly-hidden figure of Atlas, a colossal automaton whose full size was revealed when the curtain was raised (fig. 139). On either side were nymphs holding torches and shields, who descended to the stage after Atlas had stood up and sung a song. The next scene used the full depth of the stage and showed a winter scene in a rustic village (fig. 140). The climax of the action for this section of the play was the Fall of Discord, who was driven from the sky by Pallas in a headlong descent that went much faster than planned and almost fractured the actress's neck. No sooner had she vanished from sight than the Grotto of Morpheus appeared (fig. 141), and then the Chamber of Danäe, which featured a perspective view down a long file of rooms, making an effect not unlike that which Bargrave would see in the west wing of the palace itself (fig. 142).

The succeeding scene was the most spectacular and brought a fiery Inferno before the eyes of the dazzled audience (fig. 143). This gave way to a forest scene, with

138. Baccio del Bianco, *Andromeda y Perseo*, Dedication and Introduction, (Cambridge, Mass., Harvard University, Houghton Library)

139. Baccio del Bianco, *Andromeda y Perseo*, Prologue (Cambridge, Mass., Harvard University, Houghton Library)

140. Baccio del Bianco, *Andromeda y Perseo*, First Act Scene with Fall of Discord (Cambridge, Mass., Harvard University, Houghton Library)

141. Baccio del Bianco, *Andromeda y Perseo*, Grotto of Morpheus (Cambridge, Mass., Harvard University, Houghton Library)

142. Baccio del Bianco, *Andromeda y Perseo*, The Chamber of Danäe (Cambridge, Mass., Harvard University, Houghton Library)

143. Baccio del Bianco, *Andromeda y Perseo*, Inferno (Cambridge, Mass., Harvard University, Houghton Library)

144. Baccio del Bianco, *Andromeda y Perseo*, Perseus, Pallas and Mercury (Cambridge, Mass., Harvard University, Houghton Library)

145. Baccio del Bianco, *Andromeda y Perseo*, Triumph of Perseus over Medusa (Cambridge, Mass., Harvard University, Houghton Library)

146. Baccio del Bianco, *Andromeda y Perseo*, Perseus Rescuing Andromeda, (Cambridge, Mass., Harvard University, Houghton Library)

147. Baccio del Bianco, *Andromeda y Perseo*, Celebration Scene (Cambridge, Mass., Harvard University, Houghton Library)

another aerial effect, showing Mercury on a cloud that flew to all parts of the set and an airborne chariot with Pallas aboard (fig. 144). The last three sets showed a palace and garden (fig. 145), a rocky seascape with Perseus rescuing Andromeda (fig. 146), and a final celebration scene set within an elaborate architectural framework (fig. 147). The triumph of illusion was never more complete.

PASTIMES AND DIVERSIONS

It is natural that the elaborately staged productions of Lotti and Bianco should have dominated contemporary reports of festivities at the Retiro, but court theater was not limited to these grand spectaculars. In addition to the spectacle plays mounted for special occasions, private performances were also arranged for the amusement of the king and queen. Companies of professional actors were brought to the Retiro to play before the court, as in March 1639, when the annual Lent festivities were cancelled as a gesture of unusual deference to public concern about the war and high taxation. But this did not prevent a *comedia* and ballet from being performed before the royal family one Sunday evening.[91] Similarly, members of the court would write and act in their own theatrical entertainments, which provided opportunities for the coterie of royal secretaries and palace officials to make jokes about each other for the amusement of themselves and their masters.

Philip was obviously an incurable theater-goer, and Olivares, always the faithful minister, ensured that his monarch was provided with all the entertainments desired. By the mid-1630s his own enthusiasm for these entertainments seems to have diminished. A Jesuit newsletter of 1635 noted that the count–duke had spent Holy Week at the Retiro, displaying an apparently insatiable appetite for sermons—a marked change, observed the writer, from the early days of the Retiro, when he would go to three or four plays a day.[92] Olivares himself, in a letter of June 22, 1639 to the cardinal infante, wrote: "we have spent these days at the Buen Retiro in *fiestas*, which are the worst of all torments. Dancing in the midst of care and trouble, and frittering away the time on inanities."[93]

In response to a letter written to him in 1641 by don Juan Chumacero, Spain's austere envoy to the papal court, the count–duke even went so far as to write that "in twenty years I have not seen ten plays. Their Majesties (God preserve them) greatly enjoy them. I must admit to you that there is nothing good to be said for them; but in comparison with other pastimes there might well seem to be so."[94] The count–duke's agonized protest that in twenty years he had not seen ten plays appears on any reckoning more than a little strange, unless—as happened on the evening when he entertained Fulvio Testi—he talked so hard during the performance as to see nothing that happened on stage. No doubt his palate had long since been dulled, but he must at least have sat through a vast number of performances.

On one occasion Olivares even appeared on stage himself, although in a very unheroic role. It was Shrove Tuesday, February 16, 1638, and the courtiers amused themselves at the Retiro by representing the world turned upside down: "*el pobre mundo al revés.*"[95] A mock wedding was arranged between "the knight of the shining vegetable, don Suspiro de la Chanza, Marquis of Cauliflower" and doña

Grimaldina Alfonso, "daughter . . . and nearly heiress of the good Count of Parsley." All the parts were taken by members of the court, with men representing women in an all-male cast. Velázquez, as the Countess of Santiesteban, was given one line. Olivares played the part of the porter; the enormous Diego de Covarrubias represented the king, and the ugly Carbonel the queen. The occasion was obviously much enjoyed by all those present, not least their majesties.

If an increasing melancholy seems to have descended on the king during the course of the 1630s, the Retiro did not lack for resources to provide him with cheer and relaxation in the midst of personal and official cares. Masques and plays are well documented, literary evenings less so, although a newsletter of 1636 reports an unprecedented entertainment for New Year's eve.[96] The king and queen went to the Retiro for lunch, and the evening's diversions began with a poet called Atillano, who hailed from America, improvising poems on any subject suggested by the audience. Cristóbal, the blind court rhymester, followed suit, but without the erudition which Atillano had displayed. After these poetical diversions Calabazas— the jester portrayed by Velázquez—took the stage, followed by dwarfs and mummers; and the evening ended with a dance and a masque.[97]

Dancing was a popular pastime, and particularly the *sarao*. In a letter of 1635 Hopton writes: "the last night the whole court, the conde of Olivares guiding them, made a sarao (which is, to run carreras by two and two, with lamps in their hands) in very rich apparel, and very fair liveries." A newsletter of the same year reports that the king enjoyed the *saraos* more than any other festivity at the Retiro.[98] These dances were held in the Hall of Realms until the completion in 1638 of the Casón, which would serve as the palace ballroom.[99] For indoor amusements, then, the palace was well equipped; and its courtyards provided settings for open-air masques, tournaments and bullfights which could still be watched from under cover, thanks to the surrounding balconies. In May 1636 Fulvio Testi described how a torchlight cavalcade was held in the Large Courtyard in the presence of the king and queen, who then went on to watch a pageant from their windows overlooking the Principal Court.[100]

There were arrangements for other pastimes, too, in the immediate palace complex. In a letter of April 2, 1639, Monanni reports that on the preceding Sunday the king had been tilting at the ring in the Large Court of the Retiro, watched by the queen, Prince Baltasar Carlos and the Princess of Carignano from their usual low balcony, and also by anyone else who was interested, since the court was thrown open to the public for the occasion.[101] Besides equestrian exercises, the king and the courtiers could amuse themselves with games of *pelota*. In May 1635 a mason, Adrián de Flores, was contracted for 38,000 *reales* (3,450 ducats) to lay the brick floor of two *pelota* courts in the "second court"—the Large Court—to specifications provided by Carbonel.[102] Since a great game of *pelota* figures among the festivities at the end of May,[103] there must already have been *pelota* courts at the Retiro, perhaps those shown in the Prado Alto on Texeira's map.

A more exotic form of entertainment was provided by the Leonera, the lion-house or menagerie. There was a tradition of menageries in Spanish royal palaces, including the Alcázar.[104] They were constructed in such a way as to enable spectators to look down from balconies or windows on the antics of the beasts,

214

which were sometimes pitted against each other in combat to add to the excitement. On October 31, 1631 Olivares organized in the arena beside the Alcázar a fiesta in the ancient Roman manner. A number of beasts—a lion, a tiger, a bear, a bull—were released into the arena, and there was great excitement as to which would emerge victorious. The triumph went to the bull, which was then promptly felled by a single shot from the king's arquebus—a feat which called forth an effusion of extravaganzas from the court poets, eulogizing "our Christian Jupiter."[105]

The menagerie constructed at the Retiro in 1633 stood in the middle court of the range of three courts at the entrance to the palace, and is recognizable in Leonardo's painting from its oval shape (fig. 30). It was modelled on the menagerie in Florence, with a viewing gallery running around it, but it was smaller than the Florentine prototype, where animals were kept well apart from each other. The lion-house in the Retiro, on the other hand, was arranged so that if the doors were opened the animals would be forced to do battle.[106] At the beginning the menagerie contained three lions, a tiger, a bear and a few wolves, but Olivares was soon scouring the world for exotic animals. Although the menagerie might seem to have been placed uncomfortably close to the palace, it was obviously one of the major attractions, and was especially enjoyed by the young Baltasar Carlos. In November 1634 the king and his son took the Duchess of Mantua to see the animals, which included a lion and tiger cub presented by the Duke of Braganza, the premier duke in her new viceroyalty of Portugal.[107]

For the benefit of the Duke of Modena a repeat performance was staged on October 1638 of the great battle of the beasts of 1631, first with two or three animals at a time, and then with all of them thrown in together.[108] No doubt the ensuing carnage gave extra urgency to the need to replenish the stock. Monanni noted in November 1639 that Olivares had just imported some "extravagant animals and birds" from Africa, along with two Africans as keepers.[109] The chances of survival of these unfortunate beasts could hardly be rated very high, even without the Roman-style combats. Three "tigers"—presumably pumas—sent to the Retiro from Peru by the viceroy, the Count of Chinchón, survived the Atlantic crossing only to die mysteriously in the course of a single night within a few miles of Madrid.[110]

The aviary, for which the "extravagant" African birds were destined, was a still more famous, and indeed notorious, attraction. It was, after all, the Gallinero or chicken coop that had given the Retiro its popular name. But far from being demolished, in what would certainly have been a fruitless attempt to exorcize the name, it was transferred to a corner of the gardens and given an exceptionally handsome structure. Monanni describes the aviary as consisting of iron cages with cupolas, divided by partitions.[111] The court would make special expeditions to see the exotic birds, and the count–duke himself displayed an enthusiasm for his feathered friends which became a national, and international, joke. Whenever possible he would go and feed the birds himself, collecting the eggs for presentation to a favored ambassador. He was especially fond of visiting a white Cairo hen called doña Ana, to which he would solemnly bow, doffing his hat. The death of doña Ana was said by his enemies to have affected him more than the defeat of the army before Casale, and from then onwards his enthusiasm for the aviary diminished.[112]

The supreme attraction of the Retiro, however, as Bargrave pointed out, was its park and garden: "That for which the Retiro is above all famed is a large rambling garden, full of all varieties of vegetables, of fish ponds, of waterworks, and of arched walks, under which the king goes at his pleasure, in coach or on horseback, and may travel a fair journey under them, still in several ways."[113] The gardens were, indeed, enormous, even if Andrew Marvell, who may have visited them in the 1640s, would pretend to compare them unfavorably with those of Nun Appleton, the Yorkshire home of Lord Fairfax:

> For you Thessalian *Tempe's Seat*
> Shall now be scorn'd as obsolete;
> *Aranjuez*, as less, disdain'd;
> The *Bel-Retiro* as constrain'd. . .[114]

The grounds were certainly large enough to justify the making of three small coaches for the use of the royal family when they wanted to visit different parts of the gardens. The coachmaker was given his payment in 1635, at almost five hundred ducats a coach.[115] But the gardens closest to the palace in particular were designed for lingering and strolling, especially the famous Octagonal Garden, "shaped like a star with its eight paths of fine sand all converging on a central space, which has wooden arches intertwined with roses, mulberry and quince, forming a kind of green wall with occasional windows."[116]

In the years after 1633, to which this description refers, enormous efforts were made to expand and irrigate the gardens and to beautify them with unusual plants and trees. Ingenious hydraulic devices were used to give splendor and variety to the many fountains. Marble statues embellished the shady avenues. Monanni describes the king in 1639 as walking almost every morning, an hour or two after sunrise, down the specially constructed alley to his favorite church of Nuestra Señora de Atocha, and then returning to the Retiro by coach. Baltasar Carlos would do the same a little later, to be followed shortly afterwards by the queen and her ladies; and the king, if he were not busy, would come out to meet her in one of the gardens or avenues on her journey home.[117]

One of the greatest delights of the Retiro was to travel not by land but by water. The lakes and pools were linked to each other by a network of canals, completed in 1639 with the construction of the grand canal, the Río Grande.[118] Gondolas were used for moving along these canals, and in the spring of 1639 the Duke of Medina de las Torres sent twelve splendid new gondolas from Naples, which were enormously admired for their elaborate workmanship in silver, gold, bronze and glass, and were alleged to have cost over 100,000 ducats.[119] For all the pleasures of water travel, the trips were not always accomplished without mishap. There was an anxious moment in July 1636 when one of the seven or eight ponds in the gardens sprang a leak, rapidly emptying the others at a higher level, and leaving the royal gondola indecorously grounded.[120] Storms, too, were liable to blow up suddenly; and on one occasion the councillors of Castile, embarked on the canals at royal request, were overcome by seasickness, to the merriment of those who watched them from the safety of the land.[121]

On windless days the royal family could take their ease in gondolas on the Large

Lake to the gentle accompaniment of music, or go to the fishing pavilions to catch fish which had been specially acquired for the occasion.[122] The Lake also lent itself to regattas and to mock naval battles, or *naumachiae*, in the Roman style, fought by miniature fleets.[123] In July 1638 a *barco grande*— a miniature imitation of a galley, with a full complement of cannon—reached the Retiro from Seville as a gift to the king. Called *El Santo Rey Don Fernando*, and decorated with allegorical scenes by Zurbarán, it joined a toy fleet which aroused much indignation in Madrid, where it was thought that the money would have been better spent on men-of-war to fight the French.[124]

On land again the king and queen could enjoy the cool play of the fountains, lose themselves in the intricacies of the maze, or seek out the shade of one or other of the grottoes attached to the hermitages of San Jerónimo, San Bruno and the Magdalena.[125] It was, however, the hermitages themselves which constituted one of the most original and interesting features of the Retiro gardens.[126]

A contemporary description of the hermitages at Lerma describes them as adding "devotion to the beauty of the site."[127] Those at the Retiro fulfilled the same function, and the king and queen grew fond of using the hermitage chapels for private worship.[128] The idea of *retiro*, then, in the sense of a religious retreat, was carried over from the monastery of the Hieronymite monks to the palace of the king; and in 1636 there was even a scheme—which, like so many of Olivares's schemes, came to nothing—for the foundation of a combined lay and clerical fraternity of knights, with its principal convent at the Retiro.[129] This sounds like an echo of the new Order of the Holy Spirit founded in 1578 by Henry III of France, and in some respects the court of Philip IV was not unlike that of the last of the Valois. At Vincennes Henry formed, and indeed joined, a confraternity of Hieronymites who retreated into their cells for worship; and he transmuted his palace academy into a sacred academy by founding a congregation of the Oratory of Notre Dame de Vie Sainte.[130] This style of religiosity also had its attractions for Philip IV.

But in addition to the actual and projected religious functions of the hermitages, they were also much used for secular ends. A sometimes startling juxtaposition of the sacred and the profane was not infrequent at the Spanish court, as the adornment of the hermitage of San Jerónimo with statues of the Magi and of Venus and Adonis indicates.[131] The hermitage of San Juan was reserved as a residence for the governor and his guests, who included in 1634 an Italian alchemist, Vincenzo Massimi, said to be practising his mysterious arts there at Olivares's bidding.[132] The more accessible hermitages were used, too, as meeting places for foreign dignitaries and as starting points for their ceremonial entry into Madrid. But the hermitages and their gardens also provided suitably charming settings for the banquets, picnics and other entertainments with which the king and queen and other honored guests were so lavishly regaled. There was one particularly festive occasion of this kind on May 3, 1640, when Olivares arranged for all the principal military commanders then in Madrid—most of them foreigners—to spend a day at the Retiro.[133] During the morning the twenty-eight assembled generals, company commanders and colonels were given a grand tour of the palace and gardens. At four in the afternoon they found tables laid for them at the hermitage of San Antonio. Thirty different wines were served; endless toasts were drunk from unusually large glasses; and five hundred dishes were produced, laden with enough food for seven hundred people. After this gluttonous repast the gallant commanders were rather unwisely taken out in gondolas on the lake, where several of them were sick. The day ended in style with a play, the more subtle points of which are unlikely to have been appreciated.

The reception for the commanders provided a somewhat incongruous reminder that this was a time of war. There might be firework displays at the Retiro,[134] but in Flanders, Italy, and on the Spanish frontiers the cannon were thundering. It was a sign of the times when in May 1639 a troop review was held at the Retiro;[135] but it was perhaps even more of a portent that only one hundred and fifty knights of the military orders or their substitutes put in an appearance when the king held another review on September 31, 1640.[136] A few months earlier the principality of Catalonia had come out in revolt against the government in Madrid, and Olivares was now desperately attempting to find men and money to crush a domestic rebellion even while he struggled to maintain Spain's armies abroad. The evidence of the troop review was not encouraging. Morale was low, and there was no spontaneous upsurge of enthusiasm in Castile for a campaign against the Catalans. When the campaign finally got under way it failed to attain its objective; and it was a coincidence not without a certain poignancy that Pietro Tacca's martial statue of Philip on horseback was being erected at the Retiro in 1642 at the very moment when its somewhat less martial original was away in Aragon puzzling how to wage a victorious war against his own rebellious vassals.

As the shadow of war spread over the Retiro, it was clear that the days of inspired innovation, or haphazard improvisation, were drawing to an end. The king finally accepted Olivares's frequently offered resignation on January 17, 1643. The Countess of Olivares, who remained for a time in the Alcázar, replaced her husband as governor of the Retiro, as he went into exile first to Loeches, and then, further away, to Toro, where he busied himself with plans for pumping water to a waterless garden he had purchased.[137]

Once the guiding hand of Olivares was removed, the Retiro, as Monanni had predicted, quickly began to decay. In any event, the Retiro itself was seen as the relic of a discredited regime. The Committee of Works, which the count–duke had always sought to exclude from Retiro business, now tried to get its revenge by proposing that the 1,500 ducats annually assigned to its upkeep from the revenues of the Alcázar of Seville should cease to be paid. But the king, who clearly retained an affection for his palace, wrote in his own hand on the committee's report that the annual consignation was not to be touched.[138]

The 1640s, however, were to be dead years for the Retiro. The queen died on October 6, 1644, and an even more crushing blow struck the king when Baltasar Carlos died on October 9, 1646, within a few days of his seventeenth birthday. The prohibition on stage plays imposed for the period of mourning for the queen was promptly renewed, and several companies of actors were disbanded.[139] It was only in 1649, with the arrival in Spain of Philip's new queen, his niece Mariana of Austria, originally destined to be the bride of Baltasar Carlos, that the court began slowly to return to life.

By this time the Retiro had a new, if only provisional, governor. Olivares died in

1645, his widow in 1647. The estate was contested among the potential heirs, in what was to prove a long and costly lawsuit. On December 6, 1648 a royal decree stated that the Retiro was at present without a governor because of the suit between Olivares's cousin, the Marquis of Leganés, and his former son-in-law, the Duke of Medina de las Torres, over his inheritance. It was important that someone should be responsible for "repairing the ruin which has begun to overtake that structure, and that it should be restored to a state in which . . . my niece can use it for her recreation after her arrival." The king therefore appointed as interim governor the count–duke's nephew, don Luis de Haro, who has also succeeded his uncle as favorite and principal minister.[140]

The king's concern for the amusement of his young bride proved fully justified. Mariana could not abide the gloom of the Alcázar, and sought escape to the Retiro whenever she could manage it.[141] In order to humor the queen, whose attitude to the Retiro was so different from that of her predecessor, something of its former gaiety was brought back to the site. Once again there were mock naval battles on the Large Lake, and machine-plays in the Coliseo under the brilliant direction of Baccio del Bianco; and once again there was indignation at the fantastic expenditure on trivial pleasures in time of war.[142] The contrasts between profligacy and penury were as pointed as ever. When Baccio del Bianco died in 1657 it was reported that he died in extreme poverty, his wages grossly in arrears.[143]

On the surface at least, the festivities and amusements in the Retiro during the 1650s were much like those of the 1630s, but that supreme master of ceremonies the count–duke of Olivares was gone. The Retiro of Philip IV was, above anything else, the Retiro of Olivares. Its buildings, its gardens, its varied entertainments, bore the stamp of his restless spirit. Contemporaries, whether they approved or disapproved, were sharply aware of this. Identifying the Retiro with its creator, they saw it as the symbol of a minister who had ruled Spain with a heavy hand for over twenty years. Like all symbols the Retiro from the time of its inception was the subject of disputed interpretation; and the debate which raged around the palace was at heart a debate about the record and style of the minister who had brought it into being.

VIII

The Symbol of a Reign

Golden Age, Iron Age

To those who lived through the Olivares years, the Retiro seemed to fill the horizon of artistic activity. Its size, its cost, and its opulence captured the attention of Spaniards and foreigners alike. Yet for all its importance, the palace by no means exhausted the interest of Philip and Olivares in building and decorating. During the 1630s, the king and his minister promoted one of the most ambitious artistic programs of the seventeenth century.

Philip first showed a taste for major artistic enterprises in the late 1620s, when he began to redecorate some of the state rooms in the Alcázar, starting with the Pieza Nueva.[1] Then, in 1629, an important work of architecture was commissioned, the Court Prison (Cárcel de Corte). The construction of this imposing building, which now houses the Foreign Ministry, was undertaken by the team of Alonso Carbonel and Cristóbal de Aguilera, who were to be important participants in the Crown commissions of the 1630s.[2]

In the following year, the preliminary work at the Royal Apartment of San Jerónimo began, and for four years this enterprise absorbed the attention of the king and Olivares. But as soon as the Retiro was substantially finished, the two men launched three new architectural projects. The first of these was the Casa de la Zarzuela, a small hunting lodge in the grounds of the Pardo. The cardinal infante had started construction on the site, but after his departure for the Netherlands in 1632, the unfinished structure appears to have been abandoned. In October 1633, the king ordered the secretary of the Committee of Works to see what could be done to preserve the building before it collapsed.[3]

Less than a year later, it was decided to resume the work despite the cardinal infante's absence. In August 1634, Juan Gómez de Mora delivered seven handsome drawings of plans and elevations for a new building (fig. 148).[4] The Casa de la Zarzuela was conceived as an elegant country house set in a small formal garden. As drawn by Gómez de Mora, and as later constructed, the building was organized around a central patio and had reception rooms on the ground floor and small apartments above. At both sides were low wings with colonnades that masked the servants' quarters and framed the main building.

During the autumn months of 1634, the administration of the project was organized. Philip naturally put Olivares in charge, appointing him governor of the site on January 19, 1635.[5] Olivares in turn appropriated a team of assistants from the Retiro, headed by the Count of Castrillo, who was again to supply the funds from the revenues of the council of the Indies.[6] The construction contract, with a budget of 40,000 ducats, was given to Juan de Aguilar and signed by him and Castrillo on June 16, 1635.[7] Gómez de Mora was made the architect, and Carbonel, the *aparejador mayor*, or chief architectural assistant; but in 1637, after Gómez de Mora's banishment from court, Carbonel took over the project. The final member of the executive corps was Juan de Alvear, the comptroller of accounts at the Retiro, and now at the Zarzuela.

The progress of construction is reflected in the accounts of Castrillo in the archive of the Indies. It appears that the building was well advanced by March 18, 1637, when Juan García Barruelos, the roofer of the Retiro, signed a contract to cover the Zarzuela with a lead roof.[8] In the same year, the gardens were laid out and planted. Between April 1637 and March 1638, the court in front of the main facade was constructed by Gaspar Bandal. Two months later, the sculptor Bartolommeo Zumbigo, another Retiro craftsman, was paid for fireplaces.[9] By the end of the year, the Zarzuela must have been nearly finished, and in due course the obligatory complement of hunting scenes and landscapes painted by the Rubens workshop was obtained and installed.[10] Unfortunately, the completion was immediately followed by the troubles of the 1640s, which postponed the heyday of the Zarzuela to the next decade. During the 1650s, however, it was frequently used for musical plays, which came to be known as *zarzuelas* after the palace in which they had first been performed.[11]

148. Juan Gómez de Mora, Project for Casa de la Zarzuela (from Saltillo, "Alonso Martínez")

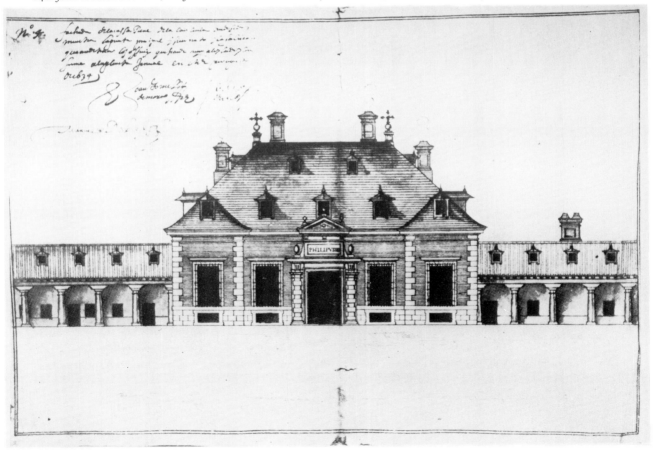

Just two months before the contract for the Zarzuela was signed, the king ordered work to start on the Torre de la Parada (fig. 149). The Torre de la Parada was a small tower located in the hunting grounds of the Pardo, and was used as a resting place for the royal party during the chase. In a contract of April 26, 1635, Gómez de Mora agreed to design a small suite of rooms to be built around the core of the existing tower. On September 13, 1636, the contractor Francisco de Mena undertook to build the structure and to have it finished by December 25, 1637, a deadline which he met.[12] Finances were arranged by Jerónimo de Villanueva, who again drew on the secret expense account. And, once again, Carbonel was present on the site as the architectural overseer.

The decoration of the Torre de la Parada was the last major commission undertaken by the Rubens workshop, which furnished a large series of scenes illustrating Ovid's *Metamorphoses*, together with hunting scenes and landscapes, numbering over one hundred in all.[13] Most of these paintings arrived in Madrid in May 1638, sent from Flanders by the cardinal infante.[14] Commissions were also given to the court painters, led by Velázquez, who did the three famous hunting portraits of the king, the prince and the cardinal infante; a series of court dwarfs; the imaginary portraits of *Aesop* and *Menippus* and the amusing version of the god *Mars*. A group of pictures of the king's country houses was executed by Félix Castelo, Jusepe Leonardo, Juan de la Corte and Pedro Núñez, all of whom had provided pictures for the Retiro. And the elderly Vicente Carducho furnished an unidentified painting for the chapel.[15]

The 1630s, then, were a remarkably fruitful decade for court patronage of the arts. A pleasure palace, a country house, a hunting lodge and the count–duke's house and convent at Loeches (fig. 150), were all simultaneously under construction. In addition, the Salón de Comedias of the Alcázar was completely remodelled and redecorated. Even Charles V's final retreat at Yuste was not forgotten. In 1638 Olivares brought to the king's attention the shameful neglect which had overtaken the emperor's old dwelling place, and was promptly named governor, so that the work of restoration could be put in hand.[16]

Construction, however, was only a part, and not the largest part, of the vigorous patronage of these years. Paintings, tapestries, precious furnishings and objects, works of sculpture large and small—all these were commissioned and purchased in impressive quantities to decorate the new buildings. The number of paintings alone obtained for the Retiro, the Zarzuela and the Torre exceeded eleven hundred.[17] Expensive tapestries were bought on the same generous scale. Then there were the gardens, with exotic plants and flowers, trees and fountains to adorn them. Finally, there were the plays, the spectacles, the entertainments and banquets, the hunts and excursions that had to be organized for the amusement of the court.

These luxurious pursuits were undertaken at a time of acute financial and economic strain, against the dark background of war. Since 1621 there had been continuous war with the Dutch; and then, from 1635, Spain found itself embroiled in what was described by one of Olivares's propagandists as a "defensive, holy and religious war" against the France of Louis XIII[18]—a France portrayed by the Spaniards as allying with heretics, disrupting the peace of Europe, and giving aid and comfort to the King of Spain's enemies.

149. (left) Anonymous seventeenth–century artist, *Torre de la Parada* (Madrid, Museo Municipal)

150. Alonso Carbonel, Church of Dominicanas Recoletas, Loeches

Olivares knew that his best, and perhaps his only, chance was to strike hard and fast at the French. Castile was in no condition to withstand a prolonged war. By May 1635 he had entered into commitments for no less than 11,000,000 ducats to be spent during the course of the year, and he was still 1,500,000 ducats short for the defense of Milan. His financial ministers protested that there was no way of raising the additional money, and argued that any attempt to raise the level of taxation could only be self-defeating. But the king and Olivares brushed aside these excuses. The money must be found; and somehow it was found, year after year, at least during the first five years of the war with France.[19]

Some of this money, but nothing like enough, came from the Indies. Over the course of the five years 1636–40 the crown received 5,500,000 ducats in American silver.[20] But the treasure fleets were now arriving with disturbing irregularity, and the sum total of the silver which they brought for the king was less than the equivalent of two years' pay for the Spanish army in Flanders. The remainder had to be extracted from the taxpayer, which meant in the first instance the taxpayer in those parts of the Monarchy where he was most defenseless—Castile, Naples and

223

Sicily. The count–duke still hoped to mobilize the resources of Portugal and the Crown of Aragon by implementing the Union of Arms, but in the meantime Castile would continue to bear the heaviest costs of the war.

By 1640 the financial and military drive of the opening years of hostilities with France was visibly faltering; but in the short term Olivares had succeeded in galvanizing Castile for yet another final effort, and it was on the short term that he was counting for a decisive victory over the French. In August 1636, when the cardinal infante's army came within striking distance of Paris at Corbie, it had almost seemed as if the count–duke had calculated correctly. But the success had proved to be transitory, and increasingly it began to look as though Spain was after all condemned to the war of attrition that it could ill afford. In spite of its massive military investment the 1637 campaigning season was disappointing, ending as it did with the loss of Breda in October. In the spring of 1638 Olivares was of the opinion that "our own forces and those of our enemies are more or less balanced today."[21] That summer French forces crossed the frontier at Irún and laid siege to the fortress of Fuenterrabía. A massive effort was organized by Olivares to repel the French; and when victory came in September a grateful king ordered that every year on the day of the victory the count–duke and his successors should dine at the royal table, with a toast being drunk from a golden goblet to Olivares as the "*librador de la patria*."[22] But what had looked like being a year of victories ended in disaster when the forces of Bernard of Saxe-Weimar captured the supposedly impregnable Rhine fortress of Breisach in December, and cut Spain's land corridor to Flanders.

From this moment there were accumulating indications that the balance of the war was beginning to tilt against the Spanish Monarchy. The cutting of the land route to Flanders was followed ten months later by the cutting of the sea route, when the fleet of don Antonio de Oquendo was destroyed by the Dutch at the battle of the Downs. By now the cardinal infante, starved of men and money, was having extreme difficulty in holding the line in the Netherlands, and the Spanish military machine was everywhere under strain. A French attack across the Pyrenees into Catalan territory in the summer of 1639 was eventually thrown back, but the long campaign only aggravated the tensions between Madrid and the Catalans caused by the government's efforts to secure a more vigorous Catalan participation in the war. By the spring of 1640 the Catalan peasantry, exasperated by the disorderly behavior of the billeted troops of the royal army, were massing with their weapons. In June the viceroy was murdered in Barcelona, and the principality, now in open revolt, was looking across the Pyrenees to France for assistance.

That same month Fulvio Testi, now back in Modena from his mission to Madrid, commented on the situation of the country that he had come to know so well: ". . . I turn now to Catalonia, and contemplate a people who have become seditious, rebellious and savage . . . I jump to Portugal and find a people discontented and little less than rebellious. Between these two extremes lies Castile, the chief of all the realms and the seat of the king, deserted, desolate, depopulated."[23] Less than six months after Testi wrote these words, a well-planned uprising in Lisbon had overthrown the unpopular viceregal government of the Duchess of Mantua, and the Duke of Braganza had been proclaimed king of an independent Portugal.

Even if France was by now in a miserable state, the condition of Spain was worse.

With a "desolate" and "depopulated" Castile caught between the two extremes of a rebellious Catalonia and a rebellious Portugal, the count–duke was no longer fighting for victory, but only to hold together a splintering Monarchy. His last two years of power, 1641 and 1642, were terrible years as he struggled to keep Spain's armies on their feet in Italy and the Netherlands, while vainly attempting to score the kind of military success against the Catalans which would persuade them to return to allegiance to the king.

It would be hard to think of a less propitious time for embarking on major building projects and for mounting lavish spectacles at court. It is true that from 1640 these activities tapered away, although the festivities were resumed again in the 1650s; but the fact remains that throughout the 1630s—a decade of continuous warfare, financial stringency and economic distress—substantial resources were allocated by the Crown, the court and the privileged classes to conspicuous consumption. The resulting golden age for the arts in Spain seemed to stand in mocking contrast to the contemporary image of a Europe torn by conflict and living in an age of iron. "This is the century of the soldiers," wrote Fulvio Testi in 1641.[24]

That a Castile at war should have been able to sustain this kind of lavish expenditure on the arts of peace may appear surprising; and the juxtaposition of golden age and iron age seems at first a startling paradox. But a population weighed down by intolerable taxation may still have at its apex an affluent elite. Madrid, as a great imperial capital, continued to draw to itself all the riches of the Monarchy. A viceroy who, like the Count of Monterrey, had shamelessly plundered his province, could easily afford to establish himself in a luxurious house in the Plaza de Santo Domingo and start construction of a picture gallery in his garden on the Pardo de San Jerónimo.[25] A successful commander—especially if, like Leganés, he had made a brilliant marriage—had no trouble in paying the highest prices for paintings that caught his fancy. The same was true of the bureaucrats in the higher reaches of the administration. When don Francisco de Tejada of the council of Castile died in September 1634 he left his heirs not only an admirable picture collection, but also an entailed estate to the value of some 15,000 ducats a year, and 150,000 ducats in cash— "as usually happens," noted Monanni, "with all ministers of comparable status, because of the opportunities they have for getting rich."[26]

The war, too, brought opportunities of its own. Increased government borrowing, war taxation, and the growth of war industries, all combined to redistribute wealth in Castilian society. Many of the old aristocratic families might find themselves hard-pressed, but others with close ties to the men of power had ample opportunity to recoup or make their fortunes. Speaking for the old families of Castile, Matías de Novoa referred contemptuously to the court of Philip IV as a court of squires (corte de escuderos).[27] He was right in the sense that this was a court in which new wealth lived on uneasy terms with old-established hierarchy, and in which the war financiers enjoyed special rights of access; a court, above all, dominated by the count–duke's men, whose power was as great as their lineage was mean.

If these men spent, and spent lavishly, it was partly to assert and confirm their new-found status. It was also in part to please the king and the count–duke, who by precept and example set the standards of entertainment, display and patronage. But it also made good financial sense at a time when constant currency fluctuation and the lack of investment opportunities in Castile's tottering economy suggested that the best employment for surplus capital was to spend it. Possessions, in the form of houses, furnishings, pictures and jewels, were at once the visible symbols of rank, and a satisfactory form of insurance against monetary depreciation.

There were risks, however, of loss by fire and theft, not to mention the danger of appropriation by the Crown. After all, the count–duke had partly furnished the Retiro from what were euphemistically known as "gifts." Members of the court and the administration stood to gain much from their position, but it was also one in which they found themselves dangerously exposed, for the king's demands for offerings of silver or valuables could not be refused.

The involuntary responses of courtiers and office-holders to royal requests helped to reduce the direct burden on the Crown's finances in time of war, and went some way toward meeting the running costs of display. By means of a system of discreet blackmail, wealth that would otherwise have been used for conspicuous consumption by the rich was often simply diverted to augment conspicuous consumption by the Crown. National resources, however, were acutely limited; and the appropriation of any part of those resources for additional court expenditure was itself an act of policy which offers an important insight into prevailing priorities.

The decision to spend lavishly on building and display, even when the times were more than usually hard, was by no means exclusive to the Spanish Crown. James I of England embarked on the remodelling of his palaces and the building of the Banqueting House in the midst of the most serious depression of the early seventeenth century.[28] Vast sums, which could ill be afforded, were lavished on the masques, spectacles and other cultural pursuits required to create the elegant Arcadia of the court of Charles I.[29] The Grand Duke Ferdinand II of Tuscany was busily improving and embellishing the Pitti palace in the 1630s at a moment when the Tuscan economy was in deep depression and the city of Florence was ravaged by plague.[30] If the court of Louis XIII of France tended to deviate from the pattern, this is largely to be ascribed to the temperament of the king. Marie de' Medici had run an opulent court during her regency, but Louis lacked the taste for this kind of display, and Richelieu, himself a great builder, could do nothing to change the austere ways of his master. "Opulence of furnishings," he told him, "is all the more necessary (in royal houses) because foreigners can only conceive the greatness of princes if it appears in external show." And yet Louis allowed the priceless pieces in his possession to be wasted and lost.[31] Although the 1630s and 1640s were times of notable building projects in Paris,[32] this was primarily the result of private enterprise. It would need Philip IV's nephew and son-in-law, Louis XIV, to create the splendid court of which Richelieu dreamed, and to play the part of star performer which Louis XIII had shunned.

In this respect it was Philip IV, not Louis XIII, who conformed more closely to contemporary expectations of the prince (fig. 151). Princes, according to Ben

151. Diego de Velázquez, *Philip IV in Brown and Silver* (London, National Gallery)

Jonson, should be "studious of riches and magnificence in the outward celebration or show."[33] Olivares had stage-managed the kingship of Philip IV with this principle in mind. He had set out to make Philip's court the center of the artistic and cultural life of the Spanish Monarchy, and in this at least he had enjoyed some success. The Retiro, for all its imperfections, epitomized the brilliance of artistic and literary activity in the realms of the Planet King.

Later generations bestowed the name of the Golden Century, the *siglo de oro*, on the sixteenth and early seventeenth centuries, as the age when Spain's political pre-eminence was accompanied by an unusual flowering of the arts.[34] The phrase was occasionally used by seventeenth-century Spaniards themselves, as when a court gazeteer wrote in 1621 that "the reign of our king, Philip IV, is a *siglo de oro* for Spain."[35] If this term was not meant to apply exclusively to the state of the arts, there was a contemporary awareness of cultural vitality which ran alongside the awareness of economic decline. In a petition to the Cortes of Castile in 1629 the royal chronicler, Tomás Tamayo de Vargas, declared that "Spain, although it came late to letters because of its commitment to the pursuit of arms, has made such progress in them in so little time that it may be suspected of having taken the lead, for it is inferior to no nation in one or the other."[36]

As a recipient of royal patronage, Tamayo de Vargas was hardly an impartial observer. But if the brilliance of Spanish arts and letters in the reign of Philip IV was primarily the work of a handful of geniuses like Lope de Vega, Velázquez and Calderón, the Crown's active encouragement of the arts of civilization in troubled times set its stamp on society as a whole. Where the king led the way, the court was bound to follow. The *siglo de oro* of the arts in Spain owed much to the Retiro. From this point of view, the palace may reasonably be regarded as cheap at the price. What from one standpoint appears a gross misallocation of limited resources then becomes from another an exceptionally successful investment. At the most it constituted no more than a tiny fraction of the Crown's expenditure on war.

Beyond the financial cost, however, there was an incalculable social cost, which was borne by the poverty-stricken taxpayers of Castile. Beyond it, too, was a political cost, and this was paid, with some justice, by the Olivares regime. For just as the Escorial stood as a monument to the regime of Philip II, so the Retiro stood as a monument to that of Olivares. It was a commonplace of the sixteenth and seventeenth centuries that princes should erect great buildings as a memorial to their fame. Alberti and Castiglione had said as much,[37] and (among Spaniards) Mariana had written that the names of princes would live longer through their buildings than if inscribed in bronze.[38] The logical corollary was that by their buildings princes were to be judged, and either praised or condemned.

POLEMICS AND PANEGYRICS

The criticism of the Retiro began even while the building was rising from the ground. "There was murmuring against this extravagant affair," wrote Matías de Novoa, "in the court and in all the kingdoms of the Monarchy. I leave on one side the people, with their uninformed views, and speak of men of affairs and learning, and people of gravity and good sense."[39] The "murmuring" is well documented in the dispatches of foreign ambassadors in Madrid; the "chicken coop" was an object of ridicule and widespread hostility. The Venetian ambassador Francesco Corner, who arrived in Madrid before the work had begun and two years later was reporting on the inaugural festivities of December 1633, explained in his dispatch that "this building has been a source of universal murmuring, and the people have been complaining loudly, in the belief that numerous taxes have been imposed for no other purpose than this. Nor is the architecture praised. . . This Retiro, then, is the subject of general criticism, although one can well imagine that in time it will die away, and perhaps tastes will change."[40]

Olivares, who prided himself on his knowledge of the rules of statecraft, might have spared himself some trouble if he had called to mind some relevant maxims in Giovanni Botero's *Reason of State* (1589). While encouraging princes to construct monumental buildings, Botero insisted that two precautions must be observed: "they must not be entirely useless, and the people must not be heavily taxed to pay for them."[41] The principal charge levelled against the Retiro was that it was an unnecessary structure built at the taxpayer's expense in times of war and hardship. But, as Corner's report makes clear, aesthetic considerations were not entirely overlooked. The Retiro, according to Matías de Novoa, was "a confusion without design (*traza*) or beauty."[42]

Yet, if the Retiro had its detractors, it also had its panegyrists. In the sycophantic world of the seventeenth century the palace provided an incomparable opportunity to lavish fulsome adulation on the king and his minister. Poets and pamphleteers hastened to record the latest fiesta, or to celebrate the completion of some new phase of the work. These effusions were for the most part devoid of literary interest. They also lacked real descriptive value, with the significant exception of the verses of Manuel de Gallegos when guiding his reader through the Hall of Realms.[43] No detailed contemporary prose description of the palace survives, and perhaps none was ever written, although there is no lack of detail in descriptions of major court entertainments, especially when Philip himself was an active participant. This reflects an order of priorities in keeping with the time. The palace was observed primarily as a setting for the king.

The copious flow of celebratory prose and verse came from poets and panegyrists who sought to please and impress the regime by drowning beneath a torrent of flattery the mutterings in the palace and the streets. It is doubtful whether these works had any effect, but certainly this was not for want of trying. No metaphor was spared, no image overlooked, that might present the king and his favorite in a brilliant light.

The literary celebrations began in style with Lope de Vega's verses in honor of the first fiesta held at the new palace, in December 1633.[44] Lope devoted most of his efforts to describing the appearance of the "royal planet" and the count–duke in the equestrian games, where, like the sun and the day, they ran side by side. But he paused for a moment to commemorate the beautiful building, which, like the young Adam, emerged perfect at birth, and was born with such rapidity that idea and execution were one and the same. Lope's device of praising the building in order to flatter its creators became the standard technique for those who haltingly followed in the great poet's steps.

When plays were written to be performed at the Retiro, like Antonio de Mendoza's *Los empeños del mentir*, some reference to the palace was clearly in order, and this gave a useful opportunity to praise the count–duke for his part in its construction.[45] In Calderón's *El mayor encanto amor*, the Retiro itself actually makes a stage appearance in the rather improbable form of a giant—although a giant in the guise of a hermit, in obvious reference to the Retiro's hermitages—who offers to guide Ulysses to a place in the temple of fame.[46] Much more remarkable, however, was Calderón's *auto sacramental*, *El nuevo palacio del Retiro*, written for performance during the feast of Corpus Christi in 1634.[47]

The *auto sacramental* was a form of liturgical play in honor of the Eucharist, which conveyed its moral or doctrinal lesson in dramatic form through a narrative that might be drawn from history, or legend, or some contemporaneous event.[48] The inauguration of the Retiro provided Calderón with a novel setting for this characteristic form of allegorical drama leading up to the public display and adoration of the sacrament. The religious message was conveyed by an allegory that moved to and fro between two planes of reality, linking the earthly order and the spiritual. One plane was represented by the Retiro itself, its gardens and its palace; the other by the Retiro as the type of the New Jerusalem.

Calderón achieved his effects through a series of complex images, equating God with the king, the Church with the queen, and Man with Olivares—the favorite of his Maker. Judaism, represented by a wandering Jew,[49] finds himself standing before a splendid palace, where once there had been only wasteland and olive groves (*el campo de olivares*). When he asks Man—Olivares—what this building is, he is told that it has been created by God (the king) for his spouse (the church), and that it is the heavenly city described by St. John in the Apocalypse. It is the home, too, of God's creatures (to be found in the Large Lake, the menagerie and the aviary respectively), and it would stand to all eternity. Foiled in his attempt to gain access—a pointed reference to the attempts of Jews and crypto-Jews to settle and trade in the king's dominions—he vows to set the palace on fire, but the way is barred by Faith, and he is forced to watch the mystery of the enactment of the Eucharist. As the Host disappears, the king is revealed inside the tower, holding the cross on high. "During this brief withdrawal (*retiro*) into the bread," he announces, "I remain for ever constant both in body and soul . . . So the law of grace may always hold me in the New Palace of the Buen Retiro . . . once a desert field, transformed into a New Palace of the New Testament." "Listen, mortals, listen!" cries Music. "Now the New Palace is the Palace of the Buen Retiro, the king's temporary abode."

Calderón, through his verbal imagery, was capable of producing symbolic metamorphoses as spectacular as those being simultaneously wrought on the stage by the great scenographer, Cosimo Lotti. Verbal and scenic ingenuity combined to reaffirm faith and to raise belivers to the heights of fervent adoration. But if, at one level—the divine—all the spectators of the *auto sacramental* were devout believers, at another—the human—there was more than a little scepticism, and not even the magical artistry of a Calderón could ensure a suspension of disbelief. The count–duke was perpetually demanding an unquestioning loyalty to himself and his works, and the poets and hacks who undertook to supply it inevitably sounded false outside the circle of the faithful.

A shining example of this kind of propaganda is provided by the *Elogios al palacio real del Buen Retiro*, the anthology of poems published in 1635 by Diego de Covarrubias.[50] The completion of the Hall of Realms provided the occasion for these verses, which sing the glory of the king by praising the decoration of the Hall. The palace itself is called *la casa del Sol*—the house of the Sun[51]—"the nest of the august royal bird";[52] the king, inevitably, becomes the Planet of Austria, and Olivares his Atlas.[53] The anthology includes a long and vapid panegyric by the royal chronicler, José Pellicer de Tovar, which depicts the Retiro as excelling the seven wonders of the world. Nothing, wrote Pellicer, strangely forgetting the war, gives such grandeur to a monarch as to "build in peace with famous monuments a lasting posterity . . . In a building there lives for ever the image of its owner." As befitted the royal chronicler, Pellicer was also anxious to present the official justification for the Retiro in his verses:

> Que para reynar atento
> Tal vez es bien que se alague
> Lo severo del Palacio
> En lo apacible del Parque.

"To reign well, it is perhaps a good thing to temper the severity of the palace with the peacefulness of the park." For this reason Philip was urged to seize the brief moments of escape from a kingly office that was little more than a prison.

Pellicer's verses are no more than a sycophantic celebration of the palace and its builders. But in 1637 Manuel de Gallegos attempted in one section of his *Obras Varias al Real Palacio del Buen Retiro* a detailed defense of the Retiro—no doubt officially inspired—which itself constitutes one of the best indications of the deep unpopularity of the project.[54] "The ignorant populace," it began, "listening to the sound of drums . . . and with all Spain at war, asks how, in these martial days, the Retiro still continues to expand." His muse then sets out to answer this delicate question. The mysteries of reason of state were not easily comprehended, nor was it incumbent upon kings to explain everything they did. Once the King of Spain had shown the world that he wanted to build a palace, it would be quite wrong for the work to cease simply because of war. What greater prize could Spain's enemies claim than the cessation of construction? No barbarous war should be allowed to interfere with royal pomp. In any event, did imperial grandeur never before combine recreation with martial fury? Recreation is part of the greatness of kings. In the midst of wars Charles V embellished the Alcázar and constructed a terrestrial paradise at Balsaín, and Philip II built the Escorial.

Although Gallegos found other justifications for the Retiro, this reaffirmation of the right of kings to indulge in what were traditionally regarded as characteristically royal activities formed the centerpiece of his argument. Behind it lay a long line of treatises on kingship, which regarded liberality and magnificence as indispensable adjuncts of princely glory.[55] But there was an alternative tradition, exemplified both by Machiavelli[56] and the neo-Stoics, which condemned excessive display as unfitting, or imprudent, or both. Justus Lipsius, that oracle of seventeenth-century Spaniards, emphasized the importance of *modestia* in the comportment of the prince.[57] If sobriety was a virtue even in princes, as Lipsius asserted, then how much more desirable was the practice of this virtue in days of war and high taxation!

The enemies of the regime seized on this idea. While in one breath they were happy enough to criticize the Retiro as a jerry-built structure unworthy of a King of Spain, in the next they were condemning it as superfluous, extravagant and totally inappropriate in time of war.[58] The same was true of the fiestas held in its courts and its gardens—fiestas described by Novoa as resembling those of Nineveh or Nero or the last days of Rome.[59] As the strain of war began to tell during the later 1630s, and as popular resentment mounted at the apparently interminable list of new taxes, so the criticism grew more bitter and the satire more savage. On December 7, 1639 Quevedo was arrested for reasons which were never made public,[60] but it was generally believed that he was the author of a scurrilous verse satire which the king found concealed beneath his table napkin. This satire, in the form of a *Memorial* addressed to Philip, condemned the ministers for their fiscal extortions, but did not spare the king himself, "great, in the way that a hole can be described as great." A principal target was the Retiro. With the heavy cost of war in Italy and Flanders, this was no time for extravagance at home—for constructing lakes, courts and palaces out of the blood and sweat of the poor. "It is lawful for a king to enjoy himself and spend, but it is only just, too, that he should pay his own way."[61]

The modifications in the design of the Retiro, and especially the construction of the Hall of Realms, may be regarded, in part at least, as a response to running criticisms of this kind. A reaffirmation of the power and splendor of the dynasty might help to banish the more frivolous overtones of a pleasure palace. But the count–duke remained extremely sensitive to attacks on the project upon which he had lavished so much care and devotion. Indeed they were strong enough to prompt the king to come to his minister's defense, in a decree dating from about 1640 in which he put the case for a new house of recreation.[62] He had, he said, entrusted the count–duke with the task of building him a royal retreat in which he could rest and relax in healthy surroundings. In this, as in everything else, the count–duke had left nothing to be desired, and had brought the work to its present state in accordance with plans drawn up to his own personal orders.

Philip was clearly attempting to shield the count–duke from the attacks of his enemies by identifying the Retiro as a royal creation. At the same time he was justifying the Retiro as best he could in terms of utility and cost, but the justification, even when it came from the king, was unlikely to go far in silencing the critics. Spain's envoy to the papal court, don Juan Chumacero, spoke of them in a private letter to Olivares, written from Rome on May 25, 1641.[63]

I cannot conceal from Your Excellency how much has been written and reported at this court over the past eight years about the cost of the Buen Retiro. One of the reasons put forward for not granting an ecclesiastical subsidy of one tenth was precisely this expenditure. In the kingdom of Sicily, and still more in that of Naples, the constant remittances for the furnishings, decorations and amusements of the palace and gardens have provoked deep discontent. The costs have been exaggerated, and have made obnoxious the recent collection of taxes for public necessities. If Your Excellency has a balance sheet prepared you will see how many military needs could have been met from those sources of revenue. I regard this as a matter of conscience at a time when taxes are a source of such impoverishment and affliction, particularly when they are levied for avoidable expenses.

Chumacero had always been a man to speak his mind, which was perhaps one reason why he now found himself in Rome. But Olivares, replying on October 22, professed himself delighted to take up the challenge and produced a lengthy justification of the Retiro. This defense of the palace, written by the man who built it, is such a remarkable document as to deserve extensive quotation:[64]

I confess that I am very happy to see you touch on this question of the Retiro . . . because, as something which seems to affect me closely, I am always pleased to see the charges and so be able to draw up the defense; and although I do not claim to excuse myself in any way, in order to avoid offending against the truth, I will say a few words. I can assure you that what was begun in the Buen Retiro, and for which I am responsible, cost closer to ten thousand than to ten million ducats. Once this was done, it was decided to continue, and in the process I lost everything I had there, and everything I had tried to construct, consisting of four rooms for passing Holy Week and those few days when His Majesty can get away to the countryside, far from the madding crowd.

Here a number of different charges arise . . . I think it can be established in the first place that there is not a king or potentate in all Europe who has not built himself a house, and a good house at that; and while I have seen judges condemned for building themselves houses, I have never heard of kings meeting such a fate. Let us now consider our own kings. . .

His Majesty's father built the palaces and gardens in Valladolid, those of Lerma, and the houses of the dukes of Lerma and Uceda here in Madrid. Look at the expense of all this to the royal treasury, and if the Retiro cost the patrimony a tenth of this sum, I am prepared to accept the criticisms . . . Now let's look at his grandfather [Philip II], the first of all kings in wisdom . . . Not one *maravedí* did he spend which was not drawn from the royal patrimony, and merely the acquisition of pasturelands cost four times more than the Buen Retiro. His great grandfather [Charles V], than whom the world has seen no greater nor more embattled monarch, built the Pardo, Aranjuez, Balsaín, Segovia, and innumerable other residences which I shall not even mention—and all this at such splendor and expense that every one of these houses cost infinitely more than the Retiro. And observe that there is probably not a single king who does not have a second residence in his capital. Here I should add that this is a positive necessity, because if there should be smallpox in the palace, all the royal family would be exposed, or else would have to take refuge in some nearby house till the epidemic ends . . . On top of this there is a host of other reasons which I shall not bother to rehearse, because if all kings have a second residence there is no need to say any more.

Let us turn now to Ferdinand the Catholic, that King of kings . . . He built an infinite number of great houses. From all of which it follows that all monarchs have two palaces in their court and capital, and that Spain's greatest kings, so far from restricting themselves to one, have built several, all of them impressive in respect both of adornment and architecture. The king, our master (whom God preserve) has built one, which is comfortable and in good taste, and he has built it with a great deal of piety, and not a trace of ostentation.

The furnishing, as regards pictures and tapestries, is of consideration, but not excessive; and if I say that the Retiro did not involve one twentieth of the costs of what Philip III built at the expense of the royal patrimony, I should have to say that it did not amount to a five hundredth of the sum spent by other kings. In fact, *señor* don Juan, I must speak out plainly. The Buen Retiro, in terms of the royal patrimony, excise dues, sales tax, royal rents and dues, benevolences and other contributions and grants, has not cost His Majesty five hundred ducats, the only exception being that the Count of Monterrey sent three or four hangings and a bed, which were paid for out of the royal treasury and patrimony.

. . . It will be said that, while the money was not drawn from the royal treasury (on this there is no dispute) it would have been possible to arrange loans with the bankers on the basis of these fiscal expedients and contributions, and so save the treasury equivalent sums. As far as this is concerned, I should say that, of all the loans arranged on the basis of such expedients, there is no evidence that a single one could have been arranged on beneficial terms, even had the expedients been of differing quality, produced in different circumstances, and solidly guaranteed. I must confess to you that, having had an inquiry made in order to reply to your letter in the terms used above, I draw consolation from the fact that the charges levelled against us can be so convincingly refuted. . .

Technically the count–duke's arguments appear to have been correct. In building the Retiro the king had carefully refrained from drawing on his patrimonial revenues and on the standard sources of income for the Crown's ordinary expenses. It is also probable that Olivares was right in arguing that fiscal expedients used for financing the construction, like the sale of offices and the excise dues of Madrid, would not have proved satisfactory instruments for negotiating loans from the bankers on advantageous terms to the Crown. But all such arguments skirted round the principal charge levelled against the new palace: that its building had been subsidized by various forms of additional taxation, of a more or less indirect nature, which fell on vassals of the Spanish Crown—whether in Naples, Sicily or Castile itself—who were already bearing an intolerably oppressive burden as a consequence of their monarch's endless wars. Taxes even for "necessary" purposes, like war, were bad enough; but when they were simply required for the amusement of the king, indignation and outrage were a natural response.

In so far as Olivares permitted himself to consider popular reactions, his arguments were couched in purely traditional terms: every king should have a second palace, on grounds both of magnificence and necessity. The defense looks lame to later generations; but, more significantly, it was already beginning to look lame to Olivares's own contemporaries. The conventional defense of royal "magnificence" had a hollow ring to it when it was voiced amidst the miseries of a seventeenth-century Europe afflicted by economic recession and heavy wartime taxation. In a world like this, the stoical virtues of restraint and sobriety acquired a new attractiveness. Olivares, in building the Retiro, was out of tune with his times.

Yet he himself was a man of notable austerity in his personal life. His own inclinations and outlook had been shaped, at least in part, by the neo-Stoicism of Justus Lipsius and his followers.[65] Why, then, did he allow his monarch to build this extravagant folly? If his letter to Chumacero is to be believed, it was done against his wishes—a mere four rooms would have been good enough for him. But was this the truth? Nothing with the count–duke was ever quite as he made it appear. There were always arguments, some of them deliberately concealed, some of them perhaps unconsciously concealed even from himself, for policies and actions which would then be defended on quite other grounds. There is no doubt that the Retiro, however untraditional in some of the manifestations it assumed, embodied a highly traditional view of the nature of kingship. For the count–duke, as indeed for his contemporaries, magnificence was the royal way of life. That kings should live in splendid palaces and disport themselves in suitably royal fashion, was entirely proper; and when the king was the King of Spain, the greatest monarch in the world, only the best would do. All this was openly avowed by Olivares in his defense of the Retiro. But behind it lay other considerations, less clearly spelled out. If at first, as is not impossible, he was genuinely reluctant to embark on the building of a great royal palace, he was quick to see the advantages in terms of the monarch whom he sought to serve. If Philip IV were to be seen as a true "King of Spain,"[66] he must be housed in a manner worthy of his greatness: not, that is, with the ostentation of a vulgar petty prince, but with the external restraint and inward splendor which betokened true royal taste. Once the decision was made, then the building of the Retiro itself became a statement about Philip and his reign. It was publicly presented as a well-earned retreat for a conscientious and hard-working monarch; and the fact that it was rising during times of hardship and war was itself a reminder to the world that Spain's resources were indeed inexhaustible, and that, as Calderón had indicated, the eternity of divinely ordained kingship transcended the changes wrought by the malicious hand of time.

But there were probably still other considerations at work, deeply woven into the complex relationship of the king and his minister. The king, not unnaturally, wished to enjoy himself. The minister, equally naturally, was anxious to ensure that his royal master was given what he desired. Once the construction of the palace was under way, Philip conceived a liking for it, and wanted to see it embellished, extended, and put to good purpose. Olivares, for his part, was happy to go along with the king, encouraging what in any event was from his point of view a conveniently harmless enthusiasm which reduced the likelihood of Philip succumbing to other enthusiasms of a perhaps more dangerous kind. In this sense, the relationship between the two men may have undergone a subtle change where the Retiro was concerned, with the king himself, usually so passive, setting the pace, and the minister, anxious to oblige, outdoing himself in his determination to keep his master satisfied.

To contemporaries, however, the Retiro was Olivares's palace. He had used it as a device for bewitching the king, and concealing from him the true state of affairs in his realms. In the *Cave of Meliso*, a dialogue in verse between Olivares and Meliso the magician which enjoyed an enormous popularity in the Spain of the 1640s, Meliso advises don Gaspar that the construction of great buildings is the proper occupation of lords. First of all he must build the king a chicken coop, and then design a garden and a palace, which would be the first wonder of the world. After this he should organize such splendid entertainments that the king would never leave his capital, and would be so distracted by diversions that don Gaspar would be left to rule alone. Then he was to found twelve hermitages, after the twelve apostles, and fill them with magicians, rabbis and alfaquis. Not a hen was to be left in Cairo, not an elephant in Africa; and nothing was to be left undone that would embellish the palace, and, with the aid of machine plays and fiestas, keep the king bewitched.[67]

The Retiro, then, had come to occupy a significant place in the mythology of the opposition to the government of Olivares, which rested on the central proposition that he had captured the king's will. There was a long tradition that favorites maintained their domination over monarchs by the use of potions and philtres, and kept them distracted with lavish diversions. This was said of the Duke of Lerma in the reign of Philip III, and now it was said of Olivares in the reign of Philip's son. The Retiro, with its gardens, its lakes, its pageants and plays, gave the charge a useful plausibility. The evidence was there for all to see. If anyone sought a monument to the mysterious influence exercised over the king by the favorite he had but to go to the Prado of San Jerónimo and look around him.

By the winter of 1642 this influence was at last beginning to wane. Olivares himself, for all his resilience, was a sick and exhausted man, suffering from terrible dizziness and headaches,[68] and perhaps already near to a mental breaking-point. His years of government had ended in disaster. Portugal and Catalonia were in rebellion, the king's Aragonese campaign of 1642 had proved a miserable failure, and the balance of power in Europe appeared to have tilted irrevocably in favor of France. Everyone, except—it seemed—the king, was convinced that Olivares must go. The king himself, returning to Madrid from Aragon on December 6, 1642 still showed every sign of confidence in his minister, but all around him Olivares's enemies were burrowing away. The count–duke's own relatives, like the Count of Castrillo, were working for his downfall, in the belief—which proved correct—that by jettisoning Olivares they could still save themselves. The king was under such intense pressure from the grandees, and from within his own intimate circle, that sooner or later he was bound to give way, not least because he was being pushed in the same direction by the logic of events. On January 16, 1643 the ever loyal Antonio Carnero wrote privately to a colleague: "My master is utterly worn down and broken, but even as the waters close over him he still keeps swimming."[69] The next day Philip, who had gone to the Torre de la Parada, sent the count–duke a note granting him permission to retire. On January 23 Olivares left the palace for Loeches, never again to return to Madrid.[70]

Once the great man had fallen, his enemies, as was to be expected, came out into the open. Amidst enormous rejoicings in Madrid, the king announced that in future he would rule without a favorite. Some of the more obnoxious features of the Olivares regime, like the juntas, began to be dismantled; and it was in the same spirit of total rejection of the immediate past that all the silver in the Retiro, including Villanueva's twelve splendid lions in the Hall of Realms, was sent to be melted down. Villanueva himself survived, at least for the time being, although with his powers sharply reduced; and so, with varying degrees of precariousness, did the other members of the Olivares circle. In the circumstances the enemies of the Olivares regime could hardly be satisfied with what they had so far achieved, and they were soon baying for the count–duke's blood.

Within a few weeks of the favorite's fall a series of charges drawn up by a member of the administration, Andrés de Mena, were circulating in the court.[71] They constituted a long indictment of the count–duke for his sins of omission and commission, and inevitably included a reference to the Retiro, built with the blood of the poor. At a time when soldiers were dying of hunger, Mena alleged, workmen were kept busy constructing and dismantling courtyards, as part of a project which was entirely unnecessary when the king already had the Escorial, Aranjuez, the Pardo, his hunting-lodges, and the Casa del Campo. Why, then, build in a desert, irrigated more by the sweat of the poor than by the canals and fountains constructed with such enormous effort?

Olivares, even in his disgrace, was not the man to let such charges go unanswered. Francisco de Rioja, who had accompanied him into exile, prepared a vigorous response, the *Nicandro*, which was printed in Madrid without a licence in May 1643, and aroused a storm at court.[72] As far as the charge about the Retiro was concerned, the count–duke's defense was predictable, and simply rehearsed the arguments already expressed in the letter to Chumacero. So far from expressing any contrition, the *Nicandro* claimed that the great care which had gone into adorning the palace, "almost without cost to His Majesty," was worthy of praise.

The count–duke's eloquent refutation of the charges against him did him no good. He was moved further away, to Toro, but at least the king saw to it that he was left in peace. It was in many ways a troubled peace, for the count–duke's memories would not let him alone. The madness that had hovered over him finally descended, and he died, his mind gone, on July 22, 1645. A vicious poem, sometimes attributed to Quevedo, was written to celebrate the event. "*Al fin murió el Conde-Duque*—now at last the count–duke is dead." Having failed to gain entry into heaven, the count–duke is turned away from purgatory by an unwelcoming devil, and pathetically asks: "For the man who built the *Retiro*, is all *retiro* then to be denied?" In the end he is appointed governor of hell.[73]

If the fall of Olivares was primarily the result of political failure and military defeat, the Retiro also played its part. For the count–duke and his colleagues it had come to stand as a symbol of the greatness of their king, of the splendor of his majesty and the distinction of royal leadership in all the arts of peace. They cherished with particular tenacity the vision of a world that revolved with perfect regularity around the splendid figure of the monarch, the earthly upholder and representative of a cosmic order. Olivares shared this vision with contemporary statesmen elsewhere—with Strafford in England demanding due decorum, with Richelieu in France protesting at the confusion in Louis XIII's household, from the kitchen to his study.[74] Struggling to prevent the fragmentation of the state under the political and military strains of the 1620s and 1630s, these statesmen sought to elevate their princes as the symbols of order and authority in times of threatening chaos.

It was a natural response on the part of hard-pressed ministers, but it precipitated new problems of its own. Authority, when elevated too high, lost touch with hard political realities; kingship, in becoming more remote, lost contact with the people. Olivares and his colleagues lived in a restricted court world, where the royal authority seemed so paramount that it was taken for granted that subjects must obey. The concerns of the king were their own concerns, and it was easy to be unaware of the nature of life outside the gilded cage of the court. This had always been true of court life, but to some extent the close proximity of the capital city had helped prevent the total isolation of ministers from the outside world. The Alcázar was part of the life of Madrid; there were shops in its patios, and courtiers, officials and populace were thrown together in the course of everyday existence.

With the building of the Retiro, however, the isolation increased. It was true that on occasions the gardens were thrown open, and the populace was invited to enjoy the pageants and plays. But the Retiro itself was a palace built on the principle of seclusion, as its surrounding wall emphasized. Essentially it was designed for private royal diversions, and for the pursuit of courtly activities away from the crowd. Within its walls courtiers and palace officials and the favorites of the favorite talked exclusively to each other, oblivious to the angry voices that were clamoring outside.

This absorption in a private world, even if it lasted for only six or seven weeks a year, could only widen the gulf between ministers anxious to emphasize the splendors of royalty, and taxpayers who could hardly fail to calculate their cost.

If the growing division between "court" and "country" was a major element in Europe's political turmoils of the mid-seventeenth century,[75] then the Buen Retiro takes its place in a wider, European, story of how that division grew. Reflecting traditional ideas of kingship and the determination of seventeenth-century statesmen to put those ideas to new and more masterful use, it challenged assumptions that were developing in society at large about the proper disposal of public resources in an age when austerity seemed both morally desirable and financially necessary. Taxes were too high, resources too scarce, for kings to indulge in expensive private pursuits. Conditions would change again, and attitudes with them, but in those harsh middle decades of the seventeenth century a pleasure palace came to seem the height of royal irresponsibility.

In the Buen Retiro Olivares created in Madrid a second royal residence which he represented as essential to the king's dignity and general well-being. The justification may seem unimpressive but the achievement was not. Taking a wilderness he turned it into a garden by the use of elaborate irrigation systems that bore witness to the growing technical ingenuity of the times. He furnished the palace superbly and helped the king make it one of the great treasure-houses of European art; and he transformed palace and gardens into a magical setting for plays and entertainments devised by some of the greatest poets and playwrights of the age. The Retiro was above all an act of the will—the will of a statesman who in everything was an instinctive architect and builder. But if he built a new palace, he signally failed to build a new Monarchy. As a result, the structure that was to symbolize all the greatness of *Felipe el Grande* was left to preside with a massive irrelevance over the ruin that was Spain.

Epilogue

With the fall of Olivares, silence descended upon the Retiro. The king's political woes, compounded by his personal tragedies, left him with no heart for merrymaking. But the partial revival of his spirits after his second marriage helped to bring the Retiro back to life. With the return of the court, there also came a few improvements to the site, the most notable of which were the frescoes executed from 1659 to 1661 by two Italians, Agostino Mitelli and Angelo Michele Colonna.[1] Another event of 1661 was the launching of a new galley on the Large Lake.[2] As it cruised the waters of the Retiro, this ship, adorned by the sculpture of José de Rates, founder of the Churriguera dynasty, and Manuel Pereira, a leading sculptor of Madrid, carried on board the memories of an age of court splendor that was now drawing to a close.

During the reign of the enfeebled Charles II, the Retiro became as much a stage for political maneuvers as for court spectacles.[3] Even before the death of Philip, quarters in the palace had been assigned to the bastard Juan José of Austria, who, as the son of an actress, must have felt very much at home in this theatrical setting. For the next twenty years, don Juan occasionally used the Retiro as a base of operations for his curiously sporadic, indecisive bid for power. Political intrigue apparently left little time to attend to the maintenance of the palace, which in 1682 was again reported to be in need of repair. On November 5 of that year, the deputy governor warned that the site would be lost if prompt attention were not paid to restoring it.[4] Over the next century and a half, a succession of court officials would make a litany of this admonition.

The disappearance of the Retiro accounts for Charles's reign makes it nearly impossible to chronicle the fortunes of the palace during this period. But at least one artist of note is known to have left his mark there. In 1692, Luca Giordano executed a splendid fresco decoration in the Casón, consisting of a ceiling painting of the *Allegory of the Golden Fleece*, which is still in place, and a series of the *Labors of Hercules* on the upper walls, destroyed in the nineteenth century.[5]

The advent of the Bourbons brought to the life of the Spanish court French ideas and French tastes, which in time were imposed on the Retiro. To the new monarch, Philip V (1700–46), and especially to his queen, the Retiro was much more agreeable than the Alcázar, which for all the attempts to disguise the fact was still a medieval castle. Once the new king had started to establish control over the peninsula, he began to explore the possibilities of remaking the Retiro into a proper French palace, on the model of Versailles.[6] The project was first discussed in 1708, but it was not until 1712 that political conditions permitted serious planning to begin. In that year, René Carlier, an assistant in the workshop of the French royal

239

architect Robert de Cotte, arrived from Paris to take the project in hand. It soon became apparent, at least to de Cotte, that Carlier's ideas for remodelling the Retiro were unworkable, primarily because they required massive excavations of the hillside on which it had injudiciously been built. In 1714, de Cotte took over the project himself and produced the design of a building whose scale and magnificence almost humiliate the existing structures and gardens (fig. 152).

De Cotte's notion was to change the orientation of the site by creating an immense circular entrance court on the Calle de Alcalá, which would lead through two more courtyards to a huge U-shaped palace. Behind the palace would be a large formal garden that extended all the way to the Calle de Atocha. In this plan, the Habsburg palace takes on the appearance of a neglected, confused stepchild shunted to one side by a brilliant new arrival. It must have been immediately apparent that de Cotte had overstepped by far the limits of the possible, because a second plan of a year later is considerably less ambitious (fig. 153). Here the architect was concerned simply with improving the garden by formalizing the design and adding a new facade to the garden wing, leaving most of the existing palace intact.

As it happened, de Cotte's second plan was also put on the shelf. But Philip did order changes to be made by the architect Teodoro Ardemans.[7] In 1712, work began on transforming the Retiro's most famous garden, the Octagonal Garden, into a formal parterre in the approved French style. Philip V also built a new church

152. Robert de Cotte, First Project for Redesign of the Retiro (Paris, Bibliothèque Nationale)

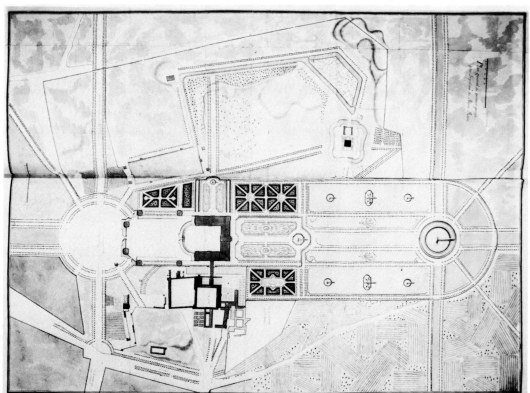

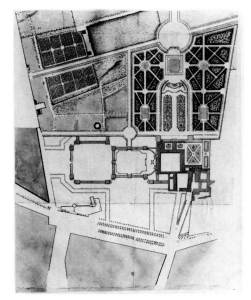

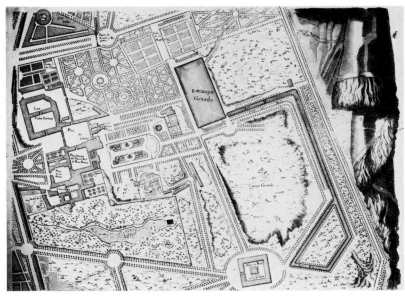

153. Robert de Cotte, Second Project for Redesign of the Retiro (Paris, Bibliothèque Nationale)

154. Antonio Espinosa, Palace and Park of the Retiro, from Map of Madrid, 1769 (Madrid, Biblioteca Nacional)

in the gardens, Nuestra Señora de las Angustias, to serve the needs of those who lived and worked at the Retiro. He found the hermitage chapels in a sad state of decay, and ordered them to be refurbished; and when San Antonio, the most impressive of them, was destroyed by fire in 1734 it was quickly rebuilt. Later that year, the Retiro unexpectedly acquired new importance. On Christmas Eve, it was the turn of the Alcázar to be ravaged by fire, and large parts of it were damaged beyond repair. Subsequently it was decided to demolish the remains and to build an entirely new structure. During the next thirty years, while the Palacio Nuevo was being built, the Retiro served as the principal residence of the Spanish royal family.[8] To tide him over the waiting period, the king ordered the remodelling of the interior in a French Rococo taste, and this work was completed by his son and successor, Ferdinand VI (1746–59).

This melancholy monarch lived primarily at the Retiro when he was not seeking solace at Aranjuez or at La Granja, where Philip V had constructed an Italianate summer palace set in French-style gardens. It was Ferdinand who was responsible for remodelling the Retiro theater to provide a suitable setting for the opera, and especially for performances by the great Italian castrato Farinelli, which helped to alleviate the royal melancholy. By the time of Ferdinand's death in 1759, the interior of the Retiro palace seems to have borne little relationship to the impressive interior designed for Philip IV. Decor, furnishings and paintings—all had been changed to suit the Bourbon taste.

Charles III (1759–88) lived in the Retiro for the first five years of his reign, but at the end of 1764 he was able to move into the new royal palace. The theater of the Retiro remained in use, but the royal apartments were increasingly abandoned. Although certain court ceremonies continued to be held there, the completion of the new palace deprived the Retiro of much of the importance it had attained in the middle decades of the century. Moreover, the costs of upkeep were high, and there was little money to spend on repairs. When Elizabeth Lady Holland visited the Retiro in 1803, she reported that "the palace is neither magnificent within nor without; the royal apartments are stripped of their furniture. A few excellent pictures alone remain."[9]

If the palace was neglected, the gardens were better cared for (fig. 154), and special arrangements were made in them for the accommodation of Art and Science, the handmaidens of the new enlightened monarch. In 1759, Charles established a porcelain factory in the hermitage of San Antonio, using workers brought from Capodimonte in Naples. Eventually Buen Retiro porcelain came to hold a distinguished place in the decorative arts of the eighteenth century.[10] Just before he died, Charles began to plan the establishment in the gardens of an astronomical observatory, which was completed in 1799. But his most important innovation was to open the gardens to the public during the summer and autumn from 1767 onwards. Regulations stipulated that men were to wear neither hats nor capes in the gardens, and women had to leave their *mantillas* at the gates. Refreshments were made available in two separate sections of the gardens, but were not to be consumed on the benches, which the public could use without charge.[11] Further attractions were added to this quarter of Madrid in the years that followed. In 1781 Charles III created the botanical garden in the Paseo del Prado and it was in his reign that work started on a Museum of Natural Sciences which was converted into a picture gallery in 1819, to become the Prado Museum.[12]

The Enlightenment had come to Madrid; public pleasure and public edification were to march to the same beat. But all too soon the Enlightenment was followed by the strains and upheavals produced by the revolution in France. It was in the Retiro in July 1807 that Canon Escoiquiz, formerly tutor to the Prince of Asturias, negotiated with the French ambassador, François de Beauharnais, for a marriage between the heir to the throne and a princess from the family of Napoleon—a negotiation that served as the prelude to the French invasion of 1808 and the proclamation of Joseph Bonaparte as King of Spain. Murat's soldiers, having placed Joseph Bonaparte on his throne, began work on fortifying the Retiro, which— occupying as it did the highest ground in Madrid—was regarded as the key to the capital. Many of its magnificent trees were felled, trenches were dug in its gardens, and the buildings were taken over to store arms and ammunition.[13] The popular uprising that drove Joseph from his new capital at the beginning of August led to the conversion of the Retiro into part of Madrid's hastily constructed defensive system against the inevitable French onslaught. This came at the beginning of December under Napoleon's direction. On December 3, following an artillery bombardment, French troops broke into the grounds of the Retiro, and occupied the porcelain factory, the observatory and the palace. The following day resistance crumbled, and Madrid surrendered to the invading army.

During the nearly four years in which the French occupied Madrid, the Retiro housed the garrison. Three lines of defense were constructed: the outer line consisting of the palace itself and the wall enclosing the Retiro park; an intermediate line with ten bastioned fronts; and a star-shaped citadel occupying the site of the porcelain factory.[14] It was inevitable, therefore, that the Retiro would bear the brunt of any attack on Madrid by the Anglo-Spanish forces under the command of the Duke of Wellington.

Following Wellington's victory at the battle of Salamanca, Joseph Bonaparte hastily left Madrid on August 11, 1812, and on the 13th the siege of the Retiro began. It was to be mercifully brief, largely because the French commander, Lafon-Blaniac, found—as others had found in more peaceful times—that the Retiro's water supply was limited. General Pakenham's men had little difficulty in breaking through the insubstantial enclosing wall and occupying the palace. Fearful of an immense conflagration if his powder-store caught fire, Lafon-Blaniac raised a flag of truce on the 14th and surrendered with his two thousand men. But the misfortunes of the now-battered Retiro were not yet at an end. With the reappearance in force of the French, the allies hastily abandoned Madrid. The French reoccupation was precarious, and on October 31 General Hill's forces entered the town, and drove the

155. Palace and Park of the Retiro, from Model of Madrid, 1830 (Madrid, Museo Municipal)

French from the Retiro, destroying the fortifications and blowing up the porcelain factory before marching out to Alba de Tormes.[15]

By the time the French had retreated across the Pyrenees in the summer of 1813, the Retiro was in ruins (fig. 155). A survey of the site made at the order of Ferdinand VII (1814–33) in September 1814 recommended that all the rooms around the garden of the bronze horse, the servants' courtyard and the southern garden be demolished; the remainder of the palace, it noted, was in urgent need of roofing to save it from collapse.[16] The repairs were not put in hand and the damaged buildings were left to crumble. Of the old Retiro there remained only the Hall of Realms, the Casón, and a pile of rubble. Having failed to save the remnants of the palace, however, Ferdinand VII made amends with the gardens. New avenues were planted, new flower-beds laid out, and new garden buildings constructed, including the little neo-classical pavilion, the *Casita del Pescador*, which still stands on its island in a pool.[17] While Ferdinand reserved part of the gardens for himself, he transferred the larger part to public use; and the process was completed after the revolution of 1868, when the entire site became the property of the municipality of Madrid. Almost two hundred and fifty years after they had paid for the Retiro, the citizens of Madrid now owned it.

The municipal authorities were at first more attracted to the park as a building site than a public amenity. In 1865, plans were drawn up for the construction of fashionable apartments in the western section of the Retiro, and the work of ground-clearing began.[18] Then in 1869, the terrain around the hermitage chapel of Santa María Magdalena was incorporated into the Plaza de la Independencia, with the impressive Puerta de Alcalá, built by Charles III, as its centerpiece.[19] In 1905, the grounds of the hermitage of San Juan, where Olivares went to seek solitude, were excavated for the foundations of a new central post office building, which is now one of the busiest places in the capital.[20] Fortunately, the Retiro has successfully withstood further erosion of its precincts.

"Few governments," observed the nineteenth-century statesman and historian Cánovas del Castillo, of the government of Philip IV, "have rendered a more useful service to Spaniards, either before or since, than in providing them with this truly marvelous park, which they have always enjoyed and still enjoy today."[21] This claim may be somewhat overstated, but there is hardly a citizen of Madrid who would care to refute it as he wanders down the tree-lined avenues of the Retiro, or lingers in the rose garden, or cruises in a rowboat around the great oblong lake—the famous Large Lake of the seventeenth century—now regrettably overshadowed by the enormous monument to Alfonso XII (fig. 156).

The Retiro gardens may have been a somewhat fortuitous legacy of the count–duke to the citizens of Madrid, but in this they were hardly unique. Many of the great civic parks of Europe first came into being as the parks of royal palaces. These splendid palaces and their spacious gardens were constructed at vast social cost to project the prince's image. But if the palace as a political symbol has long since lost its potency, it still retains a secure place in the history of civilization; for while the palace was conceived as a monument to power, it was always something more. As a showcase for the arts it displayed to the world the respectable face of absolutism.

156. The Retiro Lake today

APPENDIX I

A NOTE ON CURRENCY AND MEASUREMENTS

A. Currency

Payments in seventeenth-century Spain are sometimes recorded in units of account (ducats and *maravedís*) and at other times in silver coinage (*reales*), or gold coinage (*escudos*). The relationship between these units was as follows:

1 ducat	375 *maravedís*
1 *real*	34 *maravedís*
1 *escudo*	440 *maravedís* (from 1609)

For the sake of convenience, we have converted all payments into ducats. In the period covered by this book there were approximately four ducats to the English pound sterling.

Internal payments in Castile might be made in *vellón* currency. *Vellón* was originally a mixture of silver and copper used for fractional coins, but by the reign of Philip IV it consisted of pure copper. The inflationary policies of Philip III and Philip IV drove *vellón* to a discount, and the premiums on silver in terms of *vellón* varied from place to place and month to month, reaching fifty or sixty per cent by August 1628, when the government resorted to drastic deflationary measures. By 1640, however, the premium was almost back to the levels of the first half of 1628. (See Earl J. Hamilton, *American Treasure*, Table 7.)

B. Measurements

1 Castilian foot (*pie castellano*)	0.28 meters (11 inches)
1 *vara*	0.84 meters (33 inches)

APPENDIX II

A NOTE ON SOURCES

A. The Regime of Olivares

The study of seventeenth-century Spain has lagged far behind that of England and France in the same period. In spite of Spain's European pre-eminence, at least during the first forty years of the century, Spanish political figures, including those of the first rank, are little known in comparison with their English and French contemporaries. In particular, the Count–Duke of Olivares, who attracted at least as much contemporary attention as his rival, Cardinal Richelieu, has paid the not uncommon price of political defeat—historical neglect. The only biography of him to date, Gregorio Marañón, *El Conde-Duque de Olivares. La pasión de mandar*, first published in 1936, is a study of Olivares as a man. rather than as a statesman, and is primarily concerned to examine the count–duke's complex character and his personal relationships.

Much of the material on Olivares and his government used in our book was gathered by John Elliott in the course of researches for a comprehensive study, now in preparation, of Olivares and his policies. Some of it has now been published in a two-volume critical edition of a number of Olivares's most important state papers and letters, *Memoriales y Cartas del Conde Duque de Olivares*, by John H. Elliott and José F. de la Peña (Madrid, 1978–80). Materials relating to Olivares and his government are scattered through the major Spanish state archives, the Archivo General de Simancas, the Archivo Histórico Nacional (Madrid), the Archivo de la Corona de Aragón (Barcelona), and the Archivo de las Indias (Seville). These materials are complemented by documents in a number of private Spanish archives to which the owners have generously given access, and in archives outside Spain, notably the manuscripts section of the British Library, which contains an important collection of documents for seventeenth-century Spanish history.

On the basis of this documentation it is now possible to reconstruct certain aspects of the domestic history of the first half of the reign of Philip IV in considerable detail, although the destruction of the count–duke's own archive in two fires in the Duke of Alba's palace of Buenavista in 1795 and 1796 means that there are also enormous gaps, which can never be adequately filled. A good deal of the background to major political and court events, however, is provided by the dispatches of foreign envoys in Madrid, and we have therefore made extensive use of ambassadorial reports, particularly those of the British ambassadors and of the envoys of some of the Italian states, especially Genoa, Tuscany and Venice.

B. The Court of Philip IV

In this book we have sought to relate the development of the arts in Golden Age Spain to political life and the culture of the court. It is now almost a century since the great German art historian, Carl Justi, embarked on a rather similar enterprise in his *Diego Velázquez und sein Jahrhundert* (Bonn, 1888; English translation, *Diego Velázquez and his Times*, London, 1889). Unfortunately, Justi's pioneering lead has not been seriously followed, at least as far as the visual arts are concerned. Court history has all too often been reduced to the level of anecdote, and no one has yet made a serious attempt to study the functioning of the Spanish court as a political and social organism. Martin Hume, *The Court of Philip IV* (London, 1907) is an entertaining narrative based on quite extensive archival research, but it is not very accurate and veers wherever possible toward the merely picturesque. The Spanish historian José Deleito y Piñuela wrote a number of works on the life and times of Philip IV (*El rey se divierte*, Madrid, 1928; *Sólo Madrid es Corte*, Madrid, 1942, etc.), but these are little more than useful compilations of material drawn overwhelmingly from literary and printed sources.

Some of the most valuable work in recent years on the court of Philip IV has been done by historians of the theater, and notably by J. E. Varey and N. D. Shergold. We have found particularly helpful the articles of J. E. Varey on court ceremonial cited in Chapter II note 1, the edition by Professors Varey and Shergold of Juan Vélez de Guevara's *Los celos hacen estrellas* (London, 1970), and N. D. Shergold, *A History of the Spanish Stage from Medieval Times to the End of the Seventeenth Century* (Oxford, 1967). Between them these two authors have opened up new possibilities for the study both of court theater and of the court *as* theater—an approach which could prove particularly rewarding.

C. THE BUEN RETIRO

The Palace of the Buen Retiro, like its creator, Olivares, has not received the scholarly attention which it deserves. Part of the reason for this is no doubt the destruction of its archive during the Peninsular War, which means that no central repository of Retiro documentation survives. Any attempt to reconstruct the history of the palace must therefore be based on the very fragmentary documentation dispersed through the major Spanish archives, and on such eyewitness accounts as are available.

The first such attempt was made in 1880 by Rodrigo Amador de los Ríos, in his article, "El palacio antiguo del Buen Retiro" (*Museo Español de Antigüedades*, 11). This article drew on documents in the municipal archive of Madrid, which we have also used, and on the series of Buen Retiro documents preserved in the section of *Administraciones Patrimoniales* of the Archivo del Palacio Real of Madrid. Unfortunately this series, while relatively rich for the eighteenth and nineteenth centuries, contains only a handful of documents relating to the period of the Retiro's construction. Since the time of Amador de los Ríos, work on the Retiro has tended more toward compilation than interpretation, with the important exception of the major article of 1911–12 by Elías Tormo y Monzó reconstructing the installation of the paintings in the Hall of Realms ("Velázquez, el salón de reinos del Buen Retiro y el poeta del palacio y del pintor," reprinted in his volume of collected essays, *Pintura, escultura y arquitectura en España*, Madrid, 1949). No important new source material emerges from the pages of José Bordiú, *Apuntes para la historia del Buen Retiro* (n.d.), which is a rather slight attempt at a synthesis of received facts and assumptions. A more useful summary is provided by José M. Pita Andrade in his *Los palacios del Buen Retiro en la época de los Austrias* (Madrid, 1970), while the place of the Retiro in the history of garden architecture is discussed in a short but admirable account by Marie Louise Gothein, *A History of Garden Art* (repr. New York, 1966), I, pp. 372–80.

Such advances as have been made in the study of the Retiro since the publication of Tormo's essay have been the result of hard archival labor. The prize for this must certainly go to María Luisa Caturla, whose fifty-page book, *Pinturas, frondas y fuentes del Buen Retiro* (1947), along with a series of important articles, represents the outstanding contribution to the modern study of the Retiro. In a lifetime of investigation into the daunting notarial documentation of the Archivo Histórico de Protocolos in Madrid, she made some major discoveries about commissions and payments for artists, contractors and artisans working for the Retiro. To the best of our ability we have followed her lead in undertaking our own investigations in the same archive, and have drawn on a substantial amount of additional documentation which has not been published either by her or by the Marquis of Saltillo, who also made significant discoveries among these notarial documents. There undoubtedly remains much more to be discovered in this remarkable archive, but since the only indexing is by the names of notaries, who annually produced large registers of volumes containing a medley of business contracts, wills, inventories and marriage settlements, the process of discovery is likely to be slow and largely haphazard.

If one approach to the architecture and decoration of the Retiro is through notarial documents, another is through the various series of accounts of payments by ministers and royal officials while the work was in progress. As explained in Chapter IV we have tried to reconstruct the history of the financing of the Retiro largely on the basis of three major series of accounts: the secret expense accounts keep by Jerónimo de Villanueva; the accounts of Villanueva, Cristóbal de Medina and Sebastián Vicente in the Archivo General at Simancas; and Castrillo's accounts in the Archive of the Indies at Seville. J. Domínguez Bordona drew attention to the first of these series, and published extracts from them, in his article of 1933, "Noticias para la historia del Buen Retiro." José de Azcárate, in his "Anales de la construcción del Buen Retiro" (1966) made an extremely useful compilation on a year-to-year basis of salient facts and figures from the Simancas accounts over the period 1630–61. The existence of Castrillo's accounts in the archive of the Indies was mentioned in 1829 by Eugenio Llaguno y Amirola in Volume 4 of his *Noticias de los arquitectos y arquitectura de España* (p. 27). We found them still there, and are not aware that any use has been made of them between Llaguno's time and our own.

In addition to these first-hand sources, we have tried to round out the story by using eyewitness accounts. One major source, available in print, consists of the Jesuit newsletters from Madrid between 1634 and 1648, published in Vols. 13–19 of the *Memorial Histórico Español* (Madrid, 1861–5). There is also much valuable information to be gleaned from the newsletters for 1636 and 1637 published by Antonio Rodríguez Villa in 1886 under the title of *La corte y monarquía de España*, and from the *Avisos* of José Pellicer y Tovar in Vols. 31 and 32 of Valladares, *Semanario Erudito* (1790), although these begin only in 1639. There is also the journal of the embittered courtier Matías de Novoa, printed in Vols. 69, 77, 80 and 86 of the *Colección de Documentos Inéditos para la Historia de España* under the title of *Historia de Felipe IV, Rey de España*. Novoa is consumed by hatred of Olivares and of all his works, and while this hatred inevitably deforms his vision of the history of the period, it can also, if carefully used, provide a valuable corrective to the count–duke's panegyrists. Novoa's history constitutes, too, a mine of information, much of it regrettably tendentious and obscure, about court events and personalities.

Besides these printed contemporary accounts we have also, as explained above, sought to check Spanish documentation against the largely unpublished correspondence of foreign envoys in Madrid. For our purposes the most useful reports by a foreign observer proved to be those of Bernardo Monanni, the resident secretary of the Tuscan legation in Madrid. We have followed these reports in the Archivio di Stato of Florence all the way through from December 1631, when the new Tuscan ambassador, Francesco Medici, commendatore di Sorano, took up his duties, until September 1642, when Monanni left for home (Mediceo, filze 4959–4967). In *Diego Velázquez and his Times* Carl Justi used some of these reports, particularly in relation to the paintings in the Hall of Realms, but erroneously attributed them to the ambassador, whom he incorrectly called "Serrano," a misreading of Medici's title of "commendatore di Sorano." Ambassadors changed but Monanni endured; and since his sources of information were good, and he had a sharp eye for aesthetic matters, his almost weekly dispatches constitute a remarkable record of the building of the Retiro and of court festivities. No other foreign observer can compete with Monanni, and the Venetian ambassadors in particular proved to be disappointing for our purposes, but we did find useful the letters of Sir Arthur Hopton, who was the British agent in Spain from 1631 to 1636 and returned in 1638 as ambassador. Hopton's letter-book for 1631–6 is preserved in the British Library (Egerton Ms. 1820), and his original correspondence is in the Public Record Office, with SP.94.40–42 covering the period from 1638 to 1641. Martin Hume made extensive use of Hopton's papers for his *The Court of Philip IV* and they lend themselves readily to quotation. Hopton's sources of information, however, appear to be more limited than those of Monanni, although the fact that he served a king who was so anxious to acquire more paintings makes him an important source of first-hand artistic news, as Elizabeth DuGué Trapier demonstrated in "Sir Arthur Hopton and the Interchange of Paintings between Spain and England in the Seventeenth Century" (*Connoisseur*, 164–5, 1967). In reporting on political events Hopton was rare among ambassadors in Madrid in showing sympathy for Olivares, and was liable to be over-impressed by the achievements of the regime.

Finally, we owe to an English observer, this time not a diplomat but a merchant, the most detailed account which we possess of the appearance of the interior of the Retiro at a time close to the period studied in this book. John W. Stoye, in his *English Travellers Abroad, 1604–1667* (London, 1952), drew attention to the interest of the manuscript relation preserved in the Bodleian Library (Rawlinson Ms. C.799) of the travels in 1654–5 of Robert Bargrave in Spain (pp. 376–9). If Bargrave did not think much of Madrid, he thought sufficiently well of the Retiro to provide an eyewitness account which conveys at least some impression of how the palace must have looked in the days of its greatness.

The sources of visual information about architecture at the court of Philip IV leave much to be desired. The most serious deficiency is the lack of drawings by architects employed by the Crown, almost none of which have survived. These drawings are frequently mentioned in documents and customarily were filed with construction contracts. Their disappearance constitutes one of the great mysteries of the history of Spanish art and poses a major obstacle to studying Spanish royal architecture with the thoroughness possible for French and English works of the period. Equally unfortunate is the paucity of contemporary views of architecture and court ceremony and entertainment. For reasons which are not clear, there seems to have been little interest in recording the appearance of royal palaces and the events that took place within them.

As a consequence, the history of the construction, decoration and use of the Retiro must be written on the basis of scanty visual material. No drawings by Crescenzi or Carbonel have come to light, although they are referred to in documents. On at least one occasion, a payment was made for forty-eight sheets of "imperial" paper which were given to Carbonel for drawing plans, possibly for the Casón. Neither is there a single known view of the interior of any room of the palace.

Fortunately, however, there is enough material to allow us to recreate the exterior of the palace and parts of the garden and park. Most of the seventeenth-century views are described in the useful *Catálogo de la exposición del antiguo Madrid* (Madrid, 1926), p. 287. The earliest of them was commissioned in 1637 as part of a series of paintings of royal houses done by several artists for the Torre de la Parada. This picture (fig. 30), which is traditionally attributed to Jusepe Leonardo, shows the palace as it looked late in 1637, before the roof was put on the Casón.

Almost twenty years later, in 1656, the first complete exterior view of the palace, grounds and outbuildings was produced by Pedro Texeira in his monumental map of Madrid (figs. 2 and 31), which is discussed by Miguel Molina Campuzano, *Planos de Madrid de los siglos XVII y XVIII* (Madrid, 1960), pp. 264–79. The accuracy of Texeira's map as a whole is generally acknowledged and can be confirmed, as far as the Retiro is concerned, by comparison with other seventeenth-century views and descriptions of the site. The value of the map is increased by the detailed legend which, except for a few minor errors, permits the identification of the major parts of the complex.

A little-known French artist, Louis Meunier, provided a closer look at individual parts of the palace exterior and garden in a series of five etchings done around 1665 (figs. 46–8 and 60). Meunier's prints are discussed in the classic work by A. P. F. Robert-Dumesnil, *Le peintre-graveur français*, 5 (Paris, 1841), pp. 260–4, nos. 18–23, and in *Exposición del antiguo Madrid*, pp. 29–33. The artistic quality of the prints is only mediocre and suggests that Meunier may have been an amateur, but the general level of accuracy cannot be doubted. Meunier's prints achieved wide circulation because they were frequently copied in later compendia of views of Spain, the most important of which are Pieter van den Berghe's *Theatrum Hispaniae* (Amsterdam, n.d. [circa 1700]) and Juan Alvarez de Colmenar's *Délices de l'Espagne et du Portugal* (Leyden, 1707).

The most beautiful and evocative view of the Retiro in the seventeenth century is a large pen and wash drawing by the Italian Pier Maria Baldi (fig. 50). Baldi travelled to Spain in the retinue of the Grand Duke Cosimo III de'Medici, who visited Spain in 1668–9, and executed his drawings to illustrate an account of the journey written by Lorenzo Magalotti, which is preserved in the Laurentian Library, Florence. The drawings, including the one of the Retiro, are published in the edition of Magalotti's diary prepared by Sánchez Rivero.

The only other seventeenth-century view of the Retiro known to us is the one published as Plate 42 in *Exposición del antiguo Madrid*. The inaccuracy of this view is obvious when it is compared to other representations of the site, and it has therefore been omitted from consideration.

This assortment of visual material, when coordinated with building documents and contemporary descriptions, is sufficient to revive, at least in part, the outward appearance of the Retiro. The disposition and appearance of the interior are not as well served by the surviving evidence. There is no known representation of the interior, regardless of date. Nor is there any seventeenth century ground plan of the palace comparable to those, for example, which exist for the Madrid Alcázar. Fortunately, however, a detailed plan of the main floor of the palace was made early in the eighteenth century, before substantial changes of design had been executed. This plan was drawn by René Carlier, an assistant to the French royal architect, Robert de Cotte, who was sent to Madrid in 1712 to plan the renovation of the Retiro. Carlier's plan is preserved in the Bibliothèque Nationale, Paris, but does not reproduce well because of its poor condition. For this reason, we have had an exact copy of the plan made for use in this book.

Carlier also produced other drawings of the Retiro, the most valuable of which are precise site plans with legends that identify the various parts of the garden and park. There are also two cross-sections of the terrain which make it easier to visualize certain features of the palace. Most of these drawings were first published by Yves Bottineau, "Felipe V y el Buen-Retiro," *AEA*, 31 (1958), pp. 117–23.

The other important eighteenth-century views were produced by a Spanish military engineer, Domingo de Aguirre, in 1778. The one which was published in *Exposición del antiguo Madrid*, Plate 22, shows the southeast part of the original palace with considerable fidelity (fig. 37). But Aguirre's representation of the hermitage of San Pablo was made after the original facade had been altered.

Nineteenth-century renderings are of little use because of the extensive damage inflicted on the palace during the Peninsular War. The grounds, too, had been substantially transformed by 1800. The drawings of the site after its fortification by the French, published by Tobajas López in *Sitios Reales*, 1977, have little to say about the original appearance of the palace. And the sector of the Retiro as reproduced in the remarkable scale model of Madrid made in 1830 and now in the Museo Municipal is valuable only for illustrating the final, sad chapter of the now-devastated palace.

Two parts of the palace were salvaged from the rubble—the Hall of Realms, now the Museum of the Spanish Army, and the Casón, which has become the Museum of Nineteenth-Century Art. The exteriors of both structures were remodelled in the last century, as was the interior of the Casón, although Luca Giordano's fresco on the ceiling of the main room was fortunately left intact. But the interior of the Hall of Realms is fundamentally as it was in the great days of the Retiro.

APPENDIX III

VELÁZQUEZ AT THE BUEN RETIRO

During the course of his career as the king's painter, Velázquez participated in the decoration of three royal houses: the Buen Retiro, the Torre de la Parada and the Alcázar, Madrid. These commissions afford an opportunity to study Velázquez at work in specific settings for specific purposes, and provide a different perspective for understanding his personality as a court artist (for an example, see Chapter VI). Velázquez was represented at the Buen Retiro by eighteen paintings, which came to the palace in different ways.

The pictures of greatest interest are the ones commissioned for certain rooms in the palace, of which the Hall of Realms is the most important (discussed in Chapter VI). A second series were the six portraits of court jesters. The discovery of new information pertaining to these works has enabled us to establish their date and original location. Velázquez also painted an important picture for one of the hermitage chapels, which is one of the rare religious subjects of his post-Seville oeuvre.

In addition, the Retiro contained the two key works of Velázquez's first Italian trip, the *Forge of Vulcan* and *Joseph's Bloody Coat Brought to Jacob* (fig. 63). These paintings were in Velázquez's possession until late 1633 or early 1634, when he sold them, together with a number of paintings by other artists, to Jerónimo de Villanueva.

The Retiro also housed the masterpiece of Velázquez's early years, the *Waterseller of Seville* (fig. 87), which, as has long been known, was a gift of the Cardinal Infante Ferdinand. Two portraits of the king and queen and the enigmatic picture of *A Pelican with a Bucket and Donkeys*, rounded out the collection of pictures by Velázquez at the Buen Retiro (see above, Chapter V).

Finally, there are two paintings which represent events that occurred in the palace complex, although they appear not to have been incorporated into the decoration. These are the portrait of *Baltasar Carlos and a Dwarf* and the *Riding Lesson of Baltasar Carlos*.

By 1635, the Retiro was the repository of an excellent anthology of Velázquez's paintings to that date. There were works from Seville, Rome and Madrid, representing almost every aspect of his thematic repertory.

BALTASAR CARLOS AND A DWARF

This picture (fig. 25) is now generally considered to have been the one painted by Velázquez in 1631 upon his return from the first Italian trip, a conclusion which is based on a fragmentary inscription written about half-way up on the curtain to the right of the prince.[1] The inscription, which reads AETATIS AN.../MENS 4, has been interpreted to mean that the prince was one year, four months old when the portrait was painted. Baltasar Carlos was born on October 17, 1629 and therefore the picture would have been finished in February 1631.

This date is open to question for several reasons. One of these is that the prince appears to be older than one year, four months. More important, the inscription is fragmentary and breaks off in the middle of the word ANNUS, which logically ought to have been followed by the number of the prince's years. There is, however, evidence in the picture itself that it was painted in 1632, rather than 1631.

The oath of allegiance (*juramento*) to Baltasar Carlos was held in the church of San Jerónimo, future nucleus of the Buen Retiro palace, early in 1632. The ceremony was scheduled to take place on February 22, when the prince would have been two years, four months and nineteen days old. In the event, it was postponed for two weeks because the prince had fallen ill.[2] But an inscription that put his age at two years, four months would have been accurate if the picture were intended to commemorate the original date on which this significant ceremony was to be held.

Other evidence exists to suggest that this work is indeed the *juramento* portrait of *Baltasar Carlos*. There is the prince's costume, which shows him in the guise of captain–general, wearing an armored collar plate, a red sash and a sword, and holding the baton of command. A contemporary eyewitness account corroborates the fact that the prince wore a similar costume at the ceremony. One passage describes how the prince was carried down the nave of San Jerónimo by his uncles. "Then the infantes Carlos and Ferdinand carried the prince between them by the sleeves of his skirted costume (*vaquero*)—he was also wearing a sword at his waist and a gold, bejeweled dagger, and had on a black hat with pearly white feathers—immediately in front of the king."[3] The black hat with pearly white feathers ("sombrero negro i plumas de nacar") rests on the cushion in the lower right corner of the painting.

Finally, there is the symbolic significance of the objects held by the dwarf. Dwarfs, of course, were employed as playmates for the royal children and the apron worn by the one in this picture may be taken to indicate this role. In his hands, the dwarf holds a rattle and an apple, objects resembling the kingly symbols of the scepter and the orb. By means of these symbols, Velázquez was making a veiled and clever reference to the child's future as King of Spain, a future which was confirmed in the swearing of the oath of allegiance.[4]

LANDSCAPE WITH ST ANTHONY ABBOT AND ST PAUL THE HERMIT

This important picture (fig. 86) has been dated both to the 1630s and the 1650s. Until a document relating to the commission comes to light, the question cannot be conclusively resolved. But there are indications in the Retiro documentation that suggest the greater likelihood of the earlier date.

It is clear, because of its original semi-circular top and its subject, that the painting was intended to serve as an altarpiece. In the Retiro inventory of 1701, the first time the picture is mentioned, it was listed as installed in an altar in the hermitage of San Antonio de Padua, or "de los Portugueses." Writers have pointed out that this was an illogical location for the picture, which by virtue of its subject matter should have been in the hermitage of San Pablo.[5] Another image of *St Paul the Hermit* was made for this chapel by the sculptor G. M. Ceroni early in 1633, proving the obvious point that the hermitages were adorned with images of saints to whom they were dedicated.[6] We also know from the construction contract for San Antonio (see above, p. 81) that the chapel of the hermitage was to have altars dedicated to Sts Anthony of Padua, Elizabeth and Gonzalo, but not St Anthony Abbot.

It seems likely, then, that Velázquez's picture was commissioned for the chapel in the hermitage of San Pablo. On January 15, 1633, Monanni described the hermitage as having been finished.[7] However, work on the interior decoration including the completion of the altar continued into the spring. On May 21, 1633, a certain Miguel Viveros was paid 1400 reales on account for painting and gilding the architectural framework of the altarpieces in San Pablo and San Juan.[8] Four days later, Ceroni was paid 800 reales for the altarpiece he had made for San Pablo and the one he was making for San Juan.[9] This evidence indicates that the altarpiece of San Pablo was finished by the end of May 1633, and this presumably was when Velázquez's painting was also ready to be installed.

A possible explanation for the transfer of the picture to the hermitage of San Antonio can be found in the remodelling and redecoration of San Pablo carried out between 1659 and 1661, which involved the creation of frescoes by Colonna and Mitelli.[10] The payments to these two artists indicate that they were painting the facade and the ceiling of the "salón." The chapel is not mentioned, but perhaps the new decoration required the removal of Velázquez's picture. It is also possible that the compilers of the inventory made an error in noting the name of the chapel. In any case, it is unlikely that Velázquez's painting is related to the 1659–61 decorative campaign, precisely because the chapel was excluded from the work. Also, from October 1659 to June 1660, Velázquez was occupied with the preparations for the marriage of Maria Teresa to Louis XIV. And on August 6, 1660, he died.

THE PORTRAITS OF COURT JESTERS

In the 1701 inventory, there are listed in consecutive order six portraits of court jesters by Velázquez. Four of the originals survive: *Pablo de Valladolid, Cristóbal de Castañeda y Pernia, called "Barbarroja,"*

and "*Don Juan de Austria*," in the Prado (figs. 82–84) and *Calabazas* in the Cleveland Museum of Art (fig. 85). The fifth picture, *Francisco de Ocariz y Ochoa*, is lost but known through a copy in a private collection.[11] The sixth, the *Bufón Toreador Cárdenas*, has disappeared without a trace.

On December 11, 1634, Velázquez signed an unpublished *carta de pago* that acknowledged receipt of 797 ducats for paintings commissioned by Diego Suárez, "*para el adorno de las alcobas del Buen Retiro*."[12] There are reasons for believing that this payment refers to the jester portraits. The inventory of 1701 establishes that the pictures were hung as a series in the southern part of the palace, the part that was used as the private quarters of the queen.[13] The word *alcobas* means bedrooms or sleeping quarters and could of course refer to any bedroom in the palace. However, it also clearly connotes the private sector of the palace.

From another source, we learn that there was a room in the queen's quarters known as the *pieza de los bufones*, the room of the jesters. Around 1661, a list was compiled of paintings delivered to the Retiro by Jerónimo de Villanueva, with their locations as of that moment.[14] Only two folios of the list survive in the Palace Archive, but one of the locations described is as follows: "*Está en la pieza junto a los bufones en el q.to de la reyna.*" In other words, there was a room called the Room of the Jesters in the queen's quarters. The name could not derive from the fact that the jesters lodged in the queen's apartments; therefore it must derive from the striking series of pictures by Velázquez that adorned it. The 1701 inventory lists no other series of paintings by Velázquez in this part of the palace.

The sum of money paid to Velázquez also suggests that several paintings were involved. As a matter of fact, the valuation of the works in 1701 is roughly equivalent to the amount stipulated in 1634—720 against 797 ducats.

Nothing in the biographies of the jesters, as discovered by Moreno Villa, contradicts this date.[15] All of the jesters were in service at this time. In fact, both Pablo de Valladolid and "Barbarroja" are first documented at the court in 1633. Stylistically the works are compatible with the year 1634.

THE FORGE OF VULCAN and JOSEPH'S BLOODY COAT BROUGHT TO JACOB

In 1933, Domínguez Bordona published the entry in Villanueva's secret expense account, covering the period from October 1633 to March 1634, which recorded the sale by Velázquez of eighteen pictures, including his own works the *Forge of Vulcan* and *Joseph's Bloody Coat Brought to Jacob*[16] (fig. 63). Other paintings in the lot were Cambiaso's *Susanna and the Elders*, Titian's *Danäe* (probably a copy), five flowerpieces, four small landscapes, two kitchen scenes, and portraits of the prince and the queen, whose authors are not specified. In the list of the paintings delivered by Villanueva, both of Velázquez's pictures and Cambiaso's *Susanna* were in storage in the wardrobe (*guardarropa*).

Velázquez also made another sale of pictures in 1633.[17] This lot of three works included a painting of *St John the Baptist* by Tintoretto (whereabouts unknown) and two paintings showing processions of the pope and the grand turk. Like many a painter before and after his time, Velázquez appears to have supplemented his income by dealing in pictures.

THE RIDING LESSON OF BALTASAR CARLOS (fig. 136)

The identification of the setting of this picture as part of the palace of the Buen Retiro was first made by Michael Levey and subsequently endorsed by Enriqueta Harris.[18] Levey made the identification by reference to one of Meunier's views (fig. 60), which shows the Queen's Garden, with the *Equestrian Statue of Philip IV* in the middle ground and the eastern facade of the palace behind. With small differences apparently made for compositional reasons, the tower in the background of Velázquez's painting corresponds to the tower that terminates the wing of the palace visible at the left of Meunier's print. This wing was designated as the Prince's Quarters. It would seem, therefore, that Velázquez intended the architectural background of the picture to provide an additional reference to Prince Baltasar Carlos.

255

LIST OF ABBREVIATIONS

1. ARCHIVES AND LIBRARIES

AAE	Archives des Affaires Etrangères, Paris
ADM	Archivo del Duque de Medinaceli, Seville
AGI	Archivo General de las Indias, Seville
AGI Cont.	Contaduría
AGI Ind.	Indiferente General
AGR	Archives Générales du Royaume, Brussels
AGS	Archivo General de Simancas
AGS CH	Consejo y Juntas de Hacienda
AGS CS	Casas y Sitios Reales
AGS Est.	Estado
AGS TMC	Tribunal Mayor de Cuentas
AHN	Archivo Histórico Nacional, Madrid
AHP	Archivo Histórico de Protocolos, Madrid
APM	Archivo del Palacio Real, Madrid
APM BR	Buen Retiro
APM CR	Cédulas Reales
APM OB	Obras y Bosques
ASF	Archivio di Stato, Florence
ASG	Archivio di Stato, Genoa
ASL	Archivio di Stato, Lucca
ASM	Archivio di Stato, Modena
ASV	Archivio di Stato, Venice
AV	Archivio Segreto Vaticano
AVM	Archivo de la Villa de Madrid
BAV	Biblioteca Apostolica Vaticana
BL	British Library, London
BL Add.	Additional Mss
BL Eg.	Egerton Mss
BNM	Biblioteca Nacional, Madrid
BNP	Bibliothèque Nationale, Paris
BPM	Biblioteca del Palacio, Madrid
MSB	Bayerische Staatsbibliothek, Munich
PRO	Public Record Office, London
RAH	Real Academia de la Historia, Madrid

2. OTHER ABBREVIATIONS

AB	*Art Bulletin*
AEA	*Archivo Español de Arte*
AIEM	*Anales del Instituto de Estudios Madrileños*
BAE	*Biblioteca de Autores Españoles*
BHS	*Bulletin of Hispanic Studies*
BM	*Burlington Magazine*
BRAE	*Boletín de la Real Academia Española*
BRAH	*Boletín de la Real Academia de la Historia*
BSEE	*Boletín de la Sociedad Española de Excursiones*
BUV	*Boletín del Seminario de Estudios de Arte y Arqueología, Universidad de Valladolid*
CIH	*Cuadernos de Investigación Histórica*
Codoin	*Colección de Documentos Inéditos para la Historia de España*
GBA	*Gazette des Beaux-Arts*
Hoz	Pedro de la Hoz, *Relación diaria desde 31 de marzo de 1621 a 14 de agosto de 1640* (see Bibliography)
Jesuitas	*Cartas de algunos PP. de la Compañía de Jesús* (see Bibliography)
JWCI	*Journal of the Warburg and Courtauld Institutes*
JSAH	*Journal of the Society of Architectural Historians*
leg.	legajo
lib.	libro
MC	J. H. Elliott and J. F. de la Peña, *Memoriales y Cartas del Conde Duque de Olivares* (see Bibliography)
MD	*Master Drawings*
MEA	*Museo Español de Antigüedades*
MHE	*Memorial Histórico Español*
MKIF	*Mitteilungen des Kunsthistorischen Institutes in Florenz*
NBAE	*Nueva Biblioteca de Autores Españoles*
Novoa	Matías de Novoa, *Historia de Felipe IV, Rey de España* (see Bibliography)
RABM	*Revista de Archivos, Bibliotecas y Museos*
RS	*Reales Sitios*
RUM	*Revista de la Universidad de Madrid*
VM	*Villa de Madrid*
ZfK	*Zeitschrift für Kunstgeschichte*

NOTES

NOTES TO PROLOGUE

1. For an interesting attempt to provide an answer, see Manuel Fernández Alvarez, *Madrid en el siglo XVI*, I (*El establecimiento de la capitalidad de España en Madrid*), (Madrid, Instituto de Estudios Madrileños, 1960).
2. See Bartolomé Bennassar, *Valladolid au siècle d'or* (Paris, 1967), pp. 121–33.
3. *Ibid.*, p. 128.
4. Luis Cabrera de Córdoba, *Filipe segundo, rey de España*, I (ed. Madrid, 1876), p. 298.
5. Jerónimo de Quintana, *A la muy antigua, noble y coronada villa de Madrid* (Madrid, 1629), fo. 331v.
6. For the growth of Madrid see Miguel Molina Campuzano, *Planos de Madrid de los siglos XVII y XVIII* (Madrid, 1960); Julián Gállego, "L'urbanisme de Madrid au XVIIe siècle," in *L'urbanisme de Paris et de l'Europe, 1600–1680*, ed. Pierre Francastel (Paris, 1969), pp. 251–65; David Ringrose, "Madrid and Spain, 1560–1860: Patterns of Social and Economic Change," in *City and Society in the Eighteenth Century*, ed. Paul Fritz and David Williams (Toronto, 1973), pp. 59–75; Janine Fayard and Claude Larquié, "Hôtels madrilènes et démographie urbaine au XVIIe siècle," *Mélanges de la Casa de Velázquez*, 4 (1968), pp. 229–58.
7. Antonio Domínguez Ortiz, *La sociedad española en el siglo XVII*, I (Madrid, 1964), pp. 131–4.
8. Ramón de Mesonero Romanos, *El antiguo Madrid* (Madrid, 1861; repr. 1976), pp. xl–xli.
9. See Jean-Pierre Babelon, "L'urbanisme de Henri IV et de Sully à Paris," in Francastel, *L'urbanisme de Paris*, pp. 47–60.
10. See Antonio Bonet Correa, "El plano de Juan Gómez de Mora de la Plaza Mayor de Madrid en 1636," in his *Morfología y ciudad* (Barcelona, 1978), pp. 65–91.
11. See Gállego, "L'urbanisme," p. 261.

NOTES TO CHAPTER I

1. Andrés de Almansa y Mendoza, *Cartas* (Madrid, 1886), pp. 21–4.
2. Hoz, Mar. 31, 1621.
3. *Ibid.*, May 6, 1621.
4. Antonio de León Pinelo, *Anales de Madrid* (Madrid, 1971), pp. 235–6.
5. AGS TMC, leg. 1560, cédula, June 22, 1621.
6. *Historia general de la orden de Nuestra Señora de las Mercedes*, ed. Manuel Penedo Rey, 2 (Madrid, 1974), p. 475.
7. For this constitutional system and its implications, see J. H. Elliott, *The Revolt of the Catalans* (Cambridge, 1963), especially Chapter I.
8. *Correspondencia oficial de don Diego Sarmiento de Acuña,*

conde de Gondomar, in *Documentos Inéditos para la Historia de España*, 2 (Madrid, 1943), p. 135 (letter of Mar. 28, 1619).
9. A list prepared for the Junta del donativo in 1627 (AGS CH leg. 632) gives a total of 168 titled nobles, made up of 25 dukes (all of them grandees), 70 marquises (9 grandees) and 73 counts (7 grandees). In 1600 the total had been 119 titled nobles, and most of the increase reflects the inflation of honors under Philip III.
10. See J. H. Elliott, "Self-perception and Decline in Seventeenth-century Spain," *Past and Present*, 74 (1977), pp. 41–61.
11. For a contemporary account of Olivares's early years, see the Count of La Roca (Juan Antonio de Vera y Figueroa), *Fragmentos históricos de la vida de D. Gaspar de Guzmán* in Antonio de Valladares, *Semanario Erudito*, 2 (Madrid, 1787), pp. 145–296. For a modern account, Gregorio Marañón, *El Conde–Duque de Olivares. La pasión de mandar* (3rd ed., Madrid, 1952), and J. H. Elliott, *The Count–Duke of Olivares* (in preparation).
12. Roca, *Fragmentos*, p. 162.
13. "Historia de Felipe III, rey de España," *Codoin*, 61, p. 352.
14. References for Leganés's life and career are given in the notes to document X of John H. Elliott and José F. de La Peña, *Memoriales y Cartas del Conde Duque de Olivares*, 2 (Madrid, 1980), hereafter cited as *MC*. For a contemporary assessment, see Matías de Novoa, "Historia de Felipe IV, rey de España," *Codoin*, 69, pp. 53–4. Leganés as an art collector is studied by Mary Crawford Volk, "Profile of a Seventeenth-century Collector: the Marquis of Leganés," forthcoming in the *Art Bulletin*.
15. Archivio di Stato, Mantua. Archivio Gonzaga, serie E.XIV.3. busta 624, copy of decree of Apr. 8, 1621.
16. Angel González Palencia, *La Junta de Reformación* (Valladolid, 1932), Doc.LXVI.
17. For studies and documents relating to Olivares's proposals for reform, see Elliott and La Peña, *MC*, 1 (Madrid, 1978).
18. See Elliott, *The Revolt*, Chapter VIII.
19. N. Barozzi and G. Berchet, *Relazioni degli stati europei. Serie 1. Spagna*, 2 (Venice, 1860), p. 15.
20. ASG Lettere Ministri, Spagna 2435, Saluzzo, Jan. 20, 1629.
21. *Codoin*, 69, p. 12.
22. BPM Ms. 1817, Olivares to Gondomar, Jan. 17, 1625. For this portrait see Jonathan Brown, "A Portrait Drawing by Velázquez," *MD*, 14 (1976), pp. 46–51.
23. Marañón, *Olivares*, p. 124.
24. Roca, *Fragmentos*, pp. 245–6.
25. ADM leg. 79, Jan. 21, 1633.
26. *Fragmentos*, p. 242.
27. BL Eg.Ms. 2053, fo. 34v, Olivares to the Prince of

Carpiñano, Oct. 20, 1628.

28. BAV Barb.lat.Ms. 8599, fo. 81, Olivares to Cardinal Barberini, July 25, 1626.

29. AGS Est.leg. 2332, consulta, Sept. 25, 1631.

30. AHP 1718, *Poder de los señores condes de Olivares*, Aug. 20, 1625.

31. ASF Mediceo, filza 4959, Monanni, Mar. 26, 1633.

32. For the count–duke's library, see Gregorio de Andrés, "Historia de la biblioteca del Conde–Duque de Olivares y descripción de sus códices," *Cuadernos Bibliográficos*, 28 (1972).

33. *MC*, I, p. xlv.

34. For a biography of Rioja, see Cayetano Alberto de la Barrera, *Poesías de don Francisco de Rioja* (Madrid, 1867), pp. 1–99.

35. BAV Barb.lat.Ms. 8599, fo. 20, Olivares to Cardinal Barberini, Dec. 18, 1623.

36. AGS CH, leg. 495, unsigned note, dated May 19, 1634.

37. Francisco Tomás Valiente, *Los validos en la monarquía española del siglo XVII* (Madrid, 1963), p. 95.

38. BAV Vat.lat.Ms. 10,422, *Relazione della corte di Spagna*, fos. 76–76v.

39. *Fragmentos*, p. 246.

40. BL Eg.Ms. 1820, fo. 22, Hopton to Cottington, Apr. 14, 1631.

41. For José González, see Janine Fayard, *Les Membres du Conseil de Castille à l'époque moderne, 1621–1746* (Geneva, 1979), p. 90, and *MC*, 2, p. 129.

42. See Elliott, *The Revolt*, pp. 256–9, and *MC*, I, p. 80, n. 44.

43. Documentation in AHN Inquisición, libs. 297–8, and leg. 3687². See also Mercedes Agulló y Cobo, "El monasterio de San Plácido y su fundador, el madrileño don Jerónimo de Villanueva, Protonotario de Aragón," *Villa de Madrid*, 13 (1975), nos. 45–6, pp. 59–68, and no. 47, pp. 37–50.

44. ADM leg. 79, Olivares to Marquis of Aytona, Dec. 30, 1633.

45. Jacinto de Herrera y Sotomayor, *Jornada que su magestad hizo a la Andaluzia*, (Madrid, 1624).

46. *MC*, I, Doc. XI.

47. *Ibid.*, Docs. XII and XIII.

48. *Ibid.*, Doc. IV.

49. AV Nunziatura di Spagna 65, fo. 245, letter from nuncio, June 10, 1625.

50. AV Nunziatura di Spagna 65, fo. 371, Nov. 12, 1625.

51. See Elliott, *The Revolt*, Chapter VIII.

NOTES TO CHAPTER II

1. There is at present no comprehensive survey of ceremonial and etiquette at the court of the Spanish Habsburgs, but Antonio Rodríguez Villa, *Etiquetas de la Casa de Austria* (Madrid, 1913), provides a useful summary. For certain features of court ceremonial see Yves Bottineau, "Aspects de la cour d'Espagne au XVIIe siècle: l'étiquette de la chambre du roi," *Bulletin Hispanique*, 74 (1972), pp. 138–57, and the following articles by J. E. Varey: "La mayordomía mayor y los festejos palaciegos del siglo XVII," *AIEM*, 4 (1969), pp. 145–68; "Processional Ceremonial of the Spanish Court in the Seventeenth Century," *Studia Iberica. Festschrift für Hans Flasche* (Bern–Munich, 1973), pp. 643–52; "Further Notes on Processional Ceremonial of the Spanish Court in the Seventeenth Century,"

Iberoromania, I (1974), pp. 71–9.

2. See Lope de Vega, *El castigo sin venganza*, ed. C. F. A. Van Dam (Groningen, 1928), pp. 113–14. For Philip's nocturnal excursions, see Marañón, *Olivares*, p. 38.

3. José Deleito y Piñuela, *El rey se divierte* (3rd ed., Madrid, 1964), p. 270.

4. For the Alcázar and its renovations, see Carl Justi, *Diego Velázquez und sein Jahrhundert* (2nd ed., Zurich, 1933), pp. 183–93; Juan J. Martín González, "El Alcázar de Madrid en el siglo XVI. Nuevos datos," *AEA*, 35 (1962), pp. 1–19; Véronique Gérard, "La fachada del Alcázar de Madrid," *CIH*, 2 (1973), pp. 237–57; Francisco Iñiguez Almech, *Casas reales y jardines de Felipe II* (Madrid, 1952), which published for the first time Gómez de Mora's plans of the Alcázar.

5. Gil González de Avila, *Teatro de las grandezas de la villa de Madrid* (Madrid, 1623), p. 310; also Justi, p. 193.

6. González de Avila, p. 333. This work contains useful accounts of the duties of the principal palace functionaries.

7. *Ibid.*

8. AGS CH, leg. 494, petition of Carlos Strata (1633). For Strata's house, see Mesonero Romanos, *El antiguo Madrid*, p. 235.

9. Narciso Alonso Cortés, *La muerte del conde de Villamediana* (Valladolid, 1928).

10. José Deleito y Piñuela, *Sólo Madrid es corte* (Madrid, 1942), pp. 208–16.

11. Ruth Lee Kennedy, "Philip IV's Advocacy of San Blas on February 3, 1623," *Revista Hispánica Moderna*, 39 (1976–7), pp. 96–108.

12. Quoted in Deleito y Pinuela, *El rey se divierte*, p. 165.

13. Edward, Earl of Clarendon, *The History of the Rebellion and Civil Wars in England*, ed. W. D. Macray, 5 (Oxford, 1888), p. 79.

14. See Carl Justi, "Die Spanische Brautfahrt Carl Stuarts im Jahre 1623," *Miscellaneen aus drei Jahrhunderten Spanischen Kunstlebens*, 2 (Berlin, 1908), pp. 301–46.

15. *Declaración mystica de las armas de España invictamente belicosas* (Brussels, 1636), pp. 56–8.

16. *MC*, 2, Doc.XIIa, Olivares to Archbishop of Granada, Sept. 18, 1632.

17. ASF Mediceo, filza 4959, Monanni, Apr. 30, 1633.

18. "Autosemblanza de Felipe IV" in *Cartas de Sor María de Agreda y de Felipe IV*, ed. Carlos Seco Serrano, *BAE* 109, pp. 231–6.

19. A royal decree of Feb. 18, 1622 to the president of the council of the Indies (AGI Ind., leg. 754) informs him that a window is to be cut into the wall of his council chamber, in accordance with a design prepared by Gómez de Mora.

20. BAV Barb.lat.Ms. 8386, fos. 57–9, Mgr.Monti to Francesco Barberini, Feb. 25, 1633.

21. "Autosemblanza," p. 236. *Almas*, the word printed in the text, is clearly a mistake for *armas*.

22. For these academies see José Sánchez, *Academias literarias del siglo de oro español* (Madrid, 1961), and Willard F. King, *Prosa novelística y academias literarias en el siglo XVII* (Madrid, 1963).

23. Sánchez, p. 53.

24. Gareth A. Davies, *A Poet at Court: Antonio Hurtado de Mendoza* (Oxford, 1974), p. 60.

25. Robert Jammes, *Etudes sur l'oeuvre poétique de Don Luis de Góngora y Argote* (Bordeaux, 1967), pp. 337 and 346.

26. Davies, *A Poet at Court*, pp. 27–33.

27. Barrera, *Poesías de Rioja*, p. 288.

28. José Jordán de Urriés y Azara, *Biografía y estudio crítico de Jáuregui* (Madrid, 1899).

29. Barrera, pp. 292–319.

30. For a general introduction to Philip II as collector and patron, see Hugh Trevor–Roper, *Princes and Artists. Patronage and Ideology at Four Habsburg Courts* (London, 1976), pp. 47–83.

31. Diego Angulo Iñiguez and Alfonso E. Pérez Sánchez, *Pintura madrileña del primer tercio del siglo XVII* (Madrid, 1969), pp. 299–325.

32. For Crescenzi's family and life in Rome, see Giovanni Baglione, *Le vite de pittore, scultori et architetti* (Rome, 1935), pp. 364–7, and Anna Grelle, "I Crescenzi e l'accademia de via S. Eustachio," *Commentari*, 12 (1961), pp. 120–38.

33. For hypothetical and somewhat contradictory accounts of Crescenzi as a still-life painter, see Carlo Volpe, "Una proposta per Giovanni Battista Crescenzi," *Paragone*, 275 (1973), pp. 25–36, and Mina Gregori, "Notizie su Agostino Verrochi e un' ipotesi per Giovanni Battista Crescenzi," *Paragone*, 275 (1973), pp. 36–56.
According to the Venetian ambassador in Rome, Crescenzi's motive for the Spanish trip was to secure the support of the Spanish king for Cardinal Crescenzi's papal ambitions. See the *relazione* cited by Francis Haskell, *Patrons and Painters. A Study in the Relations between Italian Art and Society in the Age of the Baroque* (London, 1963), p. 173.

34. The fundamental accounts of Crescenzi in Spain are Juan A. Ceán Bermúdez. *Diccionario histórico de los más ilustres profesores de las bellas artes en España*, 1 (Madrid, 1800), pp. 372–6, and Eugenio Llaguno y Amirola, *Noticias de los arquitectos de España desde su restauración*, 3 (Madrid, 1829; repr. 1977), pp. 169–74. Also valuable is Elías Tormo, "Un gran pintor vallisoletano: Antonio de Pereda," in *Pintura, escultura y arquitectura en España. Estudios dispersos* (Madrid, 1949), pp. 308–26. For the documentation of the Pantheon commission, see Juan J. Martín González, "El Panteón de San Lorenzo de El Escorial," *AEA*, 32 (1959), pp. 199–213. René Taylor, "Juan Bautista Crescencio," *Academia*, 48 (1979), pp. 63–126 contains a more convincing interpretation of this documentation with respect to Crescenzi's authorship of the design of the Pantheon.

35. Angulo Iñiguez and Pérez Sánchez, *Pintura madrileña*, p. 307.

36. The date of the patent of nobility is unknown, but the title was in use by 1626. For Crescenzi's *probanza*, see AHN Ordenes militares, expte. 2209, Sept.–Oct. 1626.

37. See AGS TMC, leg. 1495, título, Oct. 14, 1630, for Crescenzi's appointment as *superintendente*, Llaguno, *Noticias*, 3, p. 373, and cédula of the same date for his appointment to Obras y Bosques. Also cited by José M. de Azcárate, "Datos para las biografías de los arquitectos de la Corte de Felipe IV," *RUM* 11 (1962), p. 534.

38. See p. 57.

39. Ben Jonson, "To Inigo Marquess Would Be," in *Ben Jonson*, ed. C. H. Herford and Percy Simpson, 8 (Oxford, 1947), pp. 406–7.

40. For example, when Crescenzi came to Spain in 1617, he brought with him the painter Bartolommeo Cavarozzi, a follower of Caravaggio. See Alfonso E. Pérez Sánchez, *Borgianni, Cavarozzi y Nardi en España* (Madrid, 1964), p. 20.

41. Angulo and Pérez Sánchez, *Pintura madrileña*, pp. 86–189, and Mary C. Volk, *Vicencio Carducho and Seventeenth Century Castilian Painting* (New York–London, 1977).

42. The competition is described briefly by Francisco Pacheco, *Arte de la pintura*, 1 (Madrid, 1956), pp. 157–8.

43. For the document recording the appointment to the position of *ujier de cámara*, or doorkeeper to the king's private chambers, see *Varia Velazqueña*, 2 (Madrid, 1960), p. 226. Shortly thereafter the documents begin to style him *pintor de cámara*. For further information on the relations between Velázquez and other royal painters, see Juan J. Martín González, "Sobre las relaciones entre Nardi, Carducho y Velázquez," *AEA*, 31 (1958), pp. 59–66.

44. Gregorio Cruzada Villaamil, *Rubens. Diplomático español* (Madrid, 1874); Ruth Saunders Magurn, *The Letters of Peter Paul Rubens* (Cambridge, Mass., 1955), pp. 283–98; Xavier de Salas, *Rubens y Velázquez* (Madrid, 1977); and Pacheco, *Arte de la pintura* 1, pp. 151–5.

45. Magurn, *Rubens*, p. 292.

46. Room 16 of the principal floor in Gómez de Mora's plan. For the king's interest in music, see Davies, *A Poet at Court*, p. 196.

47. For an admirable account of court theater in the reign of Philip IV, see N. D. Shergold, *A History of the Spanish Stage* (Oxford, 1967), Chapter 10.

48. Juan Vélez de Guevara, *Los celos hacen estrellas*, ed. J. E. Varey and N. D. Shergold (London, 1970), introduction, pp. lxviii–lxix.

49. Shergold, *Spanish Stage*, pp. 268–73.

50. Alonso Núñez de Castro, *Libro histórico político. Sólo Madrid es corte* (3rd ed., Madrid, 1675), p. 23.

51. Ruth Lee Kennedy, *Studies in Tirso, I: The Dramatist and his Competitors, 1620–26* (Chapel Hill, 1974), pp. 199–200 and 222–3.

52. AGS CS, leg. 307, fos. 356, 359, 355 and 350, petition of Lotti, consultas of Mar. 13 and Apr. 16, 1627, and order of July 4, 1628. Printed as doc. 1(a) to (d) in Norman D. Shergold, "Documentos sobre Cosme Lotti, escenógrafo de Felipe IV," *Studia Iberica. Festschrift für Hans Flasche*, pp. 589–602.

53. Shergold, *Spanish Stage*, pp. 275–6.

54. See p. 18.

55. AHN Consejos, leg. 7126, cédula, Mar. 21, 1623.

56. Ruth Matilda Anderson, *The Golilla: a Spanish Collar of the Seventeenth Century* (Hispanic Society of America, New York, n.d.).

57. BAV Barb. lat. Ms. 5689. On this diary see Enriqueta Harris, "Cassiano dal Pozzo on Diego Velázquez," *BM*, 112 (1970), pp. 364–73.

58. Ruth Saunders Magurn, *Rubens*, letter 180 (Dec. 2, 1628), p. 292.

59. Per Palme, *Triumph of Peace. A Study of the Whitehall Banqueting House* (Stockholm, 1956), p. 32.

60. Magurn, *Rubens*, letter 181 (Dec. 29, 1628), p. 295.

61. The resistance to the Olivares reform program is discussed in more detail in John H. Elliott, "El programa de Olivares y los movimientos de 1640," forthcoming in vol. 25 of the *Historia de España* (Menéndez Pidal). For *vellón* inflation see Earl J. Hamilton, *American Treasure and the Price Revolution in Spain, 1501–1650* (Cambridge, Mass., 1934), p. 94, and Antonio Domínguez Ortiz, *Política y hacienda de Felipe IV* (Madrid, 1960), pp. 255–7.

62. *MC*, 1, p. 232.

63. *Ibid.*, Doc. XIII.

64. Rafael Ródenas Vilar, *La política europea de España*

durante la guerra de treinta años, 1624–1630 (Madrid, 1967), pp. 120–2; Michael Roberts, *Gustavus Adolphus*, 2 (London, 1958), pp. 347–50.

65. For the origins of the war of the Mantuan Succession, see Manual Fernández Alvarez, *Don Gonzalo Fernández de Córdoba y la guerra de sucesión de Mantua y del Monferrato, 1627–1629* (Madrid, 1955).

66. A copy of the manifesto is to be found in Novoa, *Codoin*, 69, pp. 74–6.

67. *MC*, 2, Docs. I to X.

68. AGS Est., Leg. 2713, Oct. 30, 1629.

69. Hoz, p. 181. See also Enriqueta Harris and John H. Elliott, "Velázquez and the Queen of Hungary," *BM*, 118 (1976), pp. 24–6.

70. *Codoin*, 69, pp. 89–90.

NOTES TO CHAPTER III

1. See Iñiguez Almech, *Casas reales*, for the only comprehensive discussion of the Spanish royal houses in the sixteenth century.

2. Juan J. Martín González, "El Palacio de Aranjuez en el siglo XVI," *AEA*, 35 (1962), pp. 237–52.

3. J. García Mercadal, *Viajes de extranjeros por España y Portugal*, 1 (Madrid, 1952), p. 1479.

4. For the Pardo, see Luis Calandre, *El Palacio del Pardo* (Madrid, 1953) and Juan J. Martín González, "El Palacio de El Pardo en el siglo XVI," *BUV*, 36 (1970), pp. 5–41.

5. BAV Barb. lat. Ms. 4372, fo. 6v. *Relación de las casas que tiene el rey de España* (1626).

6. See María Cristina Sánchez Alonso, "Juramentos de príncipes herederos en Madrid (1561–1598)," *AIEM*, 7 (1971), pp. 29–41.

7. APM BR, leg. 1, no. 3, decreto.

8. For the history of San Jerónimo, see Baltasar Cuartero y Huerta, *El Monasterio de S. Jerónimo el Real* (Madrid, 1966) and Aurea de la Morena, "El Monasterio de San Jerónimo el Real, de Madrid," *AIEM*, 6 (1974), pp. 47–78. The Royal Apartment prior to 1630 is briefly described by José de Sigüenza, *Historia de la Orden de los Jerónimos*, NBAE, 8 (Madrid, 1907), p. 375, and Jerónimo Quintana, *Villa de Madrid*, fo. 399v.

9. For the construction of the Royal Apartment, see Cuartero, *El Monasterio*, p. 35; Amancio Portabales Pichel, *Maestros mayores, arquitectos y aparejadores de El Escorial* (Madrid, 1952), p. 160; and AGS CS, leg. 247, fo. 37, memorial, July 20, 1562. The documentary reference was kindly furnished by Catherine Wilkinson.

10. See AGS TMC, leg. 1560, título, Feb. 2, 1623, for Gondomar's appointment, and AGS CS, leg. 307, fo. 100, título, Nov. 11, 1626, for Arcos's appointment.

11. The earliest known payment for work at the Apartment is dated Oct. 3, 1630 (AGS, leg. 1495). This account lists Crescenzi as the supervisor of the project and Villanueva as the source of funds. The Retiro building accounts were published in summary chronological form by José M. de Azcárate, "Anales de la construcción del Buen Retiro," *AIEM*, 1 (1966), pp. 99–135, who however did not distinguish the stages of construction of the palace. Also, on the basis of an entry in AGS TMC, leg. 1495, Azcárate dated the start of construction to July 11, 1629. This date is the result of a scribe's error. The full documentation of the payment is found in AGS CS, leg. 308, fo. 293, *carta de pago*, July 11, 1632.

See Appendix II for a review of the documentation concerning the Retiro and a discussion of the literature on the subject.

12. For descriptions of the *juramento*, see the closely related accounts of Juan Gómez de Mora, *Relación del juramento que hizieron los reinos de Castilla y León al Sermo. don Baltasar Carlos, príncipe de las Españas, i Nuevo Mundo* (Madrid, 1632); Antonio de Mendoza, *Forma que se guarda en tener las Cortes el juramento que se hizo al príncipe nuestro señor. . .*, in *Discursos de don Antonio de Mendoza*, ed. Marqués de Alcedo (Madrid, 1911), pp. 25–34; and León Pinelo, *Anales*, pp. 287–90.

13. For a full discussion of this dating and interpretation, see below, Appendix III.

14. For the extent of the work carried out in 1630–1, see Gómez de Mora, *Relación del juramento*, p. 4; Duquesa de Berwick y de Alba, *Documentos escogidos de la casa de Alba* (Madrid, 1891), p. 480 and Cuartero, *El Monasterio*, p. 29.

15. Leon B. Alberti, *Ten Books of Architecture*, trans. James Leoni (London, 1755, ed. London, 1955), p. 189.

16. APM BR, leg. 2, no. 3, decreto, July 22, 1632. Cited by Amador de los Ríos, "El palacio antiguo del Buen Retiro, según el plano de 1656," *Museo Español de Antigüedades*, 11 (1880), p. 180.

17. RAH, leg. 9/1075, fos. 142–3, nombramiento, Nov. 20, 1633. Cited by Baltasar Cuartero y Huerta, "Noticias de doscientos trece documentos inéditos sobre el Buen Retiro de Madrid y otros sitios reales (años 1612–1661)," *AIEM*, 3 (1968), p. 55. The document mentions that Carbonel had been acting as master of the works since June 1632.

18. See René Taylor's significant article (cited in Chapter II, note 34) for Gómez de Mora's professional struggle against Crescenzi, and later Velázquez. See also Martín González, "El Panteón de San Lorenzo de El Escorial," who sees the relationship between Gómez de Mora and Crescenzi in another way.

19. See the *aviso* dated Oct. 18, 1636, published by Rodríguez Villa, *La corte*, pp. 44–5, and Azcárate, "Datos," p. 520.

20. There is no satisfactory study of Carbonel's interesting and important career. Fundamental documentation is found in Llaguno, *Noticias*, 4, pp. 14–16, 27, 150–2. Despite its sweeping title, Ricardo Martorell y Téllez-Girón, "Alonso Carbonel, arquitecto y escultor del siglo XVII," *AE*, 13 (1936), pp. 50–8, is limited to the publication of documents in the Palace Archive. Additional documentation is published by Cristóbal Pérez Pastor, *Noticias y documentos relativos a la historia y literatura española*, 11 (Madrid, 1914), pp. 97, 139, 150, 167, 169, 171, and Azcárate, "Datos," pp. 524–31. Albacete is named as the home town of Carbonel's parents in the supporting documentation to the last will and testament of his brother, Ginés (AHP 6751, Jan. 12, 1632). Alonso's last will and testament is in AHP 6069 fos. 667–8. His inventory was partially published by María A. Mazón de la Torre, *Jusepe Leonardo y su tiempo* (Zaragoza, 1977), pp. 419–20.

21. See Llaguno, *Noticias*, 4, p. 150, for the appointment as *aparejador mayor*, dated Nov. 9, 1630. In APM CR, tomo 13, fo. 38, a copy of the Nov. 9, 1630 document, dated Dec. 6, 1630, it is noted that Carbonel had been appointed as *aparejador de las obras del Alcázar* on Feb. 6, 1627. He became *maestro mayor de las obras reales* on Mar. 1, 1648, succeeding Gómez de Mora (Llaguno, *Noticias*, 4, p. 150).

He died on Sept. 1, 1660 (Mazón de la Torre, p. 419).

For other works by Carbonel, see below, pp. 220–2.

22. The date of Crescenzi's death is often given as 1660 by writers who have relied on Ceán Bermúdez, *Diccionario*. Tormo, in the original edition of his article on Pereda ("Un gran pintor," pp. 308–12), used Justi's reference to Monanni, cited in his *Velázquez*, and corrected the error. He also pointed out that Crescenzi's successor as *superintendente de las obras reales* was the Marquis of Torres, the similarity of whose title to that of Crescenzi, as Marquis of La Torre, has been a constant source of confusion. Torres, who held important posts in the palace, died in Mar. 1640 (ASF Mediceo, filza 4964, Monanni, Mar. 24, 1640).

23. ASF Mediceo, filza 4959, Jan. 15, 1633.

24. Construction of the menagerie was carried out early in 1633. See AGS TMC, leg. 3763, payments, Feb. 18, Mar. 24 and Apr. 2.

25. ASF Mediceo, filza 4959, Monanni, Jan. 15, 1633.

26. AGS CS, leg. 308, fo. 380, royal order, Feb. 23, 1633.

27. ASF Mediceo, filza 4959, May 14, 1633.

28. *Ibid.*

29. For the acquisition of Povar's land, see AGI Cont. leg. 70, fo. 185, referring to decreto, Aug. 29, 1636. For Tavara's property, see AGI Cont. leg. 70, fo. 184, referring to decreto, Dec. 9, 1634. The documentation of the purchase of Ayala's land is in AVM, Sección 1, leg. 162, expte. 22, decreto, Feb. 18, 1633; cited by A. Gómez Iglesias, "El Buen Retiro," *Villa de Madrid*, 6 (1968), p. 26. It is often said that Olivares owned land on which the palace was built. But, with one exception, there is no contemporary evidence of his ownership. Francesco Corner, the Venetian ambassador from April 1631 to March 1635, implies that the count–duke had property near San Jerónimo, where he kept birds (Barozzi, *Relazioni*, 2, p. 16). However, a property in this location is conspicuously absent from Olivares's document of entail drawn up Oct. 10, 1624 (AHP 1718). Both the Marquises of Povar and Tavara were relatives of Olivares, and perhaps this fact had become confused in Corner's mind with the notion that the count–duke owned land at the site.

The *huerta* belonging to the monastery had been purchased by the king for 8,000 ducats (Cuartero, *El Monasterio*, p. 29).

30. This is described by Vicente Carducho, *Diálogos de la pintura* (Madrid, 1633), p. 152v.

31. RAH sig. 9/1075, fo. 162, instrucción, Nov. 5, 1633.

32. RAH Salazar M-63, fos. 75v.–76v. *Estracto de la escritura de venta de la villa de Loeches...* (May 3, 1633); María–Amalia López, "Alonso Carbonel y la iglesia de Loeches," *AEA*, 25 (1952), pp. 167–9.

33. Novoa, *Codoin*, 69, p. 283.

34. AV Nunziatura di Spagna, 72, fo. 91, Monti, June 21, 1631.

35. ASF Mediceo, filza 4959, June 12, 1632.

36. *MC* 2, Doc. XIIc.

37. Domínguez Ortiz, *Política y hacienda*, pp. 45–7.

38. AHN Est., lib. 871, fos. 17–36v., consulta, Apr. 17, 1633.

39. Hoz, p. 208.

40. ASF Mediceo, filza 4959, Monanni, Jan. 29 and Feb. 5, 1633.

41. AGS Est., leg. 2334, consulta, Jan. 9, 1633.

42. ADM leg. 79, Olivares to Aytona, Mar. 1633.

43. For the Belvedere Court, see J. S. Ackerman, *The Cortile del Belvedere* (Vatican, 1954). For Ammannati's addition to the Pitti Palace, see Mazzino Fossi, *Bartolomeo Ammannati, architetto* (Florence, n.d.), pp. 47–61. C. Justi, "Die Einführung der Renaissance in Granada," *Miscellaneen*, 1, p. 227, mentions that the circular court of Charles V's palace at Granada, begun in 1527, was designed to be used for tournaments and festivities, although he does not cite a source for the information. The idea is certainly plausible; however, the palace was never finished or inhabited. Also, the source of its inspiration was evidently Italian, too, and it was the numerous Italian villa–theaters that must have been uppermost in the minds of Crescenzi and Olivares.

Fernando Chueca Goitia, *Casas reales en monasterios y conventos españoles* (Madrid, 1966), pp. 164–5, suggests that the Retiro was another example of the Spanish tradition of attaching royal apartments to monasteries and convents. While this hypothesis might be adequate to explain the first phase of the palace, it does not account for the addition of the Principal Court in 1633.

44. The balcony is mentioned in the description of the Retiro by Lorenzo Magalotti, *Viaje de Cosme de Médicis por España y Portugal (1668–1669)*, ed. Angel Sánchez Rivero (Madrid, n.d.), p. 103. It is also visible on the plan of the palace drawn by René Carlier (fig. 33).

45. For Aguilar and Aguilera, see Marquis del Saltillo, "Arquitectos y alarifes madrileños del siglo XVII," *BSEE*, (1948), pp. 164–7. Aguilar left in June 1635 to undertake the construction of the Casa de la Zarzuela and thereafter Aguilera became the principal building contractor of the Retiro.

46. AGS TMC, leg. 3763, payment, July 6, 1633.

47. BAV Barb.lat.Ms. 8387, fos. 2–3v.

48. ASF Mediceo, filza 4959, Monanni, July 30, 1633.

49. This was a bullfight in honor of the birth of Prince Ferdinand Francis of Bohemia. See Leon Pinelo, *Anales*, p. 295.

50. AGS TMC, leg. 3763, payment, Aug. 23, 1633.

51. ASF Mediceo, filza 4959, Sept. 17, 1633.

52. M. L. Caturla, *Pinturas, frondas y fuentes del Buen Retiro* (Madrid, 1947), p. 40, refers to a document that suggests that the work started in March 1633. However, in AGS TMC, leg. 3763, the initial payment for construction is dated May 30. Monanni reports its completion on Mar. 11, 1634 (ASF Mediceo, filza 4959).

53. BL Eg. Ms. 1820, fo. 286, Hopton to Coke, Oct. 26, 1633. For Hopton's portrait see José López-Rey, "Juan Ricci's Portrait of Sir Arthur Hopton," *GBA*, 87 (1976), pp. 29–32.

54. ASF Mediceo, filza 4959, Dec. 3, 1633.

55. BL Eg. Ms. 1820, fo. 286, Hopton to Coke, Oct. 26, 1633.

56. The king initially ordered the living quarters to be occupied on Nov. 8, 1633 (APM Cédulas reales, tomo 13, fo. 139v., cédula). But the move was delayed by a month.

57. Duquesa de Berwick y de Alba, *Documentos escogidos*, pp. 477–80.

58. León Pinelo, *Anales*, p. 295.

59. ASF Mediceo, filza 4959, Dec. 3, 1633.

60. Lope Félix de Vega Carpio, "Versos a la primera fiesta del palacio nuevo," in *Obras Escogidas* 2 (4th ed., Aguilar, Madrid, 1964), p. 247.

61. The date usually cited for the inaugural festivities, Oct. 1, 1632, is an error which originated with Ramón de

Mesonero Romanos, *El antiguo Madrid*, p. 314. The correct date is verified by Monanni, ASF Mediceo, filza 4959, Dec. 3, 1633; León Pinelo, *Anales*, p. 295, and the anonymous *Copiosa relación de las grandiosas fiestas* (Seville, 1633), the latter of which is the source of the following account.

62. ASF Mediceo, filza 4959, Monanni, Dec. 3, 1633.

63. ASL Anziani, 647 (lettere di Spagna), Jacopo Arnolfini, Dec. 3, 1633.

64. *Codoin*, 69, p. 283.

65. ASF Mediceo, filza 4959, Dec. 3, 1633.

66. BL Eg. Ms. 1820, fo. 286, Hopton to Coke, Oct. 26, 1633.

67. ASF Mediceo, filza 4960, May 13, 1634.

68. ASF Mediceo, filza 4963, Monanni, May 16, 1637. This drawing may have been the one seen and described by Llaguno, *Noticias*, 4, p. 15.

69. See Chapter 5.

70. BL Eg. Ms. 1820, fo. 357, Hopton to Coke, July 17, 1634.

71. ASF Mediceo, filza 4959, Dec. 3, 1633.

72. The design for the Plaza Grande was by Carbonel, as established in AHP 5812, fo. 774, carta de pago, Nov. 5, 1636.

73. ASF Mediceo, filza 4960, Aug. 26, 1634 and Mar. 10, 1635. The pavement is documented in AVM, Seccion 5, leg. 386, expte. 22, Sept. 21, 1634; Sept. 27, 1634; Oct. 14, 1634; Aug. 23, 1635; Oct. 5, 1635; Oct. 8, 1635; Apr. 22, 1636.

74. AGS CS, leg. 309, fo. 255, contract. Cited by Francisco Guillén Robles, "El Casón del Buen Retiro," in *Catálogo del Museo de Reproducciones Artísticas* (Madrid, 1912), pp. xxiii–xxv.

75. AGS TMC, leg. 3764, fo. 80, payment, July 7, 1638. See Shergold, *Spanish Stage*, p. 295.

76. The Crescenzi family owned a casino on the Pincian Hill which was eventually incorporated into the Villa Medici. They sold the property in 1564. See Glenn Andres, *The Villa Medici in Rome* (New York, 1976), pp. 51–67.

77. Lotti's Italian years are largely unstudied. For what is known, s.v. "Lotti," in Ulrich Thieme and Felix Becker, *Allgemeines Lexikon der Bildenden Künstler von der Antike bis zur Gegenwart*, 23 (Leipzig, 1929).

78. ASF Mediceo, filza 4960.

79. ASF Mediceo, filza 4960, Mar. 11, 1634.

80. AGS TMC, leg. 3764, fo. 43, payment, Sept. 24, 1636, mentions the work on the grotto as in progress. AGS TMC, leg. 3764, fo. 50, payment, Mar. 19, 1637, says that the Casón is to be erected in the Jardín Alto where "they had started to make a grotto."

81. The fullest seventeenth-century description of the park is found in the diary of Lorenzo Magalotti, *Viaje*, pp. 104–6, who remarks that it is "asymmetrical and irregular."

82. The acquisitions are recorded in AGS TMC, leg. 3764, fos. 77, 80–3, 85, 90–1, etc. These transactions date from June 4, 1637 to Sept. 1, 1641.

83. AGS TMC, leg. 3764, fos. 37–8, payments, May 2, 1636.

84. The hermitage that existed in the garden of the Chateau of Gaillon was illustrated by Jacques Androuet du Cerceau, *Le premier volume des plus excellents bastiments de la France* (Paris, 1607), pp. 3–4. But given the strength of the Spanish tradition of these structures, there is no need to postulate a relationship.

85. See Luis Cervera Vera, *El conjunto palacial de la villa de Lerma* (Valencia, 1967), pp. 397–9.

86. AGS CS, leg. 307, fo. 250, consulta, Jan. 16, 1627 and royal reply.

87. San Juan was designated as the governor's residence on June 23, 1633 (RAH, sig. 9/1075, fo. 338, decreto). Cited by Rodrigo Amador de los Ríos y Villalta, "El palacio antiguo," p. 185.

88. Texeira mistakenly identifies this *ermita* as San Pedro. Payments for the construction have not been found. But the *ermita* was in existence by July 24, 1636, when a silver lamp for the decoration was paid for (AGS TMC, leg. 3764, fos. 164–5).

89. Carbonel's authorship of the design of San Bruno is mentioned in the contract for the Casón; see above, note 74. Payments for construction are in AGS TMC, leg. 3764, fo. 3, Apr. 9, 1634, and fo. 7, June 3, 1634.

90. Payments for the construction are as follows: AGS TMC, leg. 3764 fo. 11, May 1, 1634; fo. 52, June 14, 1634; fo. 53, Dec. 13, 1635; fo. 55, Dec. 23, 1635. The grotto was paid for on Dec. 25, 1635 (fo. 55).

91. BNM, Sección de estampas, no. 704. See Angel M. Barcia Pavón, *Catálogo de la colección de dibujos originales de la Biblioteca Nacional* (Madrid, 1906), p. 139.

92. Its completion is noted by Monanni on Jan. 15, 1633 (ASF Mediceo, filza 4959).

93. For a discussion of this painting, see Appendix III.

94. AHP 5810, fos. 486–7, contract, Apr. 28, 1635. Cited by Marquis del Saltillo, "Artistas madrileños (1592–1850)," *BSEE*, 57 (1953), pp. 143–4. Texeira drew the hermitage of San Jerónimo on his map, but failed to give it an identifying number. It is immediately adjacent to San Bruno, to the south.

95. AHP 6432, fos. 796–806v.; cited without reference and partly quoted by Caturla, *Pinturas*, pp. 40–2. See APM CR, tomo 13, fo. 174, cédula, Aug. 2, 1635 for appointment of Carbonel as architect of San Antonio.

96. According to Magalotti, *Viaje*, p. 103, all the rooms in the palace were also tiled up to a height of a few feet.

97. Most of the construction of the waterworks was undertaken by Aguilera. See AHP 6153, *Declaraciones de los estanques y obra que hizo Cristóbal de Aguilera en el Buen Retiro*, Aug. 28, 1635.

98. ASF Mediceo, filza 4961, Monanni, Aug. 26, 1634, gives the impression that work on the Estanque Grande had just started. AGS TMC, leg. 3764, fo. 42, payment, July 20, 1636, to Aguilera as the first installment of 35,000 ducats to finish the Estanque Grande. AHP, 6153, contract, Aug. 1636, to excavate land from the "*estanque grande que nuevamente se fabrica. . .*" AGS TMC 3764, fo. 65, payment, Aug. 17, 1637, final installment to Aguilera.

99. The contract with Aguilera to build the fishing pavilions was signed on Mar. 15, 1638 (AHP 6752, fos. 74–7). The structures were to be designed by Carbonel and built for a cost of 15,000 ducats. The same contract included a provision to build four watermills, to be used to pump water to other parts of the garden. A payment of May 16, 1639, records the delivery of eighty-three pounds of live fish for the Large Lake (AGS TMC, leg. 3764, fo. 95).

100. The Grand Canal, which measured 4100 Castilian feet long, was begun on Sept. 5, 1638 (AGS TMC, leg. 3764, fos. 81–82) and finished in late May 1639 (Monanni, ASF

Mediceo, filza 4964, May 28, 1639).

101. Fulvio Testi, *Raccolta generale delle poesie*, part III (Modena, 1651), p. 16.

102. AGS TMC, leg. 3764, fo. 78, payment, June 5, 1638.

103. AGS TMC, leg. 3764, fo. 158, payment, July 3, 1641. Between March 1638 and July 1642, a sizable woodland was created in the area of the Large Lake by transplanting hundreds of mature poplars and oaks from the royal sites. See AGS TMC, leg. 3764, fo. 74, Mar. 15, 1638, for the earliest payment and fo. 75, July 20, 1642, for the final payments. The project required the recruitment of an army of laborers equal to the one employed to build the palace in 1633; see Jesuitas, *MHE*, 15, p. 367 and ASF Mediceo, filza 4964, Monanni, Dec. 3, 1639.

104. Published as pl. 17 by Sánchez Rivero in his edition of Magalotti's *Viaje*.

105. ASF Mediceo, filza 4959, Dec. 3, 1633.

106. Although the literature on the Escorial is enormous, there is no satisfactory modern study of the work. *El Escorial, 1563–1963. IV Centenario de la fundación del Monasterio de San Lorenzo el Real* (Madrid, 1963) brings together the basic information and abundant illustrations. For documentation, see Amancio Portabales Pichel, *Los verdaderos artífices del Monasterio de El Escorial* (Madrid, 1945) and *Maestros mayores*, which however draw questionable conclusions about the architect Juan de Herrera's responsibility for the building. Also useful for documents is Amalia Prieto Cantero, "Inventario razonado de los documentos pertenecientes al monasterio de El Escorial existentes en la seccion de Casa y Sitios Reales del Archivo General de Simancas," *RABM*, 71 (1963), pp. 1–127. Herrera's drawings are discussed by Francisco Iñiguez Almech, *Las trazas del Monasterio de San Lorenzo de El Escorial* (Madrid, 1965).

107. Herrera still awaits his biographer. Agustín Ruiz de Arcaute, *Juan de Herrera* (Madrid, 1936) is inadequate. Herrera's role as architect to Philip II is deftly outlined by Catherine Wilkinson, "The Career of Juan de Mijares and the Reform of Spanish Architecture under Philip II," *JSAH* 33 (1974), pp. 130–2.

108. For the use of this type of plan in the history of Spanish architecture, see Fernando Chueca Goitia, *Invariantes castizos de la arquitectura española* (Madrid, 1971), pp. 81–107.

109. This observation is made by René Taylor, in his "Juan Bautista Crescencio," p. 98.

110. For Rubens's work at the Luxembourg Palace, see Jacques Thuillier and Jacques Foucart, *Rubens' Life of Marie de' Medici* (New York, n.d.). For Cortona, see Malcolm Campbell, *Pietro da Cortona at the Pitti Palace* (Princeton, 1977).

111. ASF Mediceo, filza 4960.

112. ASF Mediceo, filza 4963, Monanni, Nov. 14, 1637.

NOTES TO CHAPTER IV

1. *Diálogos*, fo. 65v. This passage does not occur in every copy of the 1633 edition. José María de Azcárate, in "Una variante en la edición de los 'Diálogos' de Carducho con noticia sobre el Buen Retiro," *AEA*, 24 (1951), pp. 261–2 tells how a new first page of Diálogo V was inserted, substituting praise of the Retiro for the Escorial.

2. ASF Mediceo, filza 4959, July 30, 1633.

3. *Codoin*, 69, p. 285.

4. APM CR, tomo 13, fo. 139v.

5. ASF Mediceo, filza 4959, Monanni, Nov. 19, 1633.

6. Duquesa de Berwick y de Alba, *Documentos escogidos*, p. 477.

7. BL Eg. Ms. 1820, fo. 299v., Dec. 27, 1633.

8. AGS TMC, leg. 3764, royal decree.

9. ASF Mediceo, filza 4960, Monanni, May 13, 1634.

10. ASM Spagna, busta 46, letter of May 10, 1636. Printed in Fulvio Testi, *Lettere*, ed. Maria Luisa Doglio, 2 (Bari, 1967), letter 1150. Any further citations from Testi's correspondence will be taken from this edition.

11. Testi, *Lettere*, 2, letter 1151 (May 16, 1636). The poem, headed "Al signor conte duca, si descrivono le delizie del Real Retiro. . . ," is published in part III of the *Raccolta generale* of Testi's poems, pp. 23–8.

12. *Ibid.*, 3, letter 1304 (Sept. 15, 1638).

13. ASF Mediceo, filza 4960, Monanni, Apr. 28, 1635.

14. AHN Est., lib. 981, Carnero to Miguel de Salamanca, Dec. 4, 1638.

15. APM CR, tomo 13, fo. 308, June 9, 1640.

16. This diagram has been prepared on the basis of documents of appointment and the records of building operations which appear in the different sets of accounts. For Crescenzi, see above, p. 44; for Carbonel, above, p. 57. The decree appointing Juan María Forno as *pagador* is dated Dec. 22, 1631, and is in AGS TMC, leg. 1560. A *consulta* of the Marquis of Malpica, dated June 19, 1643 (AGS CS, leg. 310, fo. 382), states that Forno had been a servant in Crescenzi's household, and it is clear that his appointment was a device for ensuring that Crescenzi had control over all payments for work on the site. The appointment as *pagador* of Cristóbal de Medina, who was one of the king's secretaries, and a town councillor (*regidor*) of Madrid, dates from Jan. 7, 1633, and is recorded in AVM sección 1, leg. 162, expte. 21, and in AGS TMC, leg. 4363. Medina's appointment was made necessary by the emergence of a new source of income in the form of conciliar contributions, and his accounts, which run from Jan. 7, 1633 to Feb. 26, 1635, are to be found in AGS TMC, leg. 3763. The names of the construction contractors and subcontractors appear frequently in the accounts (AGS TMC, legs. 3763 and 3764), and also in the contract documents conserved in AHP.

17. See p. 67.

18. AHP 5808, fos. 1184–1184v., contract with Francisco Martín, *empedrador*, Oct. 12, 1633. Payments for the procurement of building materials are scattered through Medina's accounts in AGS TMC, leg. 3763.

19. AVM sección 1, leg. 161, expte. 45, order of Oct. 24, 1634 by don Francisco Antonio de Alarcón, and list of villages. The pressure under which the officials were working is indicated by a note that "His excellency" (the count–duke) "is pressing for the completion of the courtyard this month." Don Francisco Antonio de Alarcón, of the council of Castile, had been given special responsibility for seeing that the courtyard was paved.

20. See Martín González, "El Panteón," for documentation concerning these sculptors. For Zumbigo, see Angela Madruga Real, "Los Zumbigo, familia de arquitectos del siglo XVII," *AEA*, 47 (1974), pp. 338–42.

21. See, for example, AGS TMC, leg. 3763, payments, Jan. 8, 18, 19, Feb. 28, Apr. 15, 1633.

22. AGS TMC, leg. 3763, payments, Jan. 11 and Mar. 30, 1633.

23. AGS TMC, leg. 3764, fo. 2, payment, Mar. 24, 1634, and fos. 3–4, payment, May 1, 1634.
24. AGS TMC, leg. 3764, fo. 77, payment, May 22, 1638.
25. AGS TMC, leg. 3764, fo. 37, payment, Apr. 27, 1636, and fo. 3, payment, Apr. 25, 1634.
26. AGS TMC, leg. 3763, payments, July 8, Oct. 11, Nov. 3, 1633. See, for Semini, Ceán Bermúdez, *Diccionario*, 4, pp. 366–7, and Martín Gonzalez, "Sobre las relaciones," p. 60.
27. AGS TMC, leg. 3763, payment, July 30, 1633. For Núñez, see Diego Angulo Iñiguez, "El pintor Pedro Núñez, un contemporáneo castellano de Zurbarán," *AEA*, 37 (1964), pp. 179–84.
28. AGS TMC, leg. 3764, fo. 56, payment, Apr. 20, 1637.
29. See José M. de Azcárate, "Instrucción para las construcciones reales del siglo XVII," *BUV*, 25 (1960), pp. 223–30.
30. Fo. 148 (ed. Jean Paul le Flem, Madrid, 1975, pp. 101–2).
31. ASF Mediceo, filza 4959, Dec. 3, 1633. This was the same rate of pay as Andalusian laborers were receiving this year (Hamilton, *American Treasure*, p. 401).
32. ASF Mediceo, filza 4959, Jan. 15, 1633.
33. Jesuitas, *MHE*, 15, p. 367.
34. In the *Nicandro*, reprinted in *MC*, 2, Doc. XXb. This was a conventional argument which was also used in relation to the building of the Escorial and of the Plaza Mayor of Madrid (see the memoirs of Fernando de Acevedo in Mateo Escagedo Salmón, "Los Acebedos," *Boletín de la Biblioteca Menéndez y Pelayo*, 9 (1927), pp. 173–4).
35. APM BR, leg. 2, no. 5, decreto, Nov. 5, 1633, and no. 8, *primera instrucción general*.
36. AGS TMC, leg. 3764, marginal note in top margin of every folio.
37. APM BR, leg. 2, no. 8, *instrucción* for the *teniente de alcaide*, Nov. 29, 1633.
38. APM BR, leg. 2, no. 8, *instrucción* for the *tesorero*, Sebastián Vicente, Nov. 20, 1633. The subsequent history of this endowment, or *consignación fija*, of the Retiro, can be traced in an audit of Vicente's accounts, dated Sept. 18, 1657, in AGS TMC, leg. 3766.
39. The information tabulated in Table II is derived from the various *instrucciones* in APM BR, leg. 2, no. 8. Copies in RAH, Salazar, N. 69 and N. 70. The offices shown in this table were created by virtue of the authority vested in Olivares as governor, and most of the instructions for them date from November 1633.
40. APM CR, tomo 13, fo. 184, cédula.
41. APM BR, leg. 2, no. 8, *primera instrucción general*, clause 23.
42. Below, p. 166. For Feria's campaign see Golo Mann, *Wallenstein* (London and New York, 1976), pp. 735–7.
43. BL Eg.Ms. 1820, fo. 351, Hopton to Cottington, May 22, 1634.
44. Jesuitas, *MHE*, 13, p. 87.
45. Antonio Vieira, *Arte de furtar* (Amsterdam, 1652), p. 395. Vieira's authorship is generally rejected.
46. See p. 233.
47. For example, AGI Ind., leg. 759, king's marginal reply on letter from Count of Castrillo, Feb. 2, 1636.
48. AHP 6179, fos. 950–7, testament of June 24, 1632.
49. *History of the Rebellion*, 5, p. 95.
50. AGI Cont., leg. 70, *cuentas de lo gastado . . . por el conde de Castrillo en el adorno de los palacios del Buen Retiro y casa de la Zarzuela.*

51. *MHE*, 13, p. 6; ASF Mediceo, filza 4960, Feb. 4, 1634.
52. ASF Mediceo, filza 4960, Monanni, Sept. 30, 1634.
53. Manuel de Gallegos, *Obras varias al real palacio del Buen Retiro* (Madrid, 1637), "Silva topográfica," fo. 5. For Gallegos, see Tormo, *Pintura*, pp. 146–57. Tormo, in his study of the Hall of Realms, initially published in 1911–12, was the first to make use of Gallegos's verses for the study of the history of the Retiro, and printed a long extract from them. There is a modern reprint of Gallegos's poems by Antonio Pérez y Gómez (Valencia, 1949).
54. The accounts of the *gastos secretos* are preserved in part in AGS TMC, leg. 1495, and were used by Azcárate, "Anales." From the end of 1632 this series is limited to small payments, especially to Cristóbal de Aguilera. Another set of accounts of the *gastos secretos*, covering the period from October 1633 to August 1639, but with the third series, for 1635, missing, is to be found in BNM Ms. 7797, and was partially published by J. Domínguez Bordona, "Noticias para la historia del Buen Retiro," *RABM*, 10 (1933), pp. 83–90. While Villanueva controlled the secret expense account, it was kept by Miguel Tafalla, an official of the royal household (AGS CH, leg. 496, certified statement of Miguel Tafalla, Aug. 11, 1633).
55. AHP 4673, cédula, Apr. 16, 1633. The secret expense account also seems to have been fed from the chancery dues of the Crown of Aragon, estimated to be worth over 30,000 ducats a year (ASF Mediceo, filza 4959, Monanni, Nov. 26, 1633). Evidence for the diversion of these dues to the *gastos secretos* in AGS TMC, leg. 3764, fo. 2b, Sept. 1, 1634.
56. *Codoin*, 69, p. 285.
57. AGS TMC, leg. 1495.
58. BNM Ms. 7797.
59. The request of the council of finance for seating space, similar to the space allocated to other councils, is to be found in AGS CH, leg. 494, consulta, July 12, 1633.
60. A. Gómez Iglesias, "El Buen Retiro," pp. 27–8.
61. The total contributions of the different councils are listed in Azcárate, "Anales," p. 106, n. 19. The municipality of Madrid ended by paying some 16,000 ducats, as did the Junta del Reino and the council of finance. The council of Castile produced some 12,500 ducats, the councils of Aragon and the Indies about 11,500 each, and the remaining six councils substantially smaller sums. The grand total of conciliar contributions, as given by Azcárate, is 128,063 ducats.
62. AGS TMC, leg. 3764, fo. 5c.
63. Gérard, "La fachada," pp. 239–41.
64. AVM sección 3, leg. 230, expte. 6, royal order, Dec. 5, 1632. The documentation relating to Madrid's part in the financing of the Retiro is conserved in AVM sección 1, leg. 161. It was partially published by Amador de los Ríos, "El palacio antiguo," and more fully by Gómez Iglesias, "El Buen Retiro."
65. ASF Mediceo, filza 4959, Monanni, Feb. 8 and Mar. 26, 1633.
66. Núñez de Castro, *Sólo Madrid*, p. 178.
67. A statement of Oct. 1, 1637 (AVM sección 1, leg. 161, expte. 56, cited by Gómez Iglesias, p. 30) shows the extent of the Crown's liabilities incurred by that date toward the municipality of Madrid. Figures have been converted from *reales* into ducats and have been rounded off to the nearest ducat.

Total loans (excluding 4,551 ducats in silver)	130,508 ducats (in *vellón* currency)
Interest (until Sept. 30, 1643)	50,488 ducats
Total	180,996 ducats
Repayments (principal and interest) to Oct. 1, 1637	80,448 ducats
Outstanding (payable by Sept. 30, 1643)	100,548 ducats

68. For the Crown's Portuguese bankers, see Domínguez Ortiz, *Política y hacienda*, pp. 127–39, and Julio Caro Baroja, "La sociedad criptojudía en la corte de Felipe IV," in his *Inquisición, brujería y criptojudaísmo* (2nd ed., Madrid, 1972), pp. 13–180.

69. See Yosef Hayim Yerushalmi, *From Spanish Court to Italian Ghetto* (New York, 1971), pp. 105–22.

70. Pedro Calderón de la Barca, *Obras completas*, 3. *Autos sacramentales*, ed. Angel Valbuena Prat (2nd ed., Aguilar, Madrid, 1967), pp. 131–52. For a discussion of this drama, see below, p. 230.

71. For the life and career of Cortizos, see Julio Caro Baroja, *Los judíos en la España moderna y contemporánea*, 2 (Madrid, 1961), pp. 103–15.

72. Rodríguez Villa, *La corte*, p. 102.

73. ASF Mediceo, filza 4964, Monanni, June 11, 1639.

74. Shergold, *Spanish Stage*, p. 295.

75. For a description of the fire, see Jesuitas, *MHE*, 15, pp. 412–14, and the report of the Tuscan ambassador, Gabriello Riccardi, in ASF Mediceo, filza 4964, March. 3, 1640.

76. AGS TMC, leg. 3764, fos. 118–20, payments, Mar. 5, 6, 7, 1640.

77. The difficulties in arriving at a grand total are increased by the problem of overlap. This derives in particular from the attempt to centralize the Retiro's accounts in the hands of Sebastián Vicente, who had been appointed treasurer of the Retiro in November 1633. Once Vicente had begun to keep accounts, monies were handed over to him by other ministers, who recorded the transaction in their own accounts. For example, an audit was taken in 1644 of the accounts of Diego Suárez, secretary of the council of Portugal (Archivo de los Condes de Bornos, Madrid, vol. 79). From these accounts it appears that between May 23, 1633, and May 15, 1640, Suárez handed over almost 200,000 ducats to the *pagadores* of the Retiro, consisting of money which he had received from Portuguese effects. Almost all of these payments, however, show up in Vicente's accounts, and therefore Suárez's accounts, which were previously unknown, and to which we were given access through the kindness of the Condes de Bornos, do not appear in our list.

The accounts which we have used for our calculations are the following (converted into ducats and rounded out to the nearest thousand ducats):

Account	Total payment in ducats	Years covered	Documentation
Jerónimo de Villanueva (secret expense account)	270,000	1630–9	AGS TMC, leg. 1495 (1630–5) BNM Ms. 7797 (1633–9, with 1635 missing). See note 54.
Conde de Castrillo (council of the Indies)	226,000	1634–8	AGI Cont., leg. 70. See note 50.
Cristóbal de Medina (conciliar contributions)	276,000	1633–5	AGS TMC, leg. 3763. See note 16.
Sebastián Vicente (treasurer of Retiro)	875,000		AGS TMC, leg. 3764
Total	1,647,000		
Municipality of Madrid	250,000		
Total	1,897,000		

78. ASF Mediceo, filza 4963, document in cypher enclosed by Monanni with letter of Nov. 14, 1637.

79. BNM Ms. 7797, fo. 128 and AGI. Cont., leg. 70, fo. 175.

80. Modesto Ulloa, *La hacienda real de Castilla en el reinado de Felipe II* (Madrid, 1977), p. 97.

81. See the valuable essay by Antonio Domínguez Ortiz, "Los gastos de corte en la España del siglo XVII," reprinted in his *Crisis y decadencia de la España de los Austrias* (Barcelona, 1969), p. 88.

82. *Actas de las cortes de Castilla*, 55 (Madrid, 1947), p. 441.

83. *Ibid.*, p. 390.

84. Figure derived from AGS TMC, leg. 3763.

85. AHP 6432, fo. 796v., contract, July 25, 1635 (San Antonio); AGS CS, leg. 309, fo. 255, royal order of Feb. 5, 1637 (Casón); AGS TMC, leg. 3764, July 7, 1638 (Coliseo).

86. ASF Mediceo, filza 4959, Monanni, Dec. 3, 1633.

87. BNM Ms. 7797, fo. 111v.

88. AGI Cont., leg. 70, fo. 179.

89. BNM Ms. 7797, fo. 119.

90. See Nigel Glendinning, "Spanish Painting in the Golden Age," *Diamante*, 27 (London, 1977), pp. 12–13.

91. BNM Ms. 7797, fo. 119.

92. See p. 271, note 6.

93. For the incomes of the nobility, see BNM Ms. 4124, fos. 119–44, *relación de las cosas notables de la corte de España* (1623); Domínguez Ortiz, *La sociedad*, 1, Part 2, Chapter 3; Charles Jago, "The Influence of Debt on the Relations between the Crown and Aristocracy in Seventeenth-century Castile," *The Economic History Review*, 2nd series, 26 (1973), pp. 218–36.

94. Rodríguez Villa, *La corte*, p. 127.

95. BL Eg. Ms. 1820, fo. 354, Hopton to Coke, June 18, 1634.

96. Jesuitas, *MHE*, 15, p. 325, Aug. 24, 1639.

97. Sigüenza, *Orden de San Jerónimo*, 2, p. 409.

NOTES TO CHAPTER V

1. See p. 82.

2. See p. 89.

3. Magalotti, *Viaje*, p. 103. The Medici party was in Madrid

from Oct. 24 to Nov. 13, 1668.

4. AGI Cont. leg. 70, fos. 2–3, 1634; fo. 2, 1634; fo. 180, 1638.

5. AGI Cont. leg. 70, fo. 180, 1638.

6. ASF Mediceo, filza 4959, Nov. 26, 1633.

7. ASF Mediceo, filza 4959, Dec. 3, 1633.

8. AGS Est. leg. 2716, royal order to Marquis of Aytona, Sept. 1634.

9. AGI Cont. leg. 70, fo. 38, 1634.

10. ASF Mediceo, filza 4959, Monanni, Dec. 3, 1633.

11. AGI Cont. leg. 70, fo. 19, 1634.

12. AGI Cont. leg. 70, fo. 55, 1634.

13. AGI Cont. leg. 70, fo. 55, 1634.

14. "A Relation of Sundry Voyages and Journeys made by Mr. Robert Bargrave," Bodleian Library, Ms. Rawlinson C799, fos. 138–9, winter 1654–5.

15. APM OB, tomo 26, fo. 12, decreto.

16. APM BR, leg. 2, decreto. Cited by Amador de los Ríos, "El antiguo palacio," pp. 187–8.

17. APM BR, leg. 2, decreto, Apr. 11, 1635.

18. MSB, Codex Monacensis Hisp. 22, fo. 45.

19. Rodríguez Villa, *La corte,* p. 180.

20. ASF Mediceo, filza 4963, June 27, 1637.

21. AGS Sec. Prov. leg. 2445, consulta, Feb. 11, 1647. The statues were moved to the Alcázar on May 28, 1647 to be installed in the Octagonal Room; see José M. de Azcárate, "Noticias sobre Velázquez en la corte," *AEA,* 33 (1960), pp. 371–2. They are now displayed in the Throne Room and the Hall of Columns in the Palacio de Oriente, Madrid.

22. AHP 4680, obligación, Nov. 20, 1634. These silver lions are discussed by Caturla, *Pinturas,* p. 32.

23. ASF Mediceo, filza 4960, Sept. 9, 1634.

24. ADM leg. 259, no. 106, royal order, Jan. 31, 1643, to mint silver service, following example of king, who has ordered same to be done for silver in the Retiro. ASM Spagna, busta 53, Modenese ambassador, Mar. 4, 1643, reports that Retiro service has been melted down.

25. ASF Mediceo, filza 4960. The documentation is published in the valuable study by Carl Justi, "Die Reiterstatue Philipps IV von Pietro Tacca," *Miscellaneen,* 2, pp. 243–74.

26. Galileo's intervention is mentioned by Filippo Baldinucci, *Notizie de' profesori del disegno,* 10 (Milan, 1812), pp. 438–9.

27. See Francisco J. Sánchez Cantón, "Sobre el *Martínez Montañés* de Velázquez," *AEA,* 34 (1961), pp. 25–30.

28. As José López-Rey, *Velázquez. A Catalogue Raisonné of the Oeuvre* (London, 1963), p. 189, pointed out, there is nothing to support Justi's contention that a copy, now in the Palazzo Pitti, of Velázquez's *Equestrian Portrait of Philip IV* (Prado) was sent to Tacca in connection with this commission.

29. ASF Mediceo, filza 4967, Monanni, July 2, 1642.

30. ASF Mediceo, filza 4967, Pucci, Sept. 17, 1642.

31. García Mercadal, *Viajes,* 2, pp. 725–6.

32. There is no adequate study of Philip IV as collector and patron.

33. The inventories are in APM. The following figures are taken from Pedro Beroqui, *El Museo del Prado (Notas para su historia), I. El Museo Real* (Madrid, 1933), p. 34. See also Yves Bottineau, "Les inventaires royaux et l'histoire de l'art: l'exemple d'Espagne," *L'Information d'Histoire et de l'Art,* 4 (1959), pp. 69–74.

34. The inventory is published by Yves Bottineau,

"L'Alcázar de Madrid et l'inventaire de 1686," *Bulletin Hispanique,* 58 (1956), pp. 421–62; 60 (1958), pp. 30–61, 145–79, 289–326, 450–83.

35. The inventory is published by Gloria Fernández Baytón, *Inventarios reales, I. Testamentaría del rey Carlos II, 1701–1703* (Madrid, 1975).

36. These figures also come from Beroqui, *El Museo,* p. 34.

37. PRO SP 94.40, fo. 150v., Hopton to Cottington, Aug. 5, 1638. For Hopton's involvement with picture collecting, see Elizabeth DuGué Trapier, "Sir Arthur Hopton and the Interchange of Paintings between Spain and England in the Seventeenth Century," *Connoisseur,* 164 (1967), pp. 239–43 and 165 (1967), pp. 60–3. This article makes use of Hopton's letters in BL Eg. Ms. 1820.

38. See José López Navío, "La gran colección de pinturas del marqués de Leganés," *Analecta Calasanctiana,* 8 (1962), pp. 260–330.

39. Duquesa de Berwick y de Alba, *Documentos escogidos,* p. 478. On December 27, 1633 the Duke of Arschot, who had just arrived in Madrid and was living as a guest in Leganés's house, "as if in paradise," wrote back to Brussels to suggest that this was a good moment for the Estates General of the Netherlands to place Leganés under an obligation. "This is because the king has asked him to furnish some rooms in the building he is having constructed, called the Bon Retiro... He has furnished them extremely well, especially with paintings, and has already written to Olivares asking for permission to have copies made of those he gave to His Majesty." Arschot suggested that the Estates General should pay for those copies and present them to Leganés. The Estates General agreed, and arranged for copies of eight paintings to be done by March 1634. The Baron de Hoboken saw them in Antwerp in April and reported that the cost did not exceed 1,000 florins (*Actes des Etats Généraux de 1632,* ed. L. P. Gachard, vol. II, Brussels, 1866, Appendix D, document IV, and pp. 319–22 and 334).

40. See Haskell, *Patrons and Painters,* pp. 171–2.

41. In a remarkable letter to Castel Rodrigo, dated Feb. 26, 1636 (AHN Est. lib. 85, no folio number), Monterrey informs him that he is founding an Augustinian church and convent at Salamanca with the intention of interring there the bones of his uncle, don Baltasar de Zúñiga. These were at present buried in the convent of the Paular at Segovia, but the friars had failed to honor his memory in the way they had been instructed. The church was also to be used for his own burial, "and I can assure your excellency that, the way I am living now, it is a real relief to think on death." He went on to explain that he had had some marble effigies made in Naples, and also a large *retablo,* made of various expensive kinds of stone, for the high altar. He was now inquiring into the question of transportation from Naples to Salamanca, and was thinking of following the example of the Duke of Alba, who shipped back some fountains from Naples to Lisbon. From there they were sent by boat up the Tagus, which could be navigated as far as the bridge of Alcántara in the summer months. The remaining thirty-five leagues to Salamanca could be covered by ox-carts, "although there are some stretches of bad road." Monterrey wanted to find out from Castel Rodrigo whether he had a reliable agent in Lisbon to whom the consignment could be addressed, and also whether he could do something, as a native of Portugal, to secure him exemption from customs dues.

42. For the decoration of the church, see Antonio García Boiza, *Una fundación de Monterrey: la iglesia y convento de MM. Agustinas de Salamanca* (Salamanca, 1945) and Angela Madruga Real, "Cosimo Fanzago en las Agustinas de Salamanca," *Goya*, 125 (1975), pp. 291–7.

43. See Alfonso E. Pérez Sánchez, "Las colecciones de pintura del conde de Monterrey (1653)," *BRAH*, 174 (1977), pp. 417–59.

44. For the complicated history of the Haro family collection, which is still unclear, see Saltillo, "Artistas madrileños," pp. 234–40; Angel M. de Barcia, *Catálogo de la colección de pinturas del Excmo. Sr. Duque de Berwick y Alba* (Madrid, 1911), pp. 245–53; José M. Pita Andrade, "Los cuadros que poseyó el séptimo marqués del Carpio," *AEA*, 25 (1952), pp. 223–36, and Gregorio de Andrés, *El marqués de Liche, bibliófilo y coleccionista de arte* (Madrid, 1975).

45. For the 1647 inventory of the Admiral of Castile, see Cesáreo Fernández Duro, *El último Almirante de Castilla. Don Juan Tomás Enríquez de Cabrera* (Madrid, 1903), pp. 184–215. For a partial listing of the 1657 inventory of the Duke of Infantado, see Pérez Pastor, *Noticias*, 2, pp. 179–80.

46. See María L. Caturla, "El coleccionista madrileño don Pedro de Arce, que poseyó *Las Hilanderas* de Velázquez," *AEA*, 21 (1948), pp. 292–304.

47. See Alfonso E. Pérez Sánchez, *Pintura italiana del s. XVII en España* (Madrid, 1965), pp. 63–72, for a short discussion of picture collecting in seventeenth-century Spain.

48. The fundamental document for reconstructing the paintings collection of the Retiro is the inventory made following the death of Charles II and dated 1701 (APM Testamentarías, tomo II, sig. I/G-112, fos. 473–586). Unfortunately, no inventory of the palace appears to have been made at the death of Philip IV. It is obvious from the 1701 inventory, and from other sources of information, that some pictures were added and that others were removed during Charles II's reign. But it can be assumed that most of the paintings inventoried in 1701 were in the palace at Philip's death. The inventory does not list the paintings by rooms, but the path of the compilers through the palace was orderly and can be reconstructed with considerable accuracy. For a complete transcription of the inventory with annotations, see Barbara von Barghahn, "The Pictorial Decoration of the Buen Retiro Palace and Patronage during the Reign of Philip IV" (Ph.D. diss., New York University, 1979).

49. See Julián Zarco Cuevas, *Los Jerónimos de San Lorenzo el Real de El Escorial* (Madrid, 1930), p. 23.

50. For the paintings brought from Valladolid, see José Martí y Monsó, *Estudios histórico-artísticos relativos principalmente a Valladolid* (Valladolid–Madrid, n.d.), p. 617.

51. These were identified by Michael Jaffé, "Current and Forthcoming Exhibitions. Exposición Conmemorativo del IV Centenario del Nacimiento de Rubens, Museo Nacional de Escultura, Valladolid, Dec. 1977–Jan. 1978," *BM* 120 (1978), p. 349.

52. APM OB, tomo 26, fo. 33, refers to a *memorial* dated May 14, 1635, listing pictures to be sent from Aranjuez to the Retiro. This *memorial* has not come to light.

53. APM BR, leg. 3, no. 12, "*Pinturas entregadas por D. Gerónimo de Villanueva.*"

54. BNM Ms. 7797, fo. 119v. Cited by Domínguez Bordona, "Noticias," p. 85. See López-Rey, *Velázquez*, pp. 47–9, for a discussion of the works sold by Velázquez to Villanueva.

55. AGS TMC, leg. 3763, payment, Nov. 28, 1633. The papal procession may have been one of two paintings of papal ceremonies, now lost, attributed to Pietro da Cortona in the 1701 inventory. See Pérez Sánchez, *Pintura italiana*, p. 266, and Walter Vitzthum, "Review of Giuliano Briganti, *Pietro da Cortona o della pittura barocca*," *BM*, 105 (1963), p. 215.

56. BNM Ms. 7797, fo. 119. Neither of these paintings can be surely identified. There is an autograph painting of *Venus and Adonis* in the Corsini Gallery, Rome, and a version by the workshop or a follower in the Museum of Art, Cleveland, but neither can be related with certainty to the work in the Retiro.

57. BNM Ms. 7797, fo. 119. These paintings are now in the Prado, nos. 1113 and 1114 respectively.

58. BNM Ms. 7797, fo. 119. For the sale to King Charles, see W. Noel Sainsbury, *Original Unpublished Papers Illustrative of the Life of Sir Peter Paul Rubens as an Artist and Diplomatist* (London, 1859), pp. 354–5.

59. AGI Cont. leg. 70, fo. 123, 1634.

60. ASF Mediceo, filza 4959.

61. Jesuitas, *MHE*, 15, p. 58 and AGS TMC, leg. 3764, fo. 100, payment, Dec. 31, 1638, for repairs to "*quadros de pinturas que enbió del reyno de Nápoles el conde de monterey.*"

62. Monterrey's impact on the evolution of painting in Naples, although considerable, has yet to be studied.

63. Most of the extant Italian paintings for the Retiro have been identified by Pérez Sánchez, *Pintura italiana*.

64. On Dec. 10, 1637, Lanfranco wrote to Ferrante Carlo that he had just been given a commission for two paintings for the king by Monterrey, who was about to return to Madrid. The subjects of the paintings are not mentioned by the artist, but it is possible that they formed part of the series of scenes from the Roman circus, discussed below, rather than scenes from the life of the emperor. For Lanfranco's letter, see Giovanni Bottari and Stefano Ticozzi, *Raccolta di lettere sulla pittura, scultura ed architettura scritte da più celebri personaggi dei secoli XV, XVI e XVII*, 1 (Milan, 1822), pp. 307–8.

The Roman emperor paintings by Lanfranco are discussed by Pérez Sánchez, *Pintura italiana*, pp. 157–9. A fourth painting, *Triumphal Scene*, is lost, but known through an engraving.

65. For the painting by Camassei, see Ann S. Harris, "A Contribution to Andrea Camassei Studies," *AB*, 52 (1970), pp. 63–4. For the painting by Domenichino, see Richard E. Spear, "Preparatory Drawings by Domenichino," *MD*, 6 (1968), p. 127.

66. For a discussion of this series, see Walter Vitzthum, *Cento Disegni Napoletani* (Florence, 1967), pp. 39–40. Some of these paintings were commissioned by Monterrey's successor, the Duke of Medina de las Torres.

67. See Pérez Sánchez, *Pintura italiana*, p. 321 and Walter Vitzthum, "Seicento Paintings in Madrid," *BM*, 112 (1970), pp. 420–3 (Perrier). For a discussion of the attribution of the painting by Perrier, see the exchange of letters to the Editor between Erich Schleier and Walter Vitzthum, *BM*, 112 (1970), pp. 760–1.

68. See Pérez Sánchez, *Pintura italiana*, pp. 452–4 and 499.

69. AGS TMC, leg. 3764, fos. 159–60; cited by Azcárate, "Anales," p. 125, who however does not connect the shipment with the landscape paintings. Marcel Röthlisberger, *Claude Lorrain. The Paintings* (New Haven, 1961),

pp. 158–9, considered but rejected the name of Castel Rodrigo as the person responsible for the commission and proposed Crescenzi instead.

Enriqueta Harris, in an article forthcoming in *The Burlington Magazine* on "G. B. Crescenzi, Velázquez, and the 'Italian' Landscapes for the Buen Retiro," which she generously allowed us to see in typescript, adduces evidence intended to support the intervention of Crescenzi in this commission. In 1634, Crescenzi was paid nearly 11,000 *reales* from the secret account (BNM 7797) for a lot of forty-two paintings for the decoration of the Retiro (see above, note 58). Included among them were "twelve large landscapes from Italy." According to the accounts, the sale had preceded the festivals held at the Retiro on St John's day (June 24) of the same year. Harris hypothesizes that these paintings were the first installment of the decoration of the Landscape Gallery, that they were possibly obtained by Crescenzi through his relatives in Rome, and that paintings by Claude and Poussin may have been among them. The commission would have been completed by Castel Rodrigo after Crescenzi's death in 1635. There are reasons to question this hypothesis.

Crescenzi was known to be a picture collector–dealer and at this time was selling nine paintings from his collection to Charles I (see above, note 58). It is conceivable that the 1634 sale also comprised works that had long been in his possession. It is equally possible that the pictures were not acquired in Italy, but in Madrid, where there was a thriving art market . centered around the estate sale (*almoneda*). Second, there is no compelling reason to associate the "twelve large landscapes from Italy" with the commission in Rome. According to the 1701 inventory, the Retiro contained dozens of unidentified large landscape paintings, in addition to the ones obtained in Rome. The laconic reference in the secret account could apply equally well to any of these. Finally, the price paid for the pictures, 792 *reales* or an average of six ducats apiece, is extremely low if it is thought to pertain to works by Claude and Poussin, or any artist of rank.

It should also be pointed out that the pictures would have been commissioned at least a year before the delivery date in order to be on hand by June 1634. This would push the date of execution back to early 1633, with significant consequences for the reconstruction of the developments of Claude and Poussin, and for the problem of the chronological sequence of the drawings in the *Liber Veritatis.*

On balance, it seems that Castel Rodrigo is a better choice as the agent of this commission than Crescenzi. He was in Rome for almost the entire decade of the thirties, is known to have been in direct contact with Claude at the probable date when his pictures were executed and to have sent a large shipment of pictures (seventeen crates) from Rome to the Retiro. For these reasons, it is also difficult to accept the suggestion of Pérez Sánchez, "Las colecciones," p. 419, that the Count of Monterrey, who had been in Naples since 1632, had anything to do with the landscape commission.

70. See Röthlisberger, *Claude Lorrain*, p. 159, for this commission.

71. These series are discussed in part by Anthony Blunt, "Poussin Studies VIII–A Series of Anchorite Subjects Commissioned by Philip IV from Poussin, Claude and Others," *BM*, 101 (1959), pp. 389–90. Röthlisberger, *Claude Lorrain*, p. 159, suggests a date of 1636–8 for the

paintings by Claude. For a reconstruction of the installation and attributions of hitherto unidentified works, see von Barghahn, "The Pictorial Decoration."

72. Röthlisberger, *Claude Lorrain*, pp. 481–2 (*St Mary Magdalene*) and p. 483 (*Anchorite*).

73. *Ibid.*, pp. 155–61.

74. See Blunt, "Poussin Studies VIII," for these works.

75. Some of these works are discussed by James D. Burke, *Jan Both: Paintings, Drawings and Prints* (New York–London, 1976), pp. 81–90 and 221–3.

76. For Dughet's work, see Anthony Blunt, "Poussin Studies V–The 'Silver Birch Master,'" *BM*, 91 (1950), pp. 69–73. For Lemaire's work, see Anthony Blunt, "Jean Lemaire: Painter of Architectural Fantasies," *BM*, 83 (1943), pp. 241–6.

77. See Röthlisberger, *Claude Lorrain*, pp. 479–81.

78. See von Barghahn, "The Pictorial Decoration," pp. 314–28.

79. See Röthlisberger, *Claude Lorrain*, pp. 180–6.

80. See Anthony Blunt, *The Paintings of Nicolas Poussin. A Critical Catalogue* (London, 1966), pp. 118 and 176.

81. For the works by Sacchi, see Ann S. Harris, *Andrea Sacchi* (Oxford, 1977), pp. 69–70.

82. See Svetlana Alpers, *The Decoration of the Torre de la Parada* (London–New York, 1971), pp. 29–41, for a history of the commission.

83. ASF Mediceo, filza 4963, May 1, 1638.

84. Max Rooses and Charles Ruelens, *Correspondance de Rubens et documents épistolaires concernant sa vie et ses oeuvres*, 6 (Antwerp, 1909), p. 220.

85. See Matías Díaz Padrón, *Museo del Prado. Catálogo de pinturas, I. Escuela flamenca, siglo XVII* (Madrid, 1975), pp. 270–1. In 1653, a special curtain for the picture was made to hide the goddesses from general view.

86. Rooses and Ruelens, *Correspondance*, 6, p. 228.

87. See Díaz Padrón, *Escuela flamenca*, p. 364, for one of these works.

88. *Ibid.*, pp. 432–3 and 437 for some of de Vos's contributions to the Retiro decoration.

89. Prado nos. 1895, 1897, 1898 and 3208 may be identifiable with paintings for the Retiro.

90. See Díaz Padrón, *Escuela flamenca*, pp. 129–30.

91. See Appendix III for a discussion of these works.

92. See Appendix III and López-Rey, *Velázquez*, p. 135.

93. *Ibid.*, pp. 145 (*Forge of Vulcan*), 123 (*Joseph's Bloody Coat*), 163–4 (*Waterseller*).

94. *Ibid.*, pp. 210 and 237.

95. *Ibid.*, p. 173.

96. See Chapter II, note 41.

97. For Orrente, see Diego Angulo Iñiguez and Alfonso E. Pérez Sánchez, *Pintura toledana. Primera mitad del siglo XVII* (Madrid, 1972), pp. 227–358.

98. Maino's career and small oeuvre are reconstructed by Angulo and Pérez Sánchez, *Pintura madrileña*, pp. 299–325.

99. For Castelo, see *ibid.*, pp. 190–202; for Leonardo, see Mazón de la Torre, *Jusepe Leonardo.*

100. For Collantes, see Juan A. Gaya Nuño, "En el centenario de Collantes. Escenarios barrocos y paisajes disimulados," *Goya*, 10 (1956), pp. 222–8; Alfonso E. Pérez Sánchez, "Algunas obras inéditas y nuevas consideraciones en torno a Collantes," *AEA*, 35 (1962), pp. 253–63; and Jutta Held, "Die Theorie der Landschaftmalerei im frühen 17. Jahrhundert und ihre Politische Bedeutung bei Collantes," *Jahrbuch der Hamburger Kunstsammlungen*, 21

(1976), pp. 129–54, whose political interpretations of his landscapes seem implausible.

101. For Pereda, see Tormo, *Pintura*, pp. 247–336; Alfonso E. Pérez Sánchez, *D. Antonio de Pereda (1611–1678) y la pintura madrileña de su tiempo* (Madrid, 1978–9), and Jesús Urrea, "Antonio de Pereda nació en 1611," *AEA*, 49 (1976), pp. 336–8.

102. AGI Cont. leg. 70, fo. 123, 1634. A landscape signed by Pereda in the Berlin–Dahlem Museum (no. 1979) may possibly be related to this purchase.

103. See María L. Caturla, "Zurbarán en el Salón de Reinos," *AEA*, 18 (1945), pp. 292–300.

104. For an account of de la Corte's career and some of the paintings he executed for the Retiro, see Angulo and Pérez Sánchez, *Pintura madrileña*, pp. 349–68.

105. See note 48.

106. For a discussion of the arrangement of pictures in the Alcázar during the reign of Philip IV, see Steven N. Orso, "In the Presence of the 'Planet King': Studies in Art and Decoration at the Court of Philip IV of Spain" (Ph.D. diss., Princeton University, 1978).

Notes to Chapter VI

1. Covarrubias, *Elogios*, pp. unnumbered.

2. The Hall of Realms, or *salón grande* as it was usually called in the 1630s, still survives and, since 1841, has been used as the Museum of the Spanish Army. Although the exterior was remodelled in the nineteenth century, the interior structure is much as it was.

3. The balcony is mentioned by Bargrave (see p. 108) and is also visible in Carlier's floor plan (fig. 55).

4. AHP 6363, fo. 175, carta de pago, March 28, 1635, to Diego de Viana for "los bordeles que está haziendo a las 16 mesas de jaspe que se han de poner en el Salón de Buen Retiro." In the winter of 1654–5, only ten of these tables were observed in the room by Robert Bargrave (see p. 108).

5. The placement of the lions in the room is noted by Manuel de Gallegos, in "Silva topográfica," fo. 4.

6. The installation was reconstructed in the important article of 1911–12 by Elías Tormo, "Velázquez, el salón de reinos del Buen Retiro y el poeta del palacio y del pintor," reprinted in *Pintura*, pp. 127–246. An arrangement of the battle paintings and the Hercules scenes in their original sequence was not attempted by Tormo. The reconstruction presented here is based on the 1701 inventory. Although it is accurate in showing where each of the series was placed in the room, it may not coincide with the exact order of the 1635 installation. Unfortunately, there is no evidence on which to base a reconstruction of the original hanging.

7. For the documentation of the battle paintings and a discussion of the attributions, see María L. Caturla, "Cartas de pago de los doce cuadros de batallas para el salón de reinos del Buen Retiro," *AEA*, 33 (1960), pp. 333–55. The authors, titles and dates of payment when certain are as follows:

Artist	Title	Payments
E. Cajés	Recapture of St Martin (lost)	Aug. 21, 1634; Apr. 20, 1635 (final)
E. Cajés and assistants	Recapture of Puerto Rico	Apr. 14, 1635 (final)
V. Carducho	Siege of Rheinfelden	July 29, 1634
V. Carducho	Relief of Constance	
V. Carducho	Battle of Fleurus	
F. Castelo	Recapture of St Christopher	Aug. 1, 1634; Apr. 27, 1635 (final)
J. Leonardo	Surrender of Jülich	July 28, 1634; June 15, 1635 (final)
J. Leonardo	Relief of Breisach	
J. Maino	Recapture of Bahía	Mar. 26, June 16, 1635 (final)
A. Pereda	Relief of Genoa	July 28, 1634; June 15, 1635 (final)
D. Velázquez	Surrender of Breda	Aug. 13, Dec. 16, 1634; Mar. 15, June 14, 1635 (final)
F. Zurbarán	Defense of Cadiz	Aug. 7, Oct. 16, Nov. 13, 1634 (final)

The payments to Zurbarán include his paintings of the scenes from the life of Hercules. The payments to Velázquez include his royal equestrian portraits and some works by other artists that he sold to Villanueva for the decoration of the palace. All the surviving paintings are in the Museo del Prado.

It is sometimes said that a group of drawings by Vicente Carducho which show kings holding heraldic shields (Biblioteca Nacional, Uffizi, Metropolitan Museum of Art), are studies for works intended for the Hall of Realms. Except for the coincidence of the coats of arms, there is no evidence to suggest that this is correct.

8. For the Hercules paintings by Zurbarán, see Caturla, "Zurbarán en el Salón," and pp. 156–61.

9. For the equestrian portraits by Velázquez, see López-Rey, *Velázquez*, pp. 188–9, 192, 196–7; and p. 156.

10. The queen's visit is mentioned by Francisco de Quevedo, *Epistolario completo de don Francisco de Quevedo*, ed. Luis Astrana Marín (Madrid, 1946), p. 286.

11. Caturla, "Cartas," pp. 346–7 (Velázquez) and 347–8 (Maino).

12. ASF Mediceo, filza 4960, Apr. 28, 1635.

13. ASF Mediceo, filza 4960, Mar. 10, 1635.

14. The Hall of Princely Virtue, as we call it here, has yet to be considered as a type of Renaissance palace decoration, although individual examples have been studied. For brief but thought-provoking observations on the subject, see Charles Dempsey, "Review of Malcolm Campbell, *Pietro da Cortona at the Pitti Palace*," *AB*, 61 (1979), pp. 141–4.

15. For the fundamental work on this vast subject, see Frances A. Yates, *Astraea. The Imperial Theme in the Sixteenth Century* (London, 1975). A good general introduction with a useful bibliography is by Roy Strong, *Splendour at Court. Renaissance Spectacle and Illusion* (London, 1973). For the influence of Charles V on the artistic enterprises of sixteenth-century Italian princes, see Eve Borsook, "Art and Politics at the Medici Court I: The Funeral of Cosimo I de' Medici," *MKIF*, 12 (1965–6), pp. 31–54, and "Art and Politics at the Medici Court II: The Baptism of Filippo de' Medici in 1577," *MKIF*, 13 (1967–8), pp. 95–114.

16. See John Shearman, *The Vatican Stanze: Functions and Decoration* (London, 1972).

17. For the Farnese decorations at Caprarola, see Loren W. Partridge, "Divinity and Dynasty at Caprarola: Perfect History in the Room of Farnese Deeds," *AB*, 60 (1978), pp. 494–530. For Vasari's frescoes in the Palazzo Vecchio,

see Kurt W. Forster, "Metaphors of Rule. Political Ideology and History in the Portraits of Cosimo I de' Medici," *MKIF*, 15 (1971), pp. 91–9.

18. For the Banqueting House, see Per Palme, *Triumph of Peace. A Study of the Whitehall Banqueting House* (Stockholm, 1956), pp. 225–88. For the Medici cycle, see Thuillier and Foucart, *Rubens' Life of Marie de' Medici*. For the Salone of the Barberini Palace, see Walter Vitzthum, "A Comment on the Iconography of Pietro da Cortona's Barberini Ceiling," *BM*, 103 (1961), pp. 427–33. For Cortona's work at the Palazzo Pitti, see Campbell, *Pietro da Cortona at the Pitti Palace*.

19. See Heinrich Göbel, *Wandteppiche. I Teil. Die Niederlande*, 1 (Leipzig, 1923), pp. 415–16.

20. For the history of the Tunis tapestries, see Elías Tormo and Francisco J. Sánchez Cantón, *Los tapices de la Casa del Rey N. S. Notas para el catálogo y para la historia de la colección y de la fábrica* (Madrid, 1919), pp. 95–100, and Hendrick Horn, "Charles V's Conquest of Tunis: Cartoons and Tapestries by Cornelisz Vermeyen" (Ph.D. dissertation, Yale University, 1977).

21. Orso, "In the Presence," pp. 167–74, discusses in detail the significance and ceremonial uses of the Tunis tapestries at the court of Philip IV.

22. See F. W. H. Hollstein, *Dutch and Flemish Etchings, Engravings and Woodcuts* 8 (Amsterdam, n.d.), p. 241. Ernst Buchner, "Bermerkungen zum Historien- und Schlachtbild der deutschen Renaissance," in Ernst Buchner and Karl Feuchtmayer, *Oberdeutsche Kunst der spätgotik und Reformationzeit* (Augsburg, 1924), p. 204, suggested that these prints recorded the battle scenes depicted on the triumphal arch erected for the Emperor's entry into Rome, 1536. This is unlikely because several of the victories depicted by Heemskerck occurred after 1536.

23. See Julián Zarco Cuevas, *Los pintores italianos en San Lorenzo el Real de el Escorial 1575–1613* (Madrid, 1932), pp. 57–8 and 84.

24. The device of an illusionistic tapestry border for a fresco is not uncommon in the sixteenth century. See Ursula Reinhardt, "La tapisserie feinte. Un genre de décoration du manierisme romane au XVIᵉ siècle," *GBA*, 84 (1974), pp. 285–96.

25. This reconstruction is based on the 1623 Pardo inventory in AGS TMC, leg. 1560. The Pardo was severely damaged by a fire in 1604, which destroyed most of the paintings in the south wing, where the conflagration began. Pictures in the rest of the palace were safely removed and it is supposed that they were put back as they had been before. The content of the official suite of rooms discussed here glorifies the great military victories of Charles V and Philip II and contains no reference whatsoever to Philip III. On this basis, it is assumed that the decoration was arranged during Philip II's reign and restored to its original place after the 1604 fire.

26. For the tradition of dynastic portrait series in Spain, see Elías Tormo, *Las viejas series icónicas de los reyes de España* (Madrid, 1916).

27. For the history of these paintings, see Harold E. Wethey, *The Paintings of Titian, 2. The Portraits* (London, 1971), pp. 87–90 and 132–3.

28. See Borsook, "Art and Politics I," pp. 31–4, and Antonio Bonet Correa, "Túmulos del emperador Carlos V," *AEA*, 33 (1960), pp. 55–66.

29. For the emperor's columnar device, see below, p.

157.

30. The following is based on the lengthy description of the monument written by Francisco Gerónimo Collado, entitled *Descripción del túmulo y relación de las exequias que hizo la ciudad de Sevilla en la muerte del rey don Felipe Segundo*. The *Descripción* was not published until 1869 (Seville), but the details of the monument, which was the most lavish of those erected in Spain, were widely circulated.

For another important commemoration of Philip's death, see Eve Borsook, "Art and Politics at the Medici Court III: Funeral Decor for Philip II of Spain," *MKIF*, 14 (1969–70), pp. 89–114.

31. The evolution of the decoration of the Pieza Nueva and its meaning are reconstructed by Orso, "In the Presence," pp. 42–134.

32. López-Rey, p. 188, implies that the *Portrait of Philip IV* may have been damaged in the fire of 1640. This fire was limited to the southern quarter of the palace and would not have affected paintings in the Hall of Realms, which was in the northern quarter.

33. Caturla, "Cartas," pp. 341 and 343.

34. See G. Karl Galinsky, *The Herakles Theme. The Adaptations of the Hero in Literature from Homer to the Twentieth Century* (Oxford, 1972), for a useful survey of the subject, and David R. Wright, "The Medici Villa at Olmo a Castello: Its History and Iconography" (Ph.D. diss., Princeton University, 1976), pp. 306–14 for the identification of Hercules with the prince in the sixteenth century.

35. For instance, see the especially thorough identification of Hercules with Cosimo I de Medici, as explained by Hildegard Utz, "The *Labors of Hercules* and other Works by Vicenzo de' Rossi," *AB*, 53 (1971), pp. 356–61 and Forster, "Metaphors of Rule," pp. 79–82.

36. For the columnar device, see Earl Rosenthal, "*Plus Ultra, Non Plus Ultra*, and the Columnar Device of Emperor Charles V," *JWCI*, 34 (1971), pp. 204–28, and "The Invention of the Columnar Device of Emperor Charles V at the Court of Burgundy in Flanders in 1516," *JWCI*, 36 (1973), pp. 198–230. Also see Marcel Bataillon, "Plus Oultre: La cour découvre le nouveau monde," in *Les Fêtes de la Renaissance. Fêtes et cérémonies au temps de Charles Quint*, 2 (Paris, 1975), pp. 13–27.

37. For example, Hercules Rooms are to be found in the Palazzo del Te Mantua (see Egon Verheyen, *The Palazzo del Te in Mantua* [Baltimore–London, 1977], pp. 30–1, 115–16); the Villa Farnese at Caprarola (see Loren W. Partridge, "The Sala d'Ercole at the Villa Farnese at Caprarola," *AB*, 53 [1971], pp. 467–86 and 54 [1972], pp. 50–62); the Villa d'Este at Tivoli (see David R. Coffin, *The Villa d'Este at Tivoli* [Princeton, 1960], pp. 78–80). Other examples include the Sala Ducale, in the Vatican Palace; the Sala d'Ercole in the Palazzo Vecchio and the Pavillion des Poêles, at Fontainebleau. For a later but important example, there is the Camerino Farnese in the Palazzo Farnese, Rome, which is discussed by John R. Martin, "Immagini della Virtù: The Paintings of the Camerino Farnese," *AB*, 38 (1956), pp. 91–112.

The identification of Hercules with the King of France was especially strong in this period. See Corrado Vivanti, "Henry IV, the Gallic Hercules," *JWCI*, 30 (1967), pp. 176–97, for the most informative of several studies of *Hercules Gallicus*. Louis XIV also identified himself with Hercules; see Rudolf Wittkower, "The Vicissitudes of a Dynastic Monument. Bernini's Equestrian Statue of Louis

XIV," in *De Artibus Opuscula XL. Essays in Honor of Erwin Panofsky* (New York, 1961), pp. 506–7.

38. The relationship of the idea of Hercules as ancestor of the Spanish kings with Zurbarán's paintings is noted by Leo Steinberg, "Review of José López-Rey, *Velázquez*," *AB*, 47 (1965), p. 291. See also Diego Angulo Iñiguez, *La mitología y el arte español del renacimiento* (Madrid, 1952), pp. 65–134.

39. Herculean symbolism was also associated with Philip II, who owned an important series of tapestries of the Labors of Hercules, bequeathed to him by Mary of Hungary. See Paulina Junquera, "Los Trabajos de Hércules. Una serie inédita de tapices del Patrimonio Nacional," *RS*, 11 (1974), pp. 18–24. For another of many images which equate Philip with Hercules, see the scene in the pediment of the triumphal arch erected by the Genoese for the entry of Prince Philip into Antwerp, 1549. There, Atlas is handing over the globe of the world to Hercules, an allusion to the transfer of kingship from Charles V to his son (repr. in Strong, *Splendour at Court*, p. 102).

When Philip IV came to the throne, the city of Seville struck a commemorative medal with a portrait of the king on the obverse and Hercules strangling serpents on the reverse, with this motto: *Herculi Hispano S.P.Q.H.* See Angulo, *La mitología*, p. 73.

40. For the association of Hercules with the sun, see Utz, "The *Labors of Hercules*," pp. 356–60; for the sun with *Virtù*, see Cesare Ripa, *Iconologia*, 1603; ed. Erna Mandowsky (Hildesheim–New York, 1970), pp. 511–12.

41. There was also a cycle of Hercules scenes painted by Rubens for the Torre de la Parada; see Alpers, *The Decoration*, pp. 112, 274–9. During the reign of Charles II, Luca Giordano added a cycle of Hercules labors to the Cáson of the Retiro; see Oreste Ferrari and Giuseppe Scavizzi, *Luca Giordano*, 2 (Rome, 1966), pp. 208–9.

42. See Steinberg, "Review of López-Rey," p. 291.

43. For this meaning, see Tomaso Porcacchi, *Funerali antichi di diversi popoli et nationi* (Venice, 1574), and Borsook, "Art and Politics at the Medici Court I," p. 48, where Porcacchi is cited.

44. For this interpretation of Hercules, see Vivanti, "Henry IV," p. 183 and Utz, "The *Labors of Hercules*," p. 356.

45. This motif is discussed by Thomas D. Kaufmann, "Empire Triumphant: Notes on an Imperial Allegory," *Studies in the History of Art*, 8 (1978), pp. 63–75. See also Vivanti, "Henry IV," p. 183, and Utz, "The *Labors of Hercules*," p. 356. Shergold, *Spanish Stage*, p. 258, mentions the use of the motif in a royal pageant held in Valladolid in 1604.

46. Ripa, *Iconologia*, pp. 104–5.

47. The motif first appears in Rubens's work in the oilsketch *Portrait of Charles de Longueval*, c. 1620 (Leningrad, Hermitage), which was engraved by Lucas Vosterman. For its use in the Banqueting House, see Palme, *Triumph of Peace*, pp. 239–40.

48. The identification of the fallen king with Geryon is now usually rejected because, according to some antique sources, Geryon was a monstrous creature with three bodies in one. Instead he is called King Eryx. But in the influential account of Diodorus of Sicily, Geryon is called Chrysaor and is described as having a normal human body. Diodorus also refers to Eryx as the King of Sicily which, although Sicily was a Spanish possession in the seventeenth century, would have made him less appropriate in this

context. Hercules did not kill Eryx, according to Diodorus, but merely defeated him in a wrestling match. For these reasons, it is permissible to revive the earlier identification, which is also the one given in the 1701 inventory, of this scene as Hercules slaying Geryon.

49. In the print by Gabriel Salmon, on which Zurbarán based his composition, Hercules is shown on a pyre, which is indicated by several pieces of wood. Salmon's reference to the pyre is suppressed in Zurbarán's picture.

50. AGS Est., leg.2332, consulta, May 6, 1631.

51. AGS Est., leg.2332, consulta, Dec. 20, 1631.

52. AGS Est., leg.2335, consulta, Oct. 27, 1634.

53. BL Add.Ms.18,289, fo.129, *Discurso del conde de la Roca*, Sept. 1, 1628.

54. BL Add.Ms.18,289, fo.127. The *Fragmentos* were not in fact published until 1787, when they appeared in vol. 2 of Antonio Valladares, *Semanario Erudito*.

55. See above, p. 51.

56. See Jean Vilar, "Formes et tendances de l'opposition sous Olivares: Lisón y Viedma, *defensor de la patria*," *Mélanges de la Casa de Velázquez*, 7 (1971), pp. 263–94.

57. For Salazar's assistance, see Quevedo, *Epistolario*, p. 196 (note). Quevedo's pamphlet, *El Chitón de las Tarabillas* is published in Francisco de Quevedo y Villegas, *Obras Completas*. 1. *Obras en prosa*, ed. Felicidad Buendía (6th ed., Aguilar, Madrid, 1966), pp. 805–18. Mendoza's "Papel," which has apparently not previously been associated with Quevedo's *Chitón*, is included in the *Discursos* of Antonio de Mendoza, pp. 71–100.

Davies, *A Poet at Court*, p. 52, speculates that it may date from the middle or late 1630s, but late 1629 or early 1630 would seem the logical date.

58. Quevedo, p. 814.

59. Mendoza, p. 88.

60. For *El Brasil restituido* see Lope Félix de Vega Carpio, *Obras* 28, *BAE*, 233 (repr. Madrid, 1970), pp. 257–96. The play is dated Oct. 23, 1625, and was performed at court on Nov. 6. See N. D. Shergold and J. E. Varey, "Some Palace Performances of Seventeenth-Century Plays," *BHS*, 40 (1963), pp. 212–44. We are indebted to Prof. Shirley B. Whitaker for information about this play. For *El sitio de Bredá*, see Pedro Calderón de la Barca, *El sitio de Bredá*, ed. Johanna Rudolphine Schrek ('s-Gravenhage, 1957), and Shirley B. Whitaker, "The First Performance of Calderón's *El sitio de Bredá*," *Renaissance Quarterly*, 31 (1978), pp. 515–31, which makes a convincing case for composition and performance in 1625, some time before Nov. 5.

61. For discussions of the *Surrender of Breda* and the *Recapture of Bahía*, see pp. 178–90.

In the final payment to Zurbarán for his work in the Hall, dated Nov. 13, 1634, it is said that he had done two paintings of the *Defense of Cadiz*. The second picture, which is unknown, has been the subject of considerable conjecture. For Caturla, "Cartas," pp. 334–5, the picture is identical to the one lost work in the commission, which was identified by Monanni as the *Recapture of St Martin* (ASF Mediceo, filza 4960, Apr. 28, 1635). Angulo and Pérez Sánchez, *Pintura madrileña*, pp. 253–5, have convincingly argued that this painting was done by Cajés. In the circumstances, it seems reasonable to suppose that Zurbarán executed two versions of the battle, one of which, for unknown reasons, was not used.

62. *Obras*, *BAE*, 233, pp. 199–256.

63. A. P. Newton, *The European Nations in the West Indies*,

1493–1688 (London, 1933; repr. 1966), pp. 155–63.

64. The commission appears to have been given in the last months of 1633. On Nov. 13 and 23, 1633, the carpenter Gerónimo Sánchez was paid 396 *reales* for "twelve stretchers that he made for the Salón Grande de Buen Retiro"; BNM Ms. 7797, fo. 112.

65. We have not been able to find a copy either of the pamphlet or its refutation, but their existence is reported by Monanni in a letter of Oct. 15, 1633 (ASF Mediceo, filza 4959).

66. AGI Ind., leg.2658, memorandum of Mar. 23, 1633. For the Dutch occupation of St Martin and the Spanish attack, see Enriqueta Vila Vilar, *Historia de Puerto Rico, 1600–1650* (Seville, 1974), pp. 152 and 159–64, and Thomas. G. Mathews, "The Spanish Domination of St Martin, 1633–1648," *Caribbean Studies*, 9 (1969), pp. 3–23.

67. See p. 96.

68. See above, p. 30. For Olivares's original memorandum on the Union of Arms, see *MC*, 1, Doc. IX.

69. *Ibid.*, p. 187.

70. *Ibid.*, p. 185.

71. Roca, *Fragmentos*, p. 229.

72. He made his appeal to the king in a speech in the council of state on Feb. 8, 1625 (AGS Est., leg.7034, consulta).

73. Luis de Gamboa y Eraso, *Verdad de lo sucedido con ocasión de la venida de la armada inglesa sobre Cádiz el 1º de noviembre de 1625...* (Cadiz, 1626), fo. 6. For attempts to identify the figures in this painting, see G. Cruzada Villaamil, *Rubens. Diplomático español* (Madrid, 1874), p. 50, n. 1, and Cesáreo Fernández Duro, *Armada española*, 4 (Madrid, 1898), pp. 77–8, n. 2.

74. Jesuitas, *MHE*, 13, p. 22.

75. *Ibid.*, p. 139.

76. ASF Mediceo, filza 4960, Monanni, May 13, 1634. Date of final payment to Pereda, Caturla, "Cartas de pago," pp. 349–50. For Santa Cruz's career, consulta of council of state, July 28, 1640 (AGS Est., leg. 2762).

77. The copy of the manifesto in AAE Corresp. Espagne, no. 15, fo. 400 bears Sessa's name.

78. ASF Mediceo, filza 4959, Monanni, Oct. 29, 1633.

79. Jesuitas, *MHE*, 13, p. 80.

80. AV Nunziatura di Spagna 345, fo. 311, nuncio, July 15, 1634.

81. See James O. Crosby, *En torno a la poesía de Quevedo* (Madrid, 1967), pp. 34–6, for the disgrace of Don Fadrique, based on a contemporary relation.

82. Jesuitas, *MHE*, 13, pp. 115–16.

83. Quevedo, *Obras*, 2. *Verso*, p. 73. For the various drafts of the sonnet, see Crosby, pp. 31–3.

84. A. Waddington, *La République des Provinces-Unies, la France et les Pays-Bas Espagnols de 1630 à 1650*, 1 (Paris, 1895), p. 147.

85. AGS Est., leg. 2151, voto of Olivares, May 30, 1633.

86. Hoz, pp. 224 and 233.

87. ASF Mediceo, filza 4960, Monanni, Apr. 28, 1635.

88. The original is in the Prado. Numerous copies are still in existence, none of which has been identified with the picture in the Retiro. See Díaz Padrón, *Escuela flamenca*, pp. 276–7.

89. The inventory of 1701 attributes the execution of Coloma's portrait to Velázquez.

90. For Heemskerck, see Sir William Stirling-Maxwell, *The Chief Victories of the Emperor Charles the Fifth, designed by Martin Heemskerck in M.D.L.V.* (London and Edin-

burgh, 1870). For Stradano's prints, see Philipp Fehl, "Vasari e Stradano come panegiristi dei Medici. Osservazioni sul rapporto tra verità storica e verità poetica nella pittura di fatti storici," in *Il Vasari Storiografo e Artista* (Arezzo–Florence, 1974), pp. 207–24.

91. For Spínola and the siege of Breda, see especially Antonio Rodríguez Villa, *Ambrosio Spínola, primer marqués de Los Balbases* (Madrid, 1904), Chapter 22, and José Alcalá-Zamora y Queipo de Llano, *España, Flandes y el mar del norte, 1618–1639* (Barcelona, 1975), Chapter 5. For a rather confused survey of the literary and artistic ramifications of the siege, Simon A. Vosters, *La rendición de Bredá en la literatura y el arte de España* (London, 1974). We are grateful to Dr Geoffrey Parker of the University of St Andrews for his assistance with certain points relating to the siege, and to questions of military practice and dress. For the Spanish army in Flanders, see his *The Army of Flanders and the Spanish Road, 1567–1659* (Cambridge, 1972).

92. For biographical details of Justin of Nassau, see *El sitio*, ed. Schrek, pp. 66–8.

93. Rodríguez Villa, *Spínola*, p. 429.

94. See Díaz Padrón, *Escuela flamenca*, pp. 360–1, for this picture, one of three by this artist of the siege of Breda. This version was listed in the Alcázar inventory of 1636 and would almost certainly have been used by Velázquez as a source for his painting.

95. Gerrat Barry, *The Siege of Breda* (Louvain, 1627), pp. 132 and 142–3. See Hermannus Hugo, *Obsidio Bredana armis Philippi IIII* (Antwerp, 1626). For other translations of Hugo, see *El sitio*, ed. Schrek, pp. 32–3.

96. Rodríguez Villa, p. 431.

97. Barry, p. 145.

98. Although much has been written about the *Surrender of Breda*, little of value has been added to Justi's discussion in *Velázquez*, pp. 351–65. Several studies have dealt inconclusively with possible compositional sources; for a summary of this literature, see Jonathan Brown, "On the Origins of 'Las Lanzas' by Velázquez," *ZfK*, 27 (1964), pp. 240–5.

99. In addition to the painting by Snayers, Velázquez also relied on the engraving of the siege by Jacques Callot; see Fritz Saxl, "Velázquez and Philip IV," in *Lectures* (London, 1957), pp. 314–18.

The portraits of the generals and *maestres de campo* also appear to be accurate, although the identity of some cannot be verified. Spínola was certainly drawn from life because Velázquez had known him while the general was in Madrid from February 1628 to the summer of 1629, and also from the crossing to Italy they made together in September 1629. Other officers serving the Spanish Crown at Breda were Henry de Bergh, Count John of Nassau, the Marquis of Balançon, Wolfgang von Pfalz-Neuberg and Carlos Coloma. Bergh, the traitor, was obviously omitted. John of Nassau has been identified as the balding man in armor just behind Spínola. Since Balançon had lost a leg in the wars, it is possible, as Justi suggested, that he is the elderly bald man leaning on a stick behind Spínola. Wolfgang von Pfalz-Neuberg is known through a print in van Dyck's *Iconologia* (Antwerp, *c.* 1632) and may be the man in profile between Balançon and John of Nassau. Carlos Coloma was also in van Dyck's *Iconologia* and may be the man with the long hair staring out of the picture behind John of Nassau.

100. Some writers have interpreted a pentimento as indicating that Velázquez originally showed Spínola

embracing Nassau. It may be, however, that Velázquez's first idea was to show Spínola placing his left, rather than his right, arm on Nassau's shoulder. Even the radiographs do not make it clear whether Spínola's extended right arm was present from the first or whether it represents the artist's second idea for the gesture of condolence.

101. For this painting, see *Fontainebleau. Art in France 1528–1610*, 2 (Ottawa, 1973), pp. 34 and 36.

102. We are indebted to Dr Geoffrey Parker for this information, which is corroborated in many paintings of surrender scenes done in this period, including the ones illustrated here.

103. Because we interpret the *Surrender of Breda* within the tradition of surrender scenes, we are unable to accept the ingenious interpretation of James F. O'Gorman, "More about Velázquez and Alciati," *ZfK*, 28 (1965), pp. 225–8, who relates it to the tradition of scenes of reconciliation sealed by a handshake. For the same reason, the formulation of the argument in Brown, "On the Origins," no longer seems adequate to us.

104. Francisco Manuel de Melo, *Política militar en avisos de generales* (Madrid, 1638; ed. Buenos Aires, 1943), aviso 43.

105. Andrés Bernáldez, *Historia de los reyes católicos* (ed. Seville, 1870), 1, p. 302.

106. *El sitio*, ed. Schrek, p. 206; and for the circumstances of the performance, see Whitaker, "The first performance."

107. The coincidence between Calderón's play and Velázquez's picture was first noted by Justi, *Velázquez*, p. 359, and has since been referred to frequently.

108. The literature on the painting is summarized by Angulo and Pérez Sánchez, *Pintura madrileña*, pp. 319–20.

109. For a list of printed accounts, see Fernández Duro, *Armada española*, 4, pp. 467–9.

110. These contemporary representations are reproduced and discussed in Enrique Marco Dorta, *La recuperación de Bahía por Don Fadrique de Toledo (1625). Un cuadro español de la época* (Seville, 1959).

111. C. R. Boxer, *Salvador de Sá and the Struggle for Brazil and Angola, 1602–1686* (London, 1952), pp. 45–6, and see Boxer, *The Dutch in Brazil, 1624–1654* (Oxford, 1957) for the Dutch attack, and for the Spanish expedition of 1625.

112. *Compendio historial de la jornada del Brasil, Codoin*, 55, p. 167.

113. See above, note 60. The approbation is printed at the end of the play, *BAE* 233, p. 296. The relationship of Maino's painting to Lope's play was first pointed out by Pedro Beroqui, "Adiciones y correcciones al catálogo del museo del Prado," *Boletín de la Sociedad Castellana de Excursiones*, 6 (1913–14), pp. 539–45.

114. *El Brasil restituido*, p. 294.

115. *Codoin*, 55, p. 189.

116. *El Brasil restituido*, pp. 282–3.

117. *Ibid.*, p. 270.

118. This observation was made by López-Rey, *Velázquez*, pp. 56–7.

119. This figure is correctly identified by Steinberg, "Review of López-Rey," p. 291.

120. See Guy de Tervarent, *Attributs et symboles dans l'art profane 1540–1600* (Geneva, 1958), col. 129.

121. The personifications have been variously identified, with Heresy, Wrath and War being the most common. Steinberg, "Review of López-Rey," p. 290, was the first to identify Treachery or Fraud. Discord is based on Ripa, *Iconología*, pp. 104–5; also p. 160. Heresy as represented here is not found in the emblematic literature. But in type it follows the model of Heresy found in the tapestry of the *Victory of Eucharistic Truth Over Heresy*, part of a series designed by Rubens and executed in 1625–7 for the convent of the Descalzas Reales, Madrid. There Heresy is shown as a half-clad male figure sprawling on the ground beneath the personification of Eucharistic Truth. He holds a profaned host in his hands above his head which symbolizes his heresy. In Maino's painting, a cross, a common symbol of Faith, which has been broken and profaned as a sign of heresy, is held by a similar male figure.

122. In succeeding verses of the Psalm, it is said, "By thy help we will throw back our enemies, / in thy name we will trample our adversaries."

123. See Tervarent, *Attributs*, col. 290.

124. BPM Ms. 1817.

125. BPM Ms. 1817, Olivares to Gondomar, July 3, 1625.

126. Rioja translated into Castilian the Latin epigram composed by Pacheco for the painting of *St Christopher* by Matteo Pérez da Lecce, in the Seville Cathedral. See Barrera, *Rioja*, pp. 270–1, 276–7.

127. For the relations between Rioja and Pacheco, see Jonathan Brown, *Images and Ideas in Seventeenth-Century Spanish Painting* (Princeton, 1978), pp. 59–61.

128. AHP 5810, fos. 467–9, contract; cited by Saltillo, "Artistas madrileños," p. 177.

129. See Brown, *Images and Ideas*, p. 97, for a brief discussion of Velázquez as architect and decorator, with further references.

130. In Covarrubias, *Elogios*.

NOTES TO CHAPTER VII

1. Strong, *Splendour at Court*, p. 213.

2. Bargrave, "A Relation," fo. 148.

3. Barozzi, *Relazioni*, 2, p. 283. We owe this reference to the kindness of Professor Felipe Ruiz Martín.

4. *Sólo Madrid*, p. 217.

5. *Obras*, "Sextas," fo. 25.

6. AVM sección 3, leg. 230, expte. 6, Dec. 5, 1632.

7. See Romolo Quazza, *Margherita di Savoia* (Turin, 1930), p. 198.

8. Jesuitas, *MHE*, 13, p. 107; Hoz, pp. 230–1 (Nov. 4, 1634). See also Francisco Iñiguez Almech, "La casa del tesoro, Velázquez y las obras reales," in *Varia Velazqueña*, 1 (Madrid, 1960), pp. 649–82.

9. Rodrigo Mendez Silva, *Diálogo compendioso de la antigüedad y cosas memorables de la noble villa de Madrid* (Madrid, 1637), fo. 11.

10. Jesuitas, *MHE*, 14, pp. 263–6. See Victor Cousin, *Madame de Chevreuse* (7th ed., Paris, 1886), pp. 138ff. for her flight to Spain.

11. Testi, *Lettere*, 3, letter 1304 (Sept. 15, 1638). Initial plans to lodge him in the Alcázar, Jesuitas, *MHE*, 14, p. 412.

12. AGS TMC, leg. 192, *Cargos contra el capitán Tomás de Cardona*, fos. 155v.–161v. (hospedaje del duque de Módena).

13. Biblioteca Estense, Modena, Ms.a.G.6.17(3). It.685, *Relazione del viaggio fatto in Spagna da Sua A.Serma. di Modena* (anon.), fo. 6v.

14. *Obras*, "Sextas," fo. 24v.

15. ASM Spagna, busta 45, Modenese ambassador, July 4, 1637.

16. ASV Spagna, filza 70, Francesco Corner, Dec. 7 and Dec. 20, 1633; León Pinelo, *Anales*, p. 297.

17. BL Eg.Ms.1820, fo. 357, Hopton to Coke, July 17, 1634.
18. ASF Mediceo, filza 4960, Monanni, May 19, 1635.
19. Jesuitas, *MHE*, 13, p. 191.
20. *Ibid.*, p. 200. For the first performance of *El mayor encanto amor*, see Shergold, *Spanish Stage*, p. 283, and his "The first performance of Calderón's *El Mayor Encanto Amor*," *BHS*, 35 (1958), pp. 24–7. A letter from Monanni, Aug. 4, 1635 (ASF Mediceo, filza 4960), reporting the performance on the preceding Sunday, confirms July 29 as the exact date.
21. ASF Mediceo, filza 4961, Monanni, May 10, 1636; Jesuitas, *MHE*, 13, p. 438.
22. PRO SP.94.39, fo. 191. For these festivities, see below, pp. 200–2.
23. Jesuitas, *MHE*, 14, p. 139.
24. *Ibid.*, pp. 289–90.
25. ASF Mediceo, filza 4963, Monanni, May 22, 1638.
26. Jesuitas, *MHE*, 14, p. 443; ASF Mediceo, filza 4963, Monanni, July 5, 1638.
27. ASF Mediceo, filza 4964, Monanni, Nov. 27, 1638, and Feb. 12, 1639.
28. ASF Mediceo, filza 4964, Monanni, Feb. 26, 1639; Jesuitas, *MHE*, 15, pp. 180, 241 and 273.
29. Jesuitas, *MHE*, 15, p. 407; ASF Mediceo, filza 4965, Monanni, May 5 and July 28, 1640; the comments of Baltasar Carlos on Aranjuez reported by Guillermo Francisco, a French agent in Madrid, on May 16, 1640 (BNP Fonds français, 10,760, fo. 34).
30. ASF Mediceo, filza 4966, Ottavio Pucci, Aug. 21, 1641.
31. ASF Mediceo, filza 4966, Pucci, Jan. 29, 1642.
32. ASF Mediceo, filza 4966, Pucci, June 25, 1642.
33. See p. 111.
34. ASF Mediceo, filza 4960, June 30, 1635.
35. ASF Mediceo, filza 4960, May 26, 1635.
36. AGS Est.K, leg. 1416, fo. 72, consulta.
37. ASF Mediceo, filza 4963, Monanni, July 3, 1638.
38. ASF Mediceo, filza 4960, Monanni, Feb. 8, 1634.
39. León Pinelo, *Anales*, p. 295, and above, p. 68.
40. ASF Mediceo, filza 4960, Monanni, Nov. 4, 1634.
41. Ana Caro de Mallén, *Contexto de las reales fiestas que se hizieron en el palacio del Buen Retiro* (Madrid, 1637; ed. Antonio Pérez Gómez, Valencia, 1951); Andrés Sánchez de Espejo, *Discurso de las fiestas que la magestad católica del rey nuestro señor celebró en el Real Retiro . . .* (Madrid, 1637); Alfred Morel-Fatio, *L'Espagne au XVIᵉ et au XVIIᵉ siècle* (Paris, 1878), pp. 603–76 ("Académie burlesque"); and see also the sources cited in note 1 of the excellent essay on these festivities by J. E. Varey, "Calderón, Cosme Lotti, Velázquez, and the Madrid Festivities of 1636–1637," in S. Schoenbaum (ed.), *Renaissance Drama*, n.s. 1 (Evanston, 1968), pp. 253–82.
42. Sánchez Espejo, *Discurso*. For a detailed discussion of the part played by the municipality, see Varey, "Calderón, Cosme Lotti."
43. ASF Mediceo, filza 4963, Feb. 28, 1637.
44. Rodríguez Villa, *La corte*, p. 100.
45. For Olivares's propaganda campaign, see José M. Jover, *1635. Historia de una polémica y semblanza de una generación* (Madrid, 1949).
46. ASF Mediceo, filza 4963, Monanni, Feb. 21, 1637.
47. *Ibid.*; León Pinelo, *Anales*, p. 309, and the account in verse by Ana Caro de Mallén, *Contexto*, pp. 1–12.
48. Sánchez Espejo, *Discurso*; Varey, "Calderón, Cosme Lotti," p. 262.
49. Monanni, Feb. 21, 1637.
50. Rodríguez Villa, *La corte*, p. 101.
51. PRO SP.94.39, fos. 191–191v., Aston to Coke, Feb. 25, 1637.
52. Feb. 21, 1637. Unfortunately it is impossible to determine the accuracy of this figure. Varey, in the appendices to "Calderón, Cosme Lotti," prints extracts from the accounts, which suggest something of the burden on the municipality. Rodríguez Villa, *La corte*, p. 101, gives a total of 300,000 ducats or more, but this includes the costs of levelling the ground and making the Plaza.
53. ASF Mediceo, filza 4960, May 26, 1635. On the other hand he took strong exception when four foreign Jesuits whom he had urged to attend a bullfight were rebuked by the rector of the Jesuit college in Madrid for accepting the invitation (Jesuitas, *MHE*, 13, pp. 226–7, July 31, 1635).
54. Printed in Morel-Fatio, *L'Espagne*, pp. 603–76. See also Davies, *A Poet at Court* and the sources there given.
55. Morel-Fatio, p. 659.
56. AGS TMC, leg. 3764, Mar. 12, 1637.
57. Azcárate, "Anales," p. 119.
58. León Pinelo, *Anales*, p. 311.
59. Rodríguez Villa, *La corte*, p. 107.
60. Shergold, *Spanish Stage*, p. 288.
61. Rodríguez Villa, *Ibid.*, p. 108.
62. Shergold, *Ibid.*
63. *Ibid.*, p. 295.
64. *Ibid.*, p. 285.
65. AGS TMC, leg. 3764, April 27, 1636. See also Caturla, *Pinturas*, p. 34.
66. "A Relation," fo. 138v.
67. See p. 147.
68. ASF Mediceo, filza 4960, Monanni, Mar. 17, 1635.
69. ASF Mediceo, filza 4960, June 2, 1635. *La fábula de Dafne* was performed again on July 28, 1636 (see Shergold, *Spanish Stage*, p. 287, where it is identified as a work by Calderón).
70. Shergold, pp. 286–7; Emilio Cotarelo y Mori, *Ensayo sobre la vida y obras de D. Pedro Calderón de la Barca* (Madrid, 1924), pp. 171–2.
71. Jesuitas, *MHE*, 14, p. 139.
72. Testi, *Lettere*, 3, letter 1150. See above, pp. 88–9.
73. See Shergold, *Spanish Stage*, p. 380, and Hannah E. Bergman, *Luis Quiñones de Benavente y sus entremeses* (Madrid, 1965), Chapter 1.
74. ASF Mediceo, filza 4960, Monanni, June 2, 1635.
75. Bergman, p. 47.
76. *Ibid.*, pp. 315–16.
77. Luis Quiñones de Benavente, *Entremeses, loas y jácaras*, ed. Cayetano Rosell, 1 (Madrid, 1872), p. 392).
78. See note 20.
79. Quiñones 1, p. 324.
80. ASF Mediceo, filza 4960, Aug. 4, 1635; Jesuitas, *MHE*, 13, p. 224. For a description of the scenic effects, Shergold, *Spanish Stage*, pp. 280–4.
81. ASF Mediceo, filza 4964.
82. ASF Mediceo, 4965, Monanni, July 7, 1640. There was another play of this name by Calderón, Moreto and an unknown dramatist, but it had no *tramoyas*. We are grateful to Dr Ruth Lee Kennedy for advice on this point.
83. Shergold, *Spanish Stage*, pp. 328–9.
84. See p. 74.
85. Shergold, *Spanish Stage*, pp. 298–9.

86. Phyllis Dearborn Massar, "Scenes from a Calderón play by Baccio del Bianco," *MD*, 15 (1977), p. 368.
87. José Pellicer y Tovar, *Avisos históricos*, in Antonio Valladares, *Semanario Erudito*, 31 (Madrid, 1790), p. 139; Shergold, p. 299.
88. Shergold, p. 329; Cotarelo y Mori, *Ensayo*, pp. 201–2.
89. Shergold, p. 301.
90. First fully published and discussed by Massar, "Scenes," on which the following account is based.
91. ASF Mediceo, filza 4964, Monanni, March 5 and 12, 1639.
92. Jesuitas, *MHE*, 13, p. 168.
93. ADM, leg. 97, ramo 20.
94. BNM Ms. 10, 984, fo. 243, Olivares to Chumacero, Oct. 22, 1641.
95. Jesuitas, *MHE*, 14, pp. 336–7. For an excellent account of this entertainment, see Hannah E. Bergman, "A Court Entertainment of 1638," *Hispanic Review*, 42 (1974), pp. 67–81. We are indebted to Dr Bergman for providing us with a transcript of the manuscript of this *mojiganga*, which was discovered in the Biblioteca Nacional, Lisbon, by Dr Ruth Lee Kennedy.
96. Rodríguez Villa, *La corte*, pp. 7–8.
97. For another literary evening, which included pageantry and dancing, see Hannah E. Bergman, "El 'Juicio final de todos los poetas españoles muertos y vivos' (ms. inédito) y el certamen poético de 1638," *BRAE*, 55 (1975), pp. 551–610. The so-called court "academy" of Philip IV should probably not be taken too seriously. See p. 563 of this article for the word "academia" in seventeenth-century usage.
98. Edward, Earl of Clarendon, *State Papers*, 1 (Oxford, 1767), p. 219; Jesuitas, *MHE*, 13, p. 202.
99. See above p. 74.
100. Testi, *Lettere*, 3, letter 1153, May 24, 1636.
101. ASF Mediceo, filza 4964.
102. AHP 5810, fos. 565–6, escritura de obligación, May 24, 1635.
103. ASF Mediceo, filza 4960, Monanni, June 2, 1635.
104. See Agustín González de Amezúa y Mayo, "Una reina de España en la intimidad. Isabel de Valois, 1560–1568," *Discurso leído ante la Real Academia de la Historia* (Madrid, 1944), pp. 66–9, and Caturla, *Pinturas*, p. 36.
105. Collected and printed by José Pellicer y Tovar, *Anfiteatro de Felipe el Grande* (Madrid, 1631; ed. Antonio Pérez Gómez, Cieza, 1974). "Nuestro Jupiter Christiano," fo. 25v.
106. Jesuitas, *MHE*, 13, p. 5.
107. ASF Mediceo, filza 4960, Monanni, Nov. 25, 1634; APM BR, leg. 2, royal order of Nov. 30, 1633, for the feeding of these animals.
108. ASF Mediceo, filza 4964, Monanni, Oct. 23, 1638.
109. ASF Mediceo, filza 4964, Monanni, Nov. 19, 1639.
110. AGS CS, leg. 309, fo. 157, consulta, Apr. 25, 1636.
111. ASF Mediceo, filza 4960, Nov. 25, 1634.
112. Ernst Werner, "Caída del Conde-Duque de Olivares," *Revue Hispanique*, 71 (1927), p. 150.
113. Bargrave, fos. 139–139v.
114. "Upon Appleton House," stanza 95. See John Dixon Hunt, "Marvell, Nun Appleton and the Buen Retiro," *Philological Quarterly*, vol. 59/2 (Spring 1980). We are very grateful to Dr Hunt for bringing this reference to our attention.
115. AGS TMC, leg. 3764, payment, Feb. 26, 1635.

116. Jesuitas, *MHE*, 13, pp. 4–5.
117. ASF Mediceo, filza 4964, Feb. 26, 1639.
118. See p. 75.
119. ASF Mediceo, filza 4964, Monanni, May 21, 1639; Pellicer, *Avisos*, 31, pp. 9–10.
120. ASF Mediceo, filza 4963, Monanni, July 5, 1636.
121. ASF Mediceo, filza 4964, Monanni, May 28, 1639.
122. 888 *reales* on Apr. 13, 1638, to Pedro Martínez for 210 pounds of live fish for the Large Lake (AGS TMC, leg. 3764).
123. Shergold, *Spanish Stage*, p. 262, for the tradition of mock naval battles. For a *naumachia* held in June 1639, Pellicer, *Avisos*, 31, p. 36; and for a regatta in June, 1637, Jesuitas, *MHE*, 14, p. 139.
124. ASF Mediceo, filza 4963, Gabriello Riccardi, July 17, 1638. See also Caturla, *Pinturas*, p. 44, and N. Sentenach, "Francisco de Zurbarán pintor del rey," *BSEE*, 17 (1909), pp. 194–8, for Zurbarán and the *Santo Rey Don Fernando*. Payments for the ships appear in the accounts, and are noted in Azcárate, "Anales", pp. 121 and 122.
125. AGS TMC, leg. 3764, first payment of 3,000 *reales* to Eugenio Montero, *fontanero*, Sept. 24, 1636; payment for adornment of San Jerónimo, July 24, 1636; payment of 5,368 *reales* for "shells, rocks, glass and colors" for adornment of San Bruno, May 3, 1639; payment for leadwork for the rebuilt grotto of the Magdalena, Mar. 8, 1637.
126. See p. 77.
127. Cervera Vera, *El conjunto palacial*, p. 399.
128. ASF Mediceo, filza 4960, Aug. 26, 1634.
129. Rodríguez Villa, *La corte*, pp. 63–4.
130. See Frances A. Yates, *The French Academies of the Sixteenth Century* (London, 1947), esp. pp. 156–63.
131. See p. 80.
132. ASF Mediceo, filza 4960, Monanni, Nov. 4, 1634.
133. ASF Mediceo, filza 4965, Monanni, May 5, 1640; Pellicer, *Avisos*, 31, p. 167.
134. Jesuitas, *MHE*, 15, p. 168 (Jan. 11, 1639).
135. ASF Mediceo, filza 4964, Monanni, May 21, 1639.
136. ASF Mediceo, filza 4965, Monanni, Oct. 6, 1640.
137. AHN Est., lib. 869, fo. 142, Olivares to Carnero, May 2, 1644.
138. AGS CS, leg. 310, fo. 468, consulta, Aug. 6, 1644.
139. Shergold, *Spanish Stage*, p. 302.
140. APM BR, leg. 2, no. 3, royal decree, Dec. 6, 1648.
141. Jerónimo de Barrionuevo, *Avisos, BAE*, 221 (Madrid, 1968), pp. 163 and 236.
142. *Ibid.*, pp. 107 and 121.
143. *Ibid., BAE*, 222, p. 90.

NOTES TO CHAPTER VIII

1. See p. 152.
2. For this building, see Juan Bernia, *Historia del palacio de Santa Cruz 1629–1950* (Madrid, 1949). The attribution of the design to Carbonel, first proposed by Fernando Chueca, "Sobre arquitectura y arquitectos madrileños del siglo XVII," *AEA*, 18 (1945), pp. 371–4, is said to have been confirmed by a recent documental discovery.
3. AGS CS, leg. 308, fo. 411, cédula, Oct. 1633, establishes the fact, sometimes doubted, that the cardinal infante had started to build on the site before his departure from Madrid.
4. The drawings were discovered in AHP by the Marquis

del Saltillo, "Alonso Martínez de Espinar. Al margen de la Exposición de Caza," *Arte Español*, 18 (1951), pp. 123–7. They are no longer in the archive and their present location is unknown. For the Zarzuela, see also Joaquín Ezquerra del Bayo, "El Palacio de la Zarzuela," *Revista Española de Arte*, 11 (1932), pp. 123–7.

5. APM CR, tomo 13, fo. 158, cédula, Jan. 19, 1635.
6. AGI Cont. leg. 70, fos. 189–207, contains the records of Castrillo's payments for the Zarzuela.
7. For the contract, see Saltillo, "Alonso Martínez de Espinar," pp. 123–7.
8. See Saltillo, "Alonso Martínez de Espinar," p. 127.
9. AGI Cont. leg. 70, fo. 201 (Bandal); fo. 199 (Zumbigo).
10. The pictorial decoration of the Zarzuela has never been studied. For the inventory, see APM Testamentaría del Sr D. Carlos II, Registro 241.
11. For the origins of the *zarzuela*, see Cotarelo, *Ensayo*, p. 305 and Shergold, *Spanish Stage*, p. 317.
12. For these dates, see Saltillo, "Alonso Martínez de Espinar," p. 123.
13. The decoration is thoroughly discussed by Alpers, *The Decoration*.
14. See p. 130.
15. Payments to the above artists are recorded in BNM Ms. 7797, fo. 155 (1638). For a discussion of the series of country houses, see Alpers, *The Decoration*, pp. 130–3.
16. AGS Cámara de Castilla, leg. 1247, petition, July 5, 1638.
17. The royal inventories of 1700–1 list the following numbers of paintings; Retiro, 905; Torre de la Parada, 171; Zarzuela, 96. Cited by Beroqui, *El Museo del Prado*, p. 34.
18. Jover, *1635*, p. 253.
19. Elliott, *The Revolt*, pp. 307–8.
20. J. H. Elliott, *Imperial Spain, 1469–1716* (London, 1963), table 4, p. 175. Conversion into ducats of figures in *pesos* given in Hamilton, *American Treasure*, p. 34.
21. AGS Est., leg. 2053, *el Conde-Duque sobre las materias del palatinado*, Mar. 7, 1638.
22. PRO SP. 94.40, fo. 261, Hopton to Coke, Oct. 16, 1638.
23. Testi, *Lettere*, 3, letter 1414, June 21, 1640.
24. *Ibid.*, letter 1450.
25. *Ibid.*, letter 1345, Nov. 19, 1638.
26. ASF Mediceo, filza 4960, Sept. 16, 1634, and above, p. 97.
27. *Codoin*, 69, p. 91.
28. Palme, *Triumph of Peace*, pp. 42–3.
29. See Peter W. Thomas, "Charles I of England," in A. G. Dickens (ed.) *The Courts of Europe* (London, 1977), Chapter 9.
30. Campbell, *Pietro da Cortona*, pp. 15–19; Eric Cochrane, *Florence in the Forgotten Centuries, 1527–1800* (Chicago, 1973), pp. 195–200.
31. Cardinal de Richelieu, *Testament Politique*, ed. Louis André (7th ed., Paris, 1947), p. 282.
32. See Orest Ranum, *Paris in the Age of Absolutism* (New York, 1968), pp. 83–105.
33. Quoted in P. W. Thomas, "Two Cultures? Court and Country under Charles I," in *The Origins of the English Civil War*, ed. Conrad Russell (London, 1973), p. 177.
34. See Henry Kamen, "Golden Age, Iron Age: a conflict of Concepts in the Renaissance" *The Journal of Medieval and Renaissance Studies*, 4 (1974), pp. 135–6.
35. Almansa y Mendoza, *Cartas*, p. 53.

36. *Actas de las Cortes de Castilla*, 48 (Madrid, 1929), p. 323.
37. Alberti, *De re aedificatoria*, 9.1, and Castiglione, *The Courtier*, Bk. 4 (Everyman ed., London, 1956, pp. 288–9), cited by Verheyen, *Palazzo del Te*, p. 21.
38. Juan de Mariana, *Del rey y de la institución real*, *BAE*, 31 (Madrid, 1845), p. 552.
39. *Codoin*, 69, p. 284.
40. ASV Spagna, filza 70, Dec. 7, 1633.
41. *The Reason of State*, trans. P. J. and D. P. Whaley (London, 1956), p. 76.
42. *Codoin*, 69, p. 284.
43. *Obras*, "Silva topográfica."
44. "Versos a la primera fiesta del palacio nuevo," *Obras*, 2, pp. 246–9. See above, p. 68.
45. See Davies, *A Poet at Court*, p. 275. The play was probably first performed shortly after the victory of Nördlingen in September 1634, which it commemorates and describes.
46. Pedro Calderón de la Barca, *Comedias*, *BAE*, 7 (2nd ed., Madrid, 1851), pp. 385–410.
47. The *loa* which precedes the version of the play printed in the edition by Angel Valbuena Prat of Calderón's *Obras completas*, 3, is clearly of a much later date than the play, referring as it does to the hermitage of San Antonio, and Tacca's equestrian statue of Philip IV, neither of which existed in 1634. It was first published with the *auto* in 1717, and we are informed by Professor A. A. Parker that it cannot be by Calderón. We are most grateful to Professor Parker for his guidance in relation to this *auto*, which has been almost entirely neglected in Calderón studies.
48. Alexander A. Parker, *The Allegorical Drama of Calderón. An Introduction to the Autos Sacramentales* (Oxford and London, 1943), p. 79.
49. For Calderón's rather ambivalent treatment of the wandering Jew, see Alice M. Pollin, "El Judaísmo: figura dramática del auto 'El nuevo palacio del Retiro' de Calderón de la Barca," *Cuadernos Hispanoamericanos*, no. 276 (1973), pp. 579–88.
50. See p. 141.
51. Luis Vélez de Guevara, "Soneto," in *Elogios* (no folio numbers).
52. Diego Pellicer, "Octavas."
53. Vélez de Guevara, "Soneto."
54. Fos. 18–26v., "Sextas"; and see above, p. 98.
55. Eg. Francesco Patrizi (1412–94), *On Magnificence*. See Quentin Skinner, *The Foundations of Modern Political Thought*, 1 (Cambridge, 1978), p. 127.
56. Skinner, 1, p. 135.
57. *Los seis libros de las políticas*, trans. Bernardino de Mendoza (Madrid, 1604), lib. 2, Chapter 15.
58. See Novoa, *Codoin*, 69, pp. 283–8.
59. *Ibid.*, p. 285.
60. For new documentary evidence on the mystery, see J. H. Elliott, "Nueva luz sobre la prisión de Quevedo y Adam de la Parra," *BRAH*, 169 (1972), pp. 171–82.
61. Printed in Teófanes Egido, *Sátiras políticas de la España moderna* (Madrid, 1973) no. 23 ("Memorial a S. M. el rey don Felipe Cuarto").
62. See Llaguno, *Noticias*, 4, pp. 151–2 for the text of this undated *cédula* which he saw in AGI and cited without reference.
63. BNM Ms. 10,984, fos. 213–216v.
64. BNM Ms. 10,984, fos. 239–45v. The text is printed in full in *MC*, 2, Doc. XVII, pp. 213–6.

65. See *MC*, 1, pp. xlvii–xlviii.
66. Above, p. 29.
67. "La cueva de Meliso," in Teófanes Egido, *Sátiras*, no. 36, lines 723–52.
68. ASF Mediceo, filza 4966, Olivares to Ottavio Pucci, Nov. 19, 1642.
69. AGR Conseil Privé Espagnol, Reg. 1504, fo. 238v., Carnero to Pierre Roose.
70. For the fall of Olivares, see Marañón, *Olivares* Chapter 25.
71. *Cargos contra el Conde Duque* (Madrid, 1643), reprinted in *MC*, 2, Doc. XXa.
72. *El Nicandro* (Madrid, 1643), reprinted in *MC*, 2, Doc. XXb.
73. Egido, *Sátiras*, no. 38.
74. Richelieu, *Testament Politique*, p. 281.
75. See H. R. Trevor-Roper, "The General Crisis of the Seventeenth Century," in Trevor Aston (ed.), *Crisis in Europe, 1560–1660* (London, 1965), pp. 59–95.

Notes to Epilogue

1. For Colonna and Mitelli in Madrid, see Enriqueta Harris, "Angelo Michele Colonna y la decoración de San Antonio de los Portugueses," *AEA*, 34 (1961), pp. 101–5, where further bibliography is listed.
2. Azcárate, "Anales," p. 133.
3. For the history of the Retiro after the reign of Philip IV, see Amador de los Ríos, "El palacio antiguo," and José Bordiú, *Apuntes para la historia del Buen Retiro* (Madrid, n.d.).
4. Rodrigo Amador de los Ríos y Villalta, "Los jardines del Buen Retiro," *La España Moderna*, Jan. 1905, p. 111.
5. See p. 273, note 41.
6. For the information that follows, see Yves Bottineau, "Felipe V y el Buen-Retiro," *AEA*, 31 (1958), pp. 117–23, and *L'art de cour dans l'Espagne de Philip V, 1700–1746* (Bordeaux, 1960), pp. 259–68.
7. Amador de los Ríos, "El palacio antiguo," pp. 204–8.
8. For the Palacio de Oriente, see Francisco Javier de la Plaza Santiago, *Investigaciones sobre el Palacio Real nuevo de Madrid* (Valladolid, 1975).
9. *The Spanish Journal of Elizabeth Lady Holland,* ed. the Earl of Ilchester (London, 1910), p. 109.
10. Manuel Pérez-Villaamil, *Artes e industrias del Buen Retiro. La fábrica de la china. El laboratorio de piedras duras y mosaico. Obradores de bronces y marfiles* (Madrid, 1904).
11. Regulations of May 12, 1767, quoted in A. Fernández de los Ríos, *Guía de Madrid* (Madrid, 1876), pp. 360–1.
12. Fernando Chueca Goitia and Carlos de Miguel, *La vida y las obras del arquitecto Juan de Villanueva* (Madrid, 1949), pp. 285–318; and Fernando Chueca Goitia, *El Museo del Prado* (Granada, 1972).
13. Marcelino Tobajas López, "Documentos del Buen Retiro, II. Ocupación del Buen Retiro por los franceses," *RS*, 14, no. 52 (1977), pp. 57–62.
14. Charles Oman, *A History of the Peninsular War,* 5 (Oxford, 1914), p. 515.
15. Conde de Toreno, *Historia del levantamiento, guerra y revolución de España,* 3 (Paris, 1838), p. 154.
16. Quoted by Tobajas López, "La destrucción," p. 15.
17. Marquesa de Casa Valdés, *Jardines de España* (Madrid, 1973), pp. 228–9.
18. The proposed alterations to the Retiro are discussed at length by Fernández de los Ríos, *Guía de Madrid,* pp. 370–84.
19. Fernández de los Ríos, p. 166.
20. Amador de los Ríos, "Los jardines," p. 119.
21. A. Cánovas del Castillo, *Estudios del reinado de Felipe IV,* 2 (2nd ed., Madrid, 1929), p. 101.

Notes to Appendixes

1. López-Rey, *Velázquez,* p. 226.
2. Antonio de Mendoza, "Forma que se guarda en tener las Cortes y el Juramento. . . ," *Discursos,* p. 26.
3. León Pinelo, *Anales,* p. 287.
4. We are grateful to William Heckscher for his suggestion about the significance of these objects. Our proposed new date for this painting suggests that Velázquez's full-length portrait of *Prince Baltasar Carlos* in the Wallace Collection (López-Rey, *Velázquez,* no. 303), where the prince is clearly older, was probably painted later than 1632, the year to which it is usually ascribed.
5. For example, López-Rey, *Velázquez,* p. 135, who dates the picture to the middle or late 1630s.
6. AGS TMC, leg. 3763, payment, Mar. 30, 1633; cited by Azcárate, "Anales," p. 110.
7. ASF Mediceo, filza 4959.
8. AGS TMC, leg. 3763; cited by Azcárate, "Anales," p. 110.
9. AGS TMC, leg. 3763, cited by Azcárate, "Anales," p. 110.
10. See Azcárate, "Anales," pp. 130–3.
11. López-Rey, *Velázquez,* p. 268.
12. AHP, leg. 6432, fo. 558v. The relevant portion of the document reads as follows: ". . . Diego Belazquez Pintor de Su Magd. . . . confiesa aber rescibido del señor diego suarez secretario de Su Magd. en el real de Portugal setecientos y nobenta y siete ducados que el dho. señor secretario le paga por las pinturas que de orden del dho. señor secretario hizo para el adorno de las alcobas del buen Retiro. . ."
13. See von Barghahn, "The Pictorial Decoration," pp. 364–6.
14. APM BR, leg. 3. The terminus post quem for the list is established by a reference to the completion of the redecoration of the hermitage of San Pablo.
15. José Moreno Villa, *Locos, enanos, negros y niños palaciegos* (Mexico City, 1939).
16. Domínguez Bordona, "Noticias," p. 85.
17. AGS TMC, leg. 3763, payment, Nov. 28, 1633; cited by Azcárate, "Anales," p. 109.
18. Michael Levey, *Painting at Court* (London, 1971), p. 142, and Enriqueta Harris, "Velázquez's Portrait of Prince Baltasar Carlos in the Riding School," *BM,* 118 (1976), p. 272.

SELECT BIBLIOGRAPHY

This bibliography is confined to works relating to Habsburg Spain and to
the Buen Retiro and its contents.

Agulló y Cobo, Mercedes. "El monasterio de San Plácido y su fundador, el madrileño don Jerónimo de Villanueva, Protonotario de Aragón," *Villa de Madrid*, 13 (1975), nos. 45–6, pp. 59–68, and no. 47, pp. 37–50.

Alcalá-Zamora y Queipo de Llano, José. *España, Flandes y el Mar del Norte, 1618–1639*, Barcelona, 1975.

Almansa y Mendoza, Andrés de. *Cartas*, Madrid, 1886.

Alpers, Svetlana. *The Decoration of the Torre de la Parada*, London–New York, 1971.

Amador de los Ríos y Villalta, Rodrigo. "El palacio antiguo del Buen Retiro, según el plano de 1656," *Museo Español de Antigüedades*, 11 (1880), pp. 175–219.

———— "Los jardines del Buen Retiro," *La España Moderna*, Jan. 1905, pp. 80–119.

Anderson, Ruth Matilda. *The Golilla: a Spanish Collar of the Seventeenth Century*, Hispanic Society of America, New York. (Reprint from *Waffen-und Kostümkunde*, 11 [1969].)

Andrés, Gregorio de. *El marqués de Liche, bibliófilo y coleccionista de arte*, Madrid, 1975.

———— "Historia de la biblioteca del Conde-Duque de Olivares y descripción de sus códices," *Cuadernos Bibliográficos*, 28 (1972).

Angulo Iñiguez, Diego. "El pintor Pedro Núñez, un contemporáneo castellano de Zurbarán," *Archivo Español de Arte*, 37 (1964), pp. 171–84.

———— "Francisco Rizi, cuadros de tema profano," *Archivo Español de Arte*, 44 (1971), pp. 357–87.

———— *La mitología y el arte español del renacimiento*, Madrid, 1952.

Angulo Iñiguez, Diego, and Pérez Sánchez, Alfonso E. *Pintura madrileña del primer tercio del siglo XVII*, Madrid, 1969.

———— *Pintura toledana. Primera mitad del siglo XVII*, Madrid, 1972.

Astrana Marín, Luis. *La vida turbulenta de Quevedo*, 2nd ed., Madrid, 1945.

Azcárate, José M. de. "Anales de la construcción del Buen Retiro," *Anales del Instituto de Estudios Madrileños*, 1 (1966), pp. 99–135.

———— "Datos para las biografías de los arquitectos de la corte de Felipe IV," *Revista de la Universidad de Madrid*, 11 (1962), pp. 516–46.

———— "Instrucción para las construcciones reales en el siglo XVII," *Boletín del Seminario de Estudios de Arte y Arqueología, Universidad de Valladolid*, 25 (1960), pp. 223–30.

———— "Noticias sobre Velázquez en la corte," *Archivo Español de Arte*, 33 (1960), pp. 357–85.

———— "Una variante en la edición de los 'Diálogos' de Carducho con noticia sobre el Buen Retiro," *Archivo Español de Arte*, 24 (1951), pp. 261–2.

Barcia, Angel M. de. *Catálogo de la colección de pinturas del Excmo. Sr. Duque de Berwick y Alba*, Madrid, 1911.

———— *Catálogo de la colección de dibujos originales de la Biblioteca Nacional*, Madrid, 1906.

Barghahn, Barbara von. "The Pictorial Decoration of the Buen Retiro Palace and Patronage during the Reign of Philip IV," Ph.D. Dissertation, New York University, 1979.

Bargrave, Robert. "A Relation of Sundry Voyages and Journeys made by Mr. Robert Bargrave," Bodleian Library, Oxford, Ms. Rawlinson C799.

Barozzi, Nicolò, and Berchet, Guglielmo. *Relazioni degli stati europei. Serie 1. Spagna*, 2 vols., Venice, 1856–60.

Barrera, Cayetano Alberto de la. *Poesías de don Francisco de Rioja*, Madrid, 1867.

Barrionuevo, Jerónimo de. *Avisos*, ed. A. Paz y Melia, Biblioteca de Autores Españoles, vols. 221 and 222, Madrid, 1968–9.

Barry, Gerrat. *The Siege of Breda*, Louvain, 1627.

Bataillon, Marcel. "Plus Oultre: La cour découvre le nouveau monde," *Les Fêtes de la Renaissance. Fêtes et cérémonies au temps de Charles Quint*, ed. Jean Jacquot, 2 vols., Paris, 1975.

Bennassar, Bartolomé. *Valladolid au siècle d'or*, Paris, 1967.

Bergman, Hannah E. "A Court Entertainment of 1638," *Hispanic Review*, 42 (1974), pp. 67–81.

———— "El 'Juicio final de todos los poetas españoles muertos y vivos' (ms. inédito) y el certamen poético de 1638," *Boletín de la Real Academia Española*, 55 (1975), pp. 551–610.

———— *Luis Quiñones de Benavente y sus entremeses*, Madrid, 1965.

Bernia, Juan. *Historia del palacio de Santa Cruz 1629–1950*, Madrid, 1949.

Beroqui, Pedro. "Adiciones y correcciones al catálogo del Museo del Prado," *Boletín de la Sociedad Castellana de Excursiones*, 6 (1913–14), pp. 539–45.

———— *El Museo del Prado (Notas para su historia), I. El Museo Real (1819–1833)*, Madrid, 1933.

Berwick y de Alba, duquesa de. *Documentos escogidos de la casa de Alba*, Madrid, 1891.

Blunt, Anthony. "Jean Lemaire: Painter of Architectural Fantasies," *Burlington Magazine*, 83 (1943), pp. 241–6.

————— "Poussin Studies V—The 'Silver Birch Master,'" *Burlington Magazine*, 91, (1950), pp. 69–73.

————— "Poussin Studies VIII—A Series of Anchorite Subjects Commissioned by Philip IV from Poussin, Claude and Others," *Burlington Magazine*, 101 (1959), pp. 389–90.

————— *The Paintings of Nicolas Poussin. A Critical Catalogue*, London, 1966.

Boix, Félix. *El Prado de San Jerónimo. Un cuadro costumbrista madrileño del siglo XVII*, Madrid, n.d.

Bonet Correa, Antonio. "El plano de Juan Gómez de Mora de la Plaza Mayor de Madrid en 1636," *Morfología y ciudad*, Barcelona, 1978, pp. 65–91.

————— "Túmulos del emperador Carlos V," *Archivo Español de Arte*, 33 (1960), pp. 55–66.

Bordiú, José. *Apuntes para la historia del Buen Retiro*, Madrid, n.d.

Borsook, Eve. "Art and Politics at the Medici Court III: Funeral Decor for Philip II of Spain," *Mitteilungen des Kunsthistorischen Institutes in Florenz*, 14 (1969–70), pp. 89–114.

Bottineau, Yves. "L'Alcázar de Madrid et l'inventaire de 1686," *Bulletin Hispanique*, 58 (1956), pp. 421–52; 60 (1958), pp. 30–61, 145–79, 289–326, 450–83.

————— "Aspects de la cour d'Espagne au XVIIe siècle: l'étiquette de la chambre du roi," *Bulletin Hispanique*, 74 (1972), pp. 138–57.

————— "Felipe V y el Buen-Retiro," *Archivo Español de Arte*, 34 (1961), pp. 101–5.

————— *L'art de cour dans l'Espagne de Philippe V, 1700–1746*, Bordeaux, 1960.

————— "Les inventaires royaux et l'histoire de l'art: l'example d'Espagne," *L'Information d'Histoire et de l'Art*, 4 (1959), pp. 69–74.

Boxer, C. R. *The Dutch in Brazil, 1624–1654*, Oxford, 1957.

————— *Salvador de Sá and the Struggle for Brazil and Angola, 1602–1686*, London, 1952.

Brown, Jonathan. "A Portrait Drawing by Velázquez," *Master Drawings*, 14 (1976), pp. 46–51.

————— *Images and Ideas in Seventeenth-Century Spanish Painting*, Princeton, 1978.

————— "On the Origins of 'Las Lanzas' by Velázquez," *Zeitschrift für Kunstgeschichte*, 27 (1964), pp. 240–5.

Burke, James D. *Jan Both: Paintings, Drawings and Prints*, New York and London, 1976.

Cabrera de Córdoba, Luis. *Filipe segundo, rey de España*, ed. Madrid, 1876.

Calandre, Luis. *El Palacio del Pardo*, Madrid, 1953.

Calderón de la Barca, Pedro. *El sitio de Bredá*, ed. Johanna Rudolphine Schrek, 's-Gravenhage, 1957.

————— *Obras completas, 3. Autos sacramentales*, ed. Angel Valbuena Prat, 2nd ed., Aguilar, Madrid, 1967.

Cánovas del Castillo, A. *Estudios del reinado de Felipe IV*, 2 vols., Madrid, 1888; 2nd ed., 1927.

Caramuel y Lobkowitz, Juan de. *Declaración mystica de las armas de España invictamente belicosas*, Brussels, 1636.

Carducho, Vicente. *Diálogos de la pintura*, Madrid, 1633.

Ed. Francisco Calvo Serraller, Madrid, 1979.

Caro Baroja, Julio. *Inquisición, brujería y criptojudaísmo*, 2nd ed., Madrid, 1972.

————— *Los judíos en la España moderna y contemporánea*, vol. 2, Madrid, 1961.

Caro de Mallén, Ana. *Contexto de las reales fiestas que se hizieron en el palacio del Buen Retiro*, Madrid, 1637; ed. Antonio Pérez Gómez, Valencia, 1951.

Cartas de Sor María de Agreda y de Felipe IV, ed. Carlos Seco Serrano, Biblioteca de Autores Españoles, vols. 108 and 109, Madrid, 1958.

Casa Valdés, marquesa de. *Jardines de España*, Madrid, 1973.

Catálogo de la exposición del antiguo Madrid, Madrid, 1926.

Caturla, María L. "Cartas de pago de los doce cuadros de batallas para el salón de reinos del Buen Retiro," *Archivo Español de Arte*, 33 (1960), pp. 333–55.

————— "El coleccionista madrileño don Pedro de Arce, que poseyó *Las Hilanderas* de Velázquez," *Archivo Español de Arte*, 21 (1948), pp. 292–304.

————— *Pinturas, frondas y fuentes del Buen Retiro*, Madrid, 1947.

————— "Zurbarán en el Salón de Reinos," *Archivo Español de Arte*, 18 (1945), pp. 292–300.

Caxa de Leruela, Miguel. *Restauración de la abundancia de España*, ed. Jean Paul Le Flem, Madrid, 1975.

Ceán Bermúdez, Juan A. *Diccionario histórico de los más ilustres profesores de las bellas artes en España*, 6 vols., Madrid, 1800; reprinted 1965.

Cervera Vera, Luis. *El conjunto palacial de la villa de Lerma*, Valencia, 1967.

Chastel, André. "Les Entrées de Charles Quint en Italie," in *Les Fêtes de la Renaissance. Fêtes et cérémonies au temps de Charles Quint*, ed. Jean Jacquot, 2 vols., Paris, 1975.

Chueca Goitia, Fernando. *Casas reales en monasterios y conventos españoles*, Madrid, 1966.

————— *El Museo del Prado*, Granada, 1972.

————— *Invariantes castizos de la arquitectura española*, Madrid, 1971.

————— "Sobre arquitectura y arquitectos madrileños del siglo XVII," *Archivo Español de Arte*, 18 (1945), pp. 360–74.

Clarendon, Edward, Earl of. *The History of the Rebellion and Civil Wars in England*, ed. W. D. Macray, 5 vols., Oxford, 1888.

Collado, Francisco Gerónimo de. *Descripción del túmulo y relación de las exequias que hizo la ciudad de Sevilla en la muerte del rey don Felipe Segundo*, Seville, 1869.

Copiosa relación de las grandiosas fiestas que la católica magd. del rey nr. sr. mandó hacer en la villa de Madrid . . . en honra del palacio y plaza nuevo, lunes 5 de dic. de 1633, Seville, 1633.

Cortés, Narciso Alonso. *La muerte del conde de Villamediana*, Valladolid, 1928.

Cotarelo y Mori, Emilio. *Ensayo sobre la vida y obras de D. Pedro Calderón de la Barca*, Madrid, 1924.

Covarrubias y Leyva, Diego de. *Elogios al Palacio Real del Buen Retiro*, Madrid, 1635, ed. Antonio Pérez y Gómez, Valencia, 1949.

Crosby, James O. *En torno a la poesía de Quevedo*, Madrid, 1967.

Cruzada Villaamil, Gregorio. *Rubens. Diplomático español*,

Madrid, 1874.

Cuartero y Huerta, Baltasar. *El Monasterio de S. Jerónimo el Real. Protección y dádivas de los reyes de España a dicho monasterio*, Madrid, 1966.

———— "Noticias de doscientos trece documentos inéditos sobre el Buen Retiro de Madrid y otros sitios reales (años 1612–1661)," *Anales del Instituto de Estudios Madrileños*, 3 (1968), pp. 51–79.

Davies, Gareth A. *A Poet at Court: Antonio Hurtado de Mendoza*, Oxford, 1974.

Deleito y Piñuela, José. *El rey se divierte*, 3rd ed., Madrid, 1964.

———— *Sólo Madrid es corte*, Madrid, 1942.

Díaz Padrón, Matías. *Museo del Prado. Catálogo de pinturas, I. Escuela flamenca, siglo XVII*, Madrid, 1975.

Díez del Corral y Pedruzo, Luis. *Velázquez, Felipe IV y la Monarquía*, Madrid, 1977.

Domínguez Bordona, J. "Noticias para la historia del Buen Retiro," *Revista de Archivos, Bibliotecas y Museos*, 10 (1933), pp. 83–90.

Domínguez Ortiz, Antonio. "Los gastos de corte en la España del siglo XVII," *Crisis y decadencia de la España de los Austrias*, Barcelona, 1969.

———— *La sociedad española en el siglo XVII*, 2 vols., Madrid, 1964–70.

———— *Política y hacienda de Felipe IV*, Madrid, 1960.

Egido, Teófanes. *Sátiras políticas de la España moderna*, Madrid, 1973.

El Escorial, 1563–1963. IV Centenario de la fundación del Monasterio de San Lorenzo el Real, 2 vols., Madrid, 1963.

Elliott, J. H. *Imperial Spain, 1469–1716*, London, 1963; New York, 1964.

———— "Nueva luz sobre la prisión de Quevedo y Adam de la Parra," *Boletín de la Real Academia de la Historia*, 169 (1972), pp. 171–82.

———— "Philip IV of Spain," in *The Courts of Europe*, ed. A. G. Dickens, London, 1977.

———— *The Revolt of the Catalans. A Study in the Decline of Spain, 1598–1640*, Cambridge, 1963.

———— "Self-perception and Decline in Seventeenth-Century Spain," *Past and Present*, 74 (1977), pp. 41–61.

Elliott, John H., and Peña, José F. de la. *Memoriales y cartas del Conde Duque de Olivares*, 2 vols., Madrid, 1978–80.

Ezquerra del Bayo, Joaquín. "El Palacio de la Zarzuela," *Revista Española de Arte*, 11 (1932), pp. 123–7.

Fayard, Janine. *Les Membres du Conseil de Castille à l'époque moderne (1621–1746)*, Geneva–Paris, 1979.

Fayard, Janine, and Larquié, Claude. "Hôtels madrilènes et démographie urbaine au XVIIe siècle," *Mélanges de la Casa de Velázquez*, 4 (1968), pp. 229–58.

Fernández Alvarez, Manuel. *Don Gonzalo Fernández de Córdoba y la guerra de sucesión de Mantua y del Monferrato, 1627–1629*, Madrid, 1955.

———— *Madrid en el siglo XVI, I (El establecimiento de la capitalidad de España en Madrid)*, Madrid, Instituto de Estudios Madrileños, 1960.

Fernández Baytón, Gloria. *Inventarios reales, I. Testamentaría del rey Carlos II, 1701–1703*, Madrid, 1975.

Fernández de los Ríos, A. *Guía de Madrid*, Madrid, 1876.

Fernández Duro, Cesáreo. *Armada española*, vol. 4, Madrid, 1898.

Gállego, Julián. "L'urbanisme de Madrid au XVIIe siècle," in *L'urbanisme de Paris et de l'Europe, 1600–1680*, pp. 251–65, ed. Pierre Francastel, Paris, 1969.

———— *Visión y símbolos en la pintura española del siglo de oro*, Madrid, 1972.

Gallegos, Manuel de. *Obras varias al real palacio del Buen Retiro*, Madrid, 1637, ed. Antonio Pérez y Gómez, Valencia, 1949.

Gamboa y Eraso, Luis de. *Verdad de lo sucedido con ocasión de la venida de la armada inglesa sobre Cádiz el 1º de noviembre de 1625...*, Cadiz, 1626.

García Boiza, Antonio. *Una fundación de Monterrey: la iglesia y convento de MM. Agustinas de Salamanca*, Salamanca, 1945.

García Mercadal, J. *Viajes de extranjeros por España y Portugal*, 2 vols., Madrid, 1952.

Gaya Nuño, Juan A. "En el centenario de Collantes. Escenarios barrocos y paisajes disimulados," *Goya*, 10 (1956), pp. 222–8.

Gérard, Véronique. "La fachada del Alcázar de Madrid," *Cuadernos de Investigación Histórica* 2 (1973), pp. 237–57.

Glendinning, Nigel. "Spanish Painting in the Golden Age," *Diamante*, 27 (London, 1977).

Gómez de Mora, Juan. *Relación del juramento que hizieron los reinos de Castilla y León al Sermo. don Baltasar Carlos, príncipe de las Españas, i Nuevo Mundo*, Madrid, 1632.

Gómez Iglesias, A. "El Buen Retiro," *Villa de Madrid*, 6 (1968), pp. 25–38.

Gondomar, conde de (Diego Sarmiento de Acuña). *Correspondencia oficial*. Documentos Inéditos para la Historia de España, vols. 1–4, Madrid, 1936–45.

González de Amezúa y Mayo, Agustín. "Una reina de España en la intimidad. Isabel de Valois, 1560–1568," *Discurso leído ante la Real Academia de la Historia*, Madrid, 1944.

González de Avila, Gil. *Teatro de las grandezas de la villa de Madrid*, Madrid, 1623.

González Palencia, Angel. *La Junta de Reformación*, Valladolid, 1932.

Gothein, Marie Louise. *A History of Garden Art*, 2 vols., 1st Eng. ed., London, 1928; repr. New York, 1966.

Gregori, Mina. "Notizie su Agostino Verrochi e un' ipotesi per Giovanni Battista Crescenzi," *Paragone*, 275 (1973), pp. 36–56.

Grelle, Anna. "I Crescenzi e l'accademia di via S. Eustachio," *Commentari*, 12 (1961), pp. 120–38.

Guillén Robles, Francisco. "El Casón del Buen Retiro," in *Catálogo del Museo de Reproducciones Artísticas*, Madrid, (1912), pp. xxiii–xxv.

Hamilton, Earl J. *American Treasure and the Price Revolution in Spain, 1501–1650*, Cambridge, Mass., 1934.

Harris, Ann S. "A Contribution to Andrea Camassei Studies," *Art Bulletin*, 52 (1970), pp. 49–70.

———— *Andrea Sacchi*, Oxford, 1977.

Harris, Enriqueta. "Angelo Michele Colonna y la decoración de San Antonio de los Portugueses," *Archivo Español de Arte*, 34 (1961), pp. 101–5.

———— "Cassiano dal Pozzo on Diego Velázquez," *Burlington Magazine*, 112 (1970), pp. 364–73.

———— "Velázquez's Portrait of Prince Baltasar Carlos in the Riding School," *Burlington Magazine*, 118 (1976), pp. 266–75.

Harris, Enriqueta, and Elliott, John H. "Velázquez and the Queen of Hungary," *Burlington Magazine*, 118 (1976), pp. 24–6.

Haskell, Francis. *Patrons and Painters. A Study in the Relations between Italian Art and Society in the Age of the Baroque*, London, 1963.

Held, Jutta. "Die Theorie der Landschaftmalerei im frühen 17. Jahrhundert und ihre Politische Bedeutung bei Collantes," *Jahrbuch der Hamburger Kunstsammlungen*, 21 (1976), pp. 129–54.

Herrera y Sotomayor, Jacinto de. *Jornada que su magestad hizo a la Andaluzia*, Madrid, 1624.

Horn, Hendrick. "Charles V's Conquest of Tunis: Cartoons and Tapestries by Jan Cornelisz Vermeyen," Ph.D. Dissertation, Yale University, 1977.

Hoz, Fray Pedro de la. "Relación diaria desde 31 de marzo de 1621 a 14 de agosto de 1640." (Ms. in possession of J. H. Elliott. The section covering the years 1621 to 1627 published by A. González Palencia, *Noticias de Madrid, 1621–1627*, Madrid, 1942.)

Hugo, Hermannus. *Obsidio Bredana armis Philippi IIII*, Antwerp, 1626.

Hume, Martin. *The Court of Philip IV. Spain in Decadence*, London, 1907.

Iñiguez Almech, Francisco. *Casas reales y jardines de Felipe II*, Madrid, 1952.

——— *Las trazas del Monasterio de San Lorenzo de El Escorial*, Madrid, 1965.

Jaffé, Michael. "Current and Forthcoming Exhibitions. Exposición Conmemorativo del IV Centenario del Nacimiento de Rubens, Museo Nacional de Escultura, Valladolid, Dec. 1977–Jan. 1978," *Burlington Magazine*, 120 (1978), p. 349.

Jago, Charles. "The Influence of Debt on the Relations between the Crown and Aristocracy in Seventeenth-Century Castile," *The Economic History Review*, 2nd series, 26 (1973), pp. 218–36.

Jammes, Robert. *Etudes sur l'oeuvre poétique de Don Luis de Góngora y Argote*, Bordeaux, 1967.

Jordán de Urriés y Azara, José. *Biografía y estudio crítico de Jáuregui*, Madrid, 1899.

Jover, José M. *1635. Historia de una polémica y semblanza de una generación*, Madrid, 1949.

Justi, Carl. *Diego Velázquez und sein Jahrhundert*, 2nd ed., Zurich, 1933. (Eng. trans. *Velázquez and His Times*, London, 1889.)

——— *Miscellaneen aus drei Jahrhunderten Spanischen Kunstlebens*, 2 vols., Berlin, 1908.

Kaufmann, Thomas D. "Empire Triumphant: Notes on an Imperial Allegory," *Studies in the History of Art*, 8 (1978), pp. 63–75.

Kennedy, Ruth Lee. "Philip IV's Advocacy of San Blas on February 3, 1623," *Revista Hispánica Moderna*, 39 (1976–7), pp. 96–108.

——— *Studies in Tirso, I: The Dramatist and his Competitors, 1620–6*, Chapel Hill, 1974.

King, Willard F. *Prosa novelística y academias literarias en el siglo XVII*, Madrid, 1963.

León Pinelo, Antonio de. *Anales de Madrid*, Madrid, 1971.

Levey, Michael. *Painting at Court*, London, 1971.

Llaguno y Amirola, Eugenio. *Noticias de los arquitectos de España desde su restauración. Ilustrados y acrecentados con notas, adiciones y documentos por D. Juan Agustín Ceán Bermúdez*, 4 vols., Madrid, 1839; repr. 1977.

López, María-Amalia. "Alonso Carbonel y la iglesia de Loeches," *Archivo Español de Arte*, 25 (1952), pp. 167–9.

López Navío, José. "La gran colección de pinturas del marqués de Leganés," *Analecta Calasanctiana*, 8 (1962), pp. 260–330.

López-Rey, José. *Velázquez. A Catalogue Raisonné of the Oeuvre*, London, 1963.

Madruga Real, Angela. "Cosimo Fanzago en las Agustinas de Salamanca," *Goya*, 125 (1975), pp. 291–7.

——— "Los Zumbigo, familia de arquitectos del siglo XVII," *Archivo Español de Arte*, 47 (1974), pp. 338–42.

Magalotti, Lorenzo. *Viaje de Cosme de Médicis por España y Portugal (1668–1669)*, ed. Angel Sánchez Rivero, Madrid, n.d.

Magurn, Ruth Saunders. *The Letters of Peter Paul Rubens*, Cambridge, Mass., 1955.

Manuel de Melo, Francisco. *Política militar en avisos de generales*, Madrid, 1638; ed. Buenos Aires, 1943.

Marañón, Gregorio. *El Conde-Duque de Olivares. La pasión de mandar*, 3rd ed., Madrid, 1952.

Maravall, José A. *La oposición política bajo los Austrias*, Barcelona, 1972.

——— *Teatro y literatura en la sociedad barroca*, Madrid, 1972.

Marco Dorta, Enrique. *La recuperación de Bahía por Don Fadrique de Toledo (1625). Un cuadro español de la época*, Seville, 1959.

Martí y Monsó, José. *Estudios históricos-artísticos relativos principalmente a Valladolid*, Valladolid–Madrid, n.d.

Martín González, Juan J. "El Alcázar de Madrid en el siglo XVI. Nuevos datos," *Archivo Español de Arte*, 35 (1962), pp. 1–19.

——— "El Palacio de Aranjuez en el siglo XVI," *Archivo Español de Arte*, 135 (1962), pp. 237–52.

——— "El Palacio de Carlos V en Yuste," *Archivo Español de Arte*, 23 (1950), pp. 27–51, 235–51; and 24 (1951), pp. 125–40.

——— "El Palacio del Pardo en el siglo XVI," *Boletín del Seminario de Estudios de Arte y Arqueología, Universidad de Valladolid*, 36 (1970) pp. 5–41.

——— "El Panteón de San Lorenzo de El Escorial," *Archivo Español de Arte*, 32 (1959), pp. 199–213.

——— "Nuevos datos sobre la construcción del Alcázar de Toledo," *Revista de Archivos, Bibliotecas y Museos*, 68 (1960), pp. 271–86.

——— "Sobre las relaciones entre Nardi, Carducho y Velázquez," *Archivo Español de Arte*, 31 (1958), pp. 59–66.

Martorell y Téllez-Girón, Ricardo. "Alonso Carbonel, arquitecto y escultor del siglo XVII," *Arte Español*, 13 (1936), pp. 50–8.

Massar, Phyllis Dearborn. "Scenes from a Calderón Play by Baccio del Bianco," *Master Drawings*, 15 (1977), pp. 365–75.

Mathews, Thomas G. "The Spanish Domination of St. Martin, 1633–1648," *Caribbean Studies*, 9 (1969), pp. 3–23.

Mazón de la Torre, María A. *Jusepe Leonardo y su tiempo*,

Zaragoza, 1977.

Mendez Silva, Rodrigo. *Diálogo compendioso de la antigüedad y cosas memorables de la noble villa de Madrid*, Madrid, 1637.

Mendoza, Antonio de. *Discursos de don Antonio de Mendoza*, ed. Marqués de Alcedo, Madrid, 1911.

Mesonero Romanos, Ramón de. *El antiguo Madrid, paseos históricos-anecdóticos por las calles y casas de esta villa*, Madrid, 1861; repr. 1976.

Molina Campuzano, Miguel. *Planos de Madrid de los siglos XVII y XVIII*, Madrid, 1960.

Morel-Fatio, Alfred. *L'Espagne au XVIᵉ et au XVIIᵉ siècle*, Paris, 1878.

Morena, Aurea de la. "El Monasterio de San Jerónimo el Real, de Madrid," *Anales del Instituto de Estudios Madrileños*, 6 (1974), pp. 47–78.

Moreno Villa, José. *Locos, enanos, negros y niños palaciegos*, Mexico, 1939.

Newton, A. P. *The European Nations in the West Indies, 1493–1688*, London, 1933; repr. 1966.

Novoa, Matías de. *Historia de Felipe IV, rey de España*. Colección de Documentos Inéditos para la Historia de España, vols. 69, 77, 80 and 86, Madrid, 1878–86.

Núñez de Castro, Alonso. *Libro histórico político. Sólo Madrid es corte*, 3rd ed., Madrid, 1675.

O'Gorman, James F. "More about Velázquez and Alciati," *Zeitschrift für Kunstgeschichte*, 28 (1965), pp. 225–8.

Orso, Steven N. "In the Presence of the 'Planet King': Studies in Art and Decoration at the Court of Philip IV of Spain," Ph.D. dissertation, Princeton University, 1978.

Pacheco, Francisco. *Arte de la pintura*, 2 vols., ed. F. J. Sánchez Cantón, Madrid, 1956.

Palomino de Castro y Velasco, Antonio. *El museo pictórico y escala óptica*, Madrid, 1947.

Parker, Alexander A. *The Allegorical Drama of Calderón. An Introduction to the Autos Sacramentales*, Oxford and London, 1943.

Parker, Geoffrey. *Philip II*, Boston–Toronto, 1978.

———— *The Army of Flanders and the Spanish Road, 1567–1659*, Cambridge, 1972.

Pellicer y Tovar, José. *Anfiteatro de Felipe el Grande*, Madrid, 1631; ed. Antonio Pérez Gómez, Cieza, 1974.

———— *Avisos históricos*, in Antonio Valladares, *Semanario Erudito*, vols. 31 and 32, Madrid, 1790.

Pérez Pastor, Cristóbal. *Noticias y documentos relativos a la historia y literatura española*, vol. 11, Madrid, 1914.

Pérez Sánchez, Alfonso E. "Algunas obras inéditas y nuevas consideraciones en torno a Collantes," *Archivo Español de Arte*, 35 (1962), pp. 253–63.

———— *Borgianni, Cavarozzi y Nardi en España*, Madrid, 1964.

———— *D. Antonio de Pereda (1611–1678) y la pintura madrileña de su tempo*, Madrid, 1978–9.

———— "Las colecciones de pintura del conde de Monterrey (1653)," *Boletín de la Real Academia de la Historia*, 174 (1977), pp. 417–59.

———— *Pintura italiana del s. XVII en España*, Madrid, 1965.

Pérez-Villaamil, Manuel. *Artes e industrias del Buen Retiro. La fábrica de la china. El laboratorio de piedras duras y mosaico. Obradores de bronces y marfiles*, Madrid, 1904.

Pita Andrade, José M. "Los cuadros que poseyó el séptimo marqués del Carpio," *Archivo Español de Arte*, 25 (1952), pp. 223–36.

———— *Los palacios del Buen Retiro en la época de los Austrias*, Madrid, 1970.

———— "Un informe de Francisco de Mora sobre el incendio del palacio del Pardo," *Archivo Español de Arte*, 35 (1962), pp. 265–70.

Plaza Santiago, Francisco Javier de la. *Investigaciones sobre el Palacio Real nuevo de Madrid*, Valladolid, 1975.

Plon, Eugène. *Leone Leoni, sculpteur de Charles Quint, et Pompeo Leoni, sculpteur de Philippe II*, Paris, 1887.

Pollin, Alice M. "El Judaísmo: figura dramática del auto 'El nuevo palacio del Retiro' de Calderón de la Barca," *Cuadernos Hispanoamericanos*, 276 (1973), pp. 579–88.

Portabales Pichel, Amancio. *Los verdaderos artífices del Monasterio de El Escorial*, Madrid, 1945.

———— *Maestros mayores, arquitectos y aparejadores de El Escorial*, Madrid, 1952.

Prieto Cantero, Amalia. "Inventario razonado de los documentos pertenecientes al monasterio de El Escorial existentes en la sección de Casa y Sitios Reales del Archivo General de Simancas," *Revista de Archivos, Bibliotecas y Museos*, 71 (1963), pp. 1–127.

Quazza, Romolo. *Margherita di Savoia*, Turin, 1930.

Quevedo, Francisco de. *Epistolario completo de don Francisco de Quevedo*, ed. Luis Astrana Marín, Madrid, 1946.

———— *Obras Completas*, ed. Felicidad Buendía, 2 vols. (vol. 1 *Obras en prosa*; vol. 2 *Obras en verso*), 6th ed., Madrid, 1966–7.

Quiñones de Benavente, Luis. *Entremeses, loas y jácaras*, ed. Cayetano Rosell, 2 vols., Madrid, 1872–4.

Quintana, Jerónimo de. *A la muy antigua, noble y coronada villa de Madrid. Historia de su antigüedad, nobleza y grandeza*, Madrid, 1629.

Ringrose, David. "Madrid and Spain, 1560–1860: Patterns of Social and Economic Change," in *City and Society in the Eighteenth Century*, ed. Paul Fritz and David Williams, Toronto, 1973.

Roca, conde de la (Juan Antonio de Vera y Figueroa). *Fragmentos históricos de la vida de D. Gaspar de Guzmán*, in Antonio de Valladares, *Semanario Erudito*, 2, pp. 145–296.

Ródenas Vilar, Rafael. *La política europea de España durante la guerra de Treinta Años, 1624–1630*, Madrid, 1967.

Rodríguez Villa, Antonio. *Ambrosio Spínola, primer marqués de Los Balbases*, Madrid, 1904.

———— *La corte y monarquía de España en los años de 1636 y 37*, Madrid, 1886.

———— *Etiquetas de la Casa de Austria*, Madrid, 1913.

Rosenthal, Earl. "*Plus Ultra, Non Plus Ultra*, and the Columnar Device of Emperor Charles V," *Journal of the Warburg and Courtauld Institutes*, 34 (1971), pp. 204–28.

———— "The Invention of the Columnar Device of Emperor Charles V at the Court of Burgundy in Flanders in 1516," *Journal of the Warburg and Courtauld Institutes*, 36 (1973), pp. 198–230.

Röthlisberger, Marcel. *Claude Lorrain. The Paintings*, New Haven, 1961.

Rubio Pardos, Carmen. "La Carerra de San Jerónimo," *Anales del Instituto de Estudios Madrileños*, 7 (1971), pp. 61–120.

Rooses, Max and Ruelens, Charles. *Correspondance de Rubens et documents épistolaires concernant sa vie et ses oeuvres*, vol. 6, Antwerp, 1909.

Ruiz de Arcaute, Agustín. *Juan de Herrera*, Madrid, 1936.

Sainsbury, W. Noel. *Original Unpublished Papers Illustrative of the Life of Sir Peter Paul Rubens as an Artist and Diplomatist*, London, 1859.

Salas, Xavier de. *Rubens y Velázquez. Museo del Prado. Studia Rubenniana*, II, Madrid, 1977.

Saltillo, marqués del. "Alonso Martínez de Espinar. Al margen de la Exposición de Caza," *Arte Español*, 18 (1951), pp. 115–134.

———— "Arquitectos y alarifes madrileños del siglo XVII," *Boletín de la Sociedad Española de Excursiones*, 52 (1948), pp. 161–221.

———— "Artistas madrileños (1592–1850)," *Boletín de la Sociedad Española de Excursiones*, 57 (1953), pp. 137–243.

Sánchez, José. *Academias literarias del siglo de oro español*, Madrid, 1961.

Sánchez Alonso, María Cristina. "Juramentos de príncipes herederos en Madrid (1561–1598)," *Anales del Instituto de Estudios Madrileños*, 6 (1970), pp. 29–41.

Sánchez Cantón, Francisco J. "Sobre el *Martínez Montañés* de Velázquez," *Archivo Español de Arte*, 34 (1961), pp. 25–30.

Sánchez de Espejo, Andrés. *Discurso de las fiestas que la magestad católica del rey nuestro señor celebró en el Real Retiro*, Madrid, 1637.

Saxl, Fritz. "Velázquez and Philip IV," *Lectures*, London, 1957.

Sentenach, Narciso. "Francisco de Zurbarán, pintor del rey," *Boletín de la Sociedad Española de Excursiones*, 17 (1909), pp. 194–8.

Shergold, Norman D. "The First Performance of Calderón's *El Mayor Encanto Amor*," *Bulletin of Hispanic Studies*, 35 (1958), pp. 24–7.

———— *A History of the Spanish Stage*, Oxford, 1967.

———— "Documentos sobre Cosme Lotti, escenógrafo de Felipe IV," *Studia Iberica. Festschrift für Hans Flasche*, Bern–Munich, 1973, pp. 589–602.

Shergold, N. D. and Varey, J. E. "Some Palace Performances of Seventeenth-Century Plays," *Bulletin of Hispanic Studies*, pp. 212–44.

Sigüenza, José A. *Historia de la Orden de San Jerónimo*, Nueva Biblioteca de Autores Españoles, vols. 8 and 12, 2nd ed. Madrid, 1907–9.

Spear, Richard E. "Preparatory Drawings by Domenichino," *Master Drawings*, 6 (1968), pp. 111–31.

Steinberg, Leo. "Review of José López-Rey, *Velázquez*," *Art Bulletin*, 47 (1965), pp. 274–94.

Strong, Roy. *Splendour at Court. Renaissance Spectacle and Illusion*, London, 1973.

Taylor, René, "Juan Bautista Crescencio y la arquitectura cortesana española," *Academia. Boletín de la Real Academia de San Fernando*, 48 (1979), pp. 63–126.

Testi, Fulvio. *Lettere*, vols. 2 and 3, ed. Maria Luisa Doglio, Bari, 1967.

———— *Raccolta generale delle poesie*, part III, Modena, 1651.

Tirso de Molina Téllez (Fray Gabriel). *Historia general de la Orden de Nuestra Señora de las Mercedes*, 2 vols., ed. Manuel Penedo Rey, Madrid, 1974.

Tobajas López, Marcelino. "Documentos del Buen Retiro," *Reales Sitios*, nos. 51–4 (1977).

Tomás Valiente, Francisco. *Los validos en la monarquía española del siglo XVII*, Madrid, 1963.

Tormo y Monzó, Elias. *Las viejas series icónicas de los reyes de España*, Madrid, 1916.

———— *Pintura, escultura y arquitectura en España. Estudios dispersos*, Madrid, 1949.

Tormo y Monzó, Elías and Sánchez Cantón, Francisco J. *Los tapices de la Casa del Rey N.S. Notas para el catálogo y para la historia de la colección y de la fábrica*, Madrid, 1919.

Trapier, Elizabeth DuGué. "Sir Arthur Hopton and the Interchange of Paintings between Spain and England in the Seventeenth Century," *Connoisseur*, 164 (1967), pp. 239–43; 165 (1967), pp. 60–3.

Trevor-Roper, Hugh. *Princes and Artists. Patronage and Ideology at Four Habsburg Courts*, London, 1976.

Ulloa, Modesto. *La hacienda real de Castilla en el reinado de Felipe II*, Madrid, 1977.

Urrea, Jesús. "Antonio de Pereda nació en 1611," *Archivo Español de Arte*, 49 (1976), pp. 336–8.

Valencia y Guzmán, José de. *Compendio historial de la jornada del Brasil*. Colección de Documentos Inéditos para la Historia de España, vol. 55, Madrid, 1870, pp. 43–200.

Varey, J. E. "Further Notes on Processional Ceremonial of the Spanish Court in the Seventeenth Century," *Iberoromania*, 1 (1974), pp. 71–9.

———— "La mayordomía mayor y los festejos palaciegos del siglo XVII," *Anales del Instituto de Estudios Madrileños*, 4 (1969), pp. 145–68.

———— "Processional Ceremonial of the Spanish Court in the Seventeenth Century," *Studia Iberica. Festschrift für Hans Flasche*, Bern–Munich, 1973, pp. 643–52.

Varia Velázqueña. Homenaje a Velázquez en el III centenario de su muerte, 1660–1960, 2 vols., Madrid, 1960.

Vega Carpio, Lope Félix de. *El castigo sin venganza*, ed. C. F. A. Van Dam, Groningen, 1928.

———— *Obras*, 28, Biblioteca de Autores Españoles, 233, Madrid, 1970, pp. 257–96.

———— "Versos a la primera fiesta del palacio nuevo," *La Vega del Parnaso* in *Obras Escogidas*, 2, pp. 246–9, ed. Federico Carlos Sainz de Robles, 4th ed., Aguilar, Madrid, 1964.

Vélez de Guevara, Juan. *Los celos hacen estrellas*, ed. J. E. Varey and N. D. Shergold, London, 1970.

Vieira, Antonio. *Arte de furtar. Espelho de enganos teatro de verdades, mostrador de horas minguadas*, Amsterdam, 1652.

Vila Vilar, Enriqueta. *Historia de Puerto Rico, 1600–1650*, Seville, 1974.

Vilar, Jean. "Formes et tendances de l'opposition sous Olivares: Lisón y Viedma, *defensor de la patria*," *Mélanges de la Casa de Velázquez*, 7 (1971) pp. 263–94.

Vitzthum, Walter. "Letter to Editor," *Burlington Magazine*, 112 (1970), pp. 760–1.

———— "Review of Giuliano Briganti, *Pietro da Cortona o della pittura barocca*," *Burlington Magazine*, 105 (1963), pp. 213–17.

———— "Seicento Paintings in Madrid," *Burlington Magazine*, 112 (1970), pp. 420–3.

Volk, Mary C. *Vicencio Carducho and Seventeenth-Century Castilian Painting*, New York–London, 1977.

Volpe, Carlo. "Una proposta per Giovanni Battista Crescenzi," *Paragone*, 275 (1973), pp. 25–36.

Vosters, Simon A. *La rendición de Bredá en la literatura y el arte de España*, London, 1974.

Waddington, A. *La République des Provinces-Unies, la France et les Pays-Bas Espagnols de 1630 a 1650*, 2 vols., Paris, 1895–7.

Werner, Ernst. "Caída del Conde-Duque de Olivares," *Revue Hispanique*, 71 (1927), pp. 1–156.

Wethey, Harold E. *The Paintings of Titian*, 3 vols., London, 1969–75.

Whitaker, Shirley B. "The First Performance of Calderón's *El sitio de Bredá*," *Renaissance Quarterly*, 31 (1978), pp. 515–31.

Wilkinson, Catherine. "The Career of Juan de Mijares and the Reform of Spanish Architecture under Philip II," *Journal of the Society of Architectural Historians*, 33 (1974), pp. 122–32.

———— "The Escorial and the Invention of the Imperial Staircase," *Art Bulletin*, 57 (1975), pp. 65–90.

Yates, Frances A. *Astraea. The Imperial Theme in the Sixteenth Century*, London, 1975.

Yerushalmi, Yosef Hayim. *From Spanish Court to Italian Ghetto*, New York, 1971.

Zarco Cuevas, Julián. *Los Jerónimos de San Lorenzo el Real de El Escorial*, Madrid, 1930.

———— *Los pintores italianos en San Lorenzo el Real de El Escorial 1575–1613*, Madrid, 1932.

INDEX

295